PENGUIN BOOKS

CRETE

D0308789

'An admirably researched study ... In fact, when the official history of SOE in Greece is published, it should quote from this book' – Nigel Clive in the *Spectator*

'Beevor's book has a fine cast of characters, both British and German ... His facts are accurate and his judgements sound. The lively eloquence of his prose may console those who participated in one of the empire's most poignant defeats' – Sir David Hunt in *The Times*

'The cast of characters in this finely researched new history is extraordinary' – Alexander Norman in the *Daily Mail*

'Waugh is but one of the numerous cast which Beevor handles with a dexterity reminiscent of Simon Schama's technique in *Citizens*. He portrays the minor characters and the leading players with equal fidelity, even when the scene switches from military to clandestine action; and in the latter, less documented area, his assiduous research is triumphantly apparent' – Xan Fielding in the *London Magazine*

'He has made such good use of testimony by the surviving British participants that future historians of this epic will be permanently in his debt' – Sir Brooks Richards in the *Anglo-Hellenic Review*

Antony Beevor was educated at Winchester and Sandhurst. A regular officer in the 11th Hussars, he served in Germany and England until he resigned his commission after five years in the army. He has published several novels, while his works of non-fiction include *The Spanish Civil War* and *Crete: The Battle and the Resistance*, which won the 1993 Runciman Award, and *Stalingrad*, which won the Samuel Johnson Prize for Non-Fiction, the Wolfson History Prize and the Hawthornden Prize in 1999. All are published in Penguin. He is married to the writer Artemis Cooper, with whom he wrote *Paris After the Liberation* (also published in Penguin). They have both been appointed Chevalier de l'Ordre des Arts et des Lettres by the French government.

ANTONY BEEVOR

CRETE

THE BATTLE AND THE RESISTANCE

PENGUIN BOOKS

PENGUIN BOOKS

Published by the Penguin Group
Penguin Books Ltd, 27 Wrights Lane, London W8 5TZ, England
Penguin Putnam Inc., 375 Hudson Street, New York, New York 10014, USA
Penguin Books Australia Ltd, Ringwood, Victoria, Australia
Penguin Books Canada Ltd, 10 Alcorn Avenue, Toronto, Ontario, Canada M4V 3B2
Penguin Books (NZ) Ltd, 182–190 Wairau Road, Auckland 10, New Zealand

Penguin Books Ltd, Registered Offices: Harmondsworth, Middlesex, England

First published by John Murray (Publishers) Ltd 1991
Published in Penguin Books 1992
6

Printed in England by Clays Ltd, St Ives plc

For Artemis

Contents

Illustrations

Illustrations 1, 2, 3, 4 and 6 are reproduced by kind permission of the War Museum in Athens; 7, 8, 10, 11, 12, 13 and 15 by courtesy of the Imperial War Museum; 5, 14, 16 and 20 by kind permission of Patrick Leigh Fermor; 9 by kind permission of Lord Hollenden; and 17, 18 and 19 by kind permission of Hugh Fraser.

Maps

Acknowledgements

During my research, I soon learned that one should not be dismayed when people warn you that they have little of interest to offer. Sometimes a lapse of memory would be blamed – what Paddy Leigh Fermor calls 'a shot across the bows from Admiral Alzheimer' – yet those who promised little were always the ones who, often surprising themselves as much as their listener, suddenly recalled, with great clarity, incidents and individuals from half a century ago. Without their stories and insights, this book would have been very flat.

I am above all grateful to: Miki Akoumianakis, the late Lord Caccia, Dennis Ciclitira, Sir Geoffrey Cox, Gottfried Emrich, Xan Fielding, Ron Fletcher, Major General Michael Forrester, Hugh Fraser, Professor Nicholas Hammond, Professor Freiherr von der Heydte, Myles Hildyard, Brigadier R.W. Hobson, Lord Hollenden, Sir David Hunt, Lieutenant General Sir Ian Jacob, Manolis Kougoumtzakis, Patrick Leigh Fermor, Manoussos Manoussakis, Colonel Guy May, Sir Charles Mott-Radclyffe, Mark Norman, Major A.H.W. Petre Norton, George Psychoundakis, John Pumphrey, Brigadier Ray Sandover, Jack Smith-Hughes, the late Niko Souris, John Stanley, Ralph Stockbridge, Dr R.E.S. Tanner, the Rt. Rev. Stephen Verney, Michael Ward, Sir Peter Wilkinson, the late Gerry de Winton and the Hon. C.M. Woodhouse.

Many thanks are also due to Vincent Williams, the General Secretary of the UK Crete Veterans Association, and to UKCVA members and those of allied associations who kindly contributed their memories: Tom Barratt, Tom Bevan, R.B. Brown, J. Clayton, Horace Cowley, Alexander Dow, Lieutenant Commander T.J. Gibbons, Alfred Gotts, Lieutenant Commander F.M. Hutton, Clifford Pass, Kenneth

Stalder and Norman Swift; and to Vassilios Fourakis and Eleutheris
Tsinakis.

I would also like to thank those who have helped in other ways,
whether generously sharing their own research, contributing items
from unexpected sources or providing useful ideas for further delving:
Joan Bright Astley, Evangelos Christou, Antony Contomichaelos,
Michael Davie, Brigadier Christopher Dunphie, M.R.D. Foot, Imogen
Grundon, Edward Hodgkin, Penelope Hope, Charles Messenger, Sir
David Miers, Nigel Nicolson, Bernard Redshaw, Hugo Vickers and
Christopher Woods.

I owe a great debt to those who aided my research in Greece and
made it so enjoyable: John Craxton in Canea; Marion Tzanakis, the
British Consul in Heraklion; Captain Richard Evans RN, the Naval
and Air Attaché at the British Embassy in Athens; HE Richard
Woods, the former New Zealand Ambassador to Greece; and
Admiral Evangelos Sakellariou and Lieutenant Colonel Mountakis
and their staff at the War Museum in Athens.

I am also very grateful to all those who have lent me letters,
diaries, photographs and especially unpublished reports, a number of
which have proved not just helpful, but vital.

Hugh Fraser, a member of the British Military Mission in Crete,
has been extremely generous with his time in devilling and translating
useful documents and accounts of the resistance. Dr Detlef Vogel of
the Military History Research Institute in Freiburg very kindly sent
me copies of relevant German documents and passed on points
arising from his own work on the subject.

Those with first-hand or expert knowledge who read and criticized
chapters not only saved me from error, but in many cases added
further illumination. I am particularly grateful to Commander Edward
Thomas for examining all the Ultra-related sections, to Major General
Michael Forrester, to Lord Jellicoe for looking at all the passages
about SAS and SBS raids; and to all those members of the British
Military Mission in Crete and Manoussos Manoussakis who also read
Part Three, in some cases several times, and rang round their
network of resistance colleagues in Greece double-checking incidents
described in the text. Any mistakes which remain are, of course,
entirely my responsibility.

I have been extremely fortunate in all the encouragement and
assistance which I have received from my publishers, John Murray,
who have been both editors and friends to several generations of my
family. Grant McIntyre gave good advice and displayed an admirable

desk-side manner, while Gail Perkis was the perfect copy-editor, challenging muddled or clumsy passages with tact and then offering excellent solutions when my brain seized.

My greatest thanks are reserved for my wife, Artemis Cooper. If she had not borne almost the entire burden of our daughter's illness, I would never have managed to finish this book in time.

Correction

On page 194 of the first edition of this book, the commanding officer of 'A' Battalion of Layforce was given as Lieutenant Colonel J.B. Colvin. This was the name recorded in Charles Messenger's history of the Middle East Commandos published in 1988. It should, in both cases, have been Lieutenant Colonel F.B. Colvin.

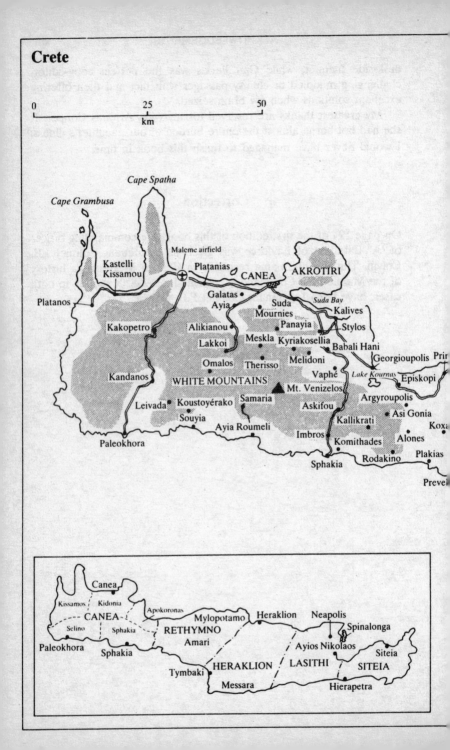

Crete

0   25   50
km

Cape Grambusa

Cape Spatha

Maleme airfield

Kastelli
Kissamou

Platanias   CANEA   AKROTIRI

Platanos

Galatas   Suda   Suda Bay
Ayia   Mournies   Kalives

Kakopetro   Panayia   Stylos

Alikianou   Meskla   Kyriakosellia
Lakkoi   Babali Hani
Melidoni   Georgioupolis   Prir
Omalos   Therisso   Vaphé   Lake Kournas   Episkopi
Kandanos   WHITE MOUNTAINS   Mt. Venizelos   Argyroupolis

Leivada   Koustoyérako   Samaria   Askifou   Asi Gonia
Souyia   Kallikrati   Koxa
Ayia Roumeli   Alones
Imbros   Komithades   Plakias
Paleokhora   Rodakino
Sphakia   Preve

Canea
Kissamos   Kidonia
CANEA   Apokoronas
Selino   Sphakia   Mylopotamo   Heraklion   Neapolis
RETHYMNO   Spinalonga
Paleokhora   Amari   Ayios Nikolaos
Sphakia   HERAKLION   LASITHI   Siteia
Tymbaki   SITEIA
Messara   Hierapetra

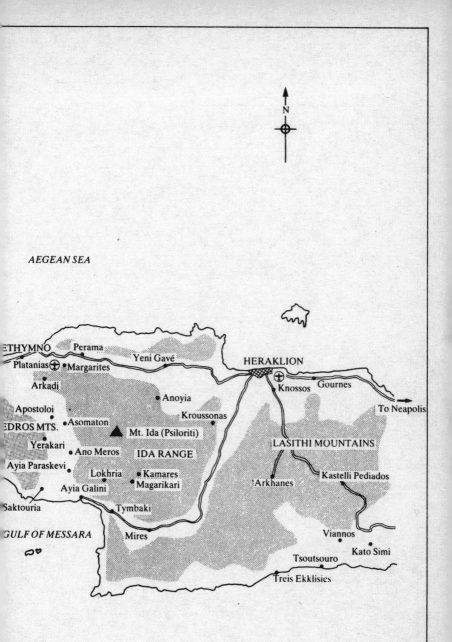

N

AEGEAN SEA

ETHYMNO
Platanias⊕ •Perama
        •Margarites   Yeni Gavé   HERAKLION
•Arkadi   ⊕
                                        •Anoyia   Knossos •Gournes
•Apostoloi   •Kroussonas
        •Asomaton   → To Neapolis
EDROS MTS.
•Yerakari   ▲ Mt. Ida (Psiloriti)
    •Ano Meros   IDA RANGE   LASITHI MOUNTAINS
•Ayia Paraskevi
    •Lokhria   •Kamares
•Ayia Galini   Magarikari   •Arkhanes   •Kastelli Pediados
•Saktouria   •Tymbaki
GULF OF MESSARA
              Mires   •Viannos
                                    Tsoutsouro   •Kato Simi
                              Treis Ekklisies

LIBYAN SEA

PART ONE
The Fall of Greece

1
Military Missions

On the night after the last British troops left the beaches of Dunkirk, a tall man with a glass eye said goodbye to his wife on the steps of the Oxford and Cambridge Club. It was the eve of his departure by flying-boat for Greece. They never saw each other again. A year later, badly wounded in the battle for Crete, he was propped against a wall by German paratroopers and shot.

Although an archaeologist, and an Old Wykehamist of conventional background, John Pendlebury was a vigorous romantic. He carried a swordstick which he claimed was the perfect weapon against parachutists. In Crete it became an even more famous trademark than the glass eye which he used to leave on his desk to indicate his absence from Heraklion whenever he left for the mountains to confer with guerrilla kapitans.

Like many dons and archaeologists, he had been canvassed in 1938 by a special department in the War Office known as MI(R) – Military Intelligence (Research) – a forerunner of Special Operations Executive. With an intimate knowledge of Crete from his time as curator at Knossos in the mid-1930s, Pendlebury was an obvious candidate for special operations. Yet no summons had arrived on the outbreak of war, and he had returned to England for a commission in a cavalry regiment.

The call had finally come in May 1940 as the German attack on the Low Countries and France began. The increasing possibility of Italy's entry into the war, and German interest in the Balkans, particularly the oilfields of Roumania, suggested that the Eastern Mediterranean would be the next region of operations. Another Greek-speaking archaeologist called to the camouflaged colours of

MI(R) in May 1940 was Nicholas Hammond, a don from Cambridge. He and Pendlebury were sent off on a rushed course in explosives, which became Hammond's speciality: an unlikely qualification for a future headmaster of Clifton and professor of Greek. Hammond was an expert on Epirus and Albania. In London, before their departure, Pendlebury insisted — more in playfulness than paranoia — that as a security measure they should always converse on the telephone in Greek: Hammond in Epirotic dialect and Pendlebury in Cretan.

Although older than the majority of those volunteering for sabotage and stay-behind groups, Pendlebury was one of the fittest. A well-known athlete from Cambridge, both as a runner and a high-jumper, and a member of the Achilles Club, he had been a friend of Harold Abrahams and Lord Burghley. In one pre-war season based at Knossos, he had walked over a thousand miles across Crete's mountainous terrain.

At little more than a day's notice, the four members of MI(R) destined for Greece and Albania were summoned to the War Office. They numbered Pendlebury, Hammond, a businessman from Zagreb, and another archaeologist, David Hunt, a fellow of Magdalen College, Oxford, who became a diplomat after the war. On 4 June, they were escorted to Victoria Station by an officer of Foot Guards in full service dress, riding breeches, gleaming boots and No.1 Dress cap. In the midst of the stream of exhausted Dunkirk evacuees his immaculate presence provided one of those surreal touches at which the British establishment inadvertently excels.

They boarded a flying-boat in Poole harbour and took off uncertain of their route. The German columns advancing deep into France forced the pilot to take a circuitous line, landing to refuel at Arcachon just south of Bordeaux, Sète, Bizerta, Malta and Corfu. At Athens, all except Pendlebury were refused entry because their covers of 'businessman' and 'civil servant' were thought suspicious. During that period preceding the Italian invasion, the Greek government was on guard against any British action which might compromise its neutrality.

Pendlebury, as a former curator at Knossos, was allowed to enter the country. He soon crossed over to Crete where he began to contact friends made during his immense marches and prepare groups to resist the invasion of such a strategically important island.

Hammond and Hunt, barred from entering Greece, had no option but to carry on to Egypt. There, they were attached to the 1st Battalion of the Welch Regiment in Alexandria. This regular battalion later demonstrated its military mettle in Crete, but for someone who had volunteered as an irregular the peacetime routine was suffocating. 'Every Sunday the officers gave a cocktail party lasting from 12 to 3 (champagne cocktails only) to the youth and beauty of Alexandria. At 3 o'clock, we all sat down to roast beef and Yorkshire pudding, although the temperature was fairly steady in the 90s.' Since Italy declared war on 10 June, two days after Hammond and Hunt reached Alexandria, this curious existence did not go on for very long.

That summer, while Britain prepared for invasion, and the first skirmishes took place in the Western Desert, the regime of the Greek dictator, General Ioannis Metaxas, acutely aware of the threat from the Italian army which had occupied Albania in April 1939, made every effort to avoid confrontation.

The government in Athens even overlooked the sinking by an Italian submarine of their cruiser *Helle* which was acting as ceremonial guardship during religious celebrations on the island of Tinos. Such exceptional moderation did them little good.

Few military campaigns have been undertaken so carelessly as the Italian invasion of Greece, launched on 28 October 1940. Mussolini originally wanted to invade Jugoslavia, but Hitler vetoed the proposal firmly. Jugoslav raw materials were almost as important to Germany's war effort as Roumania's oil. In some ways it is surprising that Hitler did not also veto the invasion of Greece. He had plenty of warning of what the Italians were up to, and Mussolini almost certainly cleared it with him during a private moment at the Brenner meeting of 4 October.

The Duce presented his prospective campaign as part of a double attack on Britain's position in the Eastern Mediterranean — supposedly the capture of Mersa Matruh followed by Italian domination of the Aegean. At the time, this accorded with Germany's 'peripheral strategy' of attacking Britain other than by a direct assault across the Channel, but Hitler had not fully appreciated the Italian regime's talent for disaster.

Emanuele Grazzi, the Italian minister in Athens, woke General Metaxas at 3 a.m. to deliver an ultimatum, without even knowing the detail of its conditions. The diplomatic charade added insult to injury since Italian troops had already crossed the Albanian frontier. General Papagos, the Greek Chief of Staff, rang Colonel Jasper Blunt, the British Military Attaché, less than half an hour later. Blunt went straight to the offices of the General Staff where he found a sang-froid that was most impressive in the circumstances.

The popular demonstrations next day showed that the country had united instinctively. Metaxas's 'No!' to Grazzi is still commemorated each year on 28 October with the national holiday known as *'Ohi Day'*. In the patriotic emotion, both Venizelist anti-monarchist liberals and the left temporarily forgot that Metaxas's royalist dictatorship had violated the constitution and suppressed all opposition.

Metaxas, with the authority of the recently restored King George II, had put an end to party politics with his decree of 4 August 1936. His rule was enforced by the police and secret police of his loyal supporter, Constantinos Maniadakis, Minister of National Security.

The endless preoccupation of Greek royalists and liberals with the constitution had long been little more than a surrogate battle enabling them to ignore the real problem of the country – the division between a self-absorbed capital and the woefully neglected countryside and islands. This failure of the two main parties, followed by the Metaxist dictatorship, which was known as the 'Fourth of August Regime', later gave the Communists their opportunity on the mainland.

Parallels with Spain were striking. The difference in the pattern of events leading to their respective civil wars lay mainly in timing. In Spain, Primo de Rivera's dictatorship in the 1920s bottled up the explosion for the late 1930s. In Greece, Metaxas's similar attempt to impose military order on civilian chaos was followed by the Albanian campaign and German occupation. This meant that the explosion was delayed until the end of the Second World War, soon after British troops arrived in Athens.

On 28 October 1940, Sir Michael Palairet, the British Minister, was cheered on the balcony of the British Legation by opponents and supporters of the regime alike. The Legation, a large pink and white mansion on Kifissia Avenue, had belonged to Eleutherios Venizelos, the great liberal statesman of the First World War, whose pro-Allied stance had helped depose the pro-German King Constantine, the father of George II. In Venizelos's native Crete, the outburst of patriotism nearly led to the destruction of the early seventeenth-century Morosini fountain in Heraklion because it was Venetian and therefore 'enemy'.

Reservists did not wait for call-up papers, they reported immediately. Wildly enthusiastic soldiery piling into troop trains fired an estimated million rounds into the air. Many units set out for the front on foot, since motor transport barely existed in the Greek army. In the Pindus mountains, men, women and children offered themselves and their pack animals to carry ammunition and supplies across the wild and roadless terrain. Within a few days the Italian advance came to a halt.

In the belief that the campaign would be little short of a triumphal march, the Italian army in Albania had not been provided with engineer units. The lack of strategy – a futile push into the mountain mass of Epirus instead of cutting across towards the key port of Salonika – exasperated Hitler as much as the incompetence with which the campaign was executed. He pretended to have had no prior knowledge of the whole venture.

Instead of a short sharp campaign which would have barred the enemy from the continent of Europe, Hitler found that Mussolini's action had triggered the British guarantee of Greek independence given in April 1939 after the Italian invasion of Albania. In Salzburg on 18 November the Führer made the Italian Foreign Minister, Count Ciano, understand that the arrival of Royal Air Force bombers in the region of his main fuel supply, the oilfields of Ploesti, was Mussolini's fault.

Hitler's concern for the oilfields increased further when it became clear that his attempts to lull Soviet suspicions aroused by German troops in Roumania had failed. On 5 December 1940, he finally decided on the invasion of Russia. The threat now of a second front on his right rear became a major preoccupation.

The original staff plan to invade Greece (Operation Marita) and Gibraltar (Operation Felix) as part of the 'peripheral strategy' against Britain's Mediterranean and imperial power had to be revised. General Franco's bland intransigence made 'Felix' impossible, and in any case Hitler, with his ambition fixed on Russia, had lost interest in the Mediterranean. 'Marita', on the other hand, had become more important than ever. He had to secure his flank for the coming advance eastwards.

Hitler's fears were exaggerated. The RAF's presence in Greece was much less of a threat than he imagined because Metaxas's government refused to allow the British to threaten the Roumanian oilfields. An improvised collection of squadrons under Air Vice Marshal D'Albiac – at first mostly Blenheims and Gladiators – was sent from Egypt to support the Greek army on the Albanian front. To avoid provoking the Germans, the bombers could not be stationed any further forward than Eleusis and Tatoi, both close to Athens.

For the advance party – who had been casually told in their mess tent in the desert, 'You're off to Greece tomorrow' – touching down in a Sunderland flying-boat at the naval air station of Phaleron near Athens was a moving moment. They were the first British forces openly back on European territory since the fall of France.

The young pilots who followed had the happy-go-lucky attitude of the time. In 211 Squadron, a number were motor-racing enthusiasts who had known each other from the paddock at Brooklands. Nicknames were compulsively applied to everything and everyone, with 'kites' called 'Bloody Mary' and 'Caminix', and pilots known as 'the Bish' Gordon-Finlayson, 'Twinkle' Pearson and 'Shaky Do' Dawson.

They soon settled into their new life. By day they carried out bombing raids on the Albanian ports of Durazzo and Valona – a dangerously repetitive pattern known as 'same time, same place' jobs. And by night they enjoyed themselves in Athens, starting at Zonar's, then going on to Maxim's or the Argentina night-club, where they rubbed shoulders, and occasionally came to blows, with unconvincing German 'holiday-makers'. At the Argentina, they used to chat up a blonde singer and dancer called Nicki after the show, unaware that she was the girlfriend of a member of Section D (another forerunner of Special Operations Executive) working under cover in the Legation.

As a further gesture of support, and to provide 'close-up information about the relative merits of the two armies', Churchill had demanded the dispatch of a British Military Mission to the Greek army. GHQ Middle East received this instruction within a few days of the Italian invasion, and at the end of the second week of November, Major General Gambier-Parry was sent from Egypt, followed by a skeleton staff.

Although the Military Attaché, Colonel Blunt, was put in a difficult position, he and Gambier-Parry got on well. But Gambier-Parry was recalled towards the end of the year for a short-lived appointment as commander of British forces on Crete. His replacement was Major General T.G. Heywood.

Heywood had been Military Attaché in Paris prior to the fall of France. His refusal to acknowledge defects in the French army was an inauspicious qualification. Harold Caccia, the First Secretary at the Legation, considered him 'intelligent, but not very wise.' Heywood was a fastidious man. He had a muscular military face, with moustache, hard, narrowed eyes and a monocle. Ambitious and 'politically minded', he increased the size of the British Military Mission from little more than half a dozen officers to over seventy at one point, a growth which convinced many in the Greek army that his organization was destined to form the nucleus of an expeditionary force.

Heywood also put his fellow gunner, Jasper Blunt, in an intolerable position. Blunt, a perceptive man, had accumulated an excellent knowledge of the Greek army. He was also the only British officer in Athens who had managed to reconnoitre the threatened north-east before the Greek General Staff vetoed further visits. Colonel Blunt, with his superior local knowledge, should have joined the mission as the senior intelligence officer, but Heywood had brought in his own man, Stanley Casson — Reader in Classical Archaeology at New College, Oxford — who although brilliant and a veteran of the Salonika front in the First World War, was rather out of touch. Perhaps the most eccentric addition was Colonel Rankin of the Indian Army in a curiously cut pair of jodhpurs and a long cavalry tunic which stuck out so much at the sides that he was known as 'the Indian evzone'.

Most members of the British Military Mission were either picked regular officers, or wartime volunteers with knowledge of the region. The chief staff officer for operations was a well-known Coldstreamer, Colonel Guy Salisbury-Jones. His number two was Major Peter Smith-Dorrien, later killed by the terrorist bomb at the King David Hotel.

The ranks of young captains and subalterns included Charles Mott-Radclyffe, a diplomat turned soldier who had served *en poste* in Athens only a few years before; Monty Woodhouse, a 23-year-old Wykehamist of stern looks and rigorous thought who a few years later in the rank of full colonel played a large part with Nick Hammond in thwarting the Greek Communists' attempt to suppress rival guerrilla groups; Michael Forrester, who was soon to distinguish himself in Crete as an almost mythical leader of irregulars in the battle against German paratroopers; and Patrick Leigh Fermor, described as 'an avatar of Byron' by Woodhouse because he had attached himself to a Greek cavalry regiment during the Venizelist revolution of 1935, and who later gave substance to the label with guerrilla adventures that were amongst the most romantic of the war.

Leigh Fermor's early career of itinerant delight has been well-chronicled in his books, yet *en route* to Athens his power of charmed survival almost failed. Coming from Alexandria, the cruiser HMS *Ajax* stopped off at Suda Bay on the north coast of Crete. He and Monty Woodhouse went into the old Venetian city of Canea for a drink and to smoke a narghile.

Afterwards, a private in the Black Watch driving a ration lorry stopped to give them a lift back to Suda, but he proved to be drunk and drove without care on roads which had 'gone artistically to ruin', in Pendlebury's phrase. The truck overturned in the ditch and Leigh Fermor, who received a head wound, had to be left behind in hospital when the *Ajax* sailed. He finally reached Athens a week later.

The mission's liaison officer with the Greek government was Prince Peter of Greece, King George II's young cousin and an anthropologist who had spent a long time in the Himalayas. As a thoroughgoing Anglophile, with 'an astonishing repertoire of bawdy songs', he was greatly liked by British officers. The mission was hardly in a position to proffer useful advice on mountain warfare. 'The Greeks were certainly brave,' observed one war correspondent, 'but mountain warfare was in their view not suited to modern methods, and they reverted almost automatically to the tactics of a century ago.' Forrester, who worked for Salisbury-Jones, described the conflict as 'like one of the Balkan wars with somewhat updated weapons.'

The nebulous task of the British Military Mission was not made clearer by the unreal environment in which it lived and worked. Immediately after the Italian invasion, the Greek government had requisitioned the Hotel Grande Bretagne on Constitution Square as its General Headquarters: it was one of the largest buildings in Athens and had extensive cellars ready to serve as air-raid shelters.

General Metaxas took over the manager's office, the King was allotted a private drawing-room, and the reputation of 'Jimmy', the barman, as the best informed man in Athens increased still further when General Mellisinos, the Deputy Chief of Staff, set up his desk opposite the rows of bottles.

'The prize show of the building', wrote Colonel Blunt in his diary, 'was Maniadakis, the public security chief. He had a huge mahogany table matching his vast bulk. On it was an outsize photograph of General Metaxas in a massive silver frame, and a battery of telephones that would not have disgraced the office of any police chief of thriller fiction or film. Maniadakis would seize a telephone receiver in his huge fist and bellow for some distant provincial prefect or police chief, shouting not only to drown the typewriters, but also because he liked to shout. While this performance was going on, all his intimate circle of officers and friends who were clustered and seated round him, would hang on his words and try to hear what was coming through from the other end.'

During the Greek army's astonishingly successful campaign against the Italians, the Joint Planning Staff and the Chiefs of Staff in London did not want British aid to go beyond the fighter and bomber squadrons already committed. One way of helping both the Greeks and British interests in the Eastern Mediterranean was to take over responsibility for Crete, which the Italians wanted to occupy as a naval and air base. Metaxas suspected the British of having their own designs upon such a strategically important island, but at that time they were clearly the lesser evil. Despite the surge of pro-British feeling, Greeks did not forget Venizelos's phrase describing their country as 'the beggar of the Great Powers'.

In London, the views of admirals, generals and air marshals were for once in agreement, and Churchill concurred. With resonances of the Grand Fleet in 1914, he demanded that the large natural harbour of Suda Bay on the north coast of Crete should be turned into 'a second Scapa'.

Admiral Cunningham, the Commander-in-Chief Mediterranean, had already planned, with Greek approval, to establish a naval base there. The first British troops to be sent, the 2nd Battalion, the York and Lancaster Regiment, received their warning order to move within forty-eight hours of the Italian invasion. The 2nd Battalion of the Black Watch, also part of the 14th Infantry Brigade, followed in the next few days.

The dispatch of British troops to guard Suda Bay allowed the Greek government to bring the Cretan 5th Division across to the mainland. Harold Caccia, deputizing for Sir Michael Palairet, passed on the categorical assurance to the Greek government: 'We will look after Crete.'

This decision — a perfectly logical move providing the British fulfilled their pledge — was later lamented by the Cretans with justifiable bitterness. 'If only the Division were here!' became an almost universal cry when the German airborne invasion of their island took place just over six months later.

The Cretan Division landed at Salonika in the second week of November 1940. Due to lack of transport, it had to march across most of Macedonia to Kastoria, some seventy kilometres south of

Lake Prespansko where Greece, Albania and Jugoslavia meet. The Cretans formed part of the reserve to the Greek army's ten divisions on a front stretching south-west across the Pindus mountains to the coast of Epirus opposite Corfu.

During the second half of November and for most of December, the Greek army advanced valiantly against the Italians, pushing them back into Albania in spite of the wild terrain, bad weather and their deficiency in aircraft and armoured vehicles. By 28 December their right flank was established at Pogradets on Lake Ohridsko.

In this mountain war, only those used to the harshest conditions survived. British officers marvelled at the resilience of the Greek soldiers, equipped with First World War weaponry – much of it taken from the Austrian army – and 'clothing and footwear of a deplorable quality'. Many were bundled in rags. During the march to the front, the luckier ones had been given civilian overcoats by pitying onlookers. It was the worst winter in living memory. Casualties from frostbite far exceeded those from enemy action. Only walking wounded stood a chance of survival. Stretcher cases were almost impossible to evacuate. Resupply, both of rations and ammunition, was erratic since virtually everything had to come up by mule-train. Pack animals that went lame were shot and their carcases stripped of flesh by the ravenous troops. On several occasions, RAF Blenheims had to drop sacks of food to starving, snow-bound units. Even water was a problem, since there was no fuel to melt the snow.

In the next phase, the Cretan Division fought on the central part of the front. In the last few days of January 1941, 5th Division distinguished itself in the fighting for Mount Trebesina and Klissoura, an important road junction. A single Cretan regiment put the 58th Leniano Division to flight. One of the other enemy formations on this sector was the 51st Siena Division, which later in the war occupied the eastern part of Crete: in 1943, after the Italian armistice, Paddy Leigh Fermor smuggled its commander off the island.

Leigh Fermor, escaping the claustrophobic atmosphere of General Headquarters in Athens, did not pay more attention to the Cretan 5th Division on his tour of the Albanian front than to any of the others. The only differences he could recall afterwards were the cheerfulness of the Cretans in spite of the savage cold, and the way they carried their rifles across their shoulders like a yoke, because that was the way the island shepherds walked with their crooks. He had no idea then how important Crete was to become.

2
Diplomatic Missions

In January 1941, the Greeks, after reinforcing their army in Albania, had only four under-strength divisions left for the Bulgarian border of Thrace and Eastern Macedonia. The Commander-in-Chief, General Papagos, hoped that an alliance with Jugoslavia would enable them to crush the Italians in a pincer so that his divisions could be redeployed should the German threat from Roumania increase. Papagos, closely supervised by Metaxas, had handled the advance into Albania with sturdy skill, but his determination to beat the Italians became a fixation, and his tunnel vision was to prove disastrous.

The Jugoslav government of the Regent, Prince Paul, in any case appeared a very uncertain ally at that stage. Armies of the Axis and its inchoate allies lay beyond six out of seven of Jugoslavia's borders: those of Italy, Austria, Hungary, Roumania, Bulgaria and Albania. And Prince Paul − Churchill later dubbed him 'Prince Palsy' − was buckling under pressure from Hitler to sign the Tripartite Pact. In spite of German assurances to the contrary, this would almost certainly mean allowing Germany to use Jugoslavia's railway system to invade Greece. The Greek government had only the British to turn to for help, but Metaxas continued in his policy of not provoking Germany. He did not have Churchill's knowledge of Hitler's intentions.

On 10 January 1941 − the same day that Hitler decided to send a force to Libya to prop up the Italians and that X Air Corps, newly arrived in Sicily, attacked the aircraft-carrier HMS *Illustrious* − Churchill received confirmation from intercepts of German signals decrypted at Bletchley Park, a source later known as Ultra, that the German build-up in Roumania formed a grave threat to Greece. He promptly ordered draft contingency plans for the commitment of a British expeditionary force to the Greek mainland.

General Sir Archibald Wavell, the Commander-in-Chief in the Middle East, was less concerned. During a flurry of signals between London and Cairo on 10 January, he argued that the Germans were basically engaged in 'a war of nerves'. Wavell felt his view was supported when General Heywood arrived from Athens the same day to say that the Greek government thought the Germans were just trying 'to warn both ourselves and [the] Russians off [the] Balkans'. But the Chiefs of Staff, following Churchill's directive, emphasized that his compliance was expected: 'His Majesty's Government have decided that it is essential to afford the Greeks the maximum possible assistance.'

Wavell flew in civilian clothes to Athens three days later for meetings with King George II of Greece, Metaxas and General Papagos. Metaxas wanted to prevent the British from sending a token force – large enough to give the Germans an excuse to invade, but too small to stop them. General Papagos, guided by Metaxas, stated that 'it would be necessary for the Greek forces on the Bulgarian front to be immediately reinforced by nine divisions with corresponding air support'. Wavell replied that this was impossible. He could make available no more than two or three divisions. Metaxas said this was quite inadequate, and to send a small advance guard of artillery, as Wavell suggested, would only provide the Germans with a pretext for attack. Papagos later claimed to have argued that British divisions would in any case be better employed in North Africa.

Wavell reiterated his offer of an advance party just before flying back to Cairo. Having faithfully followed London's instructions, he was privately relieved that the Greeks persisted in refusing such aid, for General O'Connor's forces were advancing into Libya. The Chiefs of Staff in London and the War Cabinet 'all heaved a sigh of relief' too, and so apparently did Churchill in private. Yet Churchill was conscious of broader political issues. Britain was constantly accused by German propaganda of letting down her allies and getting other countries to fight her wars for her. This latter jibe was galling at a time when 'Winston felt he must influence the Americans'.

Ultra intercepts continued to show that the German threat from Roumania was serious, and Churchill, whose view on the wisdom of sending an expeditionary force swung back and forth, refused to accept Wavell's argument that aid to Greece would be 'a dangerous

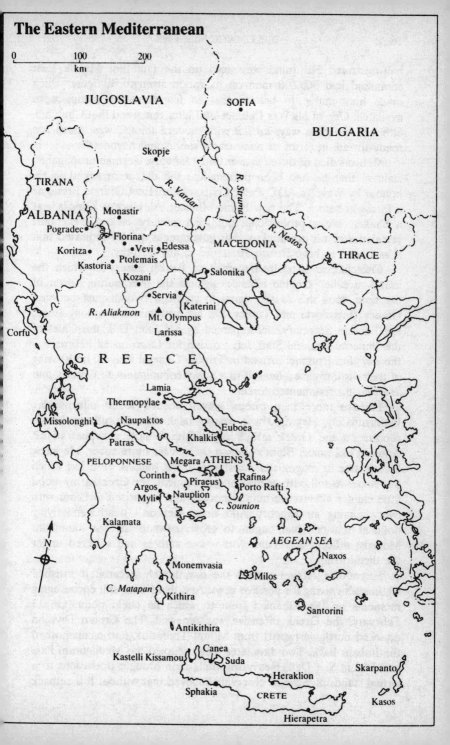

The Eastern Mediterranean

0 — 100 — 200
km

JUGOSLAVIA

SOFIA

BULGARIA

Skopje

TIRANA

R. Vardar

R. Struma

ALBANIA

Monastir

Pogradec

Florina

Koritza

Vevi

Edessa

MACEDONIA

R. Nestos

Kastoria

Ptolemais

THRACE

Kozani

Salonika

Servia

Katerini

R. Aliakmon

Mt. Olympus

Corfu

Larissa

GREECE

Lamia

Thermopylae

Euboea

Missolonghi

Naupaktos

Khalkis

Patras

PELOPONNESE

Megara

ATHENS

Corinth

Piraeus

Rafina

Argos

Nauplion

Porto Rafti

Myli

C. Sounion

Kalamata

AEGEAN SEA

Naxos

Monemvasia

Milos

C. Matapan

Kithira

Santorini

Antikithira

Canea

Kastelli Kissamou

Suda

Skarpanto

Heraklion

Sphakia

CRETE

Kasos

Hierapetra

N

half-measure'. His mind was fixed on the fact that Middle East command had 300,000 men on its ration strength, a figure which made him unable to believe that so few front-line troops were available. One of his War Cabinet staff later remarked that Churchill, although 'in some ways *au fait* with modern things', was 'much too ready to talk in terms of numbers of sabres and bayonets'.

Metaxas died of throat cancer on 29 January. German propaganda claimed that he had been poisoned at the dinner arranged in his honour by Wavell's ADC, Peter Coats, at the Hotel Grande Bretagne a fortnight before. The new Prime Minister, Alexandros Koryzis, was a banker, not a professional politician, and he lacked the robust certainties of his predecessor. His government quickly indicated that it was keen to have British assistance in any quantity.

Churchill, inspired by his sense of British history in which the island race had created alliances against the overbearing power of the time, took this as the signal to create a Balkan pact between Greece, Jugoslavia and Turkey. On his instructions, Anthony Eden, the Foreign Secretary, accompanied by Sir John Dill, the Chief of the Imperial General Staff, left London for Cairo on 12 February – the day that Rommel arrived in Tripoli. General Wavell, on hearing of their visit, resigned himself to a heavy commitment to Greece, and assessed his fragmented forces.

Perhaps more than troops Wavell needed sound information. Unfortunately, Heywood was passing back unrealistically optimistic reports on the Greek army's capabilities, almost a repeat of his delusion in France. Blunt's assessment was far more sober. He knew that despite its magnificent resistance to the Italians, an effort which had taken its toll both of men and equipment, the Greek army stood little chance against German armoured and motorized divisions with overwhelming air support. And since Metaxas's death, underlying political tensions had begun to grow between the still dominant Metaxist officers and Venizelists whose careers had suffered under the dictatorship.

Heywood's version carried the day, largely because it satisfied Churchill's craving for positive news. And there were still encouraging moments on the Albanian front to which he could point. On 13 February, the Greek offensive was renewed. The Cretan Division attacked north-westwards from Mount Trebesina, and again pushed the Italians back. Two days later they occupied the Medjigorani Pass and Mount Sen Deli. Heavy snowfalls soon brought operations to a virtual standstill. Several observers believed that without this setback the Greeks would have captured the port of Valona, and this might have brought about the collapse of the Italian army. Others were less persuaded. The Greeks had neither the supplies nor the transport to sustain their advance.

The air war did not slacken in the face of often terrible flying conditions. On 28 February, the RAF fought its most successful action of the campaign. Two squadrons, one of Hurricanes, the other of Gladiators, shot down twenty-seven Italian aircraft over the Albanian front in an hour and a half. This victory went some way towards mitigating Greek criticism of the RAF's refusal to deploy aircraft in close support of their troops, but at that stage of the war the RAF was attracting similar criticisms from the British Army: it considered itself purely a strategic arm.

At about this time, the Greeks received intelligence reports that the Italians had recovered sufficiently to plan a large counter-attack. This came in the second week of March with twelve Italian divisions deployed between the Apsos and Aöos rivers against the Greek front line of four divisions.

Mussolini, acutely aware that the German invasion being planned would put his army to shame, ordered his troops to attack 'at whatever cost'. During the week that followed, the Cretans in particular distinguished themselves by inflicting heavy losses. Their marksmanship, of which they were inordinately proud, was reputed to be the best in the Greek army. Within ten days, the great Italian counter-attack had petered out, but by then the situation in the Balkans, and indeed the whole of the Middle East, had changed. Mussolini's forces became a comparatively negligible consideration.

On 16 February, the first skirmish between British and German troops in North Africa took place near Sirte. Four days later Churchill acknowledged the dangers of dispersing forces, and signalled Eden, Dill and Wavell in Cairo: 'Do not consider yourselves obligated to a Greek enterprise if in your hearts you feel it would be only another Norwegian fiasco.' But Eden, as the generals soon discovered, would not be diverted from his course.

Churchill, with his strong and at times over-emotional sense of loyalty to the Greeks and their King, longed to help whatever the risk. On the other hand, he still wanted clear advice from senior officers on the spot, yet had given Eden plenipotentiary powers 'in all matters diplomatic and military' before leaving London. This may well have convinced Dill and Wavell that they had no option but to support the line decided by the Foreign Secretary. Eden had clearly become enamoured with the idea of surprising the world with a grand alliance – the sort of *coup de théâtre* of which diplomats dreamed. But, like Churchill, counting in 'sabres and bayonets', such illusions belonged to a past age.

Given the antiquated state of the Jugoslav and Turkish armies and air forces, a Balkan alliance could never have been anything more than a gesture. Wavell opposed Eden's attempt to draw the Turks into this scheme: it was the only time he spoke out firmly on the question. A Turkish defeat and German occupation of the Dardanelles would, he argued with justification, be disastrous. Fortunately, the Turks were clear-sighted enough not to be drawn into this deluded scheme. Aside from the German army massed in Roumania, they feared that Russia, their traditional enemy and still Hitler's ally, might repeat the stab in the back which had been practised on Poland.

On 22 February Eden, accompanied by Dill, Wavell and Air Vice Marshal Longmore, the senior RAF officer in the Middle East, flew to Athens. Before the first meeting at the Tatoi Palace, the Greek government, strongly encouraged by the King, declared its determination to resist the Germans whether the British came to their help or not. The British were impressed, even moved, by this courage. To their further approval, General Papagos conceded that a forward defence of Thrace and Eastern Macedonia was impracticable. He agreed that the bulk of Greek forces should be pulled back to the proposed Aliakmon line which ran from the northern face of Mount Olympus across and then up towards the Jugoslav border along the Vermion range. The safety of its left flank, just forward of the Monastir Gap, clearly depended on the Jugoslav army holding out against the Germans.

Eden, more excited than ever with the idea of a Balkan alliance, promised the Greeks 'formidable' resources, bumping up the figures of the forces available which had been provided in the staff brief. Colonel Freddie De Guingand, a member of the Middle East Joint Planning Staff, watched Wavell's dispirited support for the project with dismay. He, like many other officers later, found it hard to forgive him for not speaking out. After the meeting, De Guingand noted how Eden 'preened himself' in front of the fire while his subordinates congratulated him on a diplomatic triumph.

This military view of events does not tally with that of the Foreign Office. Just before the main meeting, Sir Michael Palairet organized a private lunch to give Wavell a better idea of the issues involved, and to warn him that with the death of Metaxas, the King had the real power of decision. To the surprise of Harold Caccia, who was one of the four present, Wavell, 'normally rather a taciturn man, became quite loquacious'.

He began by saying, 'Well, the situation in Greece is not that different from Egypt', and went on to compare the defensive properties of the Greek mountain ranges to the Qattara Depression. 'That means it's not really relevant to ask how many divisions are needed, since only a certain number can be deployed.' This, like many rushes of false optimism which influenced the principal characters – one suspects an almost desperate effort to conjure a virtue out of necessity – was based on the ill-founded assumption that either the Jugoslavs would stay neutral, or they would resist as fiercely and effectively as in the First World War.

Once the decision to send an expeditionary force had been taken late in the afternoon, Eden, Dill and Wavell left Athens. They paid little attention to developments in Greece for the next ten days: Eden and Dill went to Ankara pursuing the quest for an alliance, and Wavell was fully preoccupied by the problem of stretching already over-stretched resources still further. A frequent remark of his at the time was Wolfe's aphorism: 'War is an option of difficulties.' Meanwhile, De Guingand, in the guise of a journalist, toured the proposed Aliakmon line wearing a borrowed suit in a rather loud check.

On Saturday, 1 March, Bulgaria publicly joined the Tripartite Pact, and on Sunday morning the German Twelfth Army began to cross the Danube from Roumania over three pontoon bridges rapidly assembled by army engineers. Eden and Dill reached Athens a few hours later. General Heywood met them with even worse news. General Papagos had not given the orders for withdrawal to the Aliakmon line. He claimed that without transport there was not time, and that he had in any case been waiting for the response from the Jugoslavs about the security of the line's left flank.

How much Heywood was responsible for this breakdown in communications is hard to tell, but he cannot have been entirely blameless. He was not the person to provide the objective advice which Wavell so badly needed on the exhausted state of the Greek army and, above all, on Papagos's *idées fixes*: his refusal to withdraw from the Bulgarian border, and his refusal to consider the transfer of divisions from Albania, however grave the threat from the north-east.

Over the next two days, British exasperation and injured Greek pride grew in a series of fruitless meetings, which continually returned to the question of who had said what on 22 and 23 February. (General Heywood, in an astonishing oversight, had not kept minutes of the meeting for signature by both sides.) The Greek divisions in Eastern Macedonia were utterly exposed, yet Papagos still refused to move them back. His army possessed no transport and, he asserted, the British Military Mission knew that perfectly well. In any case he had been waiting for the British to inform him of the Jugoslav government's intentions, as he claimed had been agreed. Yet his obstinacy almost certainly owed more to a fear of abandoning Thrace to Bulgar cupidity; and without the port of Salonika, there was little hope of persuading the Jugoslavs to join the Greek army in his cherished project of a pincer attack on the Italians in Albania.

Whatever Papagos's reasons and whatever the cause of the original misunderstanding, the joint staff plan had fallen apart. A poor compromise over the Aliakmon line was reached – Eden compared their discussions to 'the haggling of an Oriental Bazaar' – mainly because the first troopships were leaving Egypt. Colonel Jasper Blunt described the scene in his diary:

Our representatives sat in the drawing-room of the Legation; the secretaries came and went with telegrams; Sir Michael Palairet played host, the harrassed King, the serious face of General Papagos, the deathly pallor of the Greek Premier, the suspense as the King and his advisers conferred behind the closed doors of the Minister's study. The minutes passed and I watched the scenes as a completely unconsulted onlooker. I was a spectator with a seat in the front row of the stalls at a drama as intense as any played on the classical Greek stage with the added interest that I knew the plot, the author and the players.

Blunt had guessed the outcome from the beginning, but out of loyalty to his ambassador and out of respect for the chain of command, he had not revealed his misgivings to Wavell's staff. Palairet only discovered his strength of feeling when they bade farewell to Eden and Dill at Phaleron. Blunt's quiet prediction of a débâcle shocked him deeply.

The commander designate of the British and Dominion forces, Lieutenant General Sir Henry Maitland Wilson, had already arrived in Athens. He had supposedly come incognito – a virtual impossibility for this huge, jolly general. Bald, moustached and round-faced, he had the Edwardian air of a favourite great-uncle.

Wilson and his senior officers felt that Sir Michael Palairet was over-influenced by the Greek King's Anglophilia, and that he still ignored the bleak military reality. After a fighting speech from Palairet 'full of Foreign Office optimism', Wilson was heard to say to his staff, 'Well, I don't know about that. I've already ordered my maps of the Peloponnese.'

The harbours and beaches of the south, as he rightly surmised, would soon become their evacuation points. Yet on board the troopships leaving Alexandria, officers of the expeditionary force, made up mainly of Australian and New Zealand troops, eagerly rolled out maps to study invasion routes up through Jugoslavia towards Vienna.

They were disabused of such optimism on arrival, but not even Wilson, with all his cheerful pessimism, knew that the Joint Planning Staff at Headquarters Middle East had started work in secret on evacuation details – a precaution to which Wavell acceded with reluctance and distaste.

In Cairo, the final decision on intervention was taken when Field Marshal Smuts arrived on 7 March. At an evening conference orchestrated by Eden, Smuts's firm line was that to pull out at such a late stage was unthinkable: although hardly reassuring in military terms, it proved conclusive on political grounds. Eden was clearly relieved to have his support, for Smuts's opinion carried great weight with Churchill.

The following night, when the reply finally arrived from the Jugoslav government – evasiveness permeated every phrase – Anthony Eden turned up with his retinue at the Commander-in-Chief's house overlooking Gezira racecourse. Wavell and Dill were woken on his orders. They came down and, sitting side by side on the sofa in their dressing-gowns, had to listen as Eden paced up and down composing his telegram to Churchill.

Air Vice Marshal Longmore then arrived, also in answer to a summons, and saw 'the two weary soldiers, looking like a couple of teddy-bears, trying to give the Foreign Secretary's eloquence the attention it demanded. They both went quietly to sleep, and when Eden paused for comment only their regular breathing broke the silence.'

The next morning, after his early ride and swim in the pool at

Gezira, Wavell spent a couple of hours at his desk. He then went into Longmore's office and laid the following verses in front of him without a word.

MOST SECRET AND VERY PERSONAL
The Jug
(With apologies to Lewis Carroll)

In Cairo where the Gypsies are,
I sing this song to my guitar.
('Only I'm not going to sing it really,' explained
Anthony kindly.
'Thank you very much indeed,' said Jacqueline.)*
In Athens, when I've met the Greek,
I'll tell you what it is I seek.
('It'll be nice to know,' said Jacqueline.)
I sent a message to the Jug, I told him not to be a mug.
I said he must be badly cracked
To think of joining Hitler's pact.
The Jug replied, 'But don't you see
How difficult it is for me.'
('It's difficult for me too,' said Jacqueline sadly.
'It doesn't get any easier further on,' said Anthony.)
I took a pencil large and new,
I wrote a telegram or two.
Then someone came to me and said
The Generals have gone to bed.
I said it loud, I said it plain,
'Then you must wake them up again.'
And I was very firm with them,
I kept them up till 2 a.m.
('Wasn't that rather unkind?' said Jacqueline.
'Not at all,' said Anthony firmly. 'We want Generals,
not dormice. But don't keep interrupting.')

---

* Lady Lampson, wife of the British Ambassador to Egypt, Sir Miles Lampson, later Lord Killearn.

3
Secret Missions

Irregular warfare in the Eastern Mediterranean held a strong appeal for vigorous young Britons. A cynic might easily dismiss the phenomenon as a sort of adult version of *Swallows and Amazons*, messing about in boats and treating the region as an immense adventure playground. Although many of them exulted in this new life because it provided an ideal escape from peacetime routine or frustrations, the diversity of their characters should be a warning against too simple an analysis. They ranged from Philhellenic dons to well-connected thugs, with many variations in between including a handful of good regular soldiers, romantics, writers, scholar gypsies and the odd *louche* adventurer. The vast majority belonged to SOE, Special Operations Executive, created from the amalgamation in July 1940 of Section D and MI(R). (See Appendix A.)

A process of selection, unusual in wartime, led to a preponderance of archaeologists and dons. Paddy Leigh Fermor later wrote of himself and other 'improvised cave-dwellers' that 'it was the obsolete choice of Greek at school which had really deposited us on the limestone. With an insight once thought rare, the army had realized that the Ancient tongue, however imperfectly mastered, was a short-cut to the modern: hence the sudden sprinkling of many strange figures among the mainland and island crags.'

Those recruited into special operations seem to have sensed that these war years would be the most intense of their life. 'What a lot of material for autobiographies is being provided,' a friend said to the traveller and writer Peter Fleming, who had been recruited by MI(R) shortly before war broke out. He should also have mentioned fiction. Another early member remarked that the same people kept cropping up in unlikely places round the Mediterranean: 'The whole thing was just like an Anthony Powell novel.'

Regular soldiers provided the original basis of MI(R). One of them, a sapper officer called George Young, was held at readiness in Cairo with a field company of Royal Engineers to move into Roumania to blow up the Ploesti oilfields. They were to be guided to their targets by Geoffrey Household, the author of *Rogue Male* and a more recent MI(R) recruit. Household travelled there with 'businessman' written in his passport, not author, because 'Compton Mackenzie and Somerset Maugham [both secret agents in their time] had destroyed our reputation as unworldly innocents for ever'.

The fear of forcing the Roumanians into Axis arms eventually led to the indefinite postponement of Young's mission. Soon afterwards when MI(R) in Cairo was reorganized into SOE's embryo form, Young formed a commando in the Middle East. This was eventually incorporated into Layforce, and he took part in its rearguard action in Crete described in *Officers and Gentlemen* by Evelyn Waugh, the brigade intelligence officer. In Waugh's crisis of disillusionment triggered by this retreat, Young was one of the few to retain his respect.

The most maverick enterprise of this, or perhaps any other stage of the war, was Peter Fleming's private army known as Yak Mission. Fleming, brother of Ian, traveller and author of books such as *Brazilian Adventure* and reserve officer in the Grenadier Guards, was already the veteran of one expeditionary fiasco, the Norwegian campaign. By shameless string-pulling — his father had been a great friend of Churchill — Fleming formed a party to reconnoitre Namsos by Sunderland flying-boat. Then, when the Allied forces landed, he attached himself to General Carton de Wiart who, with 'only one eye, only one arm, and — rather more surprisingly — only one Victoria Cross', was one of the inspirations for Evelyn Waugh's character Brigadier Ben Ritchie-Hook.*

During the invasion scare following Dunkirk, Fleming received orders to organize stay-behind groups known as Auxiliary Units in Southern England. Then, in the autumn of 1940, when the number of Italians taken prisoner by Wavell's forces in the Middle East began to rise, Churchill had the idea of forming a 'Garibaldi Legion' from

---

* The main ingredient for Ritchie-Hook in the *Men at Arms* trilogy was Brigadier St Clair Morford. There was also a dash of Admiral Sir Walter Cowan.

the anti-Fascists amongst them. Fleming recruited half a dozen friends including Norman Johnstone, a fellow Grenadier, and Mark Norman, a subaltern in the Hertfordshire Yeomanry, who 'didn't have a clue what it was about'. Taking their batmen with them like characters out of Dornford Yates, they went off on an intensive course in explosives and close-quarter combat at the Lochailort commando-training centre in the Western Highlands.

Their codename, 'Yak Mission', was inspired by Fleming's book, *News from Tartary*. Issued with a ton of plastic explosive, £40,000 in notes and sovereigns, and Italian pocket dictionaries (since only one of them spoke Italian), they proceeded to Cairo 'with extraordinary priority'.

Failing to obtain a single volunteer from the prison camps, Yak Mission would have been disbanded had it not been for the German threat to the Balkans. Towards the end of March, Peter Fleming persuaded George Pollock, the head of SOE Cairo, to allow them to go to Jugoslavia 'to stiffen Prince Paul's resolve'. Events forced Fleming to modify the plan. Yak Mission would instead make its way to Northern Greece to train resistance groups, and Fleming managed to find room for his men and their equipment on the next troopship sailing from Alexandria. In Athens they made contact with Harold Caccia whose wife, Nancy, was the sister of Oliver Barstow, another of Fleming's guerrilla knights.

Yak Mission, 'bristling with Tommy guns and pistols', made its way north, having bought their own transport out of the war-chest. And at the end of the first week of April, on a mountainside next to the Jugoslav border, amidst breathtaking scenery, the soldier servants pitched the tents and set up the camp-beds 'as if we were on safari'. Peter Fleming could not resist sending a signal to SOE in London – AM HOLDING MONASTIR GAP. He did not know that the Adolf Hitler Leibstandarte, the SS Division commanded by Sepp Dietrich, was heading straight for the site of their glorious picnic.

John Pendlebury, the archaeologist, was always certain that the Germans would invade Greece and then his beloved Crete. He had not been idle since he had split up with Nick Hammond and the others after their flying-boat journey from Poole harbour. Based at first back at the Villa Ariadne which he knew so well from his time as curator of Knossos, and then in Heraklion, he compiled lists of pro-British and pro-Axis citizens. At that stage, before the Italian invasion and while the Metaxas government assiduously held to its neutrality, he had to act the part of 'the most bogus Vice-Consul in the world'. But Pendlebury, like the Cretans with whom he identified so strongly, despised the discretion needed for secret operations. He was far too famous for his work. The Cretans speculated about him, endlessly intrigued by this Englishman with the glass eye and swordstick who strode about their island.

Pendlebury's directness, sense of humour and *joie de vivre* appealed enormously to them: for a Wykehamist of that generation, he was remarkably uninhibited and he seemed to relish contradictions. Pendlebury was a convivial loner with an innocent swagger, and the war − far more anarchic than dictatorial in his case − provided the perfect opportunity to throw himself into the role of a distinctly irregular soldier with irregular weapons.

After the Italian invasion, and with British troops welcomed on Crete by the government in Athens, Pendlebury took out his cavalry captain's uniform and became liaison officer between the British forces and the Greek military authorities. His real interest, however, was the creation of a Cretan force to replace in part the locally raised division sent to the Albanian front.

Pendlebury was quick to sense a slight, and his handling of superiors was not always diplomatic. 'My best rebuke', he wrote, 'was for using the word "bastard" in a wire to a Minister. In reply I pointed out that as it was in the code book the word was obviously meant to be used, that the Minister was old enough to know the facts of life, and that it was the only word that fitted the individual it referred to.'

Official rebuffs did not deter him. At Christmas in 1940, he described the Cretans' war-like spirit: 'I have been carried shoulder high round five towns and villages and have been blessed by two bishops and have made a number of inflammatory speeches from balconies. The spirit is amazing.' And he returned from a barn-storming tour into the White Mountains and round Mount Ida, claiming 'Anglophily is rampant!' Pendlebury had a passion for maps. He prided himself that he knew 'the island better than anyone in the world' and its mountains 'stone by stone'. Given the weapons, he had not the slightest doubt that the Cretans could defeat a German invasion virtually on their own. And that invasion would come as soon as Greece fell.

Pendlebury's friend and colleague, Nick Hammond, was offered work more in line with his expertise after a month in Alexandria with the

Welch Regiment and their Sunday cocktail parties. A.W. Lawrence, a professor of classical archaeology and the half-brother of Lawrence of Arabia, arrived from England, sent by Churchill to train Jews in Palestine for sabotage missions. Arnold Lawrence, Hammond and a gun-runner named Barnes established their school in a kibbutz outside Haifa. Secrecy was essential since their activities constituted a clear breach of the League of Nations Mandate. One of their first pupils was Moshe Dayan who lost his eye training there. But the project did not prosper, mainly due to Churchill's eccentric choice of leader, for A.W. Lawrence proved to be almost as ardent an Arabist as his half-brother.

For his next appointment, Hammond had to move only a few miles down the road when, in October 1940, SOE Cairo's main training-centre for agents was set up. (This camp outside Haifa, later known as ME 102, was a place which he and most SOE officers came to know well over the next four years.) In the early spring of 1941, Hammond was summoned to Athens. He arrived there on 15 March, shortly before Peter Fleming's Yak Mission. Fleming, who lacked an explosives expert, tried to poach him, but with the Wehrmacht's Twelfth Army already in Bulgaria, Hammond felt it was far too late to start training stay-behind groups, and he was already working with the two SOE men inside the Legation. Bill Barbrook was a former regular officer recalled for service because of his Albanian experience, while his companion, Ian Pirie, had been in Greece since before the war, when he was recruited by Section D.

Pirie, an Old Harrovian once described as 'not unlike a grown-up Cupid in well-cut clothes', had a colourful business career behind him which apparently included ill-fated attempts to start a dog cemetery and then a racecourse near Athens. He evidently enjoyed life in the capital with his girl-friend Nicki Demertzi, the devastating blonde at the Argentina night-club, whom he believed to be related to the former prime minister of that name.

Pirie's man-of-the-world act could on occasions be exasperating. One of his more famous remarks concerned the Greek royal family: 'How on earth can one take a dynasty seriously which isn't as old as one's wine merchant?' A number of Ian Pirie's undercover operations

---

* The Argentina's other great attraction was a dancer called La Bella Asmaro who later fell for Captain Mark Chapman-Walker of the Rifle Brigade, General Jumbo Wilson's ADC. (Chapman-Walker can be seen on the far right of illustration 4.)

strongly suggested a compulsive levity. Apparently in all seriousness, he proposed to Harold Caccia, the First Secretary, that to boost morale in the wake of a German take-over, they should import musical lavatory-roll holders which played the Greek national anthem when the paper was pulled.

One operation, which was slightly more professional at least in theory, targeted a German wireless transmitter operated from a private apartment. It broadcast messages to Berlin at regular times, so Pirie arranged to create a sudden surge of the electric current supplied to the building, hoping this would make the circuits explode. Instead, the escapade produced an explosion of protests from other occupants, including the American Minister and a dentist who was drilling a patient's tooth at the time. The Germans merely switched to a generator and carried on.

Pirie's main mission to create a resistance network in advance was unsuccessful, although this may not have been entirely his fault. With unusual frankness, since diplomats generally preferred to remain ignorant of SOE activities, he warned Harold Caccia, a contemporary from Trinity College, Oxford, about his secret work. The Metaxas government was strongly opposed to any covert activity which might upset the Germans, so Pirie felt he could not attempt to recruit anybody associated with the regime – they would denounce him to the agents of the Minister of National Security, Maniadakis. This left only the opposition groups, mainly of the non-Communist left – strict Communist Party members still had to regard Nazi Germany as the ally of 'socialism's motherland'.*

As British military assistance to Greece increased slowly in the winter of 1940 and then greatly in the early spring of 1941, so too did the involvement of all the rival intelligence organizations. David Hunt, the archaeology don attached to the Welch Regiment in Alexandria, had arrived in Athens in November 1940, accompanied by Geoffrey Household, now in a new role of field security officer. They joined the RAF intelligence staff headed by Wing Commander Viscount Forbes, who had been Air Attaché in the Bucharest Legation at the time of Household's fruitless wait for George Young's sappers.

* As an early example of the sort of political contradictions in which SOE would become involved in the region, Pirie, while recruiting left-wingers in Athens, was also sending supplies to General Mihailovic in Serbia in anticipation of Prince Paul succumbing to pressure from Hitler to sign the Tripartite Pact.

While Household liaised with Greek security officers, Hunt, as a staff captain intelligence, processed the signals intercepts, both Ultra and the lower-grade but more immediate material. Conventional military intelligence and the under-cover organizations (mainly in the form of the assistant military attachés dotted around in Balkan capitals) were seldom the best of friends. The rivalries then became further exacerbated, because General Wilson, dissatisfied with Stanley Casson of the British Military Mission, brought in Colonel Quilliam from GHQ Middle East as his own intelligence chief. When the Jugoslav army collapsed without warning in April, accusations of incompetence flew back and forth between departments with great vehemence.

4
The Double Invasion

In a vain attempt at security, the men of the 2nd New Zealand Expeditionary Force sent to Greece were not told their destination in advance. They had been issued with pith helmets, marched on to troopships, and then suffered four days of storms. 'Half the time the propellers were out of the water', they used the pith helmets as 'spew-baskets', and arrived 'sick as dogs'.

The combative optimism of those officers who rolled out maps to study invasion routes up to Austria fared little better. At the harbour of Piraeus, they found the German Military Attaché's staff on the quayside making detailed notes of their strength and equipment.* In Athens, the swastika flag flew opposite the British headquarters on the side of Mount Lycabettus. And commanding officers summoned to a briefing at the Acropole Palace Hotel heard that the whole plan of defence of the Aliakmon line had been compromised.

Yet there was little anger as units camped in the attractive hillside pinewoods ringing the north of Athens. The British and Dominion troops liked and admired the Greeks for their resistance to the Italian invasion, and in any case, CMFUs (Complete Military Fuck-Ups) were regarded as par for the course. A traditional Army fatalism took over: 'We're here, because we're here, because we're here' ran the song. Some of the Australian and New Zealand troops, on the other hand, began to wonder why they made up the majority of a doomed expeditionary force sent to honour a British obligation.

* The German Military Attaché was apparently half Scottish by birth. His English was good enough to fool some unwary officers who chatted to him quite freely.

Wavell, once the disastrous misunderstanding over the Aliakmon
line had come to light, had approached the Australian corps
commander, Lieutenant General Thomas Blamey, and the New
Zealand commander, Major General Bernard Freyberg. Although an
embarrassing refusal was unlikely, Wavell and the Chiefs of Staff in
London were greatly relieved when they and their prime ministers
separately accepted the 'additional risks involved'. But the two
Dominion governments later felt they had not been fully informed,
and both Blamey and Freyberg were to be criticized for not having
passed on their private doubts at the time.

Jumbo Wilson's command in Greece, known as W Force,
consisted of the New Zealand Division on the right of the Aliakmon
line holding the Servia Pass near Mount Olympus, the British 1st
Armoured Brigade pushed forward to the north and north-east as a
screen, and the 6th Australian Division on the left. At the last
moment, Wavell retained the 7th Australian Division and the Polish
Independent Brigade in North Africa when the strength of Rommel's
attack along the coast made itself felt. This might be described as a
fortunate piece of bad timing, since these formations would have
made little difference to the outcome in Greece, and their absence
reduced the scale of the evacuation later.

Although cold in the mountains, the days before the battle began
are remembered as idyllic. The beauty of the weather, the scenery
and the wild flowers left almost as deep an impression as the warmth
of the welcome in the villages. One officer wrote: 'I felt more like a
bridegroom than a soldier with my truck decorated with sprigs of
peach blossom and my buttonhole with violets.' While British officers
tried to communicate with their Greek counterparts in ancient Greek
ill-remembered from the schoolroom, their soldiers, surmounting the
language barrier in their own inimitable fashion, established a thriving
market to supplement rations, with empty petrol cans fetching four
eggs apiece. Lamb and wine for the officers' mess were bought
locally, while delicacies had to be fetched from Salonika. On Sundays,
Church Parade would be held in the village church at the invitation
of the priest.

On 2 April, Anthony Eden and General Sir John Dill, on their
way to confer with the Jugoslav government on the border, turned up
at the officers' mess of the Northumberland Hussars unannounced.
Dick Hobson, the 12th Lancer brigade major who accompanied the
visitors, later wrote: 'They were on the way to parley with the
Jugoslavs, who were wavering as to which side to back. Mr. Eden had

a special letter for the Duke [of Northumberland], then a captain in the regiment. (It transpired that this important missive was in fact his huntsman's report on the doings of the Percy Hounds!) At that time the cherry and other fruit trees on the plain had all been sprayed with copper sulphate and the trunks were all green. I remarked "I'm longing to see the blossom come out on the tops of those trees; what a sight that will be." Eden and Dill exchanged glances and said "I fear you won't be here long enough for that." '

On 25 March, Prince Paul, the Regent of Jugoslavia, had signed the Tripartite Pact in Vienna, after intense pressure from Hitler who wanted to use the Jugoslav railway system in his invasion of Greece. Two days later a *coup d'état* in Belgrade deposed him. Popular demonstrations of defiance followed in which a crowd insulted the German Ambassador, spitting and thumping on his car.

The news of this spectacular rebuff arrived in Berlin during the visit of the Japanese Foreign Minister, Matsuoka. Hitler, 'gasping for revenge' in the words of his official interpreter, gave immediate orders for invasion. Ribbentrop was called out from his meeting with Matsuoka – he had just suggested that the Japanese take Singapore from the British – and General Halder was immediately summoned to the Chancellery. The German General Staff, the OKH, stood by to work through the night drafting operational orders on the basis of a planning exercise carried out by Halder the previous October. Preparations for Operation Barbarossa, the projected invasion of Russia, were set aside as a total of twenty-nine divisions and nearly 2,000 aircraft were designated for the Balkan campaign. This double assault, an exercise in conspicuous over-kill, would come under the direction of Field Marshal von Brauchitsch in Wiener Neustadt south of Vienna. In the event many of these formations were not needed, and one division never even knew it had formed part of the order of battle.

The sudden turn of events in Belgrade in fact suited the Germans. The conquest of Jugoslavia would make the conquest of Greece much easier. And for Hitler's peace of mind, the subjection of the 'southern Slavs' would prevent any alliance with their Russian kinsmen after the launch of Operation Barbarossa.

But the show of Jugoslav defiance, followed by the Royal Navy's successful fleet action against an Italian naval force south-west of Cape Matapan (the centre claw of the Peloponnese), led the British into a rush of false optimism. Churchill became quite carried away.

THE DOUBLE INVASION

He cabled to the Australian government: 'Thursday's events in Belgrade show the far-reaching effects of this and other measures we have taken on whole Balkan situation. German plans have been upset, and we may cherish renewed hopes of forming a Balkan front with Turkey, comprising about seventy Allied divisions from the four Powers concerned.' His immoderate optimism was harshly exposed just over a week later.

Shortly before dawn on 6 April, the most devastating phase of the Balkan war began with the simultaneous invasion of Jugoslavia and Greece. The people of Belgrade paid for their foolhardy courage of ten days before. Several thousand died (estimates vary between three and seventeen thousand) when the city was pounded to rubble by relentless bombing, and the Jugoslav army's communication system collapsed. Later the same night, German raiders bombed the harbour of Piraeus and hit the *Clan Fraser*. Not knowing the nature of its cargo, Geoffrey Household and his sergeant major of field security went on board to inspect the blaze. They left just in time. Full of munitions, the ship exploded in the early hours, destroying most of the main harbour and sinking eleven other vessels. The effect on morale was considerable.

General Papagos's obsessive belief in a joint Greek–Jugoslav operation against the Italians in Albania proved to have been no more than a pipe-dream. The Jugoslav armed forces on which Papagos's plan had depended were found to be lamentably unprepared. Their army, almost a million strong, foolishly stretched round an immense length of frontier, managed to kill only 151 Germans in the whole campaign. Colonel Blunt's warning that the Jugoslavs would need at least a month to mobilize had been ignored amidst the official enthusiasm for the Balkan pact.

The Greek divisions on the Metaxas line, which ran along the River Nestos in the east then along the Bulgarian border as far as Jugoslavia, fought with great tenacity. Its forts were much less restrictive than the Maginot line, enabling its garrisons to sally forth unexpectedly. The German 5th Mountain Division, which later formed half the invasion force for Crete, was 'repulsed in [the] Rupel Pass despite strongest air support and sustained considerable casualties'. But the line was broken by the 6th Mountain Division: it managed to cross a snow-covered range over 2,000 metres high which the Greeks had considered impassable. One garrison fought so bravely that the Germans allowed the defenders to march out with their weapons and saluted them.

The German 2nd Panzer Division captured Salonika on 9 April and the Greek Second Army east of the River Vardar surrendered. Yet an even greater threat to the country's heartland was exposed by the Jugoslav collapse. In less than three days, the invasion route to Greece through the Monastir Gap lay open. This exposed the left flank of the Aliakmon line and the right rear of the Greek army in Albania. General Papagos later described this disaster as the development of 'an adverse situation', and tried to lay the blame on faulty intelligence from the Jugoslavs and from the British.

W Force's most exposed formation was the 1st Armoured Brigade, which consisted of the light tanks of the 4th Hussars; the Matildas of the 3rd Royal Tank Regiment; the 2nd Royal Horse Artillery with twenty-five pounders; the Northumberland Hussars, an anti-tank regiment; and the Rangers, confusingly also known as the 9th Battalion of the King's Royal Rifle Corps. From disembarkation, most of their vehicles had already covered nearly five hundred miles of bad roads to their positions between the snow-covered mass of Mount Olympus and the Jugoslav mountains. The tanks, already dilapidated and with a high track mileage, were taken by railway on flats as far as the junction at Amynteon. Centred initially on Edessa, less than thirty kilometres as the crow flies from the border, the brigade faced north-east, towards the Axios valley which led down from Jugoslavia to Salonika.

The bulk of W Force consisted of the New Zealand Division under Freyberg on the right between the sea and the Mount Olympus range, and Blamey's Australian Corps, now only a division strong at the hinge of the line south of Servia, just across the mountains from the New Zealanders. But a threat from the north through the Monastir Gap was considered so potentially disastrous that General Wilson, always dubious of Papagos's reliance on the 'Jugs', formed a composite formation under the Australian divisional commander, General Iven Mackay. Mackay Force, with two Australian battalions and part of the 1st Armoured Brigade, was pushed forward to form a line just south of Vevi to cover the exit from the Monastir Gap. The Australians especially, newly arrived from North Africa, suffered badly from the cold in their defensive positions above the snowline.

The absence of news from Jugoslavia was unsettling. Then confirmation of the German capture of Skopje arrived on the afternoon of 8 March. One commanding officer ordered to pull back rapidly to new positions felt tempted to ask, 'Facing which way?' German divisions would soon be advancing from the north and from the east. The heroic Greek defence of the Metaxas line had only slowed the German advance for a few days.

The other formations in W Force also had to adjust their positions. The New Zealand Division received orders to fall back from the coastal strip below the Aliakmon river to defend the Servia Pass, the Olympus Pass and the Vale of Tempe. Meanwhile to their north the Australian 16th Brigade manned the Veria Pass. W Force's weakest link was inevitably its connection with the Greek Central Macedonian Army, the right wing of the Greek forces on the Albanian front. Liaison and communications between British and Greek headquarters were not good enough to keep each other abreast of events. And when the German XL Panzer Corps began its rapid probes from the north, the Greek army's lack of motor transport prevented its divisions from retreating as rapidly as their allies.

Peter Fleming and Yak Mission on the Jugoslav frontier realized there was no time to accomplish their task of forming and training stay-behind groups. Deciding that withdrawal was better than a suicidal gesture on their own, they opted to become a free-lance demolition team at the service of any commander they encountered.

Starting with Mackay Force, the members of Yak Mission tackled a major bridge on the Florina road. This they followed with the marshalling yard at Amynteon, where they destroyed twenty locomotives. Driving trains and blowing them up — causing what Fleming later called 'havoc of a spectacular and enjoyable kind' — became their speciality on the retreat south from Macedonia.

Dick Hobson, the brigade major of the 1st Armoured Brigade, took little pleasure in such tasks. 'I must say as I sat in front of the wireless about to give the order for the demolitions I remember reflecting what a foul thing I was about to perpetrate. The Greeks had been wonderfully kind to us, and here we were about to lay waste their countryside and ruin their livelihood; and to run away apparently without a fight.' By chance, Hobson saw Fleming arrive at brigade headquarters near Ptolemais three days later: 'Who should turn up but Peter Fleming, immaculately dressed as a Captain in the Grenadier Guards straight out of Wellington Barracks, complete with walking stick and seemingly unmindful of what was going on.' (It should be said that Hobson greatly liked and admired Peter Fleming. One day shooting in England, he asked why Fleming was wearing hunting boots. 'I have to,' he replied. 'I broke my leg yesterday.')

On 11 April, a cold clear day, the first main engagement for the Australians and the 1st Armoured Brigade took place in the area south of Vevi. Gerry de Winton, who commanded the signals squadron, remembered the valley scene in the evening light as 'just like a picture by Lady Butler, with the sun going down on the left, the Germans attacking from the front, and on the right the gunners drawn up in position with their limbers'. However spectacular the scene, the resistance appears to have been effective. Ultra intercept OL 2042 reported, 'Near Vevi Schutzstaffel Adolf Hitler meeting violent resistance.'

In spite of bad communications, a change in the weather to freezing rain and flurries of snow brought in by the north-west wind known as the Vardar, W Force's withdrawal in the face of superior forces managed to evade enemy attempts at encirclement. These successes had little to do with brilliant intuition on the part of Jumbo Wilson, who hardly merited the description of a 'thinking general'.

Hut 3 at Bletchley Park, only established at the beginning of the year, was already providing decrypts of German radio traffic with remarkable speed, mainly thanks to the laxity of Luftwaffe radio procedure. This signals intelligence was never sufficiently immediate to lay elaborate traps for the advancing enemy – W Force in any case lacked the command and control, training and equipment to make the most of such opportunities – but it certainly helped save the British and Dominion forces from disaster. Security regulations surrounding Ultra material prevented the British from sharing this information with the Greeks, but since their army on the Albanian front was pitifully short of transport, it probably made little difference. Papagos did not begin the withdrawal across the Pindus mountains until 13 April. As a result the Germans managed to force an armoured wedge between W Force and his right-hand divisions which soon led to their encirclement.

The enemy spear-point on the Monastir front, including the Adolf Hitler Liebstandarten, never slackened in attack, but the crudity of German armoured tactics revealed how little resistance they had come to expect. In the passes between the Vernion and Vermon mountain ranges, the guns of the 1st Armoured Brigade, including the 2nd Royal Horse Artillery's twenty-five pounders fired over open sights, inflicted heavy losses on a number of occasions, but the worn-out M.10 cruisers of the 3rd Royal Tank Regiment were breaking down. Tracks designed for the desert came off regularly and spare parts generally were in depressingly short supply. With no time for anything except the simplest repair, mechanical casualties had to be abandoned at the side of the road and set on fire.

Just south of Ptolomais, the Duke of Northumberland's troop, with anti-tank guns mounted on the back of their portee lorries, faced an armoured thrust. Under heavy fire, the brigade commander, Rollie Charrington, wandered up. Not wanting to interfere in the running of the battle, he remarked to Hughie Northumberland: 'My dear fellow, how nice to see you. I've always wanted to tell you how marvellous your mother looked at the Coronation.'

Nearby, a mixed force of New Zealand machine-gunners, a troop of the 3rd Tanks and a battery of the 2nd Royal Horse Artillery opened up. The enemy thought that they represented a whole armoured division. But this was a rare success. A leap-frog retreat from gorge to mountain pass developed. In places German bombs blasted the road from the shale-covered hillside. Gerry de Winton remembered 'a hole twenty yards long which the command vehicle crew filled with dead mules rivetted with castaway Greek rifles.'

In retreat, rumours spread even more feverishly, with desperate attempts at optimism: a Canadian division had landed at Salonika to take the Germans in the rear, several hundred Spitfires had arrived. The Greeks were far more fatalistic, and also generous. British troops, touched and embarrassed, found themselves fêted by villagers each time they pulled out. One commanding officer was held up when the priest blessed his staff car with holy water. Greek feelings towards the enemy were demonstrated in a less pacific manner. Gerry de Winton, on seeing a German pilot bale out from his aircraft and parachute into a copse just outside a village, went forward to take him prisoner. A group of civilian mechanics barred his way. 'You stay out,' they told him, brandishing heavy spanners. 'We'll settle this.'

Air attacks, few in number at first, had stepped up once the rain and snow cleared. Mark Norman of Yak Mission remembered how the clarity of the sky could produce a curious optical effect. Spotting a Stuka poised to dive, he had hurled himself from their truck into the roadside ditch. Glancing back at their attacker, he saw it flap its wings. In that brilliant light 'a hawk at two hundred feet looked just like a Stuka at two thousand'.

The other bird to cause confusion was the stork. Alighting in great numbers in the course of their northern migration, they provoked wild reports of parachute landings. Other birds caused only pleasure. A member of the rearguard described listening to nightingales in a wood near Atlante until two in the morning. He and his troop of anti-tank guns were waiting for part of the Australian Division to pull back through their positions. They discovered at dawn that the unit in question had left long before, and they were in danger of being cut off. British officers in Greece had a low opinion of this particular Australian formation: one remarked that 'Their great battle-cry in Greece was "We're getting out!" ' Others observed that they had suffered most from the cold in the mountains, and added that even if they pulled out suddenly, they were just as likely to turn back again and fight.

Air attacks became frequent after the first week, once Luftwaffe air groups began to operate from advanced fields near Salonika. Few British fighters were seen opposing them. New Zealanders began to say that the initials RAF stood for Rare As Fairies. (Only 80 of their 152 aircraft were serviceable when the Germans attacked.) General Wilson noted that his men were becoming 'bomb-happy' and would abandon their vehicles at the appearance of any sort of aircraft in the distance. Yet strafing and bombing attacks on convoys were, in the eyes of British officers, astonishingly light, considering the targets presented during the often agonizingly slow withdrawal. 'Well,' said Brigadier Rollie Charrington, observing the ten-mile-long military traffic jam from a mountain pass, 'if the Boche starts bombing, that's the end of our brigade.' But most of the 1st Armoured Brigade's cruiser tanks succumbed instead to mechanical failure and were abandoned on the way.

Disengagements, when possible, were made by driving through the night. Tiredness, with drivers frequently falling asleep at the wheel during night moves, produced its own form of casualties to both men and vehicles. When the convoy came to a halt, the drivers would fall asleep so soundly that officers behind could only wake them up by firing a revolver past the cab window. Even those who stayed awake might wonder if they were dreaming, so strange were some of the sights during the retreat. A Belgrade playboy in co-respondent shoes accompanied by his mistress in an open Buick two-seater incongruously appeared in the military traffic jam. And one night, an officer of the British Military Mission saw by moonlight a squadron of Serbian lancers in long cloaks pass like ghosts of the defeated in wars long past.

Routes became clogged by broken-down vehicles, carts, horse-drawn artillery and the weary, trudging remnants of the Greek army from Macedonia. Bomb craters had to be filled in and obstructions pushed or winched off the side of the road. For one unit, a stretch of twenty-three miles took nine hours.

General Wilson realized that, with the bulk of the Greek army cut off in Albania – due to what he called 'the fetishistic doctrine that not a yard of ground should be yielded to the Italians' – all hope of holding the Germans north of Larissa had gone. Signals intelligence warned of the threat of encirclement from the west. Wilson therefore gave orders to fall all the way back to the Thermopylae line. Larissa itself was a dangerous bottleneck: already ruined by an earthquake at the beginning of the winter, it had been crushed anew by the Luftwaffe. Disengagement was difficult, particularly with the German threat to the left flank, but the real danger came on the right near Mount Olympus. The 5th New Zealand Brigade managed to hold the Vale of Tempe, the River Pinios gorge which led to Larissa, for three days against heavy attacks by the 2nd Panzer Division and the 6th Mountain Division.

Commanded by General Blamey, who was greatly liked by British officers, the newly named Anzac Corps – the 6th Australian Division and the 2nd New Zealand Division – pulled back to the line at Thermopylae. Through a disastrous oversight, a large supply dump at Larissa fell intact into the hands of the German mountain troops, giving the enemy the means to continue the advance without pause.

Determined attacks by German panzer units, and the warning from signals intelligence of a German flanking movement down the Adriatic coast and along the Gulf of Corinth, soon made the Thermopylae position untenable. On 18 April, the Prime Minister, Alexandros Koryzis, shot himself. Nobody in Athens believed the story of 'heart-failure'. Wavell flew in the following morning – his staff officers had been told to bring revolvers this time because of the uncertainty of the situation – and at another round of meetings at the Tatoi Palace, the decision to evacuate British and Dominion forces was made on 20 April.

The King had invited to this meeting General Mazarakis, a leader of the republican opposition. He wanted him to join the government, whose direction he had personally assumed after Koryzis's death. But the republicans refused to have any part in it if the hated Maniadakis remained in office. General Wilson successfully resisted their demand, arguing that no change in the direction of security matters could be contemplated at such a critical moment. The point is only important because these details were later used by the Communist Party in its contention that the British had supported 'Metaxist collaborators' from the beginning.

The same day, a *coup d'état* took place within the Army of Epirus, an act partly prompted by a perverse streak of vanity. General Tsolacoglou, the new, self-appointed commander, wanted to negotiate terms with the SS commander General Sepp Dietrich, and not with the despised Italians. 'On the Führer's birthday,' recorded the Waffen SS divisional staff, 'at about 1600 hours, two Greek officers with white flags approached our front line.'* But Tsolacoglou failed to achieve his objective. Mussolini was outraged to hear of such manoeuvres which flouted the Axis understanding that Greece belonged to the Italian sphere of influence. Although Hitler sympathized both with Sepp Dietrich and his army commander, Field Marshal List, an argument over protocol did not merit a breach with his ally. The terms accorded to Tsolacoglou were cancelled and the Italian General Ferrero was allowed to take the formal surrender alongside General Jodl two days later.

Jumbo Wilson, one of the few senior British officials to regard the Metaxist regime as truly Fascist, suspected 'fifth-column work' by 'certain individuals in Athens who had been highly placed in the late Government': there had indeed been a series of feelers put out towards the Germans since a month before the invasion. But Wilson, even less politically sophisticated than most officers of his generation, failed to see this irony in the light of his opposition to Maniadakis's removal.

For RAF squadrons, the retreat was depressingly reminiscent of the fall of France. Often the ground-crews had hardly finished pitching tents when orders — or counter-orders — came through to pull back to yet another improvised landing ground. Due to lack of spare parts, aircraft had to be cannibalized ruthlessly in their task of 'patching and dispatching', and several times a day they would be harried by Messerschmitt 109s and the twin-engined 110s on strafing missions.

For anti-aircraft defence, there was only the odd Lewis gun mounted on what looked like an exceptionally tall music-stand. In most cases, ground-crews had nothing but rifles. At Eleusis aerodrome, between Athens and the isthmus of Corinth, three 'erks', as aircraftmen were known, managed to down a Messerschmitt 109,

---

* Thanks to an Ultra intercept (OL 2128) — 'Commander of unidentified Greek Army believed ready to capitulate' — the British were forewarned.

but that was a fluke. And later at Argos, Air Commodore Grigson was seen 'standing in the centre of the field with rifle to shoulder. An aircraftman loaded for him, and they stood there as calmly as if they were on the grouse moors.'

The last major air battle took place on 20 April, Easter Day in the Greek calendar, when fifteen fighters – all that remained of the three Hurricane squadrons – took on over 120 German aircraft above Athens and Piraeus. Between them, pilots such as 'Timber' Woods, 'Dixie' Dean and 'Scruffy' Dowding – shot down twenty-two enemy machines for the loss of ten of their own.

In Athens, once the sirens fell silent, there was a curious air of normality. Optimistic rumours circulated that the Thermopylae line would hold. On the evening of 21 April, Theodore Stephanides, an Anglo-Greek doctor serving in the Royal Army Medical Corps – also a writer and friend of Lawrence Durrell from Corfu – had dropped in at the Officers' Club, just opposite the Hotel Grande Bretagne, then dined at Costi's restaurant with hardly a care in the world. Next morning, the order for evacuation was given.

The news came as a shock. Stephanides was not alone in assuming that a stand would be made in the Peloponnese. Yet the British civilian community in Greece had few illusions. A crowd of them had virtually tried to storm the Legation gates as early as 17 April, demanding to know the plans for their evacuation. According to the correspondent Clare Hollingworth, it was 'not an impressive sight'.

Over the next two days W Force withdrew, screened by a strong rearguard. Under cover of dive-bombing attacks, the German armour made probing attacks on the Thermopylae road. The 5th New Zealand Artillery and the Northumberland Hussars between them knocked out sixteen tanks on 24 April. Only their well-sited positions saved them from the full effect of the Germans' skilful combination of synchronized air and ground attack.

That night the rearguard pulled out. They reached Athens the next morning 'having driven with the devil at their heels'. The last defensive position of the anti-tank guns was next to the house of the First Secretary at the American Embassy. He offered the officers drinks on his veranda, but said he could not invite them inside without compromising United States neutrality. Soon afterwards, a senior police officer from Athens arrived to ask the detachment to move on since resistance so close to the capital might provoke German reprisals. They immobilized their guns near the Palace at

Tatoi, removing breech-blocks and sights, then followed on to the evacuation points.

Once again, touched and embarrassed by the embraces, flowers and gifts of wine from those they were abandoning, the departing troops were cheered on their way: 'Come back with good fortune! Return with victory!'

5
Across the Aegean

For the British and Dominion forces, the need to escape before the Germans arrived produced a form of waking anxiety-dream: a school-corridor fear of being late combined with a child's fear of being left behind. At the camp at Kokinia, outside Athens, 'lorries were being hurriedly packed, stores and equipment were flung about anyhow, officers' valises and suitcases were lying open with their contents scattered around as if the owners had made a hasty choice of their more valuable belongings at the last moment'.

The surrender of the Army of Epirus allowed the Germans to push round the Thermopylae line from the Adriatic coast, and advance on Athens along the north shore of the Gulf of Corinth. To protect the Peloponnese, General Wilson moved two squadrons of the 4th Hussars to Patras to oppose any attempt to land on the southern shore. And to delay the enemy's right hook on Athens, he sent Yak Mission to block the road along the north side of the Gulf between Naupaktos and Missolonghi. By then Fleming's band had run out of explosive, so they had to fetch some 500lb. bombs from a dump just across the isthmus at Corinth and sail them to their target by caique (the classic fishing or trading schooner of the region with an engine added in case the wind failed). This improvised demolition, although not wholly successful, was enough to slow the German advance from that direction while the evacuation proceeded apace.

The main harbour of Piraeus was filled with blackened wrecks, and the houses along the waterfront were little more than burnt-out shells. Only the surrounding docks were fully serviceable. Early in the evening of 22 April, about forty German prisoners, mainly Luftwaffe pilots, were marched on board the SS *Elsi* and put in the hold. The

Australian soldiers, who guarded them from above, had grenades ready to lob down if there was trouble. Amongst the civilian passengers, Professor A.R. Burn of the British Council and his wife welcomed the presence of the enemy in their midst. So certain were they of the fifth column's efficacy in Athens that they believed Goering would know immediately and give orders to spare the ship. The *Elsi* crossed the Aegean, and everyone disembarked safely at Suda Bay before the Luftwaffe sank her there on 29 April; so their faith was not confounded.

The same day, most of the Royal Household − not forgetting Otto, the royal dachshund − boarded a Sunderland flying-boat at Phaleron. The ship on which they had been due to leave the previous day had been sunk at its moorings. The party included Crown Princess Frederica, her two children, Constantine, who later lost the throne of Greece, and Sophia, the present Queen of Spain, together with their Scottish nanny. King George's mistress, the admirable Mrs Britten-Jones, was designated lady-in-waiting to the Crown Princess Frederica.

Joyce Britten-Jones was one of the very few royal mistresses in history for whom no one seems to have had anything but praise. Harold Caccia described her as the very best sort of Army wife, thoroughly sensible, never involving herself in intrigue and excellent in a crisis. Her husband, a captain in the Black Watch who drank too much, had been ADC to the Viceroy when the King of the Hellenes visited India not long before his restoration to the throne. A close relationship had soon developed, and in 1936 Mrs Britten-Jones had rather appropriately acted as the King's hostess when entertaining Edward VIII and Mrs Simpson during their summer cruise on the *Nahlin*.

Joyce Britten-Jones's steadying effect on King George had prompted Eden to demand in March that her air passage from London to Greece, via Cairo, should be facilitated in every way. But the attempt to keep her journey secret had foundered on her arrival at Heliopolis aerodrome, when General de Gaulle, arriving on the same aeroplane, had insisted that she should precede him, just as the band struck up with the Marseillaise. Sir Miles Lampson, the proconsular British Ambassador to Egypt, entertained her discreetly. By chance, he had known her father-in-law, 'Jerky' Jones, the manager of the Hongkong and Shanghai Bank in Yokohama. Finally, she had reached Athens at the beginning of April, only a few days before the German invasion of Greece.

Crown Prince Paul ('Palo') watched the flying-boat containing his family take off from Phaleron. He left for Crete the next day, with his brother the King on another Sunderland accompanied by Emmanuel Tsouderos, the Prime Minister, Sir Michael Palairet and Colonel Blunt, the Military Attaché.

The British Legation and the Hotel Grande Bretagne reeked of burnt paper – that unmistakable smell of retreat – as diplomats and staff officers hurriedly destroyed documents.* Officers of W Force later complained that the only records brought out of Greece had been their mess bills. But the 1st Armoured Brigade's signal squadron, based alongside the Palace of Tatoi, made up for this disadvantage. The royal chamberlain telephoned the King in Crete to ask for instructions, and was told to distribute wine from the cellars, two bottles for each officer and one for each soldier.

The evacuation date for most of the Military Mission and headquarters staff still in Athens was 24 April. The chief intelligence officer of British Air Forces Greece, Wing Commander Lord Forbes, accompanied by David Hunt, waited at the aerodrome in the early hours of the morning. He had been asked by the Greeks to fly one of their Avro Ansons on to Crete. Forbes waited his turn to take off at dawn, but an unusually early Luftwaffe strike forced them to throw themselves into a slit trench, from where they watched the destruction of their aircraft.

Forbes and Hunt returned to Athens, killed time at Forbes's apartment, then drove down that evening to the Piraeus through streets in which people stood around uncertainly. At the quayside, they joined the *Kalanthe*, a steam yacht originally requisitioned by the Greek navy from its English owner, and now assigned to the British Legation. The Naval Attaché acted as captain, and the passengers also numbered Harold and Nancy Caccia, their children, dogs and Chinese amah; Colonel Jasper Blunt's wife, Doreen; various members of the Military Mission including Charles Mott-Radclyffe; and a number of prominent Greeks. A subsequent and most surprising addition to this company was the exiled Communist leader, Miltiades Porphyroyennis, whom Harold Caccia allowed to join them from exile on the island of Kimolos. Caccia, who dubbed this curiously-named Communist 'old born-in-the-purple', encountered him again across a negotiating table during the Greek civil war.

* Ultra signal OL 2142 of 22 April ordered: 'take greatest care to burn all deciphered material this series. Vital security our source.'

Peter Fleming's Yak Mission, having loaded their remaining weapons and explosives, were to defend the *Kalanthe* in the event of air attack, with an officer and his soldier servant operating each of the four Lewis guns. Several very dubious allegations were made against Fleming at this time. According to one story, Colonel Blunt and Fleming had a row the day before the *Kalanthe* sailed, with Blunt insisting that since Yak Mission had come to Greece as a stay-behind force, Fleming would be a deserter if he left. Another claimed that Fleming fastened a bandage unnecessarily to his head on arrival in Egypt and tried to wangle himself a DSO. Fleming, it must be remembered, had stirred up a considerable measure of righteous jealousy with his string-pulling in London and Cairo, so these accounts should be treated with some caution.

There was no doubt about the dispute in which General Heywood, the head of the Military Mission, became involved. Having received urgent orders from Cairo to destroy the RAF's fuel tanks containing over 30,000 tons of petrol and aviation spirit, a valuable prize for the Luftwaffe, Heywood took a party of sappers down to carry out the task at night, but found the site guarded by Greek troops posted there to prevent just such an attempt. Since they were prepared to open fire, Heywood withdrew, not wanting to precipitate a battle between allies. This decision was later condemned by GHQ Middle East, and Heywood's career suffered. The possibility that this was a way of punishing him for his earlier failures, without embarrassment, cannot be discounted. Heywood died in an air crash in India two years later.

Nick Hammond, leading a team of four sappers, had also engaged in scorched-earth missions during the retreat. While Fleming's band enjoyed themselves blowing up rolling stock and ramming locomotives into one another, he had concentrated on industries useful to the German war effort. On his last day, he destroyed the stockpiles of cotton at Haliartus, then returned to Athens, where he rejoined Ian Pirie and David Pawson, the third clandestine officer in the Legation. They prepared their escape, having destroyed the last traces of MI(R) and Section D activity, and packed up any useful material. Pirie and Barbrook left behind two radio sets – one with a Venizelist group, whose activities soon petered out, and one with a radical republican, Colonel (later General) Bakirdzis who, under the code-name of 'Prometheus', became SOE Cairo's first contact in Greece.

Before his departure, the King had requested General Wilson to look after Prince Peter; Admiral Sakellariou, the Minister of Marine;

and Maniadakis, the Minister of National Security. So, after a final meeting with General Papagos on 25 April, Wilson and his party drove down from Athens to the Peloponnese in a convoy of motor cars; one of them was the limousine left behind by Prince Paul, the *ci-devant* Regent of Jugoslavia, on his journey into exile. Although they did not suffer the same dangerous indignity as Colonel Salisbury-Jones and Captain Forrester, whose staff car was shot at by discontented Australian infantrymen, bombed buildings and craters slowed their progress to such an extent that they finally crossed the bridge over the Corinth canal two hours before dawn the next morning. They were only just in time.

Shortly after daybreak on 26 April, German paratroopers landed on the south side and stormed the bridge, which was guarded by some light tanks of the 4th Hussars and New Zealanders manning Bofors guns. The fighting was chaotic. A convoy with two hundred walking wounded commanded by Captain Guy May from Force Headquarters had just crossed on its way to Nauplia and became caught up in the battle.

The Germans swiftly crushed all opposition, but the two officers who had prepared the bridge for demolition apparently crept back to the canal bank and managed to detonate the charges by rifle shots. This feat (so beloved of scriptwriters) was afterwards challenged as impossible, but the bridge was destroyed with many Germans on it, and Wilson awarded the two officers the Military Cross.

The 4th New Zealand Brigade, on its way to the Peloponnese to embark, was extremely fortunate at a time when communications had almost collapsed. The Middlesex Yeomanry signal squadron with the 1st Armoured Brigade headquarters managed to pass on a message warning them about the capture of the Corinth isthmus by German paratroopers. Brigadier Inglis promptly turned his brigade round and the New Zealanders made their way to the eastern coast of Attica. They destroyed their vehicles and heavy equipment, and formed perimeters for defence at Porto Rafti and Rafina under perfect spring skies. At nightfall, the troops made their way to the port or beach, taking only their personal weapons and packs. There they waited anxiously for dark shapes to appear offshore.

Ferrying them out to the cruisers, destroyers and requisitioned merchantmen took a long time — far too long for the Royal Navy captains who knew their likely fate from dive-bombers if the ships were not well under way, and out of dangerous waters before first light. The 1st Armoured Brigade, which to its disgust had been held back as a 'Base Sub Area' and rearguard, was the last to arrive at the beach at Rafina. After a slow embarkation, mainly by rowing boats, nearly a thousand men were left stranded. When the beachmaster suggested to Brigadier Rollie Charrington that he could get him aboard before the rest, Charrington exploded with anger: 'Who do you take me for?' He would be the last to leave, and Dick Hobson, the brigade major, the second from last.

Charrington and his men withdrew into the woods to hide. There were remarkably few complaints. At brigade headquarters, Hobson was 'just about to throw myself down onto the ground where I stood, when Sgt Blythe, our mess sergeant, popped up and said "Whisky and soda, sir?" I said, "Sgt Blythe, I don't believe it." "Well, sir," he said, "it's not soda; only water." He then produced a bottle sized flask of whisky and a water bottle. I don't think I have ever enjoyed or needed such a drink before — or since. Sgt Blythe, an ex-12th Lancer who had been butler to Willoughby Norrie* before rejoining was rather special.'

Attempts to find a way to the other embarkation beach at Porto Rafti failed. The Germans had reached the coast in between. That night Charrington and his men had resigned themselves to the fate of prison camp, and most of them fell into an exhausted sleep. But at about one in the morning, they were shaken awake to be told that a ship had appeared offshore. It was the destroyer, HMS *Havoc*, sent on to help them by the last of the 4th New Zealand Brigade at Porto Rafti.

On board, the sailors handed out the Navy's standard panacea in the wake of disaster: cocoa, bully beef sandwiches and blankets. Throughout the evacuation, the Army's gratitude and praise was well-deserved. Admiral Sir Andrew Cunningham, the Commander-in-Chief Mediterranean, had committed six cruisers and nineteen destroyers to the task, almost all his ships of that size.

While most of the formed troops left by warship, other parties of officers and soldiers left in smaller boats. On 22 April, a party from the British Military Mission including Paddy Leigh Fermor and some signallers had pushed their truck over the cliff at Cape Sunion. They had arranged to take over the *Ayia Varvara*, a caique converted into

---

* Later General Lord Norrie and Governor-General of New Zealand. Joined the 11th Hussars, commanded the 10th Hussars, and subsequently the 1st Armoured Brigade, 1938–1940.

a handsome yacht, which they armed with Lewis guns. Their mission
was to sail it round to Myli in the Gulf of Argos to evacuate General
Wilson and his entourage in case other means failed.

To avoid the ubiquitous Luftwaffe, they could only move safely at
night. On the morning of 26 April, the party reached Myli and
searched for Peter Smith-Dorrien who had come down from Athens
with General Wilson and Prince Peter. They could see the line of
abandoned military vehicles stretching back several miles from the
small harbour. Jumbo Wilson was at the end of the mole sitting on
his bed-roll chewing the end of his stick. He was waiting for a
Sunderland flying-boat. Somebody asked him what he intended to do,
and Jumbo Wilson jovially replied: 'I'm going to do what many a
good general has done before — I'm going to sit on my luggage.' In
the end he did leave by Sunderland that evening. His luggage — to
which he seemed greatly attached, to judge by the attention it
received in his memoirs — together with his driver and several
members of his staff, including Smith-Dorrien bearing several bottles
of champagne, and Wilson's second ADC, Philip Scott of the 60th
Rifles, decided to go with the *Ayia Varvara*. At least the General's
belongings did not include another large American car, one of Jumbo
Wilson's most surprising weaknesses. In any event, the caique was
sunk the next day off Leonidion with the loss of all kit, but
fortunately no hands.

Amongst the last to leave Athens — only a few hours before the
Germans raised their flag over the Acropolis — had been Nicholas
Hammond, David Pawson, Ian Pirie and Nicki Demertzi. To ensure
Nicki's safe-conduct in the face of British officialdom, the couple had
hurriedly married. Leaving Athens at dawn, they drove to the yacht
harbour of Tourkolímono. Their load included a large batch of
German uniforms, which Pirie had been hoarding, and the remains
of Hammond's plastic explosive.

After Attica's rapid occupation by the Germans, evacuation
continued during the last nights of April from the ports and beaches
of the Peloponnese. Every form of transport available was pressed
into service: destroyers and cruisers of the Royal Navy, requisitioned
merchant vessels, caiques and aircraft. Blenheims ran a shuttle service
to Crete with men packed with dreadful discomfort in the bomb-bays
and turrets of each aircraft, while Sunderlands took them off the
beaches in the Gulf of Argos and round Kalamata. One somehow
managed to take off from the Gulf of Argos with eighty-four men on

board, nearly three times the maximum permitted on its civilian equivalent, the Imperial Airways flying-boat. But vessels hired and requisitioned by the British were barred to Greek troops, including Cretans from the 5th Division trying to return home to continue the fight. Such officious rigidity caused astonishment and dismay after all the acts of spontaneous generosity displayed by the Greeks.

The last stage of the evacuation became chaotic. The road between Argos and Nauplia was a solid jam of abandoned military vehicles. And nearly two thousand RAF ground crew and administration personnel concentrated at Argos were 'getting out of hand' as their hope of escape diminished and German air attacks increased. Most of their officers had already left by air, and the RAF later complained that they had not even been on the distribution list of evacuation instructions. The mass of disconsolate airmen was diverted to Kalamata, but so were 8,000 men of the Australian Division, joined by 1,500 dispirited Jugoslavs.

No defence was organized. During the day, the demoralized and exhausted troops stayed under cover in olive groves outside the town to avoid the bombing. They were outflanked by a small German force, which had crossed the Gulf of Corinth and the whole Peloponnese undetected and had slipped in to capture the port under their noses. Although counter-attacks led by some determined officers and NCOs eventually succeeded – Sergeant Hinton, a New Zealander, won a Victoria Cross – the Navy held back in the belief that the Germans were still a threat, and very few men were taken off during that last night.

Air attacks during the voyage to Crete were for many even more harrowing than their experiences on the mainland. The *Julia*, like the *Elsi* carrying the Luftwaffe prisoners, was one of the luckier ships. This 1,500-ton collier had departed before two in the morning on 23 April soon after the *Elsi*. Her time of departure was just inside the Royal Navy's guidelines for clearing dangerous waters before daylight, but the *Julia* was capable of no more than seven knots. They were only thirty miles down the coast of Attica when dawn broke, revealing a calm sea and a clear sky. Shouts announced the first Stuka attack which came almost immediately from the north-east – seven black specks 'grouped in two V's of three planes each with a solitary plane a little distance ahead'. In a chaotic rush, Pioneer NCOs with rifles, the only weapons on board, took up position.

The Stukas, according to Theo Stephanides, 'formed themselves in a line and as each plane arrived nearly overhead it flipped over on its side and then on its nose and seemed to fall vertically down on us. [They] made a most terrific screaming sound as they dived and, what with the banging of our thirty rifles, the din was deafening. When each plane had swooped down to about one thousand feet, one saw a black speck detach itself from the undercarriage and plummet towards us with a fiendish whistling.' Each bomb – all fortunately were near misses – sent up a huge column of spray, 'and each time the whole vessel reeled and there was a shock and a curious metallic clang caused by the compression wave hitting the side'. The Stukas then went through the same cab-rank circuit to drop their second bomb, and finally strafed the ship with machine-gun fire before turning for base to replenish. There were surprisingly few casualties for Stephanides to treat; one was an Australian sergeant whose watch had been smashed into his wrist by a bullet.

During the course of the day, the *Julia* was bombed five times without receiving any direct hits. Seaweed was blasted up on to the deck, and the crew, determined to make the most of their troubles, netted up some fish killed by the shock-waves. After sheltering in a little cove off the island of Cythera throughout the next day, they finally reached Crete on the morning of 25 April, and sailed into the immense natural harbour of Suda Bay.

The *Julia* had indeed been lucky. In all, twenty-six vessels were sunk including two hospital ships, and over two thousand lost their lives. Virtually all the civilian refugees and wounded Greek soldiers on the ferry *Hellas* were burnt to death. For those who dropped the bombs, the horror below remained distant, if not abstract. 'A sunny day,' recorded the pilot of a Junkers 88 on 25 April, 'and we were sent to look for ships embarking British troops in the Athens, Corinth and Nauplia areas.' He tried to identify Mycenae. 'I told my crew that we were passing over a territory which had seen at least 3,000 years of Greek history . . . The villages and the little towns looked like a playground of white dots.' Over Nauplia harbour, 'everything looked peaceful and untouched. But there was something which made my heart beat faster'. A passenger liner at anchor – a 'fascinating sight' – offered 'a unique target'. The bomb-aimer prepared as the aircraft banked, then dived. The pilot lifted the aircraft's nose at the crucial moment and pushed the red button. The radio-operator and the gunner, craning their heads, spotted the explosions. 'We've hit her! Two full hits, two bombs near misses. Water cascades and high flames. What did I feel? Relief after maximal tension, pride that a

junior crew had been successful. Sorrow, that a beautiful ship was
gone. Satisfaction that she would no longer transport British Forces,
and that was all that counted on this day.'

The worst disaster of the evacuation also began at Nauplia. A
Dutch merchantman, the *Slamat*, continued to take on troops until
four in the morning in spite of warnings that she would never clear
the Antikithera channel by daybreak. Caught by dive-bombers at
seven o'clock and badly damaged, she sent out distress signals. The
destroyer HMS *Diamond* went to her rescue and picked up survivors.
But *Diamond* was sunk, so HMS *Wryneck* went to help and was also
sunk. Altogether 700 men were lost from the three ships. Fifty
survived, including some wounded sailors from the *Wryneck* whose
whaler was rescued by Nick Hammond's group.

Hammond, Pirie and Nicki had sailed from the yacht harbour of
Tourkolímono to the Peloponnese, where one of their two caiques
had been sunk by air attack. In the second boat, the one carrying
Hammond's plastic explosive and Pirie's stock of German uniforms,
they had reached the uninhabited islands of Anana. There, they had
found the sailors, and took them on to hospital in Crete.

Leigh Fermor's caique party, having had the *Ayia Varvara* with
Jumbo Wilson's kit bombed from under them, bought another. They
carried on round the Peloponnese to the island of Antikithera,
picking up stragglers on the way including a dozen New Zealanders
in an open boat and later ten Australians. The second caique proved
a bad buy. The engine failed after leaving Antikithera to cross the
channel to Crete, and they had to turn back, improvising desperately.
At Antikithera they found the *Amalia,* a three-masted schooner which
a Greek infantry officer had taken from a fellow-countryman 'of
doubtful loyalties' at pistol-point. They sailed, this time without
trouble, to the north-west tip of Crete, where they landed at the old
Venetian harbour of Kastelli Kissamou.

Michael Forrester, who set sail at about 8 p.m. on a caique with
a mixed cargo of civilians and soldiers from Monemvasia, should have
followed a similar course. He awoke in the early hours of the
morning with the sensation that something was wrong. Checking his
prismatic compass, he found they were sailing due east. The captain
and owner of the caique, whom the beach-master at Monemvasia had
recommended as a thoroughly reliable fellow, turned out to be so
drunk that his hold on the wheel was all that kept him upright.
Forrester called a couple of Australians to help him, and they secured
the man safely in the hold. Unable to make more than the roughest

guess at how far they had gone in the wrong direction, Forrester turned the ship about and, using his prismatic compass, hoped to reach the island of Kithera.

During daylight, they heard aero-engines. Forrester told all the soldiers to hide below deck or under tarpaulins and asked the women to sit at the front of the boat and wave. A Messerschmitt 110 swooped over the masthead, taking a close look, then banked and turned back as if on a strafing run. The Greek women never flinched. They waved as hard as they could. The pilot swooped round once more, waved back from his cockpit, then set off after other prey.

The British Legation's steam yacht, the *Kalanthe*, with its distinguished yet very assorted passenger list, had left the Piraeus at dusk on 24 April. Through the night they steamed towards the small archipelago of Milos. There, they sheltered for the next day in the bay of an uninhabited island called Poliaigos, because any ship or small boat on the open sea would soon attract the attention of German aircraft.

The passengers were rowed to the beach where they spent a happy carefree day, with the Blunt and Caccia children playing together so rowdily that Nanny Blunt threatened to give notice. The Greek crew remained on the ship to carry out repairs and keep up steam in case of attack. They were protected by Lewis gun teams from Yak Mission. Eating omelettes from the large supply of eggs purchased that morning and drinking gin and lime on the bridge in nothing but a pair of shorts, Peter Fleming spent almost as pleasant a day as the party on shore. Late in the afternoon, the *Kalanthe* was sighted by three Junkers 88 bombers. Someone sounded the siren to warn those on land, and three gun teams went into action – Mark Norman and Oliver Barstow on either side of the bridge, each with a soldier servant, and Fleming in the stern with a Guardsman.

But the bombers were not deterred by the three Lewis guns blazing at them, and after several near misses, one of them scored a hit amidships. The *Kalanthe* blew up, killing nine of those on board, including Nancy Caccia's brother Oliver Barstow, and wounding six. Mark Norman was severely injured and Peter Fleming concussed. Harold Caccia and Norman Johnstone, the Grenadier subaltern in Yak Mission, rapidly rowed out to the blazing wreck – with munitions exploding in the heat, it was a courageous act – to take off the wounded. Burnt and blackened men were saved by the prompt action of the three women in the party with VAD experience. They tore up their shirts to clean the wounds and burns. For Nancy Caccia, who by then knew for certain that her brother was dead, the urgency of the work at least forced her to concentrate on other things.

Helped by the nearby islanders on Kimolos, and picked up three days later by a caique brought to their rescue from Crete, the party set off again.* But headwinds and the slowness of the caique forced them to make for the volcanic island of Santorini. A minor eruption just after their arrival made them think they were being bombed again. Mark Norman, who was still in great pain from his wounds, later claimed that at Santorini he had been laid on the altar steps of the little church and fed communion wine as a substitute for anaesthetic.

Fortunately, at Santorini there lay a small cargo boat which a detachment of military police had commandeered. Twice as fast as the caique, it could reach the coast of Crete in the course of a night. The following morning at daybreak they saw the snow-capped peak of Mount Ida off the starboard bow and a couple of hours later entered the harbour of Heraklion, the city the Venetians called Candia. On the quayside, Colonel Jasper Blunt waited for them, having been warned of their arrival. Doreen Blunt's fellow passengers tactfully moved aside, expecting a poignant reunion after all she had been through, but the first thing her husband demanded was what on earth she had done with the key of the piano before leaving Athens.

After the evacuation from the Greek mainland, Churchill signalled to Wavell, 'we have paid our debt of honour with far less loss than I feared.' The loss of men was indeed mercifully lighter than it might have been: 2,000 had been killed or wounded and 14,000 made prisoner out of the 58,000 troops sent to Greece. But the loss in *matériel* was disastrous: 104 tanks, 40 anti-aircraft guns, 192 field guns, 164 anti-tank guns, 1,812 machine guns, about 8,000 transport vehicles, most of the signals equipment, inestimable quantities of stores and 209 aircraft – of which 72 were lost in combat, 55 on the ground and 82 destroyed on evacuation.

Was such a heavy cost worth the salvation of Britain's bad conscience at having let down allies in the past? From a purely military point of view the decision to dispatch an expeditionary force

* According to Harold Caccia, the surname of Rodney Bond, their rescuer and a member of the Secret Intelligence Service, was later suggested by Peter Fleming to his brother Ian when he was searching for a name for his fictional secret agent.

was calamitous. Metaxas once said to Colonel Blunt: 'Few realise how easy and how dangerous it is to mix sentiment with strategy.' Churchill's idea that supporting Greece influenced the United States was more wishful thinking than fact, even though Greece's heroic resistance to the Italian invasion had helped sway opinion before the Lend-Lease debate on Capitol Hill. And in recent years, the firm belief that the Balkan campaign delayed the launch of Operation Barbarossa with fatal consequences has come under attack.*

Whatever the arguments against sending an expeditionary force, it is hard not to sympathize with Geoffrey Household's verdict. 'I am proud,' he later wrote, 'and I was proud then that we had permitted generosity – whether real or a political gesture to overcome common sense.' Monty Woodhouse, acknowledging the benefit of hindsight, has argued that without British intervention, the Greek government – as opposed to the Greek people – might have given in to the Germans without a fight, and the Communist hegemony over the resistance would have been complete.

For the Cretans, the disaster was more personal. Their division, with sons, husbands and brothers, had been trapped on the Albanian front. General Papasteriou, commanding the division, managed to escape to Crete, but his salvation was short-lived. He was assassinated in Kastelli Kissamou by a sergeant of gendarmerie during a violent protest at his desertion.

---

* Martin Van Creveld in his book *Hitler's Strategy 1940–1941 – The Balkan Clue*, published in 1973, argued most convincingly that Operation Barbarossa was delayed not by the redeployment of formations after Operation Marita, but by the slow distribution of mechanical transport, much of it captured from the French the year before, to units destined to lead the advance into Russia. Recently, the Barbarossa question began to attract attention again. Professor Hagen Fleischer disproved the theory that bad weather had delayed the launch. The whole debate then erupted at a symposium in Salonika in May 1991. To the anger of Greek academics, Professor Poog of the Military History Research Institute in Freiburg declared that there was no futher doubt on the matter: Barbarossa's delay was due to the Luftwaffe's tardy preparation of airfields in Poland. When Monty Woodhouse expressed strong scepticism, Poog said that Hitler had not informed Goering of his plans. United States historians meanwhile claimed that oil distribution was the key problem. Whatever the true reason, or rather combination of reasons, for the delay, the Balkan campaign and the subsequent invasion of Crete helped confirm Stalin's false sense of security by giving him the impression that Hitler was aiming for the Suez Canal, not Russia.

PART TWO
The Battle of Crete

6
'A Second Scapa'

For those exhausted evacuees from Greece heading towards Crete, the White Mountains just above the horizon provided a first sight of the island. The vast majority of vessels with troops on board sailed into Suda Bay, a natural harbour eight kilometres long guarded on the north by the rocky hump of a large peninsula, the Akrotiri, and on the south by the great Malaxa escarpment.

At the mouth of the bay stood the ruins of a Venetian castle, but the evacuees' attention was more likely to focus on the hulk of a small steamship, bombed by the Luftwaffe. This was merely a foretaste of the scene within — the funnels and masts of sunken vessels, always one or two ships burning steadily after an air raid, and damaged superstructures on most of the rest. The cruiser HMS *York* lay beached, stern awash, after a daring attack by the Italian navy using six small motor boats loaded with explosive. The quay-front village of Suda, a row of low houses, bombed and abandoned, was not an encouraging sight.

Four battalions of the 2nd New Zealand Division arrived at Suda Bay on 25 April: Anzac Day twenty-six years on. The memory of British planning at Gallipoli could not have been encouraging for Dominion troops. They had come from Porto Rafti on HMS *Glengyle*, a combined operations troopship, and the cruisers *Calcutta* and *Perth*.

Activity on the quay had a nervous air since bombers were likely to return at any moment. A British staff officer on a launch came out to their ships yelling instructions that all weapons apart from rifles and sidearms were to be piled on the jetty. Brigadier James Hargest, the commander of the 5th New Zealand Brigade, knew very well that they would never again see all this equipment which they had brought with such difficulty out of Greece, and refused point-blank. The staff officer screamed back that he was in charge of this base area and insisted on his orders being obeyed. 'I am not surprised', retorted Hargest, 'that you are in charge of a *base* area if this is the way you go on. I tell you my men will retain their weapons.' In spite of Hargest's refusal, a detachment of British Military Police on the jetty still managed to relieve many companies of their heavy weapons. The New Zealanders were not alone. Nearly all units, British and Dominion, disembarking at Suda were greeted with this memorable lesson to soldiers that to care for their weapons during a withdrawal was not worth the effort.

Companies were formed up on the quayside, then marched off, but after starting in 'fairly good order', the attempt at smartness collapsed. Men still exhausted from Greece fell out and took off their boots at the side of the road. Inland towards Canea, away from the harbour area and the smell of burning oil, the troops found trestle tables set up where British troops already on the island doled out bars of chocolate, tea and packets of biscuits.

The sight of the smartly turned-out regulars of the Welch Regiment, part of the garrison based on the 14th Infantry Brigade, had a heartening effect on many of these dispirited survivors. Those who trudged away from Suda along Tobruk Avenue, as the British had renamed it, were unshaven, dirty, dishevelled and tired. Many were bare-headed because they had thrown away their steel helmets in the retreat, and their battledress was unbuttoned in the warm sun. Cretan boys selling ice-creams at two drachma each did good business.

To disperse this unwieldy assembly – 27,000 men in the course of less than a week – troops were marched out behind Suda and Canea and settled along the stretch of coast between the foothills of the White Mountains and the sea. They spread themselves in the olive groves – the designated camps were no clearer than mining claims on a map – and settled themselves as best they could. The warm spring days could be deceptive: nights were cold for those who had dumped their greatcoats during the retreat.

Once units had a recognizable dispersal area, the 'Annie Lorry' came round dropping off rations: tins of bully beef, and cans of jam to go with the hard-tack biscuits which otherwise turned to plaster of Paris in the mouth. Bread was scarce because of the shortage of field bakeries, but when the Greek army offered Italian bakers out of their pool of prisoners of war, the British officer in charge refused: 'But we couldn't allow that. They might poison our chaps.' The Greeks, with admirable tolerance, then offered their own bakers, saying that they would use the Italians.

The bully beef or 'corned dog' had to be gouged out with a clasp-knife and eaten off the blade. Oranges generously given by the Cretans followed, but the sudden consumption of large quantities of fruit had its effect. The olive groves quickly became fouled and the Army ritual of latrine-digging was not made easy by the lack of entrenching tools.

The best drinking vessels were the round tins of fifty Player's Navy Cut, but most had to use empty bully beef tins instead for brew-ups, and also for drinking raki and wine. Short rations on tea and sugar – delivered in a sandbag per company – combined with Cretan hospitality greatly increased the consumption of the local red wine. The Greek word *krassi* – as in 'got krassied up' – lingered in regimental slang for a long time after Crete.

The overcrowding round Canea became acute. There were also several thousand civilian refugees mixed in with both formed troops and the 'odds and sods': RAF personnel without aircraft, fitters without tools, drivers without vehicles, pioneers without picks, and stragglers from every regiment, corps and minor unit imaginable.

The appearance of a reconnaissance aircraft – known as the shufti-plane – would send the new arrivals diving pell-mell into slit trenches. A couple of RAF pilots found themselves piled on top of a very attractive young woman. As they extricated themselves on the all-clear, they recognized Nicki from the Argentina night-club. 'Good afternoon, Nicki,' one of them said with a grin. 'Mrs Pirie, please!' she answered rather haughtily to emphasize her new status.

For most civilians, Crete was no more than a resting place on their flight into Egypt. They often had even less reason for trusting in authority than the soldiers. When General Wilson's force retreated to the Thermopylae line, Lawrence Durrell in Kalamata telegraphed his British Council boss in Athens asking for instructions. He received the reply: 'Carry on! Rule Britannia!', only to discover later that the author of this flippant message had then slipped away on his own.

Durrell, his wife Nancy and baby daughter Penelope escaped from the military chaos in Kalamata only because a former Merchant Navy man with a caique, an acquaintance from Corfu, took them on board. After disembarking in the old Venetian port in Canea, Nancy Durrell mentioned to some Australian soldiers that she had no milk for the baby. With cheerful vandalism, they smashed open the dingy green shutters of nearby shops using their rifle butts, and presented her with enough tins of condensed milk to last for six months. The Durrells' troubles were not entirely finished. After ten days in Canea, they left for Egypt, where civilians unable to prove their identity were kept in a wired compound. Durrell, unable to send a cable to England to tell his mother of their escape, spotted a reporter from the *Daily Mail* through the wire of the cage. He called him over and gave him the story of their adventures.

Grander refugees, especially the Greek royal family, encountered none of these difficulties. On reaching Heraklion by flying-boat, the King stayed first at the Villa Ariadne at Knossos, where he was welcomed by the curator, R.W. Hutchinson, always known as 'the Squire'. This Edwardian villa, with shaded gardens of palm trees and plumbago, was built by Sir Arthur Evans after the King's uncle, Prince George, had in 1900 secured his right to buy the freehold of the main Minoan site. As Evans took a less active part, he turned it into a base for British archaeology in Crete. From 1930 to 1934, in the years following Evans's retirement, John Pendlebury had lived there as curator, his wife's presence breaking the monastic tradition.

King George was joined at Knossos by Princess Katherine, Mrs Britten-Jones and the Prime Minister, Tsouderos. But after a few days at Knossos, the King and his advisers decided that they should move to the other end of the island, since Canea was now officially the seat of the Greek government.

Princess Katherine, although reluctant to leave her brother, was persuaded to depart for Cairo in a flying-boat. Crown Prince Paul and Princess Frederica with their children, Constantine and Sophia (both suffering from the onslaught of Cretan bedbugs), and Mrs Britten-Jones in her ever-discreet guise of lady-in-waiting flew to Alexandria, then on to Cairo on 2 May in the same Sunderland flying-boat as General Wilson.

The King and Tsouderos were joined in Canea by Maniadakis, still the Minister of National Security, who had arrived in Crete with a large number of his hated secret police. This was regarded as so provocative by the Cretans that the former British Vice-Consul in Athens and his counterpart in Canea approached Tsouderos and the King to warn them. Maniadakis was sent on to Egypt where his fifty secret policemen soon sowed hatred and fear amongst the largely pro-Venizelist Greek community there. The two British Vice-Consuls believed that the King and his government lost much prestige during their short time on the island. On the whole, British diplomats tended to be blind to the dislike the King aroused, presumably because he felt able to unbend in their company in a way he could seldom manage with his own countrymen. He once remarked to Charles Mott-Radclyffe with engaging simplicity that 'the most essential piece of equipment for any King of Greece was a Revelation suitcase'.

The King's presence in such a republican stronghold as Crete, loyal to the liberal memory of its most famous son, Venizelos, was unpropitious. Tsouderos, as a Cretan and a monarchist, was a relatively rare bird, but as a banker and a politician, he had in Cretan eyes virtually become an Athenian by profession.

The Cretans, more than any other Greeks, never forgave King George for having granted a dubious legitimacy to the dictatorship of Ioannis Metaxas on 4 August 1936. Traditional Venizelist sympathies were affronted, and on the second anniversary of the August Decree, the Cretans had risen in revolt. Afterwards, their weapons – both the agent and the symbol of resistance to foreign oppression – were confiscated. That aroused more than disgust when the Cretan population then found itself practically unarmed in the face of the German invasion. After the war, in the plebiscite on the monarchy of 5 September 1946, Crete returned an absolute majority against the King. And yet the Communists in Crete, unlike their comrades on the mainland, never stood a chance of gaining power.

The Cretan character – warlike, proud, compulsively generous to a friend or stranger in need, ferociously unforgiving to an enemy or traitor, frugal day-by-day but prodigal in celebration – was, of course, strongly influenced by the landscape of dramatic contrasts in which the islanders lived. Rich coastal strips on the north coast, endless olive groves on the foothills, fertile valleys and odd little plains hidden in the highlands, all were overshadowed by the island's spinal mass of limestone cordilleras – the White Mountains, the Kedros range, the Mount Ida or Psiloriti range, and finally the Lasithi or Dikti mountains in the east. From sub-tropical vegetation with banana trees, carobs and orange groves, a mountain village, only fifteen kilometres away as the crow flew, but probably sixty on foot, seemed to exist in a different world and a different climate.

Mountain villages in the sheep-rearing (and sheep-stealing) regions of the centre consisted of little more than a cluster of white-washed houses round a simple Orthodox church. Often they had only a floor of beaten earth and a few pieces of home-made furniture, including a large dowry chest of clothes and sheets. The diet of sheep's and goat's cheese, potatoes and erratically cooked meat was as hard and monotonous as the life, but the air was invigorating and so clean that wounds healed with astonishing rapidity.*

In the highlands a man was known by the number of sheep he owned, in the lowlands by the number of his olive trees, of which Crete was reputed to have twenty million. Villages in the valleys and lowlands had pollarded mulberry trees down each side of the street, their trunks lime-washed against insects. The houses had plants and flowerpots, cherry trees behind and vine-covered arbours. Life was less harsh, but the people were no less generous. Only in the large cities of Heraklion and Canea were the inhabitants likely to have lost some of those Cretan qualities which had survived, even thrived, over the centuries of foreign occupation with its cycle of repression and revolt.

For Canea to become the new capital of Greece struck the Cretans as a rather unconvincing idea. They maintained an air of normality as the rent for villas shot to previously unimaginable figures. This money did not seem to make its way down to the under-stocked little shops with dingy shutters. And Cretan men did not forsake their café routine of newspapers and cups of Turkish coffee.

The men, mostly middle-aged since the young ones had been trapped with the Cretan Division in Epirus, presented a curious contrast to the newcomer. Those from the town wore shapeless suits, while those from the hills wore moustaches of cultivated ferocity and traditional Cretan costume consisting of a black bobbled head-cloth – a *sariki* – embroidered jacket and waistcoat, a mulberry-coloured cummerbund over dark, capacious breeches – British soldiers called them 'crap-catchers' – and high boots which completed an impression that was half pirate, half irregular cavalry.

The Cretans welcomed the British soldiers as distant relatives who had arrived unexpectedly from another country. Stephanides saw a group of Cretans dancing the Pentozali – a highly energetic dance – stop to invite soldiers to join them. The self-conscious British, uncomfortable in their prickly battledress, tried to learn the movements and were soon laughing with the dancers at their own clumsiness.

For those who had escaped from the fighting in Greece, the island of Crete was a glorious haven – a place of great beauty and of great

---

* Even on the coast at Rethymno, a German paratrooper who received a bullet sideways through the nostrils during the battle found he could blow his nose normally a week later.

friendliness where glasses were perpetually lifted to the common cause. Cretans, although robust drinkers themselves, were astonished at the Anglo-Saxon compulsion to get drunk. According to the degree of their inebriation, drunken soldiers wandered round bawling out ribald songs or mawkish ones. If the BBC was playing popular songs, such as 'The Banks of Loch Lomond' or 'There is a Tavern in the Town', homesick troops would crowd round a radio immediately.

The effects of drink were also likely to bring out some of the underlying tension between Dominion troops and British symbols of authority, whether military policemen or officers. The New Zealanders and Australians in Crete were neither regulars nor conscripts, but volunteers for the duration, and their lack of reverence − almost a point of Antipodean honour − made British officers steer clear of them whenever possible. On arrival in Egypt, one New Zealander had greeted a rather languid British officer carrying a fly-whisk with: 'Hey! What've you done with the rest of the horse?' The New Zealanders certainly had their share of 'wife-dodgers' and 'one-jumpers' (volunteers one jump ahead of the police) but, unlike Australian soldiers, they did not strike fear into British officers.

A yeomanry captain, who had already encountered Australians in Greece, remarked only half in jest of the 6th Australian Division: 'I think they must have been recruited from the prisons.' In Canea, a British officer, seeing an Australian filling his pockets with fruit from an old woman's stall and refusing to pay, remonstrated with him, only to find the muzzle of a looted German pistol thrust into his face. And a Cretan recounted how when a British colonel (probably Jasper Blunt) accompanying the King of Greece had gone to quieten a disturbance outside the window where they were talking, the Australian responsible for the row promptly seized him by the throat and nearly strangled him.

At night, Australian air-raid precautions consisted of shooting at any light they saw, whether a match struck for a cigarette or the correctly dimmed headlamps of a vehicle. Harold Caccia remembered a drive past one of their areas at night as 'one of the most anxious moments of my life'. Soon afterwards, this ill-disciplined rabble fought the German paratroopers at Rethymno with savage exuberance.

A rather more orderly regime was soon established in the Canea area. Bell tents and EPIP (European Personnel, Indian Pattern) were erected under the olive trees for the rear echelon. Most of the stragglers from Greece were transported on to Egypt, while formed units were moved out to their designated defence positions. They had been given little chance to sample the delights of Canea's thirty-seven brothels — 'thirty-six of them owner-driven' according to the New Zealand Division Provost-Marshal.

The bulk of the Australian troops were moved eastwards to Georgioupolis, Rethymno and Heraklion. The New Zealanders, on the other hand, marched westwards to take up positions along the coast between Canea and the airfield of Maleme, where the Blenheims of 30 Squadron were now based to fly shipping patrols over the Aegean to chase off Stukas.

The Maori battalion set a cracking pace which some officers found hard to follow. In the village of Platanias the mayor and his daughters welcomed them with tables set out offering bread and white goat's cheese and red wine. A young woman holding a child began to weep when she saw the soldiers. A New Zealand subaltern asked a Cretan why she cried. Her husband and brothers had been with the Cretan 5th Division in Epirus.

Few of those marching out to their positions had been impressed by the preparations they had seen from the moment they landed. The dockside at Suda was a shambles. Only two small ships could be unloaded at the same time, so the rest had to wait at anchor in the bay, easy targets for air attack as the half-sunken wrecks testified. Churchill's call the previous November to turn Suda Bay into a 'second Scapa' had not been taken seriously by GHQ Middle East at a time of more urgent demands on other fronts.

Churchill's phrase had not been a mere figure of speech. He believed strongly in the importance of turning Suda into 'the amphibious citadel of which all Crete is the fortress' and had not forgotten the task during the winter. But the emphasis on Suda allowed Wavell to believe that, with all his other commitments, he could get away with reinforcing only the port area.

The most recent commander of the island, Major General E.C. Weston, had arrived in Crete at the end of March. His command, part of a Royal Marine formation known as the Mobile Naval Base Defence Organisation, consisted mainly of anti-aircraft and searchlight batteries. Before the German invasion of Greece, the raids were carried out by Italian torpedo bombers. Almost every gun on every ship in harbour banged away at them, the civilian gunners on merchantmen and Royal Fleet Auxiliaries perhaps even more enthusiastically than the Royal Navy. But the scream of Stukas, once the Luftwaffe took over from the Italians, announced a far more frequent and less sporting event.

The Palestinian Pioneers and a misnamed Dock Operating Company which consisted of shipping clerks in uniform, not stevedores, had the worst job, unloading ammunition and fuel from the ships in Suda Bay under one air attack after another. The red warning flag hoisted over naval headquarters on the quayside could not be seen from the hold of a ship, so often there was no warning of a raid until the Bofors guns opened up. The lack of warning made dockyard parties nervous, which did not help productivity. And the officer in charge of unloading foolishly refused to allow them to take cover, saying that they must consider themselves front-line soldiers. Not surprisingly, a very high proportion began to report sick.

Harold Caccia, having arrived at Heraklion with the other survivors from the *Kalanthe*, moved to join a skeleton version of the British Legation transposed to Halepa, next to Canea. On the way he saw what appeared to be one group of soldiers repainting a bridge and another preparing to demolish it. For him this typified the appalling lack of preparation. 'We'd been there for six months. What had we been doing?' The strength of his feeling stemmed from the failure of the British to honour their assurance that they would look after Crete which he had delivered to the Greek government when the Cretan Division was sent to the mainland.

While the old city of Canea consisted of narrow streets and tall Venetian houses each topped with a Turkish *hayáti* (a wooden extension with shuttered windows), Halepa, extending on its east side towards the Akrotiri, had spacious villas with gardens of palm trees, Persian lilac, bougainvillea and oleander. The British Legation was installed not far from the former residence of Prince Peter's father when he had been Governor-General. And alongside the residence stood the house of the Venizelos family.

Caccia, whose clothes had gone down with the *Kalanthe*, received some replacements when Peter Wilkinson of SOE arrived on Crete. Wilkinson, mainly responsible for Poland and Czechoslovakia, had come to see if an 'underground railway' into Central Europe was still possible up through the Balkans. He was also on the island to watch the parachute invasion, whose imminence had been confirmed by Ultra, and report back to Colonel Colin Gubbins at SOE's Baker Street headquarters. SOE at that stage was examining the wild idea of parachuting large formations of Pole and Czech forces back into their countries without any hope of being able to support them.

From Suda Bay, Wilkinson hitched a lift to Canea and searched for the British Legation. To his surprise, he found Harold Caccia clipping the hedge. Even more surprising was his attire: patent leather shoes with rubber soles, striped morning-coat trousers, a black cycling jacket and a Panama hat with the ribbon of the Eton Ramblers. They went off for lunch at a good restaurant, then Caccia proposed a walk to Venizelos's birthplace – a respectable distance. They soon found themselves passing 'some extremely bolshie Australian troops'. Wilkinson, in uniform, was a little uneasy about the reception that 'this fairly improbable Englishman' beside him might receive, but Caccia was unruffled by the barracking, and they strolled rather than ran the verbal gauntlet.

As well as trousers for Harold Caccia, Wilkinson had also brought a wireless set for Ian Pirie, the less respectable face of British diplomacy. Pirie and Barbrook had established themselves in another, even grander, villa not far away in a street lined with Persian lilacs then flowering luxuriantly. Pirie, as Nicholas Hammond observed, was 'a great chap for getting good accommodation.' This centre for secret operations, dubbed Fernleaf House, was filled with wireless sets, the German uniforms brought over from Athens in the caique and crates of machine guns humped about by Greeks in and out of uniform. Pirie's and Barbrook's piratical crew included a former rum-runner and a warrant officer with waxed moustache, a Mauser pistol in his belt and a Browning in a shoulder holster. The thoroughly irregular set-up was completed by the blonde Nicki, who although newly married and stand-offish with RAF pilots in slit trenches, had not lost any of her unselfconscious sexuality. It left the local Cretan women, young and old alike, 'speechless with amazement'.

They were joined at Fernleaf House first by Wilkinson and then by Geoffrey Cox, a foreign correspondent turned subaltern in the New Zealand Division, who had been told to establish a daily newspaper for the troops called *Crete News*. Wilkinson's interest in the undergound route into the Balkans soon dwindled when it became clear that Pirie's fleet of clandestine caiques organized by a shadowy figure called Black Michael owed more to imaginative optimism than reality. So while waiting to study the parachute invasion at first hand, Wilkinson decided that the most useful and entertaining employment open to him was to sit on the terrace with a selection of rifles from the armoury which littered the house and, comfortably installed with a loader, take pot shots at the Stukas as they climbed, belly exposed, from their dive-bombing attacks on Suda Bay just over the hill. Wilkinson's running commentary on his shooting — 'made that blighter turn' — was on one occasion accompanied by a rather wistful sigh from the fearless Nicki on the balcony above as she watched the unopposed bombing. 'No good RAF. Come along Hurricanos.'

Nick Hammond, having left Ian Pirie and Bill Barbrook in Canea, had signed on with a character whose exploits soon became legendary in the Eastern Mediterranean, Mike Cumberlege. Cumberlege, a bearded naval officer with a gold ring in one ear, commanded a caique from Haifa renamed HMS *Dolphin* and fitted with a two-pounder gun and a pair of Oerlikons for defence against aircraft. The rest of the crew consisted of Cumberlege's cousin, Cle, a major in the Royal Artillery, who had demoted himself to gun-layer on this extraordinary vessel, a South African private in the Black Watch called Jumbo Steele, and Able Seaman Saunders. The *Dolphin* sailed to Heraklion, where Hammond met up with John Pendlebury for the first time since their separation in Athens the previous summer.

He found Pendlebury in his element. Apart from his swordstick, he had learned a form of stave-fighting in Egypt at the archaeological dig at Tell el-Amarna. He half-pictured himself as a sort of Cretan Lawrence of Arabia, but lacked Lawrence's disturbing tenacity.

After the Italian invasion, and with British troops welcomed on Crete by the government in Athens, Pendlebury no longer had to play the part of Vice-Consul. He took out his captain's uniform, and became liaison officer between the British forces and the Greek military authorities. His real interest was the creation of a force to replace the Cretan 5th Division sent to the Albanian front. At that time there were less than four thousand Greek soldiers left on the island, and fewer than one in five of them was armed.* Pendlebury therefore requested 10,000 rifles in November 1940 from GHQ Middle East in Cairo. He did not seem to realize that he was echoing the Prime Minister.

Churchill had recently told the CIGS: 'Every effort should be made to rush arms and equipment to enable a reserve division to be

---

* The Communists in 1946, during the Civil War, tried to exploit the dispatch of the Cretan Division to the mainland in November 1940 as a plot by the 'Fourth of August' regime of General Metaxas to crush the Cretans (*Voice of the People*, Canea, June 1946).

formed in Crete. Rifles and machine guns are quite sufficient in this case. To keep a Greek division out of the battle on the Epirus front would be very bad, and to lose Crete because we had not sufficient bulk of forces there would be a crime.' This order was not ignored, nor did it sink in the bureaucratic morass of GHQ Middle East, as many seemed to think. Although the Metaxas regime, with the Cretan revolt of 1938 in mind, can hardly have been keen to rearm a population from whom it had recently confiscated all arms, it appears to have accepted the idea. 'The Greek General Staff', wrote Colonel Salisbury-Jones in his subsequent report on the Battle of Crete, 'agreed to raise a reserve division, requesting us to provide the equipment. The provision of complete equipment was, of course, impossible but it was agreed that 10,000 rifles should be provided.' Only 3,500 American carbines arrived because German air raids on the Midlands had destroyed small arms factories, and production did not recover until late in 1941. Such practical considerations did little to moderate Pendlebury's righteous enthusiasm.

Pendlebury had not confined his activities to Crete. He had worked closely with 50 Middle East Commando, sent to the island in December to bolster the garrison after the departure of the Cretan Division and to carry out raids on Italian-held islands in the Dodecanese, first Kasos and then Castelorizzo. Early in the year, SOE Cairo sent two younger officers to help him: Terence Bruce-Mitford and Jack Hamson who, by a curious coincidence, had a glass eye like Pendlebury's. Bruce-Mitford, a lecturer in classics at the University of St Andrews, with an academic air and thinning sandy red hair, was austere and very tough. His idea of fun in Cairo was to go out into the desert and spend the night in the sand dunes. Hamson, who later became Professor of Comparative Law at Trinity College, Cambridge, was very different if only because of his exotic background. He came from a Levantine English family, jewellers in Constantinople who lived in princely style on the island of Prinkipo. Their well-connected Catholicism even brought Hamson a beautiful new pair of boots after his capture in Crete: his mother managed to send them via Cardinal Roncalli, the future Pope John XXIII.

Both took part in one of the raids on the Dodecanese. Hamson described the scene of embarkation on a moonlit night: 'past the Venetian fort and down to the water . . . as we went in silence with equipment and rifles and bombs and knives through the ruins of other wars: a scene in a boy's story-book.' But then he went on to blast the 'confusion, incompetence, ineptitude and mess'. The débâcle was not entirely the fault of 50 Middle East Commando, but they were soon withdrawn to Egypt.

Pendlebury's life of relished contrasts continued. Having organized an Old Wykehamist dinner in Heraklion, Pendlebury, accompanied by his faithful muleteer and bodyguard Kronis Vardakis, set off into the mountains wearing a black patch, having left that glass eye on the table in his room to warn friends who dropped by that he was away on guerrilla work.

The room itself was truly chaotic: rifles, not brooms, fell out of cupboards, and secret papers spilled on to the floor. After his execution by paratroopers, a German report – which insisted on calling him 'Pendleburg' – stated: 'In his house in Heraklion documents concerning his organisation were found, the financing and the arming, as well as the names of his assistants. Arms, munitions and explosives were found there in a considerable quantity.' But John Pendlebury had accepted his death in advance: not in any way as a suicide, but with his heart set on an exultant finale of self-sacrifice. On 17 March, over three weeks before the German invasion of Greece, and two months before the invasion of Crete, he had written his last words to his wife: 'love and adieu'.

7

'The Spear-point of the German Lance'

For British and German planners alike, study of a map of the Eastern Mediterranean in the autumn of 1940 led to two conclusions: Crete was a key air and naval base for the region; and the Axis could only capture it with airborne forces. The strength of the Royal Navy made a seaborne assault too dangerous.

As soon as plans for the invasion of Britain were set aside, General Halder suggested on 25 October that 'mastery of the Eastern Mediterranean was dependent on the capture of Crete, and that this could best be achieved by an air landing'.

General Jodl, the architect of the 'peripheral strategy' – to throttle Britain in the Mediterranean – then recommended that if the Italians invaded Greece they should be sure to take Crete to pre-empt a British occupation of the island. And on 28 October 1940, the day both of Italy's invasion of Greece and of the Axis leaders' meeting in Florence, Hitler told Mussolini that 'Germany could make available a division of airborne troops and a division of parachute troops' should he wish to invade Crete.

The strategy was so self-evident that Brigadier Tidbury, who was appointed commander of the British troops in Crete on 3 November, correctly identified every German objective and their four dropping zones on the island six and a half months before the attack came. The possibility that the British might work this out for themselves does not seem to have occurred to the Germans.

The proposal of a German airborne invasion of Crete was put to Goering by General Kurt Student, the architect of the paratroop division and commander of the XI Air Corps. Student came from a family of impoverished Brandenburg landowners, part of that Prussian class of 'ditch-barons' who formed the backbone of the Wilhelmine officer corps. From a light infantry regiment he transferred to flying duties, and when the First World War came, he flew a scout-plane over the Russians before the Battle of Tannenberg. One of the few German fighter pilots to survive the war, Student later became part of that secret cadre of officers in the Central Flying Office which laid the foundations for the Luftwaffe in violation of the Treaty of Versailles.

Student, known for his 'brusque good humour', irony and drawling voice, was a tireless worker, not a party man or corridor politician. Promotion came slowly. His assistant at Central Flying, Hans Jeschonnek, rapidly outstripped him to become Chief of Staff of the Luftwaffe. But this proved an advantage, for General Jeschonnek backed Student's appointment to form parachute regiments and helped him develop his more daring ideas, such as the use of gliders, later employed to spectacular effect in the capture of the Belgian fort of Eben Emael in May 1940.

Student believed passionately in his creation of a new strategic arm, rather than in the original idea of sabotage groups that would be dropped in the wake of a Luftwaffe bombing raid. Goering's feat of empire-building, which enabled a Luftwaffe division to be created, aroused great jealousy within the Wehrmacht. Military orthodoxy decried Student's ambitious schemes and the resources they required. Yet such a revolutionary form of warfare clearly appealed to Hitler's sense of military surprise and symbolic imagery. Even before Student's men had a chance to prove themselves, he chose Colonel Bruno Bräuer's 1st Parachute Regiment to lead the march-past on his birthday parade in 1939.

Just over a year later, Wehrmacht critics had to fall silent after Captain Witzig's gliders landed within the defences of Eben Emael, and Student's paratroop drops paralysed the Dutch army. Yet the operation against Rotterdam nearly cost Student his life when a sniper's bullet penetrated one side of his brain. A Dutch surgeon saved him from death or paralysis.

Student, although he had grown flabby during the months of inactivity in hospital, was entirely recovered when Goering took him to see Hitler at the Mönichkirchen headquarters, south of Vienna. They arrived on 21 April 1941, the day after the Führer's fifty-second birthday and General Tsolacoglou's offer of surrender to General Sepp Dietrich in Greece. Hitler was openly sceptical of Student's visionary plan to use Crete and then Cyprus as stepping stones across the Mediterranean, with a paratroop assault on the Suez Canal just as Rommel reached the outskirts of Alexandria. This was the most dramatic expression yet of Jodl's peripheral strategy, which Hitler had abandoned in December to concentrate on the invasion of Russia. Hitler asked rather pertinently whether the paratroopers might not be more effectively deployed in the capture of Malta. Student repeated the same arguments with which he had convinced Keitel and Jodl: that Malta's size and shape meant that the garrison could deploy rapidly to counter-attack the dropping zones. Crete, on the other hand, was long and thin, with bad communications. Hitler, less easily persuaded than his generals, predicted heavy casualties. When not obsessed with a project, his military and psychological intuition was often very accurate.

Yet after a few days Hitler gave in to Goering's repeated requests for approval of what was to be called Operation Merkur, or Mercury. Martin Van Creveld defined the circumstances thus: 'Far from being part of any coherent strategy, therefore, Merkur was little more than a sop to Goering, whose air force was destined to play a subordinate role in the coming Russian campaign.' But in this context Professor Van Creveld overstates his case about the Balkan campaign and its effect on Operation Barbarossa. Hitler, unlike those of his generals who still hankered after the peripheral strategy, was indeed uninterested in Crete as a stepping stone to the Middle East, but his lingering concern for the Roumanian oilfields and his atavistic Austrian fear of invasion from the south-east made him see the island as a useful offshore rampart.

Führer Directive No. 28 of 25 April began: 'The occupation of the island of Crete (Operation Merkur) is to be prepared in order to have a base for conducting the air war against England in the Eastern Mediterranean.' There was one qualification: 'The transport movements must not lead to any delay in the strategic concentration for Barbarossa.'

Student had already flown back to the airborne headquarters at Berlin-Tempelhof to set in motion the transfer to Greece of the 7th Parachute Division from eleven different camps in Prussia. For the divisional chief of staff, Major Count von Uxküll, the administrative complications allowed little time to think of the operation, whose objective they had been told in the strictest confidence. Secrecy only stimulated the rumours further when the warning order to move reached the barracks.

The Parachute Division, as part of the air force and not the army, was very conscious of jealousy and scepticism within the Reichswehr's officer corps. 'Our formation is young,' Captain Freiherr von der Heydte told his men in the 1st Battalion of the 3rd Parachute Regiment when presenting them with the divisional badge of a diving eagle with a swastika in its claws.* 'We must create tradition by our actions in the future. It depends upon us whether or not the sign of the plunging eagle – the badge which unites us – will go down in history as a symbol of military honour and valour.'

They were all volunteers, a number of them 17-year-olds who had seen magazine articles about the *Fallschirmjäger* regiments and longed to belong to this new élite. Heydte said that his men had joined for 'idealism, ambition or adventure'. The idealists, former members of the Hitler Youth 'saturated with national slogans' were the most likely to crack up. According to Heydte, the adventurers made the best soldiers.

One volunteer called Martin Pöppel managed to be both a former member of the Hitler Youth and an adventurer. He was constantly in trouble throughout the 'unbelievably hard' training when Hauptfeldwebel Zierach 'reigned supreme with his fat punishment book, which he kept jammed between the first and second button on his chest.' The sentence was always physical exertion until the culprit dropped: 'running on the spot, marching and falling flat, marching and punishment routines to music'. But 'a bit of spirit, something out of the ordinary was what the paratroops wanted.' Success on passing-out and after the first jump was celebrated with sausages and beer and chatting up girls impressed by the paratroop uniform and their reputation as a *corps d'élite*.

The persistent notion that the Parachute Division represented only the flower of Nazi youth is misleading. A number of private soldiers and lance corporals came from old Prussian families: in the British Army, where NCOs instinctively distrusted 'gentleman rankers', this would have been unthinkable. The three brothers, Counts Wolfgang, Leberecht and Hans-Joachim von Blücher, provided the most striking example. Wolfgang, aged 24, was a lieutenant; the other two aged 19 and 17, sergeant and private. All three were to die on Crete fighting the Black Watch on the rust-coloured terrain round the airfield of Heraklion.

---

* Each regiment, with three battalions of 550 men, was equivalent to a weak infantry brigade. The Storm Regiment had four battalions, each 600 strong.

Parachute officers provided an equally marked contrast in backgrounds. Heydte described a fellow battalion commander as a man who had been 'a very good NCO; but even as an officer, he remained an NCO.' Amongst the hard-bitten fighters who had risen from the ranks, the most outstanding was Colonel Hermann Ramcke who had started as a ship's boy. During the First World War he fought in the trenches, and after the Armistice he joined one of the most brutal of the Freikorps – General von der Goltz's Iron Division which terrorized the Baltic states in 1919 on the fringe of the Russian Civil War. He finally became an officer in the Reichswehr during the inter-war years.

On the other hand Major General Wilhelm Süssmann, Major Count von Uxküll (from a family of Baltic landowners) and Captain Baron von der Heydte all belonged to the anti-Nazi faction within the armed forces. Uxküll, who recruited Heydte, was a second cousin of Colonel Count Claus von Stauffenberg.

Einer von der Heydte, who had been a friend of Patrick Leigh Fermor in Vienna in 1934, 'had become a regular cavalry officer,' wrote Leigh Fermor, 'rather like *ancien régime* Frenchmen, who followed the profession of arms in spite of their hatred for the government.' After the plot to assassinate Hitler in July 1944, Heydte, who had known a number of the conspirators, escaped only because his 'name was misspelled in the papers the Gestapo found. Instead, a major called von der Heyde was arrested, and later freed by the Russians.'

In the eyes of the men, an officer's origins seem to have been more or less irrelevant: those with a well-earned reputation for bravery were idolized. Captain Gericke, a battalion commander, they regarded as 'a real god of war' following his exploits in Holland. And the eldest Blücher was admired more for his Knight's Cross, also won in Holland, than for his family name.

The 2nd Parachute Regiment and the divisional staff led by General Süssmann had left for Bulgaria on 26 March, before the invasion of Greece. And although no parachute units were called on to capture the island of Lemnos, as planned, they were used at short notice to seize the Corinth isthmus on 26 April.

On 2 May, the rest of the paratroopers followed by train, a thousand-mile, thirteen-day journey from their moorland training grounds in North Germany down through Austria, Hungary and Roumania to the Bulgarian border, then to Salonika and down the

Aegean coast by lorry. They felt 'rather on holiday than on a journey into battle'. Only in Greece did they see signs of war: 'knocked-out tanks, gutted vehicles and the freshly-dug graves of soldiers'.

Their lorries took them to bivouac areas near airfields in Attica: Dadion, Eleusis, Megara, Tanagra, Topolia and Corinth where the 2nd Parachute Regiment had remained after their action. Heydte's battalion of the 3rd Parachute Regiment pitched their tents at Topolia. Early on 15 May, the morning after their arrival, an order arrived for regimental and battalion commanders to report to the Hotel Grande Bretagne in Athens by eleven o'clock. General Student had taken over the hotel as his headquarters within a week of its abandonment by the Greek high command and the British Military Mission.

As a Luftwaffe operation, Mercury came under the command of General Löhr's 4th Air Fleet, not Field Marshal List's XII Army headquarters. Senior German army officers were opposed to the operation. They were certain that the British would defend such a strategically important island to the end, and they feared the diversion of more troops just before Operation Barbarossa. The Parachute Division's privileged treatment, and Student's unprecedented plan to capture a major island from the air, with little hope of the usual ground support, promised some inter-service *schadenfreude* should the operation run into trouble.

The 22nd Division had been the air-portable formation allocated to the XI Air Corps, but Field Marshal List's headquarters decided that to move it down from Roumania, where it guarded the oilfields, was too complicated. In its place, List's staff suggested the 5th Mountain Division consisting of Bavarian and Austrian alpine regiments. This formation, which had suffered heavy casualties at the Rupel Pass, was resting at Chalkis. The 5th Mountain Division disliked the Prussians in the parachute division, and called them *Saupreussen* — or 'pigs of Prussians'.* Their commander, Major General Julius Ringel, an Austrian Nazi from before the *Anschluss*, was a jaunty Styrian squire with a dark moustache and imperial beard.

Student also encountered opposition within the Luftwaffe. He resented not having sole command of the operation, including control of the VIII Air Corps which was to provide close support to the paratroopers with about 570 aircraft — Stukas, Junkers 88s, Dorniers,

* For the full order of battle, see Appendix B.

Heinkels, Messerschmitt 109s and Messerschmitt 110s. The VIII Air Corps was commanded by Student's rival, General Freiherr Wolfram von Richthofen, a cousin of the 'Red Baron'. This Richthofen's fame was less romantic. He first attracted international attention when he directed the Condor Legion in Spain. His infamous battle honours — Guernica and, more recently, Belgrade — did not augur well for the ancient cities of Crete.

The concentration of transport planes, the largest ever seen, reached its peak on 14 May. Just over five hundred Junkers 52s, solid slow tri-motors of corrugated metal, were assembled on seven airfields in Attica and Boetia ready to ferry waves of paratroopers south for three hundred kilometres over the Aegean to drop on what were thought to be weakly defended objectives. But Student was then forced to delay Operation Mercury, originally scheduled for 17 May, to Tuesday, 20 May. Extra time was needed to bring the tanker *Rondine* with 5,000 tons of aviation fuel down the Adriatic.

Any doubt in German officers' minds as to the identity of their objective vanished the moment they entered the ballroom of the Hotel Grande Bretagne. A huge map of Crete had been fastened to the far wall. They took their seats and looked around. Daylight was excluded. The shutters and windows along the outer wall had been fastened, and the lights of the chandeliers were reflected in the mirrored doors along the opposite side.

'In a quiet but clear and slightly vibrant voice', wrote Heydte later, 'General Student explained the plan of attack. It was his own, personal plan. He had devised it, had struggled against heavy opposition for its acceptance, and had worked out all the details. One could perceive that this plan had become a part of him, a part of his life.' Student had rejected advice to concentrate his forces on one objective: instead he preferred to spread his bets and attack all three airfields on the north coast, each of which had a nearby port for resupply if the attack was successful. But this dispersal of effort left him with insufficient paratroop reserves to reinforce a particular sector rapidly.

The Storm Regiment, his largest formation, would drop on and around the airfield of Maleme in the west of the island. Not far from there, the 3rd Regiment and the engineer battalion would drop in the valley running north-east towards Canea to attack Suda and tie down any Allied reserve forces. Fifty kilometres to the east, most of the 2nd Regiment would drop on the airfield next to Rethymno, and a further sixty-five kilometres to the east, the 1st Regiment would take Heraklion and its airfield. Glider-borne troops would land first near Maleme and Canea to attack key anti-aircraft batteries. As soon as the airfields were secured by paratroop forces on Day 1 or Day 2, the transport planes would fly in the 5th Mountain Division. Motorcycle troops, mountain artillery and engineer units would follow.

On the second day, two *Leichten Schiffsstaffeln*, or groups of light ships – altogether 7 small freighters and 63 motor-assisted caiques – would bring reinforcements, supplies and pack-animals for the mountain regiments. The reinforcements consisted of two battalions of mountain troops and anti-aircraft batteries. The first flotilla would sail with one battalion to Maleme, or Suda Bay if it was captured on the first day, and the second flotilla to Heraklion with the other. Some light tanks and motor transport would come later as part of 'the follow-up' once 'shipping communications between the mainland and Crete' had been established. The seaborne part of the plan had only been added as an insurance policy at Hitler's insistence.

General Student's intelligence staff, led by Major Reinhardt, then produced one of the most inaccurate briefings of the whole war. Their photo-reconnaissance 'line-overlaps' along the coast, which recreated an aerial picture of each objective and dropping zone, had failed to pick out the vast majority of the well-camouflaged positions. General Student after the war claimed that the Dornier pilots had reported that 'the island appeared lifeless.'

The Germans, during their period of seemingly unstoppable conquest, paid relatively little attention to the art of intelligence. Such over-confidence was revealed in the language of their summaries which phrased mere suppositions with the cast-iron confidence of undeniable truths. That of 19 May, on the eve of battle, categorically stated that the British garrison on Crete was no more than 5,000 strong, with only 400 men at Heraklion, and none at Rethymno. All the New Zealanders and Australians from Greece had been evacuated directly to Egypt and there were no Greek troops on the island.

Most astonishing of all, Reinhardt's summary predicted an enthusiastic welcome from the civilian population, even that a pro-German fifth column would emerge, and in reply to the challenge 'Oberst!' would utter the password 'Bock!'. He and his staff had either dismissed out of hand or failed to read the general briefing document completed on 31 March for the invasion of Greece. There the relevant passage read: 'The Cretans are considered intelligent, hot-blooded, valorous, excitable as well as obstinate and difficult to govern. The agricultural population is accustomed to using arms, even in everyday life. Vendetta and abduction are still customary and criminality is high. In case of invasion account must be taken of obstinate resistance by the civilian population.'

After dismissal from the briefing, which had gone on to emplaning instructions and other administrative details, battalion commanders wandered out into the glaring light of mid-afternoon. They could not yet digest the full import of the operation ahead of them. This perhaps would be their only chance to see Athens, but little enough time remained for a late lunch in a taverna before returning to their regimental commanders for another session of orders.

Although unimpressed by the 'overloaded donkey-carts, and the overcrowded old tramcars which tried to force their way through the crowds with their bells clanging and their sides festooned with black bunches of sleek and agile street-arabs', officers wanted to go for a proprietorial stroll on the Acropolis where a huge scarlet and black swastika flag drooped in the windless heat. Many of them exulted in the conquest of Greece as if their New Order had absorbed its ancient civilization by martial triumph. Some wrote in lyrical terms of the shadows of their aircraft passing over the Parthenon.

Other vital steps were taken at the last moment purely to preserve secrecy. On 17 May, two days after the briefing at the Hotel Grande Bretagne, members of Student's staff commandeered the Aspiotis printing works to run off maps of Crete using paper and plates brought down from Germany. Everything was present except the aviation fuel. Even with Student's three-day postponement of the operation to 20 May, the timing was very nearly too close. The tanker *Rondine* carrying the aviation fuel had come down the Adriatic to Patras, but when she reached the Corinth Canal, her captain refused to proceed unless the length of its bottom was searched for unexploded bombs and cleared of underwater obstacles. Engineers and divers from both Wehrmacht and Luftwaffe units were hastily called in, and the task was completed in less than a day. The fuel only reached the airfields a few hours before take-off.

For reasons of security, battalion commanders were told not to brief their men until the very eve of operation. But the evening before, when quartermasters provided beer and brandy, the paratroopers knew the moment of action was close. The swagger and jokes were muted by thoughtfulness. Even the 17- and 18-year-olds, as yet without any experience of battle, sat round the campfires playing mouth organs and singing songs of home rather than of war.

At ten o'clock on the morning of 19 May, a final conference of officers commanding air force units took place at Eleusis aerodrome. They had no idea that an Ultra intercept about this meeting, followed by a warning that 'today Monday may be day minus one', had gone off from London in the early hours to General Freyberg.

In the heat of the day, wearing nothing but PT shorts and boots, the paratroopers cleaned their sub-machine guns, rifles and Spandau bipod machine guns ready for the most rigorous inspection. Then, bent over parachute canisters with coloured markings, they packed their weapons with almost as much care as they repacked their parachutes. Their final task was to put their own belongings into small crates, and fill in forms so that personal effects could be sent to next-of-kin in the event of death.

Towards dusk, company commanders assembled their men for briefing. The objective was announced as the first of a series of Mediterranean islands to be taken. 'We are almost foolish with enthusiasm', a young corporal wrote in his diary.

8

'Most Secret Sources'

Major General Bernard Freyberg VC, the commander of the New Zealand Division, only reached Crete on 29 April. With characteristic determination, he had refused to leave Greece until the last moment to ensure that as many of his men were evacuated as possible. He looked forward to reassembling the New Zealand Expeditionary Force in Egypt as a single formation. His 6th Brigade had gone on to Alexandria, and he assumed that the other New Zealand units evacuated to Crete would follow in the next few days. The possibility that he might be asked to stay to command the island's defence never occurred to him. But for Churchill, Freyberg was the obvious choice. And Wavell was urged to appoint him — tantamount to an order in the circumstances.

Freyberg's career was endowed with the muscular morality of the Edwardian hero. At school in New Zealand, he proved himself a champion swimmer, but his academic performance did not indicate a reflective or enquiring mind. He studied to be a dentist but, on the prospect of war in 1914, made his way to London to volunteer. He had no military experience other than as a territorial subaltern in New Zealand. The story that Freyberg, on his way to Europe, had joined Pancho Villa's army in Mexico and 'reached the rank of General' was a preposterous exaggeration which Churchill helped circulate. This canard, which gave him 'a certain amount of notoriety', lasted until after the Second World War. 'The truth is', Freyberg said in 1948 when Governor-General of New Zealand, 'I have never bothered to contradict it.'

Churchill, as First Lord of the Admiralty, secured Freyberg a commission in the Royal Naval Division, and took pride in his deeds of cold courage – swimming by night to a hostile shore near Gallipoli with flares to confuse the Turks, and winning a Victoria Cross after leading the Royal Naval Division's Hood Battalion to capture Beaucourt in Flanders.

Freyberg, who had been a slightly incongruous comrade of such aesthetes of the lost generation as Rupert Brooke, Patrick Shaw-Stewart and Charles Lister, was lionized by hostesses after the Armistice. Fascinated by his lack of fear, Churchill describes in a curious paragraph how, during a country house weekend, he had asked Freyberg to strip to allow him to count his twenty-seven wounds. Freyberg modestly explained before taking off his clothes that 'You nearly always get two wounds for every bullet or splinter, because mostly they have to go out as well as in.'

During the inter-war years Freyberg settled down. He married a remarkable woman, both well-connected and greatly liked, and left behind the ostentatious bravery of his youth when his ambition to win medals had been ingenuously proclaimed. He retired from the Army in 1934. Five years later, on the outbreak of war, Churchill lobbied on his behalf when the future command of New Zealand's expeditionary force was discussed. But Churchill's intervention made little difference to the deliberations: the New Zealand forces at that time had no other obvious candidate.

In the early days, Freyberg was not popular, especially with his staff officers. He had acquired the formalism of the British Army of that time and lost touch with the New Zealand of his youth. To the irritation of his officers, he busied himself with details which he should have left to them. But as the war progressed, they grew to admire his strengths: on top of his bravery he had a genuine interest in the welfare of his men and he was a first-class trainer of troops. And they developed a humorous, although occasionally exasperated, affection for his weaknesses.

These failings – chiefly obstinacy, muddled thinking and an extreme reluctance to criticize subordinates – became especially important in the circumstances of Crete. Freyberg was famous for his inability to sack a useless officer, even after promising his staff that he would go through with it. 'He could not bear to be unkind,' one of them wrote later. On numerous occasions he went to great lengths to avoid such a distressing duty. This was perhaps part of that soft-heartedness very often found in large men of prodigious physical courage.

Bernard Freyberg was indeed large, and the description barrel-

chested for once fitted perfectly. Churchill called him 'the great St
Bernard', which suggests also his rather endearing schoolboyish
enthusiasms. When he wore his 'lemon-squeezer' hat, he really did
look like 'a huge scoutmaster', as another of his staff officers
remarked.

Freyberg provides yet another example of how storybook heroes
seldom make good generals. A member of the War Cabinet staff felt
that Churchill was too impressed by men of action. 'Winston was a
bad judge of character. He didn't seem able to relate the task to the
man needed to do it. He automatically went for men who had been
tremendous fire-eaters in their youth, almost thinking "Who is most
like I was then?" '

On 30 April, the day after he reached Crete on board HMS *Ajax*,
Freyberg was summoned to a conference with his two immediate
superiors, General Wilson and General Wavell. This meeting took
place at Ay Marina in a large seashore villa with a rooftop balcony
sheltered by an awning which flapped in the breeze.

The Commander-in-Chief arrived by car from Maleme airfield
where he had landed after an uncomfortable flight from Egypt in a
Blenheim. Churchill had sent the following signal two days before: 'It
seems clear from our information that a heavy airborne attack by
German troops and bombers will soon be made on Crete. Let me
know what forces you have in the island and what your plans are. It
ought to be a fine opportunity for killing the parachute troops. The
island must be stubbornly defended.'

Having accorded Crete the lowest priority possible for the last six
months, despite Churchill's instructions, Wavell was depressed by his
renewed pugnacity. 'Winston is always expecting rabbits to come out
of empty hats,' he said to Chips Channon. Disastrous aircraft losses
during the fall of Greece meant that there were not enough
Hurricanes left to provide adequate fighter cover. As a result, both
the Royal Navy and the RAF had rather lost interest in the island as
a forward base. The opportunity to develop aerodromes for long-
range bombing of the Ploesti oilfields seems to have slipped from
strategic thinking at this stage. Meanwhile the Army needed every
battalion and tank available to cope with Rommel's advance in North
Africa, and Wavell now had to put together a force to relieve British
bases in Iraq besieged in an uprising which the Germans had
promised to support.

First of all Wavell took Jumbo Wilson on one side and told him,

'I want you to go to Jerusalem and relieve Baghdad.' Then he called Freyberg over and, having complimented him on the performance of the New Zealand Division in Greece, said that he wanted him to command Creforce.

Freyberg did not conceal his dismay. 'I told him', he wrote later in a report to the New Zealand government, 'that I wanted to get back to Egypt to concentrate the Division and train and re-equip it and I added that my Government would never agree to the Division being split permanently. He then said that he considered it my duty to remain and take on the job. I could do nothing but accept . . . There was not very much to discuss. We were told that Crete would be held. The scale of attack envisaged was five to six thousand airborne troops, plus a possible seaborne attack. The primary objectives of this attack were considered to be Heraklion and Maleme aerodromes.'

Freyberg was the seventh commander of British forces on the island since their arrival the previous November. He was appointed over Major General Weston of the Royal Marines, who had recently arrived to command the various elements of the Mobile Naval Base Defence Organisation. Weston, who had displayed considerable energy during his four days in office, believed that the appointment of General Officer Commanding had been offered to him, so he felt aggrieved by the abrupt change. This senior Marine officer was a curious mixture. He possessed an analytical mind and a much clearer view of enemy strategy than his successor, yet was self-important and liable to behave unreasonably over small incidents.

That afternoon Creforce Headquarters was established in a quarry above Canea on the west side of the neck of the peninsula that formed the shelter of Suda Bay. The site was perfect. It looked down the coast towards Maleme and, swinging a few degrees left, over the valley leading to Canea which Brigadier Tidbury had correctly identified six months before as the second enemy dropping zone in the area of Canea.

Weston jealously held on to his personnel so Freyberg found himself without a headquarters staff. 'There weren't even clerks and signallers,' he later recorded, 'only an officers' mess.' Freyberg, even though he was no prima donna, may well have been privately upset by Weston's behaviour, but friction between them seems to have had little influence on events, perhaps because Freyberg backed away from any unpleasantness.

Freyberg clearly wondered what he had been landed with. In spite of Churchill's command of November 1940 and repeated demands, basic measures for the defence of the island had not been taken. The subsequent excuse of GHQ Middle East that there were not enough resources to go round, although true, was also disingenuous. No effort was made to think things through: that fatal British vice of compromise, spreading the jam so thinly that it did no good anywhere, was all too evident. The will and energy for hard decisions were in even shorter supply than materials.

Peter Wilkinson, the SOE officer who had come to Crete to observe the parachute invasion, wrote in his report to Colonel Colin Gubbins at SOE's headquarters in London: 'Our staff appeared to suffer from complete inertia. Not even the most elementary preparations had been made. Although we have now been over six months in Crete, there is not a single road from Canea to the south coast that can be used for military transport – though there were only four miles to complete when they arrived here.'

Crete, with its mountain ranges like battlements facing Africa, could only be resupplied through ports on the north coast. With German airfields in Greece, this was a grave weakness, as the constant pall of black smoke over Suda Bay demonstrated: ten merchant ships totalling fifty thousand tons were sunk by air attack in under a month.

Only strong air cover could protect shipping, and Middle East command did not have enough Hurricane squadrons to allow them to be destroyed on pathetically vulnerable airfields. Nobody doubted the bravery of the RAF pilots. Soldiers watched in anguish at the odds they faced. One of the last Hurricanes at Maleme rose into the sky alone against a swarm of Messerschmitts which fell on it, in the words of a Bofors gunner, 'like a horde of hawks on a single sparrow'. But tardy and half-hearted attempts to construct fighter pens and satellite airfields protected by the mountains attracted fierce criticism. 'The attitude of the RAF beggars description,' Wilkinson continued in his report to Gubbins. 'Their excuses are not borne out by fact, and if the Germans can improvise aerodromes from which Junkers can take off six hours after landing, one feels something might have been done in six months of peaceful occupation. Because whatever the results of the Greek Campaign it must have been obvious to a schoolboy that Crete was the natural half-way house.'

Similarly, the courage of Royal Navy and Merchant Navy crews was not matched by administrative will-power on land. 'There was no foam fire fighting apparatus in Suda Bay,' Wilkinson continued, 'although it had been a so-called naval base for six months.'

Freyberg, understandably concerned to discover the true state of affairs, sent a signal to Wavell in Cairo. 'Forces at my disposal are totally inadequate to meet attack envisaged. Unless fighter aircraft are greatly increased and naval forces made available to deal with seaborne attack I cannot hope to hold out with land forces alone, which as a result of campaign in Greece are now devoid of any artillery, have insufficient tools for digging, very little transport, and inadequate war reserves of equipment and ammunition. Force here can and will fight, but without full support from Navy and Air Force cannot hope to repel invasion.' On the same day he sent his own government a similar message: 'There is no evidence of naval forces capable of guaranteeing us against seaborne invasion and air force in island consists 6 Hurricanes and 17 obsolete aircraft.'

The use of phrases such as 'seaborne invasion' assumed that the enemy intended to mount a beach-storming operation, rather than reinforce his airborne troops by sea on a part of the coast he had already captured. They were, of course, very different matters. So different were they in the context of the Battle of Crete, that this misunderstanding completely distorted General Freyberg's view of enemy intentions to the point that he misread an Ultra signal on the second day of the battle with disastrous, and almost certainly decisive, consequences.

Wavell, with Admiral Cunningham's assurance, replied that the Navy would support him and that even if the decision to hold Crete were reversed, there was little time left to evacuate the island. To judge by his signal to London of 1 May – 'our information points insufficient sea-going shipping left Aegean for large-scale sea-borne operations' – Wavell clearly did not share Freyberg's concern with the sea. Churchill's view of the threat was also different from Freyberg's, as his signal to the Prime Minister of New Zealand on 3 May shows: 'Our information points to an airborne attack being delivered in the near future, with possibly an attempt at seaborne attack. The Navy will certainly do their utmost to prevent the latter, and it is unlikely to succeed on any large scale. So far as airborne attack is concerned, this ought to suit the New Zealanders down to the ground, for they will be able to come to close quarters, man to man, with the enemy, who will not have the advantage of tanks and artillery, on which he so largely relies.'

As Wavell's ADC, Peter Coats, observed, Freyberg was 'a man of quickly changing moods, easily depressed and as easily elated.' Only four days after his very pessimistic messages to Wavell and the New Zealand government, Freyberg signalled to London: 'Cannot understand nervousness; am not in the least anxious about airborne attack; have made my dispositions and feel can cope adequately with the troops at my disposal. Combination of seaborne and airborne attack is different. If that comes before I can get the guns and transport here the situation will be difficult. Even so, provided Navy can help, trust all will be well.'

The Chiefs of Staff in London appear to have been disconcerted by Freyberg's back-to-front analysis of the enemy threat. The following day this signal was sent to Cairo: 'Please enquire from General Freyberg whether he is receiving Orange Leonard [Ultra] information from Cairo if not please arrange to pass relevant OL information maintaining utmost security.'*

Since Freyberg's misreading of Ultra at the crucial moment of the battle has never before been fully explored, it is important to look closely at how it happened.

The invasion of Crete represented the first major test of Ultra in operational conditions. The possibility that the Germans were considering a Mediterranean island as a target for a major parachute assault was understood from signals intercepted in mid-April during the Allied retreat in Greece. An indication that the target was Crete came on 25 April, a few hours before Hitler's headquarters issued the Führer Directive for Operation Mercury. Over the next few days, the enemy intention to invade from the air became increasingly clear: Mercury was a Luftwaffe operation and the Luftwaffe's lax cypher discipline greatly helped Hut 3 at Bletchley. On 28 April, London arranged to send a resumé of relevant Ultra intercepts to the senior RAF officer on the island, Group Captain George Beamish, and then to Freyberg when he took command of Creforce two days later.

In the course of the meeting of 30 April, Wavell briefed Freyberg on 'most secret sources' or 'most reliable sources', as Ultra intelligence was euphemistically termed, but did not disclose exactly what this source was. He gave Freyberg the impression that the information came from a well-placed spy of the Secret Intelligence Service. (Freyberg's son and biographer, the present Lord Freyberg,

---

* The text of relevant Ultra messages will be found in Appendix C.

claims that his father knew from the beginning what the true source was, but his version is unconvincing. Yet whatever General Freyberg believed the OL or 'Orange Leonard' source to be, it will always be known as Ultra material here.)

The rules governing the use of Ultra material were unclear. Jumbo Wilson, presumably with Wavell's blessing, used Ultra to avoid entrapment during the German advance on the mainland. It is thus very hard to imagine Wavell forbidding Freyberg to make use of it in Crete, especially after the Chiefs of Staff signalled on 9 May – 'So complete is our information that it appears to present heaven sent opportunity of dealing enemy heavy blow.' And on Churchill's orders, a senior staff officer, Brigadier Eric Dorman-Smith, was flown to Crete on 11 May to brief Freyberg on the accumulated intelligence. Dorman-Smith was impressed by Freyberg's courage but depressed by his tactical sense and 'ruefully put him in his "Bear of Little Brain" category'. Dorman-Smith took back to Cairo a letter from Freyberg to Wavell which read: 'If they come as an airborne attack against our aerodromes I feel sure we should be able to stop him if he attacks after the 16th. If however he makes a combined operation of it with a beach landing with tanks, then we shall not be in a strong position.'

Freyberg's confusion about the relative strengths of the airborne and seaborne forces had begun at that first meeting with Wavell on 30 April. The figure of 'five to six thousand airborne troops plus a possible sea attack' appears to have been a rather conservative reading of a Joint Intelligence Committee report of 27 April which stated: 'The Germans could transport up to 3,000 parachute or airborne troops in the first sortie or possibly 4,000 if gliders are used. Two or possibly three sorties per day could be made from Greece.' Neither Wavell nor Freyberg grasped the point that this estimate of the Germans' air transport capacity was merely for the first day. Wavell should have had a clearer idea since the first report on the airborne force initially allocated to the operation – the 7th Parachute Division and the 22nd Airlanding Division – reached Cairo on 26 April.

The first formal estimate arrived from London in Ultra signal OL 2167 on 6 May (see Appendix C). It gave the proposed invasion date of 17 May, and an enemy airlanding strength of two divisions plus corps troops and added elements. This was an accurate forecast. Confusion then arose from the Twelfth Army's decision to keep the 22nd Division up in Roumania and send Major General Ringel's 5th

Mountain Division instead. And because of their heavy losses in the fighting at the Rupel Pass, part of a mountain regiment from another division was added to Ringel's two regiments. Later the same day, a correcting signal, OL 2168, was sent to Cairo and Crete. 'Flak units further troops and supplies mentioned our 2167 are to proceed by sea to Crete. Also three mountain regiments thought more likely than third mountain regiment.'

Somehow, this signal seems to have given the Directorate of Military Intelligence two wrong ideas: first, that three mountain regiments were now coming in addition to the 7th Parachute Division and the 22nd Airlanding Division; and second, that three mountain regiments were coming by sea. Wavell's signal doubting the enemy's ability to assemble sufficient ships does not appear to have had much effect. And the possibility of an airbridge by Junkers 52, like the one which brought General Franco's Army of Africa from Morocco to Seville in 1936, does not seem to have been considered.

A much more detailed signal sent the next day, an accurate analysis by the Air Ministry (OL 2170), clearly indicated that the seaborne contingent represented a very minor element of the whole operation. But the damage was revived by a subsequent signal, OL 2/302 on 13 May, in which the compiler again assumed that both the 22nd Airlanding Division and the 5th Mountain Division were taking part. As a result Freyberg was told that the 'invading force . . . will consist of some thirty to thirty-five thousand men, of which some twelve thousand will be the parachute landing contingent, and ten thousand will be transported by sea.' As a comparison of the signals (in Appendix C) will show, this was a case of rearranging figures to fit a hypothesis. Little differentiation was made between speculation and hard intelligence.

Freyberg, the commander on the ground, did not spot that anything was wrong. Although he possessed an excellent memory (a useful talent since the messages were supposed to be burnt after reading) he lacked the analytical intellect and the scepticism necessary to identify inconsistencies. The notion of a seaborne invasion became fixed in his mind even though the information he received pointed only to the transport of reinforcements. Such was his preoccupation that he came to regard a maritime operation as a greater threat than all the airborne troops who, even in the figures of the mistaken report, represented a far more immediate and much greater threat.

Apart from the confusion over the 22nd Airlanding Division, few commanders in history had enjoyed such precise intelligence on their opponent's intentions, timing and objectives. Churchill's comment after the war, although magnanimous, is clear: 'Freyberg was undaunted. He did not readily believe the scale of air attack would be so gigantic. His fear was of powerful organised invasion from the sea. This we hoped the Navy would prevent in spite of our air weaknesses.' And Freyberg himself later acknowledged: 'We for our part were mostly preoccupied by seaborne landings, not by the threat of air landings.'

Freyberg, having been misled a certain distance in one direction, was unable to see things in proportion. He firmly seized the stick by the wrong end and, as later events showed, he could not let go. His obstinacy and lack of comprehension were something of a joke amongst his fellow generals. General Sir Brian Horrocks, later Freyberg's corps commander in the desert, told a friend that he used to put a couple of obvious but unimportant points into his orders which he knew Freyberg would contest, and which he could concede.

The revisionist theory of events propagated by the present Lord Freyberg – that his father was deeply shocked to discover the true nature of the airborne threat on 7 May, but could not move any troops to reinforce Maleme airfield in case this betrayed the secret of Ultra – is hard to accept, if only because General Freyberg's letter to Wavell on 13 May and his subsequent behaviour contradict it. His continuing preoccupation with invasion from the sea, his calamitous misreading of what turned out to be the most important signal of the battle, and his relative lack of interest in Maleme until the morning of 22 May (two days after the invasion, by which time the Germans had captured the airfield and landed reinforcements) do not suggest a man who had recognized the enemy's intention, yet found himself frustrated by security precautions.

Most ironically of all, Freyberg appears to have helped preserve the secret of Ultra better by having misunderstood the contents than by his painstaking preservation of secrecy. The German report on the Battle of Crete, *Gefechtbericht XI Fl.Korps – Einsatz Kreta*, later recorded: 'One thing stands out from all the information gleaned from the enemy (prisoners' statements, diaries and captured documents) that they were on the whole very well informed about German intentions, thanks to an excellent espionage network, but expected that the bulk of the invasion forces would come by sea.'

General Freyberg's misreading of the threat inevitably produced a damaging compromise both in the disposition of his troops and in his

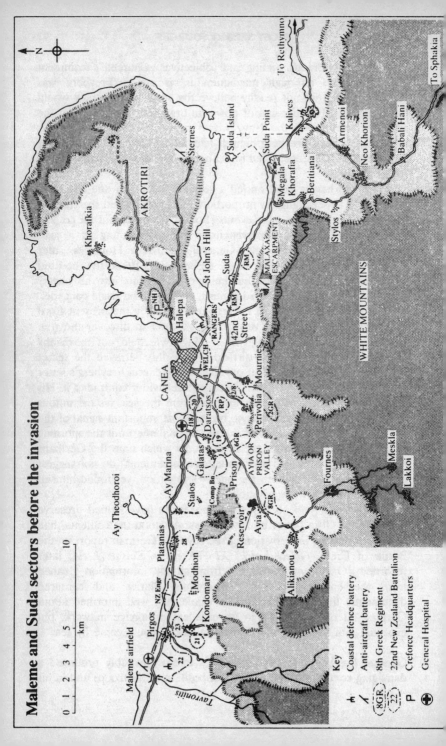

Maleme and Suda sectors before the invasion

N

0 1 2 3 4 5 10 km

Maleme airfield

Pirgos
Tavronitis
Platanias
NZ Engr
Kondomari
Modhion
Ay Marina
Ay Theodhoroi

Stalos
Galatas
Comp Bn
Prison
Reservoir
Ayia
Alikianou

CANEA
Daratsos
AYIA OR PRISON VALLEY
Perivolia
Mournies
Fournes
Meskla
Lakkoi

WELCH
RANGERS
42nd Street
Halepa
St John's Hill
AKROTIRI
Khorafkia
Sternes

Suda
Suda Island
Suda Point
Kalives
Megala Khorafia
Beritiana
Stylos
MALAXA ESCARPMENT
Neo Khorion
Armenoi
Babali Hani

To Rethymno
To Sphakia

WHITE MOUNTAINS

Key

- Coastal defence battery
- Anti-aircraft battery
- 8GR — 8th Greek Regiment
- 22 — 22nd New Zealand Battalion
- P — Creforce Headquarters
- ⊕ — General Hospital

operational orders, which confused priorities. Brigadier Tidbury's plan – to combat airborne assaults on the three north coast airfields of Heraklion, Rethymno and Maleme, and in the Ayia valley south-west of Canea – was adapted in the Maleme and Canea sectors to face an assault from the sea.

At Heraklion, Freyberg had Brigadier Chappel's 14th Infantry Brigade with regular battalions of the Black Watch and the York and Lancaster Regiment reinforced by an Australian battalion, and a Greek regiment of three battalions. They were joined at the last moment by the 2nd Leicesters and, finally, by a battalion of the Argyll and Sutherland Highlanders who were landed on the south coast at Tymbaki (see Appendix B for full order of battle).

At Rethymno there were two Australian battalions and two Greek battalions guarding the airfield, and in the town a very effective force of Cretan gendarmes who were properly armed. Two main groups of reserves were organized: another two Australian battalions with most of the motor transport at Georgioupolis, between Suda and Rethymno, and the 4th New Zealand Brigade as well as the 1st Battalion of the Welch Regiment close to Canea and Creforce Headquarters.*

Along the crucial sector between Canea and Maleme, the New Zealand Division was deployed to defend the coast as well as the airfield and the valley. This allowed little depth to their defences. Also the divisional reserve, the 20th Battalion, and the main force reserve were both positioned close to Canea rather than near Maleme airfield, the enemy's main designated objective.

Freyberg had jumped to the conclusion that he faced 'a seaborne landing bringing tanks', yet he ordered no study of likely beaches. A rapid examination of naval charts would have shown that in the Suda, Akrotiri, Canea and Maleme sectors, only the beach from Maleme to Platanias could have been considered possible for a landing in any strength, and then only if the Germans had assault ships and landing craft, which they did not.**

A number of regimental officers noticed this flaw in their orders.

---

* From west to east by road, the distance from Maleme to Canea was 18 kilometres, Canea to Suda 6 kilometres, Suda to Georgioupolis 31 kilometres, Georgioupolis to Rethymno 36 kilometres and Rethymno to Heraklion 75 kilometres.

** I am most grateful to Captain R.G. Evans RN in Athens for obtaining and analysing the relevant charts.

The Welch Regiment, which had been based on that stretch of coast since February, considered an 'invasion by sea' a 'somewhat unlikely possibility'. But the only senior officer in the New Zealand Division to spot it was Colonel Howard Kippenberger, commanding the improvised 10th Brigade to the west of Canea, and he did not raise the question at the time: he just reduced his troops watching seawards.

Most astonishing of all, Freyberg's extended line of defence came to a halt on the far edge of Maleme airfield, which General Wavell and intelligence reports had identified from the beginning as one of the enemy's principal objectives. Brigadier Tidbury had pointed out over five months before, on 25 November, that the site of this airfield had been badly chosen because it was acutely vulnerable to attack. Brigadier Puttick, who had taken Freyberg's place as divisional commander, soon became conscious of the threat to his flank. He asked for reinforcements to cover the river-bed of the Tavronitis on the west side of the airfield, since it offered an ideal assembly area for enemy paratroops.

Creforce Headquarters apparently applied for permission from the Greek authorities to move the 1st Greek Regiment from Kastelli Kissamou, but only received agreement on 13 May. (This seems strange since Freyberg had already been given full command of all Greek forces.) Freyberg then said that the airborne attack was imminent, so there would not be time for them to march to the Tavronitis and dig trenches. It is possible, but not probable, that he thwarted this move in the belief that it might betray 'most secret sources', a perhaps exaggerated fear since he already had one battalion round the airfield and two on the eastern side.

Freyberg spent little time studying the ground at Maleme. Colonel Jasper Blunt urged him to move more troops there, but Freyberg refused, either to safeguard the secret source of their intelligence, or because he did not want to diminish his coastal defences. In any case, he considered Heraklion a more important objective for the enemy, and he lacked confidence in the abilities of the commander there, Brigadier Chappel of the 14th Infantry Brigade. His reconnaissances were also limited 'owing to policy matters holding me at HQ'.

One distraction was the question of whether the King should remain on Crete or leave before the German invasion began. Wavell, the Foreign Office and the War Cabinet in London believed he should stay as an example to neutral countries. General Heywood, on the other hand, argued that the indignity and danger of having to run away the moment the enemy landed should be avoided by his immediate withdrawal to Egypt. The King seems to have had little say in his own fate.

Freyberg was understandably dubious at the idea of the King remaining on the island, since defending a group of civilians against parachutists was the most uncertain calculation of all. He felt that they were far too exposed out at Perivolia, where they were staying in an old Venetian country house called Belakapina (a corruption of Bella Campagna), and invited them to move within the perimeter of Creforce Headquarters. But during their visit on 17 May to the building earmarked for them, a heavy air raid forced the King and his companions to take cover in slit trenches. King George decided to refuse the accommodation offered. Two days later, on the eve of the invasion, he moved instead with his entourage to another house near Perivolia, closer to the foothills of the White Mountains over which they would have to escape.

Freyberg's responsibility for all the Greek forces on the island included feeding and arming them. Weapons were handed out in a random manner from the Greek army headquarters in Canea — Steyers, Mausers, Mannlichers, Lee Enfields and a few antiquated St Etienne machine guns; a handful of cartridges, often of the wrong calibre, was pushed across at the same time. Few men received more than three rounds apiece.

Freyberg did not share the prejudices of some of his officers who deprecated the worth of these Greek units, mostly withdrawn from the mainland and supplemented by ill-trained recruits. Kippenberger described those attached to his brigade as 'malaria-ridden little chaps from Macedonia with four weeks' service'. Freyberg appointed Colonel Guy Salisbury-Jones from the Military Mission in Greece to take over the task of organization and liaison. Eight Greek regiments were formed from 9,000 men. Some of their battalions collapsed at the shock of battle, either due to poor leadership, or because their training and armament were inadequate to face determined attacks by German paratroop forces. But others astonished their detractors by their staunchness. In a fierce defence towards the end of the battle the 8th Greek Regiment, strengthened with Cretan guerrillas, saved the Commonwealth forces from envelopment at the most critical stage of their retreat.

It is greatly to Freyberg's credit that he quickly recognized how 'the entire population of Crete desired to fight'. Some British officers clung to the presumption that their regular troops would still perform better in an irregular battle than Cretans fighting in defence of their native land with an unbeatable knowledge of the ground and generations of guerrilla warfare behind them. Their least forgivable disservice to the Cretans was their failure to give volunteers some form of uniform and thus afford them an official status to protect them from being shot on capture as *francs-tireurs*. Even if they thought there were no weapons to hand out – in Canea, 400 Lee Enfield rifles remained locked up in the ancient Venetian galley sheds beside the harbour – the idea of handing over captured enemy weapons does not seem to have occurred to many officers until they saw what the Cretans could achieve with the crudest of weapons and virtually suicidal bravery.

Freyberg's lack of confidence in Brigadier Chappel at Heraklion has never been satisfactorily explained. Chappel, a regular officer from the Welch Regiment of great experience, may not have been a very charismatic figure but he was by no means inferior to most of his New Zealand counterparts.

Distance, shortage of transport and the bad condition of the coast road between Heraklion and Canea made Chappel's command there virtually independent. Installed in a quarry, like Creforce itself, 14th Infantry Brigade's headquarters personnel were drawn mostly from the Black Watch which provided the defence platoon, the brigade major, Richard Fleming, and Lieutenant Gordon Hope-Morley, one of the two intelligence officers.

The other intelligence officer was Patrick Leigh Fermor, who spoke Greek as well as German. After his semi-piratical adventures on the island of Antikithera, Leigh Fermor had reached Kastelli Kissamou. Soon afterwards, he met up with Prince Peter of Greece and Michael Forrester, his fellow member of the British Military Mission. The three of them spent several days based at Prince Peter's house on the coast north of Galatas. Then, when Leigh Fermor continued eastwards to Heraklion, Forrester acted as Colonel Salisbury-Jones's liaison officer, checking on the needs of the Greek regiments. The two men met up for dinner in Heraklion on the night of 18 May when Forrester visited the two Greek regiments grouped within and without the town's huge stone ramparts.

Another brief visitor to the British headquarters at Heraklion was John Pendlebury, still in search of spare weapons for the guerrilla kapitans. Leigh Fermor described how his 'handsome face, his single sparkling eye, his slung guerrilla's rifle and bandolier and his famous swordstick brought a stimulating flash of romance and fun into that khaki gloom'.

Even the sceptics among the regular officers of the 14th Infantry Brigade soon came to realize the fighting potential of 'Pendlebury's thugs'. There were three principal guerrilla kapitans with whom he worked in the region of Heraklion — Manoli Bandouvas, a rich patriarchal peasant of great influence who had moustaches like the horns of a water buffalo; Petrakageorgis, the owner of an olive-oil pressing business, lean-faced with deep-set eyes and a fearsome beak of a nose; and the white-haired Antonis Grigorakis, better known as Satanas, the greatest kapitan of them all.

'Satanas', wrote Monty Woodhouse, 'owed his name to the general belief that nobody but the devil himself could have survived the number of bullets he had in him.' But according to another version, this name dated from the day of his christening. The priest apparently was just saying 'I baptize thee', when the baby seized his beard, causing him to exclaim: 'You little devil!' Another of Satanas's distinguishing features was a mutilated hand. Furious with himself at losing heavily at dice, having promised to play no more, he had shot off his rolling finger. In the heat of the moment he forgot that the offending object was also his trigger finger.

The subject of Pendlebury's last days still attracts enormous interest. Many plans were discussed and he seems to have been in constant movement, although always coming back to Heraklion. He sent Jack Hamson with a hundred Cretan volunteers up to the Plain of Nida on the eastern flank of Mount Ida in case German paratroops dropped there, and with Herculean efforts they shifted boulders down on to its smooth areas to prevent aircraft landing.

Mike Cumberlege was asked to take his armed caique HMS *Dolphin* round to Hierapetra to see if a cargo of weapons and ammunition could be salvaged from a ship sunk in the harbour there. He found a sponge-diver from the east coast of the island, and arranged his temporary release from the Greek army. On the eve of their departure, Pendlebury gave a dinner at the officers' club overlooking the harbour of Heraklion. Ignoring the club's protocol of rank, he insisted that their crewman, Able Seaman Saunders, should also come. Over the meal, which consisted of fish concussed by German bombs that morning, they discussed a raid against the Italian-occupied island of Kasos for the night of 20 May, after the *Dolphin* returned. Cumberlege and his crew would ferry Pendlebury and his Cretans over to seize a few prisoners for interrogation. These guerrillas, known in Greece as *andartes*, were a fearsome bunch. Hammond recalled how they 'breathed blood and slaughter and garlic in the best Cretan style'.

If the Germans overran Crete, Pendlebury was determined to stay behind to organize guerrilla warfare. He regarded himself as virtually a Cretan. Life for him at this time consisted of secret arms dumps, guerrilla groups, sites for ambushes and demolition targets. His pet project – a far-sighted one as events proved – was to convince the 14th Infantry Brigade of the need for snipers to cover springs and wells. Water was the first vital commodity the paratroopers would need to replenish. But it does not seem that the British followed his advice. For Cumberlege and Hammond, that evening at the officers' club was their last sight of Pendlebury. They left on the *Dolphin* for Hierapetra the next morning.

In the last few days before the German invasion, Freyberg proved a perfect figurehead: his tours of inspection shortly before the battle were really an exercise in morale-boosting. He exuded a burly confidence, and his reputation for bravery gave him presence in the eyes of his soldiers, who referred to him with affectionate admiration as 'Tiny'. With his rasping voice, he told them, 'Just fix bayonets and go at them as hard as you can.'

But some officers suspected that his stirring words were not borne out in the Creforce operation order. Several inconsistencies made them uneasy. Freyberg himself had also advised troops 'not to rush out when the paratroops come down', and he had placed much emphasis on barbed wire as a defence. As most junior commanders and soldiers instinctively recognized, the only way to deal with an airborne assault was to counter-attack immediately. Much had also been made of the force reserves in the operational order, yet their deployment at the right time depended on several elements: accurate information; good communications; proximity to the objective; motor transport, of which there was very little; and the ability to move to the threatened sector without unnecessary exposure to air attack. The Luftwaffe's superiority in fact restricted the movement of reserves to the hours of darkness, and any attack had to be completed by first light. That in itself should have cast doubt over the strategy of holding back a large proportion of the total force in a battle which was bound to be rapidly decided. But Freyberg's eyes were fixed on the sea, not on the sky.

Creforce's weakest link was its ramshackle communications. Field telephones depended on wires run loosely along existing telegraph poles: they were vulnerable to bombardment and to paratroopers dropping between headquarters. The wireless sets available, mostly those brought back from Greece, were unreliable and in short supply. Nothing had been done to ship or fly in enough replacements in the three weeks before the invasion. Freyberg did not even mention radios in his list of urgent requirements sent to Cairo on 7 May. Signalling lamps had no batteries, and those capable of working off mains electricity were of the wrong voltage. The possibility of using heliograph between the Maleme sector and Creforce Headquarters was apparently never considered.

The last RAF fighters had been withdrawn, yet Creforce Headquarters rejected recommendations to mine or block the runways, mainly because the Air Ministry had demanded that landing grounds should be kept operational for a sudden deployment from Egypt. The historian Ian Stewart (the Welch Regiment's medical officer) has also suggested that because Freyberg believed that the troop-carriers would be able to crash-land almost anywhere, 'he was not according supreme importance to the airfields themselves.' However, the validity of this argument is hard to judge. Freyberg should have realized the importance of the airfields to the Germans, if only because Ultra signal OL 2167 warned that they wanted to use the runways at Maleme and Heraklion for their dive-bombers and fighters. Whatever the case, he appears to have been most reluctant to take any initiative.

Freyberg, as Churchill observed, was not downcast by the impending airborne assault. His secret signal to Wavell on 16 May hardly carries the tone of a man imprisoned in a decision he knew to be wrong – the failure to defend the ground to the west of Maleme airfield – in case such a redeployment betrayed the source of his intelligence.

Have completed plan for defence of Crete and have just returned from final tour of defences. I feel greatly encouraged by my visit. Everywhere all ranks are fit and morale is high. All defences have been extended, and positions wired as much as possible. We have forty-five field guns placed, with adequate ammunition dumped. Two Infantry tanks are at each aerodrome. Carriers and transport still being unloaded and delivered. 2nd Leicesters have arrived, and will make Heraklion stronger. I do not wish to be over-confident, but I

feel that at least we will give excellent account of ourselves.
With help of Royal Navy I trust Crete will be held.

Maleme, although officially taken over by the RAF, was a Fleet Air
Arm station with a collection of unserviceable Fulmar fighters and
Brewsters grounded by lack of spare parts. The two services co-
existed quite happily. A ship's bell serving as air-raid alarm hung
outside the dispersal tent, while the deck-chairs belonged to RAF
officers based there after the fall of Greece, when Maleme became
the base for 30 Squadron's Blenheims patrolling over the Aegean. A
slightly anti-military insouciance amongst RAF ground-crew – they
apparently took little interest in weapon training lessons – tended to
exasperate the New Zealanders of the 22nd Battalion, especially after
the surviving Blenheims and Hurricanes had left for Egypt.

In the Maleme sector, as elsewhere, troops dug their slit trenches
as deep as the ground permitted. They did not spend the night in
them in case lizards fell on their faces. Instead they rolled themselves
in blankets, and slept in groups round the trunk of the nearest tree.
By day, the men in greatest danger were the Bofors gunners round
the airfield and those who drove the ration lorry, as the cloud of dust
raised on the dry dirt-roads soon attracted a Messerschmitt or two.

Churchill had been right when he said in his telegram to the New
Zealand government that the men of its division were keen to 'come
to close quarters' with the enemy. Well-rested in the idyllic shade of
olive groves, and invigorated by the spring sunshine and by frequent
swims in the jade and cobalt-blue waters of the Aegean, they had
recovered entirely from the effects of the Greek campaign.

The key commanders in the coming battle had not recuperated so
easily. Veterans of the First World War, they were much older –
Lieutenant Colonel Leslie Andrew VC, commanding officer of the
22nd Battalion on Maleme airfield, and one of the very few regular
officers from New Zealand; Brigadier James Hargest of the 5th
Brigade, a round-faced politician with toothbrush moustache and a
tubby frame usually clad in pullover and voluminous shorts; Brigadier
Puttick, the new divisional commander, loquacious and instantly
recognizable by his red hair and thick black eyebrows; and finally
Freyberg himself. All of them were brave men, but not one of them
was bold any more. Several were apt to fuss over irrelevant details.
Their notions of warfare had been formed by hard pounding in the
trenches of Flanders. Yet the Battle of Crete, a revolutionary
development in warfare, was to be a contest in which fast reactions,

clear thinking and ruthless decisions counted most. The mentality of
linear defence and holding on which lingered in some minds from the
First World War was to prove a grave handicap. Of all the formation
commanders, only Colonel Kippenberger of the 10th New Zealand
Brigade and Brigadier Inglis of the 4th New Zealand Brigade, both
lawyers, demonstrated a grasp of the essentials.

During the evacuation from Greece, Lieutenant Geoffrey Cox had
been surprised to find Hargest, 'a man who presented himself as a
blunt, no-nonsense farmer', reading *War and Peace*. Yet Hargest's
interest in the book was not out of character. 'I've been reading
about this fellow Koutouzow,' he said. 'He's the kind of general to
study. He knew that in war steadiness and endurance are more
important than any amount of strategic flair.'

Soon after nightfall on 19 May – the eve of battle – when flames
from a burning tanker in Suda Bay lit an area far beyond the Malaxa
escarpment, Hargest confided in Cox again. 'I don't know what lies
ahead,' he said. 'I know only that it produces in me a sensation I
never knew in the last war. It isn't fear. It's something quite different,
something which I can only describe as dread.

9
'A Fine Opportunity for Killing'
20 May

At one o'clock in the morning of 20 May, Colonel von Trettner, the chief staff officer for operations, ran up to General Student's bedroom in the Hotel Grande Bretagne to wake him. Trettner, clearly concerned, told him that strong British naval forces had been sighted south of Crete.* Might this not mean that the British knew of their plans, and were bringing up warships as anti-aircraft gun platforms to engage the slow-moving Junkers 52 troop-carriers? A decision had to be taken quickly. The first aircraft were due to take off in three hours. Student, at first bemused, thought for a moment, then replied: 'That is not a good enough reason to change our plans, or to wake me up. Good-night.'

The thirteen parachute battalions camped near their different airfields in Attica, had by then been ferried with their equipment in columns of lorries to the waiting aeroplanes. In just under four weeks, the German military authorities had cleared, extended and, in some cases, constructed completely new runways with the ruthless use of forced labour.

The night was hot and heavy, and the paratroopers sweated in their jumpsuits of grey camouflage, the same weight of clothing as used in the jump over Narvik the year before. Confusion was inevitable with so many men milling around in the dark. A number of weapon canisters were dropped and split open, orders were hard to hear against the roar of engines being tested — the fuel had only

* Admiral Cunningham had deployed a total of two battleships, five cruisers and sixteen destroyers to attack any troop convoys and block off the Italian fleet.

just arrived – and dustclouds partially obscured the green-filtered torches used to marshal platoons and companies to assembly points for emplaning. Chaos was overcome mainly by the efforts and curses of sergeant majors.

When already lined up to board, officers in the Storm Regiment's glider group received a disquietening report. 'Contrary to previous assumption of enemy strength on the island, one will have to reckon not with about 12,000 but with about 48,000.'

The first aircraft taxied into position, then waited. When eventually these Junkers tri-motors lumbered forward, they bounced heavily along the runway of beaten earth, engines straining at full throttle to lift full loads of up to a dozen paratroopers and their canisters.

The dust thrown up by their propellers obscured the view of pilots in the next wave; they had to wait until the cloud abated. Even then a film of terracotta powder remained on the cockpit windscreens. This unforeseen complication – a surprising oversight – had disrupted the rhythm of take-off.

After each troop-carrier lifted from the ground with a last lurch, the streak of dawn on the eastern horizon became more visible to its pilot and passengers. In those aircraft which flew over Athens, young heads craned at windows to catch a glimpse of the pale Acropolis raised to the light above a hazy, grey city.

Inside the corrugated fuselage of the Junkers, the paratroopers in their life-jackets, high-collared doublets which appeared to be made of canvas sausages sewn together, welcomed the drop in temperature. Then, striving against the noise of the engines, a voice, almost instantly followed by others, broke into the *Fallschirmjäger* marching song, *'Rot scheint die Sonne'*.

Red shines the sun, prepare yourselves!
Who knows if it'll shine for us tomorrow?
Fly on this day against the enemy!
Into the 'planes, into the 'planes!
Comrade, there is no going back!

For the seventy-odd gliders, each with ten men of the Storm Regiment, there was certainly no going back. As the first wave, they had set off soon after four o'clock in advance of the parachute troop-carriers. One company under Lieutenant Genz was to attack the anti-aircraft guns and a wireless station south of Canea; another, led by

Captain Altmann, was to tackle the battery on the neck of the Akrotiri behind Suda Bay; and three companies were to land across the Tavronitis from Maleme airfield.

Inside the claustrophobic gliders, alternatively wallowing and then jerking on the cable from their tow-plane, the curious motion produced a sensation unlikely to encourage martial ardour. Part of the Parachute Division's headquarters also set off this way, but the cable attached to the glider carrying its commander, General Süssmann, with members of his staff, snapped high over the island of Aegina. Süssmann crashed to his death, a fate inevitably compared to that of Icarus.

The main fleet of troop-carriers, wave after wave of Junkers 52s, flew low over the Aegean, its surface glimmering in the oblique light of early morning. Eventually those in the cockpit caught sight of the peaks of the White Mountains above the horizon. Their silhouette, at first softened by distance, increased in size and definition. Then the coastline could be distinguished. Word was passed back.

The roaring throb of the engines, both hypnotic and disturbing, was altered by the rush of wind when the dispatcher opened the door in the side of the fuselage. On the command to prepare, the paratroopers stood up to go through the drill they had practised so often.

While they secured the chin-straps of their helmets – rimless, close-fitting versions of the Wehrmacht coal-scuttle – they held in their teeth the white plaited cord with safety clip to be fastened to the bar above their heads. Each man adjusted his knee pads and harness and checked his Schmeisser sub-machine gun, his only means of defence until he found a weapons canister after landing.

Some closed their eyes to compose themselves as they waited for the order to prepare to jump, others cracked nervous jokes and could not resist bending or twisting round for a glimpse of mountainside through the side windows or the cockpit windscreen. All of them could feel the aircraft vibrate as it gained altitude, then bank as it swung round on the approach to the dropping zone.

The dozen paratroopers, having fixed their lines to the metal bar, formed a queue down the inside of the fuselage. The klaxon sounded, and the dispatcher yelled 'Go!' The line of closely packed men jostled forward as, in rapid succession, they grabbed the vertical handrails on either side of the door to launch themselves into a flat, spread-eagle dive — 'the crucifix' — the next man's face momentarily behind the bootsoles of the one in front until the slipstream tore him away back towards the tailplane of the aircraft.

For the New Zealand infantry company and the RAF and Fleet Air Arm personnel stranded at Maleme airfield, dawn stand-to on 20 May had been little different from previous days. The early morning was quiet in its gentle haze. Cigarettes were cupped in hands below the parapets of slit trenches.

The airborne invasion predicted for 17 May had not materialized; many therefore convinced themselves that it would not take place at all. Yet over the last couple of days, the eight o'clock routine visit of the 'shufti-plane' — the reconnaissance Dornier known as the 'flying pencil' because of its long thin fuselage — had been followed by intense waves of air attack.

Stukas and Messerschmitts had concentrated on anti-aircraft positions. The heavier guns on Hill 107 just south of the coastal road were manned by General Weston's Royal Marines, while the ten Bofors crews round the airfield were either gunners from a Royal Artillery light battery, or Australians who mobbed the dispirited RAF ground crews. 'Where's the bloody Air Force, Poms?' they yelled across the runway.

Weston had insisted on controlling all anti-aircraft fire from a centre on the north side of Suda Bay. Unlike at Heraklion, the ill-concealed Bofors crews were not allowed to play possum and wait for the most important and the easiest targets of all: the troop-carriers. As a result, the relentless air attacks had knocked them about so much that none of the survivors were in a state to engage the enemy at the crucial moment.

On Tuesday, 20 May, the raids along the coastal plain westwards from Suda Bay began soon after six o'clock, earlier than usual. Just before their arrival, the 22nd Battalion war diary recorded: 'Usual Mediterranean summer day. Cloudless sky, no wind, extreme visibility: e.g. details on mountains 20 miles to south-east easily discernible.'

The first air raid was similar to those of previous days, then there was a respite at about 7.30 a.m. and the defenders were told they could stand down. Freyberg, to protect his secret information, did not tell anyone that the Germans had postponed the operation scheduled for 17 May: few people therefore regarded the morning's events as significant.

'So accustomed', continued the war diary of the 22nd Battalion, 'were the troops to the daily "hate", that as soon as the planes disappeared out to sea the men began to move to breakfast which had been cooking during the raid.' Many of the RAF fitters at Maleme did not bother to take their rifles with them.

The New Zealanders responsible for turning them into temporary infantrymen had in any case enjoyed little success: the only point on which both parties agreed was that they should have been evacuated when the last aircraft were ordered back to Egypt a few days before.

Just before eight o'clock the sound of heavy engines was heard: 'an angry throb'. Communications were so ineffectual that warning of this enemy force, which had been picked up well in advance by the radar station on a hill a few kilometres to the rear of Maleme, had not arrived from Weston's air defence centre at Suda Bay. The ship's bell hanging outside the dispersal tent was now rung vigorously again to sound the alarm.

This second wave from Richthofen's VIII Air Corps consisted of twin-engined bombers, Dornier 17s and Junkers 88s, followed by strafing fighters. There was a mad rush for slit trenches under tamarisk and olive trees on the edge of the airfield. Once again the Bofors gun pits were the main target. Their crews were so badly shaken by these attacks that only one gun returned fire, and then inaccurately. With conspicuous bravery, a medical team drove an ambulance across the runway at the height of the attack to the aid of a badly wounded group.

The shock-waves from each exploding bomb could be felt like a muffled blow to the stomach, and heads began to ache from the relentless percussion. Much has been written of the effect of the Stuka dive-bomber, whose siren was designed to increase the fear of its victims. Yet for many on Crete, the heart-stopping scream of a Messerschmitt fighter appearing from nowhere at tree-top level was far more terrifying.

Just after the raid finished — one sergeant described the brief silence as 'eerie, acrid and ominous' — strangely shaped aircraft with long tapering wings swept low over the airfield. Those New Zealanders of the 22nd Battalion who saw them through the cloud of smoke and dust yelled 'Gliders!' virtually in unison.

As these gliders crossed their field of vision, most of them sweeping in to land on the stoney river-bed of the Tavronitis, the infantrymen in their slit trenches opened up with small arms of every sort. This produced a noise like a mass of fire-crackers set off simultaneously. Several gliders smashed on the stones of the broad, almost dry river-bed, injuring many of their occupants. One bounced off the bridge itself. In a couple of cases, the New Zealanders succeeded in hitting the pilot. One glider, whose pilot was shot, crashed nose up with the belly striking a rock. This broke the fuselage in half. The only man to survive was a war correspondent and veteran of the Western Front, Franz-Peter Weixler, who had been in the tailplane section.

Altogether about forty landed at the mouth of the Tavronitis and further up the river-bed. They contained the rest of I Battalion, the Storm Regiment, commanded by Major Koch who had led the attack on Eben Emael the year before; regimental headquarters; and part of the III Battalion.

Soon there came a louder throbbing of engines, almost too slow to be those of aircraft. These were the Junkers 52s, nicknamed 'the trams' during their inexorable bombing shuttles over Madrid five years before.

At General Freyberg's villa, the atmosphere was one of business as usual when Monty Woodhouse arrived before eight to deliver a message. The General invited him to stay to eat.

'It was not a luxurious breakfast,' Woodhouse recalled, 'but it was better than I had had for some time.' Half-way through, he 'looked up and saw the blue sky full of German aircraft . . . The General continued quietly eating his breakfast. What should I do? It seemed impolite, not to say insubordinate, to interrupt.'

When Woodhouse finally plucked up the courage to speak, Freyberg raised his head and grunted, then looked at his watch. 'They're dead on time!' he said. 'He seemed mildly surprised at German punctuality, then returned to his breakfast.'

Freyberg's sang-froid at the sighting of an enemy armada was in the best British tradition. 'His attitude', wrote Woodhouse, 'was that he had already made all the necessary dispositions on the basis of his information, and there was now nothing more for him to do except leave his subordinates to fight the battle.'

This unflappability had been admirable during the sudden panics of the Greek withdrawal, but a relaxed manner on the morning of an airborne invasion perhaps did not convey the proper sense of urgency when the battle's outcome would be decided by each side's speed of reaction to events. For some reason, word of the long-awaited assault was not passed to the forces at Heraklion, where the 14th Infantry Brigade was to remain in complete ignorance of the fighting round Canea until after two o'clock in the afternoon.

Staff officers at Creforce Headquarters were more demonstrative than their chief when they spotted some of the glider force, released at a high altitude out over the sea, circle in over the coast. A dozen swept low over the Creforce quarry with a swish of wings to land on the rocky terrain of the Akrotiri less than a mile to their north. Six came down next to the tomb of Venizelos at Profitilias and the regimental headquarters of the Northumberland Hussars. Another four landed by a dummy battery of anti-aircraft guns only a quarter of a mile from the quarry.

Although severely understrength and ill-equipped, B Squadron of the dismounted Northumberland Hussars engaged Captain Altmann's company without delay. One glider was set alight in mid-air and crashed; the three men who emerged miraculously from the flames were shot down immediately. Another glider exploded after a lucky shot hit a case of grenades inside. A ten-man crew surrendered after a quick charge led by an ordnance corps fitter. Another section was also shot down mercilessly after one of the Germans waved a white flag and others then opened fire. Altmann's body was never identified.

Some of the surviving paratroopers escaped into an olive grove behind Venizelos's tomb, and later in the morning they had to be flushed out by very cautious drives. Before crossing one dry-stone wall, the second-in-command, Major David Barnett, raised his helmet on a stick as a precaution before emerging. There was no reaction. As he raised himself to peer over the wall, a bullet struck him through the forehead and he died instantly.

The paratroopers nearest to Creforce Headquarters went to ground in the wired and sandbagged positions of the dummy anti-aircraft battery. The Northumberland Hussars lost several men attempting to attack; without hand-grenades they could not hope to dislodge the well-armed Germans. Their other squadrons were spread around the peninsula, mainly guarding other gun positions, so assistance eventually had to be sought from the Welch Regiment beyond Creforce Headquarters.

While the action against the glider troops was beginning on the top of the hill above the Creforce quarry, Freyberg's staff officers observed the panoramic view over the coastal plain with a mixture of astonishment, dread and professional fascination. The air fleet approached over the sea, and 'the heavens shook with the roar of their engines'. When they first saw the stream of black shapes coming out behind the troop-carriers, several observers thought for a moment that the aircraft were trailing smoke after being hit, but the shapes separated and sprouted canopies with a jerk, white for paratroopers, and red, green or yellow for weapon canisters, equipment or supplies. David Hunt, standing next to Group Captain Beamish, heard him murmur 'What a remarkable sight! Looks like the end of the world.'

Within a matter of minutes, the outburst of firing up and down the coastal strip transformed the tranquil Mediterranean vista into a disturbingly ill-defined battlefield. Through their binoculars, Hunt and Beamish could see puffs of smoke rising above the olive groves and the odd patch of white where a parachute had caught in a tree or snagged on a telegraph pole.

While senior officers thought of H.G.Wells and feared the chaos of warfare without lines, younger officers and soldiers were much less awed. They recovered their aplomb and set to killing paratroopers as if it were a dangerous and exhilarating fairground sport.

New Zealand officers told their men to aim at the boots of the paratroopers since their descent was deceptively rapid. This seems to have worked well to judge by the number who jerked, dangled limply, then crumpled on hitting the ground. They were covered by their own parachutes as by instant shrouds.

The design of the German parachute harness does not seem to have helped. Lines were attached centrally to a webbing yoke across the shoulder-blades, so each soldier was suspended, 'like a kitten held by the scruff of the neck'. And although their hands were left free to fire their Schmeissers – or in one case to sound a bugle call – they had little control over their descent. Yet their fate depended more than anything on where they fell: on to undefended ground, or on to the muzzles of the New Zealand infantry waiting in the Maleme and Galatas sectors.

For most parachutists, the idea of jumping from the air and then floating down to attack their enemy gave a sensation of invincibility. To find themselves so vulnerable instead was the most disorientating shock of all. That the defenders should shoot at them when helpless struck many of them as an outrageous violation of the rules of war.

At Maleme, the attacking aircraft had avoided the runway on purpose. The dispersal tent with deck-chairs outside had been slashed and riddled by the bullets of strafing fighters, and the perimeter had been bombed, leaving large clouds of dust hanging in the still air. This prevented many of the New Zealanders in trenches round the airfield from seeing the gliders sweep over to land in and around the bed of the Tavronitis.

Some members of the RAF ground-crew, still sheltering from the air attack, did not even look up when the troop-carriers thundered overhead in threes discharging their loads. Those who did raise their heads saw the 'brollies', as they called them, open at about 300 feet. Several parachutes opened so soon that they snagged on the tailplane, and in a few cases soldiers jumping from the lead aircraft of the V formation were struck by the next plane behind.

In the first few minutes of the battle, C Company of the New Zealand 22nd Battalion, its three platoons north, west and south of the runway, engaged any targets which came their way. The platoon on the western edge next to the Tavronitis river-bed had to switch their fire to the groups advancing from the gliders which had landed close to the beach. In the course of the next hour, they killed the company commander, Lieutenant von Plessen, and a dozen of his men.

Already the German plan was clear: they were trying to drop their forces beyond the Tavronitis, and then use the dead ground of the river-bed as the start line for their attacks on the airfield. Major Stentzler's II Battalion and Captain Gericke's IV Battalion dropped by parachute well beyond and out of sight of Colonel Andrews's command post of Hill 107.

Brigadier Eugen Meindl, the commander of the Storm Regiment, jumped just behind Gericke. Meindl had refused to accompany his own staff in their glider. He insisted on jumping to prove himself as fit as any young subaltern.

The New Zealanders of D Company on the west side of Hill 107 overlooking the river-bed kept up a rapid and accurate fire which caused considerable slaughter amongst Major Koch's glider troops. The company commander's suggestion that the two 4-inch coastal defence guns on Hill 107 should be used against the glider landing zone round the Tavronitis bridge was refused because this battery was 'sited for targets at sea'.

The other artillery pieces to the east of the hill — most of the forty-nine guns shipped to the island from Egypt were captured Italian 75s without sights — could not help since their view was limited to little more than the beach.

Soon Major Braun of the Storm Regiment's headquarters staff managed to infiltrate men across the river-bed either side of the bridge. The New Zealand platoon responsible for that sector had a limited field of fire, and the chaos of the RAF camp immediately behind them did not help. Brigadier Meindl grasped the situation with impressive speed. He deduced that whatever the reports from aerial reconnaissance, the bulk of the enemy's unexpected strength lay between Maleme and Canea. For some extraordinary reason they had not reinforced the line of the Tavronitis. The airfield was the key to German reinforcement and survival, and Hill 107 was the key to the airfield. So while Braun's men kept pushing at the airfield flank, he sent Stentzler's II Battalion round on a right-flanking movement to take Hill 107 from the rear.

But Meindl, within an hour of landing, was wounded twice, lightly the first time, then in the chest. And at about the same time, Major Koch was struck down with a severe head wound in the unsuccessful attempts to attack Hill 107 from the Tavronitis river-bed. The Storm Regiment had begun to lose most of its commanders: Koch's battalion alone was to lose sixteen officers killed and seven wounded. Yet the comforting theory of British officers that German troops went to pieces when things did not go according to plan was soon proved wrong.

While the Storm Regiment troops landing to the west of Hill 107 could shelter from the worst of the fire in the river-bed, Major Scherber's III Battalion, dropping two kilometres or so along on the Canea side of the airfield, faced a massacre from the moment they jumped.

Most of Scherber's men landed on the well-concealed positions of the New Zealand Division's Engineer Detachment and 23rd Battalion. One group dropped on battalion headquarters. Colonel Leckie killed five and his adjutant, seated at a packing case which served as his desk, shot two without standing up.

Exultant cries of 'Got the bastard!' could be heard on all sides. Nowhere was it heard with greater glee than amongst the former inmates of the Field Punishment Centre at Modhion, just inland from the Engineer Detachment. The soldiers under sentence there were given rifles and the promise of a pardon if they fought well, then let off the leash to hunt down paratroopers scattered in their area. Sixty prisoners killed a hundred and ten in less than an hour.

Those Germans who survived the descent through crossfire arrived doubly disorientated by the unexpected resistance. Some crashed on to roofs, others through the branches of olive trees. There they were shot before they had time to wriggle out of their harnesses. Suspended bodies twisted gently as if from the macabre gibbets of a previous century.

Even those who landed unwounded and unseen in a vineyard or field of barley could not fight back effectively until they found their weapons. And if a container had fallen in the open, retrieving it was like a murderous game of grandmother's footsteps. Scherber, his adjutant, and three out of four company commanders were killed, along with nearly four hundred men. Lieutenant Horst Trebes was the only key officer to survive unwounded.

The other main German objective in the Maleme and Suda sectors was the Ayia valley south-west of Canea, known during the battle as Prison Valley because of the low, white buildings of Ayia jail. The prison was overlooked by the heights of Galatas a kilometre to the north, which formed part of a range of round dry hills separating the cultivated valley from the sea.

Galatas was the central position of the New Zealand Division's scratch 10th Brigade, which only possessed a single truck. Colonel Kippenberger, its commander, did not even have a wireless set in his headquarters. The largest unit in this very mixed formation was the Composite Battalion comprising the remnants of two New Zealand regiments of field artillery, the Divisional Petrol Company, and a transport company, all reassigned as infantrymen: the gunners were known as the 'infantillery'.

Kippenberger also had two Greek regiments, both ill-armed and ill-led. The 6th Greek Regiment, with only three rounds of ammunition per man due to a mix-up, straddled the valley leading towards Canea, while the 8th Greek Regiment, armed with Steyers captured from the Austro-Hungarian army in the First World War, were placed in a dangerously isolated position south of Lake Ayia. When Kippenberger visited the liaison officer he had sent to advise the Greek colonel, he did not 'tell him that I had argued elsewhere that 8 Greek was only a circle on the map and that it was murder to leave such troops in such a position.' (This Greek regiment proved their pessimism wrong by its astonishing resistance.)

Also up the valley, but on the north side, was the Divisional Cavalry nearly two hundred strong acting as infantry. Kippenberger's battalion in Greece, the 20th, comprised part of yet another reserve against a seaborne invasion, 'where', he later lamented, 'they did nothing all the vital first day'.

Kippenberger, although one of the ablest New Zealand officers, made a crucial mistake. He put no defending force in the prison itself: 'a solid rectangle of buildings impervious to our little guns. Its Governor was suspected of being pro-German, and so he proved. I have no recollection that we ever considered garrisoning it.'

After the bombing and strafing attacks of the early morning, Kippenberger shaved, then began to eat a very unsatisfactory plate of porridge under the trees outside the little house which acted as his headquarters in Galatas. Suddenly, he heard oaths and exclamations, and lifted his head to see four gliders: 'in their silence inexpressibly menacing'. He shouted 'Stand to your arms!' and dashed back upstairs for his own rifle.

These gliders, bearing the now leaderless headquarters of General Süssmann, landed between the prison and Lake Ayia. They were followed almost immediately by the waves of troop-carriers dropping the three battalions of the 3rd Parachute Regiment and the Engineer Battalion.

Rather like Brigadier Meindl, the division's chief of staff, Major Count von Uxküll refused to come by glider and insisted on parachuting instead. With great style, he fixed his monocle firmly in place before launching himself from the aeroplane, and later claimed that it stayed in place, even on landing.

But for many in the 3rd Parachute Regiment, the drop was far from jolly. A large part of its III Battalion came down on the well-camouflaged positions of the 18th and 19th New Zealand Battalions and suffered a similar fate to Scherber's men east of Maleme. The trenches of the 19th Battalion were so well-concealed that Corporal Fletcher and his section watched in mounting excitement as one of the first paratroopers to land leopard-crawled towards them across a small field, thinking he was concealed by the furrows. They held their fire until he popped his head up three yards away. The first shot only wounded him. 'He yelled and squealed like a pig with its throat cut and pleaded for mercy – we gave him mercy all right – one clean through the nut.' Most accounts of this action, like those of the fighting elsewhere, boast about tallies and compare the slaughter to duck-shooting and potting rabbits. Kippenberger records: '19 Battalion told us that they had killed 155 parachutists and, rather apologetically, that they had taken nine prisoners.'

The 6th Greek Regiment, whose position ran from Galatas across the valley, found the enemy dropping all round. But since their colonel had not issued the ammunition received the day before, the ill-trained soldiers not surprisingly scattered.

Kippenberger's brigade major, Captain Bassett, tried to rally as many as he could. The next morning, two hundred of those who remained were handed over to 'a blond hero' — Captain Michael Forrester of the Queen's and the British Military Mission. The New Zealand official history and most other works incorrectly describe Forrester as taking over that morning and leading a charge. In fact he had returned from Heraklion the evening before to Prince Peter's house overlooking the bay north of Daratsos. Here he found only Marcos, the cook.

During his pre-breakfast shave, he had seen the paratroopers begin to drop, and grabbing a rifle, first took part in the battle against a group of paratroopers who attacked the 7th General Field Hospital just across the bay, then joined the coastal flank of the Composite Battalion manned mainly by drivers.

Only a light troop of Royal Artillery remained in the valley below Daratsos, utterly exposed. A group of Captain von der Heydte's men raided them from the flank and, having no personal weapons, they were beaten back losing several men and one of their field guns, which the paratroopers gleefully turned on a nearby farmhouse held by British soldiers.

Nearly five kilometres up the valley, Major Liebach's Engineer Battalion dropped to the west of Lake Ayia, some of its detachments falling on the 8th Greek Regiment, most of whose men held their ground with a bravery and effectiveness that Kippenberger had never expected. The rest of Heydte's I Battalion and Major Derpa's II Battalion landed virtually unopposed between Lake Ayia and the prison which they promptly occupied. Unable to believe their good fortune, they had a secure base, a medical station and a source of water.

From 'Pink Hill', just in front of Galatas, it looked as if 'the whole valley was covered with discarded parachutes, like huge mushrooms'. Kippenberger and the men of the Divisional Petrol Company could see paratroopers running about collecting themselves and their weapons from the containers. They were out of effective range. Only scattered paratroopers had landed near enough to engage. In the first moments of the battle, Kippenberger had stalked a sniper on the edge of the village and shot him at point-blank range.

Less than two kilometres to the north-east of Galatas, was leaguered part of a squadron of the 3rd Hussars. These recently arrived cavalrymen were not yet fully accustomed to the morning air raids known as 'the daily hate'.

Every spare moment had been spent on badly needed maintenance and repairs to their light Whippet tanks. The vehicles – described by one of their officers as 'armoured perambulators' – were already in a deplorable state when shipped from Alexandria: they represented a hasty selection from those sent back from the desert to be refitted in base workshops round Cairo. To make matters worse, the ship carrying them had been bombed on arrival in Suda Bay, and the tanks had to be winched from the hold of the half-sunken vessel.

Squadron headquarters and two troops (each of three or four tanks) had concealed themselves in an olive grove. The officers and NCOs were sitting round a table under a tree having breakfast when the second wave of bombers and fighters attacked the coastal strip. The Messerschmitts came low overhead strafing at random, the bullets ripping through the canopy of leaves. Everyone scrambled for cover behind tree-trunks.

A few minutes later, with bodies packed uncomfortably on top of one another, somebody shouted 'The bastards are landing!' They looked up through the branches and saw the parachutes. The squadron leader screamed, 'Tank crews!' Another mad scramble followed, and the crews became mixed up in their haste.

Lieutenant Roy Farran led his troop charging up the road to Galatas. They passed a group of Greek soldiers who begged for ammunition. Farran threw them a belt from his Vickers, but later realized that it was the wrong calibre for their rifles. The cavalrymen experienced a surge of exhilaration as New Zealanders yelled encouragement and gave them the thumbs-up sign.

Beyond Galatas, the lead tank came under fire from a Schmeisser. Traversing the turret, Farran spotted a grey figure charging towards them up the road. He yelled the order to fire and the gunner let off a burst, but their target proved to be a peasant woman in a long dress. One bullet hit her in the shoulder, another in the head, but she ran on past the tank screaming. Farran was frozen in horror until the German parachutists began firing again.

Back through the village the tank halted when a Cretan hidden in a ditch waved to them with a handkerchief. He put his fingers to his lips and pointed to the opposite ditch. Straining out of the top of the turret, Farran saw a German parachutist in full gear lying face-down. He called on him to surrender, but the man did not move, so he fired his heavy service revolver at him. The shot missed, but the German could not stop himself from tensing visibly. Farran traversed the turret and turned the Vickers on him.

A few yards further down the road they shot two more Germans, then five suddenly appeared out of the trees from another direction, their hands up. Fearing a trick, Farran gave the order to fire and three were cut down. The other two, although hit, managed to escape back into the trees. 'I do not think that I would make a practice of shooting prisoners', he wrote in his memoirs, 'but Crete was different, and in the heat of the moment I had not time to think.'

Crete was indeed different. In the speed, uncertainty and fear of battle, neither side showed much regard for the Geneva Convention. There were numerous incidents when soldiers and officers on both sides killed prisoners. Yet when paratroopers from the 3rd Parachute Regiment's III Battalion attacked the field hospital on the coastal promontory two kilometres north of Daratsos and allegedly forced patients taken prisoner to walk in front of them as a screen, Farran was surprised at 'German callousness towards the Red Cross at this period of the war, for generally speaking they were most meticulous in their observance of the rules.'

Crete's greatest difference, to the horror of the Germans, was the part played by 'unrecruited civilians'. The Cretan resistance, unlike those underground movements in the rest of Europe which did not start to develop until a year or so after the German occupation, began literally in the first hour of the invasion.

Boys, old men and also women displayed a breath-taking bravery in defence of their island. German soldiers were doubly scandalized at the idea of women fighting them. They would rip the dress from the shoulder of a suspect. If she had a bruise from the recoil of a rifle, or was caught knife in hand, she would be shot along with the men.

Scattered paratroopers landing near Perivolia were, in the words of the New Zealand official history, 'despatched by civilians with axes and spades'. One of the first examples of spontaneous mobilization was an attack on the rear of the Parachute Engineer Battalion which had landed round Lake Ayia by Cretan irregulars advancing from the large village of Alikianou.

Within a short space of time, according to a German report, the 16th Company of the Storm Regiment 'which had been ordered to protect the south of the aerodrome of Malemes [*sic*] continually had to fight against *francs-tireurs*'.

Although the Cretans had their own proud traditions of resistance to the Turk, their ferocity and reckless bravery in 1941 were more reminiscent of the Second of May Rising against Napoleon's forces in Madrid, of a *guerra al cuchillo*: war to the knife.

Some priests led their parishioners into battle. Father Stylianos Frantzeskakis, hearing of the airborne invasion, rushed to the church to sound the bell. Taking a rifle, he marched his volunteers north from Paleokhora and later fought German motor-cycle detachments when they reached Kandanos.

An intelligence officer from the 14th Infantry Brigade's headquarters remembered several priests, keen duck-shooters and therefore 'pretty good shots', who almost certainly took part in the fighting. At the time of the battle, one went around with a rifle down his trousers waiting for the chance of a pot-shot at German paratroopers. And at Rethymno, Ray Sandover, one of the Australian battalion commanders, saw a monk on the second day of the battle armed with a rifle and an axe in his belt. On the third day the monk appeared accompanied by a little boy acting as gun-bearer with a Schmeisser sub-machine gun and other trophies he had won in the battle against the paratroopers.

Also on that first morning, one of the companies of II Battalion of the Storm Regiment, which landed several kilometres south-west of Maleme, was surprised by Cretan irregulars when sent on to secure the pass near Koukouli. But the most contentious episode of the whole battle concerned Lieutenant Mürbe's detachment. This group, seventy-two strong, which dropped on the edge of Kastelli Kissamou to capture the port, was ferociously engaged by the 1st Greek Regiment and Cretan irregulars. Mürbe and fifty-three of his men were killed, the rest became prisoners. A number of German corpses were hacked about by civilians, but there is little evidence to support the claims made afterwards by Goering and Goebbels that many wounded paratroopers were tortured and mutilated while still alive.

The Germans, partly lulled by the intelligence prediction that the Cretans would welcome them, were completely taken by surprise. And the scale of their losses enraged them. On the first day alone 1,856 paratroopers had been killed. That figure must have swelled to over 2,000 as the mortally wounded died. To assess how many the Cretans had killed is impossible, but the shock to the Germans was unmistakable. They had come to expect their chosen enemy to cave in at the approach of what they liked to call *der Furor Teutonicus* in imitation of the Spanish infantry's *furia española* in the fifteenth century. Civilian resistance, while an ancient tradition in Crete, so deeply offended the Prussian sense of military order that brutal reprisals were taken against the local population.

10
Maleme and Prison Valley
20 May

General Freyberg had done his best to get inessential people off the island before the battle started. Colonel James Roosevelt, son of the US President, had been persuaded to leave by Sunderland flying-boat only thirty-six hours before the invasion. But the King of Greece was still on Crete.

The royal party had left the Belakapina and moved to another villa near Perivolia on 19 May. Prince Peter joined them there that evening from his house on the coast north of Galatas, only a few kilometres away. Next morning, Colonel Jasper Blunt, who knew the enemy plan having served as Freyberg's chief intelligence officer after his arrival from Greece, began telephoning Creforce Headquarters for news from seven o'clock, when the first air raids began along the coast. Anxiously watching the sky through binoculars, he spotted the first wave of Junkers transport planes and the first sticks of paratroopers. Blunt cranked the field telephone in an urgent attempt to ring Creforce Headquarters again, but without success. A bomb had already severed the landline.

One group of paratroopers landed less than a kilometre away. Blunt ordered the escort platoon of New Zealanders to grab their weapons, and leave their bedrolls and blankets. There was not even time to pack up the wireless set. He chivvied his charges, who included the King, Prince Peter, Colonel Levidis, the court chamberlain, a long-standing friend with whom the King quarrelled as if they were 'an old married couple', and the Prime Minister, Mr Tsouderos.

They had to hurry up the hill behind the house, leaving most of their belongings. The platoon, commanded by Lieutenant Ryan, then deployed around the party, sections forming advance, rear and flank guards.* Another parachute drop made them veer to the left, and scrambling up the hill behind Perivolia, they came under fire from an outlying detachment of the 2nd Greek Regiment. The King and Prince Peter went forward to prove their identity to the wary soldiers.

Later, when the party stopped to rest, the King was clearly preoccupied. He had left behind some important papers and medals, including the Order of the Garter. (This oversight was curiously reminiscent of an incident in 1620. Fleeing from imperial troops after the Battle of the White Mountain, Frederick, King of Bohemia and the husband of the Winter Queen, left behind on their bed the Garter, which his father-in-law James I had given him.) A section of New Zealanders under the platoon sergeant was sent back for King George's decorations, but they found that German paratroopers had already occupied the house.

Blunt was concerned. With such a vulnerable and unwieldy group, the escort was only adequate against a handful of paratroopers, yet their number was large enough to attract the attention of German aircraft. And their rapid departure without the wireless set meant that he had no way of contacting Creforce Headquarters to find out about evacuation plans from the south coast. He needed information on parachute drops, but Creforce's ignorance of events was almost as great as that of the party wandering on the mountainside.

At Maleme, the 22nd Battalion's command post could no longer speak by field telephone to brigade headquarters, and Colonel Andrew knew nothing of what was happening to his two forward companies, C and D, on the airfield and on the Tavronitis side of Hill 107. They could not be seen either from his command post or from neighbouring company positions, and they lacked a wireless set. Thus no reports were available on the enemy's progress against the airfield, one of his main objectives.

Colonel Andrew's area of responsibility round the airfield and Hill 107, the main objectives of the enemy attack, consisted of about five

---

* Prince Peter's story of paratroopers landing with special maps showing the Bella Kapina, which the party had left the day before, marked with an arrow and 'Koenig hier!' is a little fanciful considering the scarcity of German intelligence. Fifth-column fever gripped a number of British and Greek officers in Greece and Crete, but much less so than in France where rumours had circulated of paratroopers dressed as nuns.

square kilometres of very uneven terrain with dead ground. Visibility was further impaired by the bamboo thickets, vineyards and olive trees. To make matters worse, he still had no idea of the size of the parachute forces which had landed beyond the Tavronitis. Nothing had been heard from his observation posts which, since they also lacked wireless sets, were unable to send a warning. Enemy air attack was too heavy and too constant for a runner to stand a good chance of getting through.

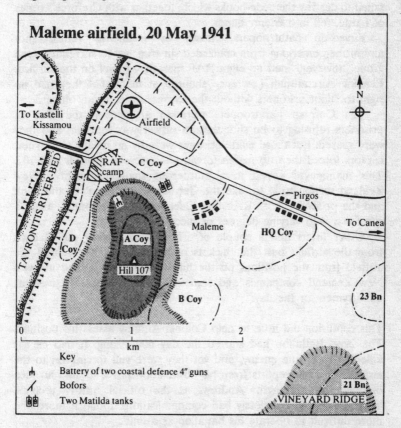

Maleme airfield, 20 May 1941

Key

⛏ Battery of two coastal defence 4″ guns

╱ Bofors

🔫🔫 Two Matilda tanks

The platoon on the airfield nearest to the sea managed to repel attacks along the beach from the mouth of the Tavronitis. But 15 Platoon defending the western end of the airfield was hard-pressed. Only twenty-two strong, lacking machine guns, and responsible for a front over a kilometre wide, they held on with great tenacity.

At ten o'clock, when Braun's paratroopers began probing on to the edge of the airfield, Captain Johnson, the company commander, called for help from the two Matilda tanks of the 7th Royal Tank Regiment. A pair had been hidden next to each airfield. But Colonel Andrew refused: he did not want to play his 'trump card' too early.

Soon, the German paratroopers probing round the Tavronitis bridge broke through between the two New Zealand companies and overran the camp. An RAF officer, in an unforgivable oversight, failed to destroy the code-books which, together with Creforce's order of battle, fell into enemy hands.

Keyed-up paratroopers, mostly by instinctive reflex, shot aircraftmen emerging from concealed slit trenches to surrender. One group, however, lined up eight RAF men they found on the surface. Leading Aircraftman Lawrence shouted at them that they had no right to shoot prisoners without the express order of an officer.

The German paratroopers were so amazed at the idea of prisoners refusing to be shot that an officer was sent for, and they were spared. But those made prisoner were by no means safe. Their captors forced them to march forward as a screen towards Hill 107. This manoeuvre ended in a murderous shambles when a New Zealand section tried to take the German paratroopers in the flank and the prisoners, both RAF and Fleet Air Arm personnel, made a run for it with varying degrees of success.

Other fitters and a couple of officers had already pulled back from the airfield past the thickets of bamboo which obscured the airfield from the positions on the hill behind. They joined up with New Zealand companies and some of them fought effectively as infantrymen for the day.

This confusion did little to help Colonel Andrew assess his position. The 22nd Battalion had started the day 600 strong. It had clearly killed many of the enemy, and yet they were still forcing on to the airfield. Without reports from his observation posts, he had no idea of their true strength. Andrew, as the official history records, 'handicapped by hopelessly bad communications, found it more and more difficult to operate his battalion as a unit'.

The battalion's plight would have been even worse if Major Stentzler and his two companies, trying to attack Hill 107 from the rear, had not clashed with a fortuitously placed platoon. This forced his exhausted and dehydrated men to take an even longer detour through the heat of the day. Their grey parachute overalls had been designed for Northern Europe, and each man's load of weapons, ammunition and emergency pack weighed heavily under the hot sun. Many had drunk most of the water they carried, having sweated almost continuously since the night before.

Colonel Andrew, ignorant of Stentzler's manoeuvre, was far more preoccupied with the fate of his two forward companies. He began to suspect that they had been overrun, and his requests for support became more urgent. At 10.55, he warned brigade headquarters – his wireless set was working intermittently – that contact had been lost with C and D Companies.

Around midday, the Germans brought into action their mortars and a light field-piece parachuted with them. The British artillery batteries could not be used because the field telephone lines from their forward observation officers on Hill 107 had been cut. These gunner officers instead took command of the Fleet Air Arm and RAF personnel.

Colonel Andrew, once again out of contact by wireless, began sending up white and green flares, the emergency signal to the 23rd Battalion, which had been specially designated as the counter-attack force. But the observers positioned to watch for the flares never saw them. Semaphore was also tried. A message, however, got through to Hargest's headquarters – inexplicably sited six and a half kilometres along the coast at the furthest point from Maleme within the brigade area – at 3.50 p.m. There was no reaction.

Andrew became increasingly concerned. He had been slightly wounded, although not enough to affect him. With mortar shells falling round his command post, and without news of the forward companies, he began to assume the worst.

At five o'clock, still with no sign of support from Colonel Leckie's 23rd Battalion, he managed to contact Hargest's command post by wireless. But Hargest's reply to his urgent request for support claimed that the 23rd Battalion was engaged with enemy paratroops, an assertion that was unverified and untrue.

Hargest's state of mind is hard to fathom. Either he was hopelessly confused and misinformed or, reflecting Freyberg's priorities, he still regarded attacks on Maleme as secondary in importance to the threat from the sea.

Faced with Hargest's refusal, Colonel Andrew decided that he had to play his trump card. The two Matilda tanks of the 7th Royal Tank Regiment, backed by his reserve platoon which had been made up to strength with some gunner volunteers, were ordered into action. As the ungainly Matildas manoeuvred from their hide on to the coast road, their steel tracks squealed and screeched, a noise inspiring dread in the German paratroopers. But this psychological advantage did not last long.

With extraordinary rashness, the two tanks ignored the enemy on the airfield and in the RAF camp. Instead, they headed straight for the Tavronitis river-bed. On the way, the crew of the rear tank found that they had the wrong ammunition and that their turret could not traverse properly – a rather tardy discovery – so they turned back, leaving the other Matilda to go on alone.

The lead tank rumbled on towards the bridge, then bumped and lurched down on to the river-bed. This Matilda turned to attack the German paratroopers in the flank, but almost immediately its armoured belly stuck on a boulder: the tank now resembled a stranded turtle. The crew then found that they too could not traverse their turret, and abandoned the vehicle. Their exposed infantry escort was beaten back with several losses.

At about six o'clock, Andrew contacted Hargest by wireless to tell him of the failure, and that without support from the 23rd Battalion, he would have to withdraw. Hargest replied: 'If you must, you must.' But he also said he was sending two companies to his aid. Andrew assumed that they would arrive 'almost immediately'. But as darkness fell, with no sign of help, with ammunition running low and still no message from his forward companies, he began to consider a full withdrawal.

It is easy to sympathize with Colonel Andrew's state of mind, but harder to understand why he did not leave his command post, blind on the rear slope of the hill, and attempt to study the scene through binoculars. The forward slope, raked by machine-gun fire, bombed and virtually stripped of vegetation, was certainly a dangerous place, but Andrew's bravery is not in doubt. Like his superior officers in the chain of command upwards – Hargest, Puttick and Freyberg – his imagination and instincts seem to have become shackled to his command post. This did not mean that Andrew was behaving like an ostrich – he did not try to belittle the threat – but his thought processes had jammed.

If Colonel Andrew had gone forward before nightfall to observe the coastal strip and the western slopes of Hill 107, he would have seen that Captain Johnson and his men in C Company were still resisting strongly on the airfield, as was Campbell's D Company above the Tavronitis. They had suffered considerable casualties, but

having inflicted far greater losses on the enemy, their thoughts were
not on withdrawal.

In the area of Prison Valley, the situation was much clearer, partly
because Kippenberger, the brigade commander in Galatas, observed
the battle in person.

Confusion had existed only around the edges. Genz's glider group,
which landed south of Canea to attack the wireless station and anti-
aircraft batteries, was soon tied down; the catastrophic drop of much
of the 3rd Parachute Regiment's III Battalion on top of strong New
Zealand positions had created another fine opportunity for killing;
and the paratroopers who attacked the 7th General Hospital on the
coast had all been killed or taken prisoner. But in Prison Valley itself,
the rest of the regiment was well established and had begun to make
strong probing attacks along the Galatas and Daratsos heights.

General Weston's rapid decision to bring an Australian battalion
from the reserve at Georgioupolis to strengthen the line where Prison
Valley opened into a small plain behind Canea was entirely correct.
He put them between the mixed force from the transit camp north
of Perivolia (they were dubbed the Royal Perivolians for supposedly
saving the King) and the 2nd Greek Regiment on the foothills of the
White Mountains.

The 8th Greek Regiment, that exposed 'circle on the map' as
Kippenberger called it, held their ground against the German
Engineer Battalion extraordinarily well despite their poor armament,
and they soon seized the weapons of paratroopers they had killed.
Local irregulars, mostly villagers with old sporting guns, fought fiercely
to repel an attack on Alikianou. 'Civilians', recorded a German
report, 'including women and boys of a total number of 100
approximately participated in the defence.'

On the north side of the valley, the New Zealanders of the Petrol
Company on 'Pink Hill' in front of the village of Galatas were forced
back by an impetuous attack soon after ten o'clock. But this assault,
led by Lieutenant Neuhoff, ended in the virtual destruction of his
company.

Pink Hill was so named after the colour of the earth, on which
grew couch grass, weeds and lines of yucca like huge caltrops to keep
goats out of the vineyards. The trenches there had been dug by the
Black Watch six months before, during that energetic period under
Brigadier Tidbury. But although Pink Hill formed a strong centre to

the 10th Brigade's defence, all the Petrol Company's officers had already become casualties. Kippenberger realized that the drivers and fitters of this composite battalion could not be expected to do more than hold off the enemy; they did not have the training to mount a counter-attack.

Two hours later, Colonel Heidrich, the commander of the 3rd Parachute Regiment, who had set up his headquarters in the prison, directed a scratch force from three companies and Major Derpa's battalion headquarters against the left flank of the Petrol Company and Cemetery Hill, which stuck out between Galatas and Daratsos. They too were repulsed, although with greater difficulty.

There was a lull around lunch-time, almost as if the Anglo-Saxon and German soldiery had become infected by a Mediterranean rhythm. One of Kippenberger's concerns at that time was the fate of the Divisional Cavalry detachment he had positioned up the valley beyond Lake Ayia. But after he had sent out a patrol to bring them in from their isolation, they appeared on their own late in the afternoon, having followed a long, circuitous trek over the coastal hills. They had been able to do little good where they were. Kippenberger immediately put them into the line to replace the Greeks between the Petrol Company at Galatas and the 19th Battalion at Daratsos.

In the valley during that afternoon, platoons from Heydte's battalion attacked up the right-hand side against the 2nd Greek Regiment. They took a hill with an old Turkish fort on top, but soon attracted artillery fire of unpredictable accuracy. The Italian 75s manned round Perivolia had no sights, save an improvisation of wood and chewing gum which might have surprised even Heath-Robinson. They also had no mechanical means of elevation. According to one gunner: 'We just found a bigger stone to shove underneath, if we wanted to increase the range.'

More of Heydte's men probed ahead towards Canea, but they faced the newly arrived Australian battalion as well as the Royal Perivolians from the transit camp. Most of these gunners and rear echelon soldiers, such as fitters and drivers, had never received any infantry training. Some hardly knew how to handle a rifle. But a number of them demonstrated a remarkable instinct for this stalking warfare in the deceptive shadows of the olive groves.

After the lull in the early afternoon, Richthofen's fighters suddenly reappeared, strafing indiscriminately. The German air force's vast expenditure of ammunition and bombs caused much more noise than casualties. Theodore Stephanides, with both medical and human curiosity, observed the phenomenon of a man panicked by an air attack literally running in circles, or ellipses to be exact. That evening many men were too tired to eat. They just fell asleep once the enemy aircraft departed.

On the German side too, the paratroopers, having dug shallow trenches, bedded down rolled in a parachute. Those cut off behind British lines took advantage of the dark to slip through, ready to whisper *'Reichsmarschall'*, the password chosen by General Student in honour of Goering.

Lieutenant Genz, whose glider group from the Storm Regiment had kept the anti-aircraft guns south of Canea out of action for most of the day, led his survivors after nightfall through British units north of Perivolia. They marched openly in a body, but without helmets so as not to be recognized by their silhouettes. Next morning, after a wide sweep, they made contact with elements of Heydte's battalion in Prison Valley.

As night fell on 20 May, the few German commanders who survived in the Maleme–Galatas sector felt they had lost. They had taken neither the airfield of Maleme nor the port of Canea; they had not even taken the small port of Kastelli Kissamou. Their losses had been so disastrous that they believed the strong counter-attack, expected at any moment, would scatter them completely. General Student in Athens was alone in wanting to continue. Richthofen the commander of the VIII Air Corps, Löhr the commander of the IV Air Fleet, and List the commander of the XII Army were convinced that the airborne invasion had been a débâcle and that the operation would have to be aborted.

Freyberg's failure to launch a vigorous counter-attack that night is one of the most vexed questions of the battle. One reason is that he was misinformed by Brigadier Hargest, whose persistent refusal to take Colonel Andrew's warnings seriously still cannot be explained satisfactorily. Yet Freyberg seems to have shown little interest in Maleme, some say because he had become convinced that the Germans intended to crash-land their transports and that therefore possession of an airfield was irrelevant. That even the Germans could afford to be so profligate – their whole transport fleet would have been destroyed in two days – was indeed a curious idea.

Only one counter-attack was attempted. This took place at dusk on Puttick's orders following an inaccurate report that paratroopers

were trying to construct a landing strip in Prison Valley. Amid much
confusion, two companies and three light tanks — a pathetically
inadequate force — were sent against Heidrich's parachute battalions
numbering nearly 1,300 men. Attempts to cancel the operation failed
at the last moment, and patrols roamed throughout the night trying
to find the company commanders to tell them. Platoons lost contact
with each other in the dark, and the outcome was a number of
random and chaotic clashes, fortunately with the enemy rather than
each other.

11
Close Quarters at Rethymno and Heraklion
20 May

At Heraklion on that first morning, the 'daily hate' did not turn out to be the prelude for parachute drops as at Canea. Companies were stood down for breakfast, and the skies remained clear of aircraft. As the morning progressed uneventfully, the 14th Infantry Brigade relaxed. General Freyberg had not dared pass on to his brigade commanders the information gleaned from Ultra that the Germans had finally fixed the operation for 20 May. In any case, it was assumed that an airborne invasion would come soon after first light, and no word had arrived from Creforce Headquarters of glider landings or parachute drops at their end of the island.

Members of Chappel's headquarters staff not on duty received permission to leave the quarry. One of the intelligence officers, Gordon Hope-Morley, a keen botanist, set off in search of wild flowers: he took his camera, which later came in useful, but not his rifle or steel helmet which would have been more appropriate. Officers in the three British infantry battalions also set off, some to pay purely social calls on friends in other companies, others on the more serious purpose of reconnoitring the surrounding countryside. The Leicesters, who had arrived at the last moment, badly needed to 'walk the course'. Their commanding officer, on the other hand, decided that this was the ideal opportunity to slip into Heraklion for a bath in the principal hotel.

On the mainland, the commanders of the 1st and 2nd Parachute Regiments became increasingly impatient as they waited beside their airfields. Colonel Bruno Bräuer, charged with the assault on Heraklion, did not hide his displeasure at the delay. Bräuer, shorter than most paratroopers, was known for his slight stammer, his cigarette-holder and his bravery. During the capture of Dordrecht in Holland, he had ignored advice to shelter from enemy fire with the curious dictum: 'Paratroopers never come under fire!'

Colonel Alfred Sturm, an older man inclined to stand on his dignity, resented the low priority accorded to his attack on the town of Rethymno and its landing strip. His 2nd Parachute Regiment had captured the Corinth isthmus, yet now he had to hand over a battalion to Bräuer.

The delays during the early morning departures for Maleme and the Ayia valley accumulated during the course of the day. And when the Junkers returned from their mission, the bullet holes in fuselage, wings and tailplane were not only chastening to behold, they also required time to repair.

Since there were no petrol bowsers, the tri-motors had to be refuelled by hand. To speed up the operation, paratroopers were told to lend the ground crews a hand. This order provoked angry disbelief, but the soldiers stripped off to their gym shorts and sweated away at the work with the temperature at forty degrees centigrade in the shade. The sun had become so hot and evaporation so rapid that attempts to water the runway and dispersal areas to keep down the red dust proved futile. For the paratroopers still in their full jumping gear, the discomfort was considerable. And the planes, when the time eventually came for boarding, were like ovens.

Most of the paratroopers had not even emplaned at two o'clock, the time they were supposed to be over the Heraklion and Rethymno dropping zones. And when the first wave took off, the dust clouds caused even more hold-ups than the night before. In a couple of cases aircraft collided on the runway. The times between take-offs became crucial at the other end, since every extra minute gave the defenders more time to deal with one drop before the next wave was upon them. Once airborne, few paratroopers in Group East felt like singing 'Rot scheint die Sonne'. Bräuer was on the last wave of fifteen aircraft to leave. He was furious. Because of a shortage of aircraft, 600 men had had to be left behind: Group East now had only 2,300 men.

Colonel Sturm, although he resented losing one of his battalions to Bräuer, faced less fearsome odds at Rethymno. He decided to keep a reinforced company under his personal command, and divided the rest of his force into two battle groups, one led by Major Kroh and the other by Captain Wiedemann. Both were based on battalions which had captured the Corinth isthmus the month before. Kroh's battle group was to land to the east of the airfield then take it. Wiedemann's slightly stronger force was to land between the airfield and Rethymno to capture the town and port dominated by a strong Venetian fortress.

The defence of the Rethymno area was the responsibility of a young, recently promoted Australian regular – Lieutenant Colonel Ian Campbell. He left the defence of the town itself to 800 members of the Cretan gendarmerie, a well-disciplined and very effective force. The defence was directed by Major Christos Tsiphakis, a Cretan officer who was to play a major part in organizing the resistance during the occupation. To hold the airstrip, which lay eight kilometres east of the town between the coast road and a line of hills, Campbell had two Australian battalions and two machine-gun platoons – some 1,300 men – together with 2,300 Greek soldiers, as ill-armed and inexperienced as their counterparts elsewhere.

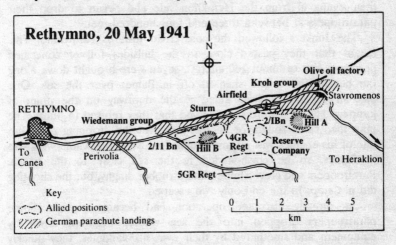

Rethymno, 20 May 1941

N

Olive oil factory

Kroh group

Airfield

Stavromenos

RETHYMNO

Sturm

Wiedemann group

2/1Bn   Hill A

2/11 Bn   Hill B   4GR Regt   Reserve Company

To Canea

Perivolia

5GR Regt

To Heraklion

Key

⌒⌒⌒ Allied positions

▨▨▨ German parachute landings

0 1 2 3 4 5
km

Campbell's own battalion, the 2/1st, and half a dozen field guns, well-hidden in the terraced vineyards on the hillsides, could cover the landing strip while remaining concealed. Aerial reconnaissance spotted only one of their positions, and that was changed. The other battalion, 2/11th, commanded by Major Ray Sandover, was sited on another coastal hill three kilometres closer to the town. A Greek regiment filled the gap. The rest of the Greeks and two Matilda tanks were hidden in olive groves on the rear slope of the ridge.

To give their soldiers a break in the days of waiting before the invasion, Campbell and Sandover sent them off to swim in parties of less than twenty at a time in case of air reconnaissance. On their return, with the forward platoons stood to, they had to try to creep back without being seen. This enabled the defenders to identify in advance pockets of dead ground and likely routes of attack. The ridge's many gullies, which following their desert experience the Australians called wadis, were numerous and dangerous.

With few other diversions to occupy the time, Campbell and Sandover had to get a grip of their heavy-drinking and pugnacious men. The town of Rethymno, where several fights had broken out in cafés, was put out of bounds and provost patrols were instituted.

On 20 May, the air attack began at four o'clock in the afternoon. With no more than twenty fighters and light bombers, it was a desultory affair. A few of the Greek recruits panicked, but a handful of Australian NCOs sent across by Campbell soon brought them back into line. At 4.15 p.m. the troop carriers appeared over the sea. They then swung in from the Heraklion side and began to drop their paratroopers at between three and four hundred feet.

The Junkers followed the coast road towards Rethymno. This meant that they passed close to the hillsides full of concealed positions. Out of about 160 aircraft, seven were brought down along the beach, and others sheered off in flames over the sea. One platoon commander was killed in the doorway on the point of jumping. His men were so unnerved that they refused to jump. The pilot then came round for another run over the dropping zone, but one of his engines was hit and caught fire. Soon the whole wing was in flames, so he crash-landed in the sea close to the beach. Paratroopers and crew climbed into a rubber dinghy, but the shooting did not stop. In the end only two escaped.

An already disrupted operation had became chaotic. Some paratroopers dropped into the sea where, weighted down by equipment and smothered by their own silk canopies, they quickly drowned. Many of those who fell slightly inland suffered injury landing on the rocky terraces. The most horrific fate befell about a dozen men who came down in a large cane-brake where they were impaled on bamboos.

Out of the whole force, only two companies were dropped in the right place. They were part of Kroh's battle group, destined for the airfield, and thus landed directly in front of Campbell's positions. The survivors of this disaster had slipped into the scrub and gone to ground. One lieutenant wanted to give the order to surrender, but a sergeant curtly replied: 'Out of the question.' The survivors were later assembled by Lieutenant von Roon who led them on a circuitous journey inland to join up with Major Kroh's men.

The main part of Kroh's force fell round the olive oil factory at Stavromenos, two kilometres to the east. Kroh, who had come down even further along the coast, gathered his men as quickly as possible and marched in to attack the main hill — called Hill A — which formed Campbell's flank. On the way, he encountered Lieutenant von Roon, who had gathered more men in spite of skirmishing attacks from Cretan irregulars. Kroh's paratroopers, with local superiority and better weapons, overcame the defenders and killed most of the field gun and machine-gun crews. The vineyards provided good cover for attackers as well as defenders.

Campbell did not lack decisiveness. He deployed half his reserve company and the two Matildas in a rapid counter-attack. The tanks, in another anti-climactic appearance, proved themselves as useless on rough ground as at Maleme, but the rapid deployment of infantry managed to prevent the Germans from advancing. That evening, he contacted Creforce Headquarters by wireless to ask for help but Freyberg did not want to commit the remaining Australian battalion at Georgioupolis. Campbell, knowing that everything would depend on the next morning, prepared to use every spare man he had in a counter-attack to throw the Germans back off Hill A.

Colonel Sturm's group of nearly two hundred men had dropped in front of Sandover's battalion and suffered a fate similar to that of those landing on the airfield. All twelve members of a stick from one aircraft were dead by the time they touched the ground. Sturm and his immediate headquarters staff were saved only because they dropped into a small patch of dead ground. Shortly before nightfall, Sandover advanced with his whole line to clear the area. Eighty-eight prisoners were taken and a large quantity of weapons collected. Sturm himself was captured the next morning.

The same morning, 21 May, Campbell launched his counter-attack on Hill A using all reserves, with the two Greek regiments supporting on each flank. Just before the assault commenced, a German bomber pilot mistook a paratroop position and killed sixteen men. This sight encouraged Campbell's Australians who soon charged with ferocious determination. Kroh's paratroopers were swept back and withdrew to the olive oil factory at Stavromenos, which they used as a fort.

Both Australian battalions then carried out a mopping-up operation and managed to capture most of the survivors. Only a few small groups were left. Major Sandover, walking down a track afterwards, came across a message chalked on the road in German: 'Doctor urgently needed'. Sandover's companion spotted a small cave and, finding that it contained six wounded paratroopers, pulled out a grenade to finish them off. Sandover stopped him, and called for them to be taken to the regimental aid post. The paratroop medical unit had also been captured, and within a few days a joint field hospital developed tending several hundred patients, German, Australian and Greek together.

Colonel Sturm, 'a very shaken man' on capture, was further dismayed when, during Major Sandover's interrogation in German, he discovered that the Australians had found a full set of operational orders on the body of one of his officers. Sandover found him trying to look over his shoulder to see who could have committed such a blunder. From another officer, Sandover discovered that there were no paratroop reserves to come. 'We do not reinforce failure,' said the German.

Meanwhile, Wiedemann's battle group, which had landed a couple of kilometres closer to Rethymno, did not fall into a trap like the others but soon came up against the Cretan gendarmerie from the town and 'unrecruited civilians' on the southern side. Unable to advance without crippling loss, Wiedemann ordered his men to prepare a 'hedgehog' defence round the seaside village of Perivolia.

News of the parachute drops on Maleme and Prison Valley finally reached Brigadier Chappel's headquarters outside Heraklion at 2.30 p.m. The Leicesters managed to retrieve their commanding officer from his bath in town, but many of the other officers absent from their units remained out of contact.

At four o'clock, German bombers arrived in large numbers, and a few minutes later the warning 'Super Red' arrived from the radar station on the ridge two kilometres to the south-east of the airfield. Stuka dive-bombers began to attack at 4.12 p.m., and at 4.34 p.m., according to the Black Watch war diary, twin-engined Messerschmitt 110s started strafing.

Casualties were few. The positions were well camouflaged, as captured maps and aerial reconnaissance photographs later proved. And soldiers, in a measure designed mainly to conserve ammunition, were forbidden to open fire on aircraft with small arms. (Later in the battle this order was rescinded in the interests of morale.) More importantly, the anti-aircraft guns around the airfield perimeter – a

dozen Bofors manned by Australian and British gunners, and a Royal
Marine battery of 3-inch guns and pom-poms – had remained silent,
unlike at Maleme. Chappel's ruse managed to convince the Germans
that their previous raids on the gun emplacements had put them out
of action.

After less than half an hour, the Stukas returned to their base on
the island of Skarpanto to the east of Crete and the Messerschmitts
turned back over the Aegean; neither could wait for the long-delayed
troop-carriers.

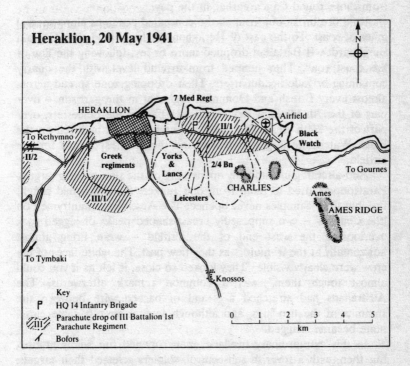

Heraklion, 20 May 1941

HERAKLION

7 Med Regt

Airfield

To Rethymno

II/2

Greek
regiments

Yorks
&
Lancs

II/1

Black
Watch

2/4 Bn

To Gournes

III/1

Leicesters

CHARLIES

Ames

AMES RIDGE

To Tymbaki

Knossos

Key

P   HQ 14 Infantry Brigade

III/   Parachute drop of III Battalion 1st
         Parachute Regiment

/   Bofors

0   1   2   3   4   5
          km

N

Those British officers away from their units, whether on official or
unofficial business, breathed a sigh of relief that this had been just
another air raid. But shortly before 5.30 p.m., the company
commander of the Leicesters out with his platoon commanders was
horrified to hear a bugler in the distance sound 'general alarm'. This

was the signal for an imminent parachute attack: by wireless or field line, the code was 'Air Raid Purple'. His dismay was greatly increased by the fact that Brigadier Chappel had given the Leicesters the task of immediately mounting any counter-attack that might be required.

The slow rumble of the approaching wave of Junkers increased to an oppressive roar as the specks out over the sea grew to recognizable silhouettes. In their flat 'V' formations of three, the troop-carriers banked to turn for their run along the coast, spilling out long dark streaks which, with a sudden jerk, blossomed into canopies. The gasps of astonishment at the sight were no different from those round Canea earlier in the day.

Rifle fire broke out from all the concealed positions along several miles of coast. To the east of Heraklion on the airfield side, Captain Burckhardt's II Battalion dropped more or less following the line of the coast road. They jumped from around level with the quarry containing brigade headquarters. Their dropping zone spread across almost every British and Dominion regiment in the garrison — over part of the 7th Medium Regiment, over part of the Leicesters, over part of the 2/4th Australian Battalion, and then the bulk fell on the Black Watch, the largest battalion and the one responsible for the airfield.

Anti-aircraft guns suddenly opened fire on the slow-moving targets. Paratroopers tried to jump from one Junkers 52, which had caught fire, but their canopies never opened. The Australian infantrymen on 'the Charlies' — two supposedly breast-shaped peaks of jagged rock overlooking the west end of the airfield — were firing almost horizontally at the tri-motors as they flew past. The white faces of the crew were clearly visible. 'They looked so close, it felt as if you could almost touch them,' was a common remark afterwards. The Australians had stretched a strand of barbed wire between the summits of the two hills, and although several aircraft came close, none became snagged.

In this extraordinary fusillade, many opened fire wildly at first, but then, with a feverish self-control, soldiers selected their targets, whose gentle swaying camouflaged the speed of their descent. They fired, reloaded and fired again at paratroopers who may already have been dead. Unlike the terrain round Maleme and Prison Valley, there were few trees or telegraph poles to snag chutes, but there was little cover. Germans were riddled as they struggled free of their harnesses.

The battle was of course not restricted to front-line sections and platoons. Paratroopers were just as likely to come down on top of a company or battalion headquarters, where officers used rifles as well as service revolvers. For officers and soldiers alike it offered a perfect opportunity for laconic humour in the thick of a fight. When one Black Watch command post at last received official notification of the parachute attack, the 'signaller said solemnly to Captain Barry (who had just shared three Germans with Lieutenant Cochrane): "Air-raid warning Purple, sir." '

Because of the delays that disrupted take-off from the mainland, the drop continued for two hours. Without Messerschmitts and Stukas to worry about, the Bofors gun crews traversed on to the lumbering Junkers 52 troop-carriers with grim glee. The Black Watch war diary recorded at 7.07 p.m. that eight of them could be seen going down in flames at the same time: but since the Germans lost a total of fifteen aircraft in two hours, this figure is probably more enthusiastic than reliable. Yet even fifteen aircraft lost to groundfire in one action must still have been a record. It was more than double the combined total of those shot down at Maleme, Suda and Galatas.

Burckhardt's paratroopers who fell in the open spaces round the aerodrome, such as a turnip field, had to run for their weapon containers in full view. Those who fell into low cover, such as the field of barley near the runway, survived a little longer. Movements in the corn and frantic animal rustlings indicated their positions, and soon incendiaries were used to flush them out like rabbits at harvest time. A company with Bren gun carriers went hunting in a vineyard, but the Germans there were able to stalk them in return and lob grenades.

At 6.15 p.m. Brigadier Chappel told the Leicesters to send fighting patrols to comb 'Buttercup Field' east of the quarry. Out of Captain Dunz's reinforced company, only five survivors managed to escape. Throwing themselves into the sea, they shed their kit and swam round to rejoin Major Walther's I Battalion eight kilometres further east along the coast at Gournes, where it had been dropped to capture a wireless station.

But the fighting towards the airfield was not a complete walk-over. Chappel had made a mistake similar to Kippenberger's failure to occupy the prison in Ayia valley. He had not put troops into buildings on either side of the coast road, including an abandoned barracks and a slaughter-house. These soon provided shelter and defence for a few groups of survivors who needed winkling out later. On the other hand, Chappel's forces wasted no time in counter-attacking. The two Matildas of the Royal Tank Regiment and the six

Whippets of the 3rd Hussars were unleashed almost immediately: the Germans never had a chance to recover. Lieutenant G.D. Petherick, the troop leader of the 3rd Hussars at Heraklion, claimed that at least thirty paratroopers had been dealt with at close quarters 'by the revolvers of his tank commanders, and many others were killed by running over them.'

Neither Campbell's Australians at Rethymno nor the 14th Infantry Brigade at Heraklion suffered from that fateful indecision over the commitment of reserves which was so disastrous at both Maleme and Galatas. Chappel saw that the outcome of the battle would be decided in the first couple of hours and sent in his reserve battalion seventy-five minutes after the first troop-carriers were sighted.

The Black Watch, the Australians and the Leicesters were so successfully occupied with the destruction of Burckhardt's battalion — over 300 killed, more than 100 wounded and several dozen prisoners — that they did not have a chance to take note of the other landings outside their area.

At Gournes, Bräuer dropped to join Major Walther's battalion, already depleted by the numbers left behind on the mainland. He found that no wireless contact had been established with the other groups: Burckhardt on the airfield; the half battalion from the 2nd Regiment dropped as a blocking force well to the west; or Major Karl-Lothar Schulz's III Battalion which had landed to the west and south of Heraklion with the objective of taking both the city and the port.

Bräuer now realized that to have sent single battalions on such missions was far too ambitious. Although still lacking definite news, he sensed that the operation had run into serious difficulties. Misinformed about enemy strength, General Student had dispersed his forces dangerously. And Group East's sector was the most widespread of all with four dropping zones along nearly twenty kilometres of coast.

At nightfall, Colonel Bräuer decided to move westwards to join up with Burckhardt and see the battle round the town of Heraklion for himself. As escort, Walther gave him the platoon commanded by Lieutenant Count Wolfgang von Blücher, who had won the Knight's Cross of the Iron Cross in the drop on Holland. Around midnight, after a rapid march, Blücher's point section sighted troops ahead on the hill to the south-east of the airfield. Optimistically convinced that they had encountered pickets thrown out by the II Battalion of their regiment, they called forward the password *'Reichsmarschall'* only to receive a ragged volley in reply. Blücher's platoon, which had outstripped Colonel Bräuer, found itself well inside the Black Watch perimeter. Coming under fire from other positions, they had no alternative but to go to ground.

Black Watch officers were particularly pleased with their tally, which continued to mount after dark. According to one regimental account: 'Mungo Stirling, the Adjutant, and Andrew Campbell, the Intelligence officer, wandered down to call on one of the companies and shot a couple on the way.' Shooting parlance permeated a running joke that became increasingly laboured and unattractive. The morning after 'the shoot' was referred to as 'the pick-up'. Officers in different companies discussed their bags over the field telephone. One recorded the following snatch of a conversation: 'I nearly came along and offered myself as an extra loader. What did you get – 20 brace? And did you lay them all out on the road afterwards? And did they come over nice and high? And did you send your keeper after the runners?'

For the scattered survivors of Burckhardt's battalion, many of them wounded and almost all desperate from thirst, it was a grim night. The British heard them whistling and hooting to each other to establish contact. In return they were made to listen to Pipe Major Roy's bagpipes. To judge by German accounts, the wailing pipes seem to have been a very effective form of psychological warfare.

Major Schulz's battalion dropped round the west and south side of Heraklion on to maize fields and vineyards just outside the huge Venetian ramparts. Schulz's habitual insistence on jumping at the head of his men saved his life. The moment after he threw himself out in the crucifix position, the troop-carrier exploded in flames behind him after a direct hit on a fuel tank from an anti-aircraft gun.

His scattered companies had great difficulty collecting themselves. A number were killed on landing by Greek soldiers from the garrison of three large but ill-armed regiments, and by Cretan civilians, some of whom knifed paratroopers caught in the trees, rather as Henry V's Welshmen cut the throats of dismounted French knights at Agincourt. The battalion of the York and Lancaster Regiment was positioned further round on the south-east edge of the town and the 64th Medium Regiment – gunners serving as infantry – between them and the port.

The part played by Cretan 'unrecruited civilians' in this battle was as great as that in the province of Canea. A German report stated that 'south and west of the town, considerable fighting against *francs-tireurs* took place: these fought in groups of 7 to 8 men, one of which was led by a Pope [*sic*] who was subsequently shot'. Perhaps this was the priest with a rifle down his trousers, whom Gordon Hope-Morley met just before the battle.

Schulz, having collected as many of his men as possible, divided his force into two. He took one half against the Canea Gate while Captain Count von der Schulenburg swung round to the left with the other to find another less obvious opening. Schulz's force soon became embroiled in a form of warfare which many participants later compared to wars long past. A furious battle took place at the Canea Gate, where civilians, Greek soldiers and Cretan gendarmerie under Captain Kalaphotakis lined the massive Venetian city walls. Both Schulz's and Schulenburg's groups managed to fight their way in, but along the narrow streets an equally bitter guerrilla battle harried them at every turn.

John Pendlebury, although the senior SOE officer at Heraklion, had had as little warning of the invasion as the commanding officer of the Leicesters. At lunchtime, he had a drink with friends at his favourite meeting place – the basement bar of the Hotel Knossos – just round the corner from where a German bomb had hit a British ration truck with several thousand eggs on board thus creating 'the biggest omelette in Europe'.

In many ways it is surprising that he stayed in the town with the paratroop drop expected any day, but from Jack Hamson's account Pendlebury had received orders to remain, having sent his two lieutenants – Hamson and Bruce-Mitford – up into the hills on 16 May to hold strategic points with Cretan volunteers. Perhaps he also felt the most urgent battle would be in Heraklion: Satanas too was in the town that day with some of his *andartes*.

No doubt Pendlebury and Satanas were with the defenders in that battle at the Canea Gate, reminiscent of a Renaissance siege, and took part in the street-fighting against Schulz's III Battalion. The paratroopers fought their way well into the town; some even reached the quayside of the old Venetian harbour at about 10.30 that night.

If one pieces together the various accounts of Pendlebury's last movements (often having to take an average of those which do not match) he appears to have slipped back through the fighting to his office the next morning. Although the battle in the town had not yet finished, he wanted to leave Heraklion to co-ordinate the bands of *andartes* in the surrounding hills.

Major Schulz, who had earlier taken the surrender of the city from a Greek major and the Mayor, an elderly man in a linen suit and boater, was furious to find himself under renewed attack when reinforcements arrived from the Leicesters and the York and Lancaster Regiment. Since his men were very short of ammunition, he would have to withdraw. He called back the Mayor to warn him that as soon as his men had pulled out of the city, he would call on the Luftwaffe to destroy it. Then the two now intermingled groups of paratroopers fought a rearguard action out beyond the ramparts, and remained more or less concealed to the south and west.

Armed with a rifle and, according to most versions, wearing uniform, Pendlebury left through the Canea Gate in the afternoon, not far behind Schulz's men. He was accompanied by his driver and a small group led by Satanas, the guerrilla kapitan from Kroussonas on the eastern flank of Mount Ida. Outside, he said goodbye to Satanas, having arranged to join forces later. He set off by car with his driver down the road towards Canea, an inexplicably rash move since paratroopers were known to be all over the area. Almost immediately they ran into a section of Germans at Kaminia, less than a kilometre from the city walls. In the fight that ensued, Pendlebury is said to have killed three of the enemy before being wounded high in the chest. The Germans took him, bleeding heavily, to a house beside the road and left him there in the care of two women. A German doctor arrived that evening and bound his wounds.

Next day, 22 May, another group of paratroopers came to the house. They are said to have recognized Pendlebury by his glass eye. (This is unlikely: Pendlebury's lack of discretion has to be weighed against the poverty of German military intelligence.) The two women were taken to a temporary internment camp and Pendlebury was hauled out and shot against the wall of the house. Another version says that the second group of parachutists shot him out of hand as a *franc-tireur* because they found him in a civilian shirt, probably one given him by the women because his uniform was soaked in blood.

To confuse matters further, the part of the German report of December 1942 dealing with 'Captain Pendleburg [*sic*]' said: 'Seriously wounded in the fighting on May 20 near HERAKLION, he died two days later and was buried there.' For Pendlebury to have attempted to leave the town just after the paratroop drop on the afternoon of 20 May, but before Schulz's battalion stormed the town, would have been more logical, but this course of events conflicts with eye-witness accounts.

Pendlebury acknowledged in his diaries – later found by the Germans – that his preparation of armed resistance by the civilian population was presumably against international law. And Hamson wrote soon after the event: 'He knew that for him there was no issue but success or death.' Whether or not the paratroopers who shot Pendlebury knew who he was, the German military authorities took great pains afterwards to identify the corpse for certain. His body is said to have been dug up a couple of times to check the glass eye and once to cut a sample of material from the shirt, presumably to prove that he had not been in uniform.

The number of Cretans claiming to be the last person to have seen Pendlebury alive is bewilderingly impressive. Tom Dunbabin, an archaeologist and friend, and from 1942 the senior British liaison officer with the Cretan resistance, wrote after the war: 'Many wild tales circulated at the time and later, and the story of his last days has inevitably been worked, in Cretan belief, into something like saga.' So strong was the myth of Pendlebury that Brigadier Shearer, the chief of military intelligence in Cairo, reported to Churchill on 28 August, three months after the battle was over: 'We also tried to drop a wireless set by parachute to Pendlebury, who at the moment is largely controlling the guerrilla activities in the Crete hills.'

On 21 May, while fighting still continued in the city, Mike Cumberlege and Nick Hammond reached Heraklion in the *Dolphin* on their return from Hierapetra. They had tried to telephone Pendlebury from Sitia – at their last dinner together they had planned to raid Kasos on the night of 20 May – but could not get through.

On being fired at from the dockside, Cumberlege put in alongside the extreme end of the mole which formed the new harbour outside the Venetian port. His cousin Cle and Nick Hammond jumped ashore, each armed with a Mauser pistol. They approached until the sight of the swastika flag flying from the power station gave the impression that the enemy controlled most of the town. Clearly the *Dolphin* and her crew could do little to help – all the approaches seemed to be covered by machine-gun fire – so Cumberlege turned her round and sailed out north-east to the island of Dia.

The next morning, preoccupied by the fate of Pendlebury and other friends in the fighting, they continued on along the north coast, waving to any German aircraft which flew close to investigate. At the entrance to Suda Bay, Cumberlege anchored near the island on which stood the ruins of a Venetian castle. From there, they engaged Stukas coming out of their dive after attacking ships in the harbour. It was a good position. The *Dolphin* claimed five confirmed kills and a number of 'probables' in addition. Cumberlege and his crew were not to know that their guns would have been even more welcome at Heraklion when the bombers of Richthofen's VIII Air Corps returned to destroy the city.

12
First Night and Second Day
20 and 21 May

Night seemed to fall more rapidly than usual. Columns of smoke from bombed shipping in Suda Bay gave the impression of storm clouds blacking out an evening sky. But exhaustion as much as a lack of visibility brought the fighting to a close. Men in the firing line sank to the ground or to the bottom of their slit trenches in numb relief, their skin taut from dried sweat and dust. Others, whether defenders cut off or paratroopers scattered in drops over strongly held positions, crept out of their hiding places to rejoin their own side.

Danger made the sense of hearing acute in the dark. Every now and then a Very light shot upwards with a muffled crack and then a hiss as it slowed into its dazzling shaky parabola of magnesium white or green, casting a ghostly glare over the countryside. There were outbreaks of shooting started by nervous sentries, and occasionally the elegant curve of tracer rounds would appear in the distance followed by the rattle of the machine gun which fired them.

Those out in the unmapped no-man's land slipped past each other avoiding a fight by instinctive consent, like different species of animal after a fire or flood. Also reminiscent of the wild were curious jungle noises, rustling in bushes, or whistles, hoots and calls, as isolated paratroopers tried to make contact.

For the wounded, darkness brought little relief except from the sun. All suffered from a choking thirst as they lay on the hard and still warm ground. A group of Greek soldiers, who lay wounded in an isolated house hit by a bomb, were discovered only by chance three days later, tortured by pain and thirst. An RAF squadron leader near Maleme, with both his forearms shattered, tried to shoot himself with his pistol, but his fingers had not even the strength to pull the trigger and thus release him from his agony. For the Germans fear increased as Cretan irregulars stalked the battlefield for arms. All they could do was to crawl under bushes to hide.

In the lingering warmth of that first evening the thyme-scented air was still pure: on subsequent days it became increasingly corrupted by the stench of decomposing flesh.

At ten o'clock, Freyberg signalled to Cairo: 'Today has been a hard one. We have been hard pressed. So far, I believe, we hold aerodromes at Retimo [Rethymno], Heraklion and Maleme and the two harbours. Margin by which we hold them is a bare one, and it would be wrong of me to paint optimistic picture. Fighting has been heavy and we have killed large numbers of Germans. Communications are most difficult.'

He then added to his signal, 'A German operation order with most ambitious objectives, all of which failed, has just been captured.' Geoffrey Cox, one of his intelligence officers, had discovered this document when sifting through papers collected from dead and captured members of the 3rd Parachute Regiment. Cox's rapid translation showed that the Germans had expected to take the airfields and the ports in the course of the first day's fighting. Freyberg was elated by this news. He did not know that the margin by which they held Maleme was disappearing at that very moment.

That night, most Germans believed that they were beaten because the British would launch a counter-attack. Such large numbers from their ranks had been killed that, according to Weiksler, the war correspondent with them, only fifty-seven men remained capable of fighting in the area of the Tavronitis bridge and airfield. The loss of platoon and company commanders was the most disastrous. Major Stentzler and Captain Gericke were the Storm Regiment's only battalion commanders still on their feet.

The web of misunderstanding which led to the loss of Maleme, and ultimately the whole island, was partly due to the 'most difficult' communications: the defenders on the airfield had no wireless set, and Colonel Andrew's command post, which did, could not see the airfield. But muddled thinking before the invasion, compounded by fatigue and confusion once the battle started, contributed still more.

Colonel Andrew had told Brigadier Hargest shortly before nightfall that after the failure of the attack with the tanks, he would have to withdraw. Hargest's reply — 'If you must, you must' — was accompanied by a promise to send two companies to reinforce him.

Dismay at their non-appearance, on top of Hargest's very unhelpful reaction in a critical situation, inevitably had a disorientating effect on Colonel Andrew. His superior officers had emphasized the importance of counter-attacking the enemy, yet now seemed inexplicably reluctant to act. Combined with the order of Creforce Headquarters before the battle that the runway should be left intact and the mines laid on the airfield should be left unprimed, that would make any commanding officer wonder whether a fundamental change in priority had been decided without his knowledge.

Out of contact with his forward companies, convinced that the Germans had broken through on to the airfield from the bridge and overrun the platoons on the west side of Hill 107, and finally threatened by the probing attacks of Stentzler's companies which had swung round to attack his rear, Andrew felt that without support he must extricate his men before dawn brought the return of the Messerschmitts. Not long after nine o'clock, he warned Hargest by wireless that he was withdrawing to the subsidiary ridge to the south-east of Hill 107. Hargest does not seem to have felt that a reaction was required to this news, though it signified an end to any effective control over Maleme airfield. Hargest even informed divisional headquarters that the situation was 'quite satisfactory'.

Andrew sent out runners to his companies to warn them of the move, but the runners sent to C Company on the west of the airfield, D Company on the Tavronitis slope of Hill 107 and HQ Company by the village of Pirgos did not get through. Meanwhile, the two companies eventually sent by Hargest to reinforce the defenders – one from the 28th (Maori) Battalion and the other from the adjacent 23rd Battalion – had no contact with each other. The Maoris reached the airfield in the dark, and proceeded carefully on hearing German voices. Afterwards, it was estimated that they had got to within two hundred metres of C Company's command post when they decided that the defenders must have been overrun and turned back.

The other company, from the 23rd Battalion, eventually found Colonel Andrew's new position, but after a certain amount of confusion and indecision, Andrew concluded that this rear ridge was also too isolated and exposed to hold. He would take his surviving companies another kilometre east to join up with the 23rd and 21st Battalions. There was barely a hint of *reculer pour mieux sauter*, in any case the worst possible strategy in the face of a paratroop attempt to capture an airfield. Following this course, the only hope of preventing the Germans from landing reinforcements on Maleme airfield would have been either a counter-attack by night, a risky venture for even the best trained troops, or an advance in full daylight facing the far greater perils of enemy air superiority. But the cruellest twist of Andrew's decision did not become apparent until after the war when it transpired that a single platoon, even a single Bren gun left in place on the airfield, could have swung the course of the whole battle.

The forward companies, not reached by runners, had no idea of Andrew's order to withdraw. Conditions varied from one platoon to another. Some had suffered heavily and were short of ammunition, others remained virtually intact. Battered but unbeaten, with their morale sustained by the far heavier losses they had inflicted on the enemy, they were mainly dismayed by the length of time the 5th Brigade was taking to put in its counter-attack and sweep the remnants of the Storm Regiment back beyond the Tavronitis.

Before midnight, Captain Campbell of D Company on the Tavronitis slope of Hill 107 heard from a straggler, a marine gunner, that the rest of the battalion had withdrawn: he refused to believe him. Thirst was their main problem, so Campbell and his company sergeant major crept off into the night festooned with felt-covered water-bottles. They were shocked to discover that the marine had been right. Battalion headquarters had left Hill 107. Not surprisingly, spirits fell as soon as this news spread in the company. Campbell felt that he had no alternative but to fall back as well.

A German propaganda myth grew out of this withdrawal from Hill 107 making a national hero out of the Storm Regiment's senior medical officer, Dr Heinrich Neumann. Neumann, a notorious disciplinarian in steel-rimmed spectacles, was a frustrated warrior of intense seriousness. He had flown twenty missions in Spain as a rear gunner in Heinkel bi-planes of the Condor Legion until told to stick to his duties as a doctor. After the slaughter of the Storm Regiment's officers, Neumann decided that his moment of destiny on the field of battle had come. He told his assistants in the regimental aid post to carry on without him, then assembled a force of twenty-odd paratroopers and, to the bemusement of combat officers, sent a dramatic note announcing his intention to capture Hill 107.

Neumann's group set off and eventually encountered a company commanded by Lieutenant Horst Trebes. A couple of accidental clashes in the dark, resulting in the death of one German sergeant, were later woven into a story of savage battle and heroic conquest by an unconventional leader, later presented with the Knight's Cross of the Iron Cross. Whatever the ludicrous aspect to this episode, the Germans were in possession of Hill 107 by dawn.

On the airfield, C Company stayed alert in their trenches listening to German voices in the surrounding darkness. Fortunately for them, the paratroopers' lack of enthusiasm for fighting at night became clear: most were so exhausted that they fell asleep as soon as the shooting stopped. Captain Johnson, the company commander, did not find out about Andrew's decision to withdraw until the early hours of the morning. One of the patrols he sent out returned with news that the Germans now occupied the battalion command post on the rear slope of Hill 107.

Johnson's dilemma was not an enviable one. He knew that if his men remained on the airfield their fire could prevent troop-carriers landing. But soon after dawn, they would be the focus for attack by the remainder of the Storm Regiment and the mass of Stukas and Messerschmitts, now that their positions were identified.

He knew nothing about the reasons for Colonel Andrew's withdrawal, and doubted whether a counter-attack by the rest of the brigade would be mounted in daylight. His men could not possibly survive another twenty-four hours unless resupplied and reinforced. At 4.20 a.m., he told them to take off their boots and tie the laces to hang them round their necks, then they moved as cautiously and as silently as possible, circumnavigating the snoring groups of German paratroopers on the airfield. Finally, after sheltering in trees during the early morning blitz, they joined up with the 21st Battalion. By dawn on 21 May, no New Zealand troops remained within the airfield perimeter. From their new positions direct fire was only possible on the eastern end of the runway. Maleme airfield was lost before the second day of the battle had started.

Both Puttick and Freyberg were gravely misled by Hargest's message that the situation at Maleme was 'quite satisfactory'. But considering their reluctance to devote sufficient forces to retake Maleme even after German troop-carriers began to land, it is unlikely that Hargest's failure made much difference. Hargest almost certainly had not wanted to move the 23rd Battalion, the one earmarked for a counter-attack on the airfield, because of its responsibility for coastal defence. This only emphasizes the impression that the whole operational plan had been fatally muddled by Freyberg's misunderstanding over the enemy's seaborne reinforcements.

Kippenberger, on the other hand, had begun within a few hours of the first parachute drop to ask for the 20th Battalion, the divisional reserve, to launch a counter-attack on Prison Valley. Brigadier Inglis was equally frustrated. His 4th Brigade, which Freyberg had released to Puttick from Force Reserve, had waited expectantly with nothing to do after the initial flurry of fighting after breakfast. Inglis wanted to use the whole of his brigade to attack Prison Valley to clear it of Heidrich's 3rd Parachute Regiment, then swing north-westwards on Maleme.

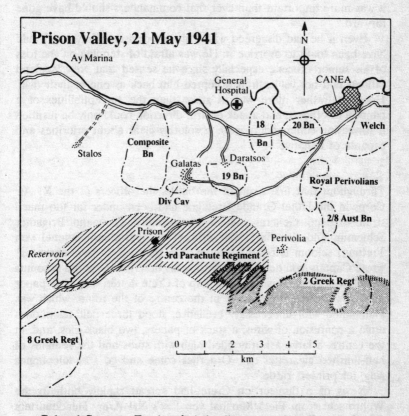

Prison Valley, 21 May 1941

Colonel Stewart, Freyberg's brigadier general staff, and Colonel Gentry, Puttick's own chief of staff, added their voices to urge action. But Puttick, backed by Freyberg, set his face against all pleas to counter-attack, despite the emphasis on such a course in operational orders. After the war Puttick argued that an attack on Prison Valley would have left troops exposed to enemy aircraft at dawn, but one can only conclude that he and Freyberg were in fact so preoccupied by the seaborne reinforcements that they did not want to move any units from their coastal positions.

Colonel Stewart also pointed out after the war that 'A striking feature of the battle was the tendency for senior officers to stay in their headquarters. In subsequent campaigns it was the accepted practice in the Division for commanders to be well forward . . . In Crete where communications were always bad and often non-existent, it was more important than ever that commanders should have gone forward.'

Even if he had disagreed with Puttick's decision, Freyberg would have been loath to override it. He was afraid of stepping on the toes of his senior officers, especially since he sensed that New Zealand officers had not yet entirely accepted him back as one of their own. However, rather more was at stake than the susceptibilities of a handful of officers, and a lack of firm direction could only be justified if formation commanders were absolutely clear about priorities and capable of initiative.

Throughout that first night of the battle, the officers of the XI Air Corps in the Hotel Grande Bretagne had been under far too much strain to sleep. General Student, his second in command, Brigadier Schlemm, and the chief staff officer for operations, Colonel von Trettner, seldom left the ballroom. 'On the wall, in semi-darkness', wrote Captain von der Heydte basing his description on the accounts of fellow officers, 'was the large map of Crete dotted with little paper flags . . . On the broad table in the centre of the room, which was illuminated with unnecessary brilliance, stood three field-telephones amid a confusion of wires, a stack of papers, two black files, and, in the centre, a large ash-tray piled high with stubs and the remains of half-finished cigarettes . . . Orderlies come and go . . . telephones ring, teleprinters rattle.'

News of a disaster on Crete had spread rapidly both in the Wehrmacht from Field Marshal von List's XII Army Headquarters and in the High Command in Germany as well as in the Luftwaffe via Richthofen's VIII Air Corps.

The losses had been so great and the gains so small that Student was under heavy pressure to abort the whole operation. Although casualty figures were not yet available, he had a fairly accurate idea of the scale of the slaughter. The total of 1,863 killed on the first day over the four sectors happened to match the number of men landed in the Maleme–Tavronitis area.

At nightfall on 20 May, none of the objectives of Operation Mercury had been met. Colonel Sturm's force at Rethymno was out of wireless contact, while Bräuer's now appeared far too weak to overcome the entrenched battalions of the 14th Infantry Brigade. Heidrich's 3rd Parachute Regiment in Prison Valley was thwarted by the defence of Galatas. Only the Storm Regiment at Maleme was close to taking an airfield, but it was not in a strong enough state to hold the perimeter and protect the landing of the 5th Mountain Division. Above all, it lacked both ammunition and leadership.

Major General Süssmann had been killed, Brigadier Meindl seriously wounded, Major Scherber killed and Major Koch wounded. The losses amongst company commanders had been equally disastrous. Student immediately decided to send Colonel Ramcke, that Freikorps veteran and leader of crude vigour, with reinforcements to re-form the Storm Regiment as an effective fighting unit. To get enough men together – his level of reserves had been perilously low in the first place – he would send all those held back from Colonel Bräuer's force at Heraklion due to the shortage of aircraft. Fearing that the operation would be halted in the next few hours, Student does not appear to have told his superior, General Löhr, of his final gamble.

Even with Ramcke and the reinforcements, General Student knew that unless he could land and deploy the fresh troops of the Mountain Division by the second evening of the battle, he would have lost: the seaborne force which Freyberg feared so much had been delayed. Careful study of the contours on the map combined with air reports on the New Zealand positions suggested that with Hill 107 in German hands the Tavronitis end of the airfield might be out of the line of direct fire. Two Junkers had tried to land on the airfield during the afternoon of 20 May, but vigorous fire from the New Zealand company had forced them to sheer off out to sea again. Everything therefore depended on whether the original defenders were still dug in on the western perimeter. There was only one way to find out.

Student summoned Captain Kleye, an intrepid aviator on his staff, to the ballroom in the Hotel Grande Bretagne. He explained the problem and asked Kleye to attempt a touch-down and take-off at first light on the western edge of the airfield. Captain Kleye set off in the early hours and carried out his test landing. Although light artillery fired on his aircraft, he could confirm that the western edge at least was not covered by direct fire. The last of the defenders had withdrawn from both the airfield and Hill 107.

Another Junkers 52 also took off alone early that morning. Having heard a wireless message from the Tavronitis that the Storm Regiment survivors were virtually out of ammunition and that Brigadier Meindl would die without hospital treatment, two pilots, Koenitz and Steinweg, loaded their aircraft and, without asking permission, flew south across the Aegean. They managed to land on the beach west of the river-bed. Paratroopers ran out to the aeroplane and offloaded the ammunition. Then, once the already delirious Brigadier Meindl and seven other stretcher-cases were on board, and volunteers had cleared boulders from the very improvised runway, Koenitz just managed to take off again.

On receiving Kleye's encouraging news, General Student sent orders to General Ringel's 5th Mountain Division. A first battalion of mountain troops must be ready to fly to Crete at a moment's notice from Tanagra airfield. First, another wave of troop-carriers would take off with Colonel Ramcke and the paratroop reserves. But Student made a serious mistake in his plan aimed for mid-afternoon. While Ramcke and two and a half companies were to be dropped west of the Tavronitis where their landing would be protected by the survivors of the Storm Regiment, two more companies from the 2nd Parachute Regiment were to be dropped east of the airfield. Curiously, he does not seem to have imagined that they might be massacred like Major Scherber's battalion the day before.

The New Zealand 5th Brigade spent the morning of 21 May sorting itself out. Colonel Andrew's survivors were reorganized in two companies, one each attached to the 21st and 23rd Battalions. Hargest allowed the three commanding officers to carry on as they felt best. He made no attempt to go forward from his headquarters at Platanias to see for himself, and did not urge them to mount a counter-attack on the airfield.

The New Zealanders in the front line, now behind the road which led from the coast up to the village of Xamoudohori and the destroyed radar station, could not at first see the Storm Regiment's cautious advance as far as the hamlet of Maleme.

At about three in the afternoon, the Luftwaffe began bombing and strafing. This was a prelude to the attack of the Storm Regiment due to coincide with the parachute drop. As soon as the air raid stopped, detachments of the Storm Regiment advanced towards Pirgos, but they were repulsed after ferocious fighting in which the New Zealanders used some captured Spandau machine guns to great effect.

Three kilometres behind the New Zealand lines, twenty-four troop-carriers in their now familiar trios came over dropping the two parachute companies. But the area Student had chosen straddled the positions of the New Zealand Engineer Detachment and the 28th (Maori) Battalion. Those who were not killed in the air were just as likely to be shot before they struggled free of their harnesses. 'At one stage', recalled a captain, 'I stopped for a moment to see how things were going and a Hun dropped not ten feet away. I had my pistol in my hand and without really knowing what I was doing I let him have it while he was still on the ground. I had hardly got over the shock when another came down almost on top of me and I plugged him too while he was untangling himself. Not cricket, I know, but there it is.'

The Maoris fixed bayonets and went straight in at the paratroopers dropping in their area. One of their officers described the scene. 'As we got to him [a German playing dead] I told the Maori to bayonet him. As he did so, he turned his head away not bearing the sight. We rushed out among the Germans scattered every 15 or 20 yds. One at about 15 yds instead of firing his tommy gun started to lie down to fire. I took a snap shot with a German Mauser. It grazed his behind and missed between his legs. My back hair lifted, but the Maori got him (I had no bayonet). We rushed on . . . Some tried to crawl away. A giant of a man jumped up with his hands up like a gorilla, shouting "Hants Oop!" I said: "Shoot the bastard" and the Maori shot him. That was because many others were firing at us.' Every German officer and NCO from that company was killed. Only eighty men out of the two paratroop companies – a third of the whole force – survived, mostly by hiding, then slipping back westwards along the beach after dusk.

Although both attacks had been failures, the perimeter of Maleme airfield remained in German hands and at about five o'clock, the first troop-carriers with the II Battalion of Colonel Utz's 100th Mountain Regiment arrived from Tanagra. They landed, stopped to disgorge with their engines still running, then immediately took off again. But many aircraft did not survive. Maleme airfield came under random artillery fire from the sightless 75s in the 5th Brigade area. The nine field guns, mostly Italian pieces without sights which had been taken in Libya, opened up on the runway — a 'gunner's dream' — with some success, but not enough to stop the shuttle of Junkers 52s coming round over Cape Spatha on the western horizon.

For the mountain troops who felt the shock waves of bursting shells while still inside the Junkers fuselage, it was a nightmarish and disorientating experience. Even before the aircraft had come to a halt they were leaping on to the dusty red runway — General Student likened it to a clay tennis-court — holding on to Mauser rifle and steel helmet. They usually preferred their peaked caps with the silver badge of an edelweiss on the side, and only wore the coal-scuttle helmets when under bombardment.

Platoons and sections became mixed up, as they hurried to the side to escape the shell-fire. One company was immediately pushed forward to strengthen the Storm Regiment. The others, once assembled, moved to take up positions to defend the airfield from any counter-attack on the south and south-west flank.

About twenty troop-carriers were hit or crashed. But with a ruthless single-mindedness and energy which the British would never have contemplated, the Germans kept the runway open. They used captured Bren gun carriers to tow crashed aircraft out of the way and dragooned prisoners of war at gunpoint as work parties to fill in craters: several are said to have been shot out of hand for refusing to comply with this flagrant breach of the Geneva Convention.

There is a story on the German side that General von Richthofen's nephew, a Stuka ace, also landed on the western corner of the airfield, then ran up Hill 107 with a pair of strong binoculars, identified the artillery batteries firing on Maleme, and took off again to lead his group to dive-bomb them. Ramcke's paratroopers also engaged British batteries with the mobile Bofors guns they had captured at Maleme, using them like German 88s against targets on the ground.

That afternoon a German bomb hit a petrol and ammunition dump. A huge pall of smoke blotted out the sky and the surrounding olive groves began to burn. The shuttle rhythm of aircraft landing and taking off appeared alarmingly impressive to staff officers watching through binoculars from the Creforce quarry. Freyberg's artillery commander, an Australian colonel, timed them. 'Seventy seconds to land and clear its men and gear,' he observed.

The need for a counter-attack on Maleme was at last accepted by those senior officers who had been so reluctant to react. Hargest had first discussed the subject by field telephone with Puttick during the morning. He strongly recommended that it take place at night to avoid air attack. Puttick agreed. But the inadequate force they were prepared to devote to it undermined the operation before it began. That prescription of too little too late was once again disastrously adopted. Two battalions, the Maoris and the 20th, with Lieutenant Farran's three 'armoured perambulators', were expected to defeat a fresh battalion of mountain troops and the re-formed and well-armed Storm Regiment in a few hours after a long march at night.

Hargest, Puttick and Freyberg all accepted the principle of counter-attack, yet showed little enthusiasm for the enterprise. A more disastrous state of mind for commanders preparing such an operation is hard to imagine. Without action to prevent a German build-up and attack from Maleme, a German victory became inevitable. But the official New Zealand history points out that for Puttick and Freyberg, 'the impression prevailed that the sea attack was the one most to be feared'. And yet Freyberg had some 6,000 formed troops in the Canea–Suda area in addition to the New Zealand Division in the Maleme and Galatas sectors.

Not only was the force allocated to the counter-attack on Maleme perilously small, a fateful condition was also imposed. The remaining Australian reserves at Georgioupolis had to be brought round to take the place of the 20th Battalion before the advance could begin.

13
'The Seaborne Invasion'
Night, 21 May

'Our attention in the quarry', wrote one of Freyberg's staff officers, 'in this counter-attack was overshadowed by an impending event closer at hand. The seaborne invasion was under way.'

Freyberg's *idée fixe* had retained its grip to such an extent that he misread a crucial Ultra signal on the afternoon of 21 May and believed that an enemy fleet was heading straight for Canea. This signal, like all the other intercepts, was for his eyes only, so he could not discuss it with anyone. In any case he does not appear to have been in a mood to listen. Freyberg would not accept the assurances of Captain Morse RN, the Naval Officer-in-Charge at Suda Bay, that the Mediterranean Fleet was indeed capable of dealing with any seaborne threat.

The only description of this threat in Ultra messages – 'Fourthly. Arrival of the seaborne contingent consisting of anti-aircraft batteries as well as of more troops and supplies' – did not suggest a beach-storming operation with tanks. And apart from the confusion, described in Chapter 8, over the number of troops involved, no hint of an invasion fleet had been made in Ultra signals – the only specific reference had been to 'sea transport'. Finally, there had been no indication from any intelligence source that the Germans or the Italians possessed assault ships or landing craft. Wavell, as has already been pointed out, informed the War Office on 1 May: 'Our information points insufficient sea-going shipping left Aegean for large-scale sea-borne operations.' Leaving aside the question of the unsuitable coastline round Canea, it should have been hard to imagine an enemy risking an opposed landing when he could bring ashore reinforcements and stores behind his own lines.

On the first night of the battle, Freyberg had been most excited when Geoffrey Cox had discovered amongst a mass of papers taken from enemy dead the 3rd Parachute Regiment's operation order. This revealed their objectives and added that the Light Ships' Group would land west of Maleme. But he must have pushed this from his mind when on 21 May, the following signal, OL 15/389, reached Crete:*

Personal for General Freyberg   Most Immediate

On continuation of attack Colorado [Crete], reliably reported that among operations planned for Twenty-first May is air landing two mountain battalions and attack Canea. Landing from echelon of small ships depending on situation at sea.

Freyberg appears to have confused the two sentences. One can only suppose that it did not occur to him that 'attack Canea' might refer to a proposed attack from the south-west by paratroopers in Prison Valley or an air raid. In his fixation with a seaborne assault, he seems to have seized upon the words 'Canea' and 'Landing' while forgetting the full stop between them. The idea that an 'echelon of small ships' intended to land a large force with tanks on a hostile coast or storm Canea harbour proved a serious mistake. It was clearly the main element in the disastrous train of events which befell the counter-attack on Maleme planned for the same night. Soon after receiving the Ultra signal, Freyberg issued the following order:

Reliable information. Early seaborne attack in area Canea likely. New Zealand Division remains responsible coast from west to Kladiso River. Welch Battalion forthwith to stiffen existing defences from Kladiso to Halepa.

Not only did Freyberg keep the Welch Regiment, his largest and best equipped battalion, in Canea to man the seafront, he would allow no more than the 20th Battalion out of Inglis's 4th Brigade to join the counter-attack on Maleme, and then only after it had been replaced

---

* Although dispatched at 0900 hours GMT, Freyberg did not receive this message until later 'owing to temporary stoppage of communications' reported to Cairo in OL 389. To judge from the New Zealand official history (Davin, pp.195–6), it arrived that afternoon during Freyberg's conference with Puttick, Inglis and Vasey.

by an Australian battalion from Georgioupolis. The counter-attacking force was both too small and too late when in fact Freyberg could have spared five battalions with ample time to crush the enemy at Maleme.

Even after the war, Freyberg never realized that the German flotilla had been heading for Maleme, not for Canea. 'I could not leave this covering position near Canea unheld', he wrote of the tardy release of the 20th Battalion, 'because had the Germans landed as they planned, we should have lost all our supplies and ammunition; besides the enemy lodgement would have cut the whole New Zealand Force off from Suda Bay. I gave the order; neither Puttick nor Inglis was responsible for the delay.'

Far from an invasion fleet, the First Light Ships' Group proved to be a collection of nineteen caiques and two rusty little steamers escorted by an Italian light destroyer, the *Lupo*. It transported only the III Battalion of the 100th (Reichenhall) Mountain Regiment with heavy supplies, especially ammunition, and flak batteries. A second *Schiffsstaffel* escorted by another light destroyer, the *Sagittario*, had also assembled to carry the II Battalion of the 85th Mountain Regiment to Heraklion.

These two flotillas had been laid on as a back-up to the airborne invasion on the assumption that the defenders would render the airfields unusable. General Ringel, to emphasize the expedition's low priority, asserted that for navigation the caiques only had 'a 1/500,000 map and a pocket compass'. Soldiers later claimed to have seen their caiques as 'death-traps' even before they set off. But this may have been hindsight, for during the crossing most of them sang 'Marching against England' lustily enough, played concertinas and waved enthusiastically as German aircraft on their way to attack the island came down low over the water to greet them.

After loading in the Piraeus, this improbable armada had set out for the island of Milos, the largest of the south-westerly islands in the Cyclades and half way to Crete. The plan was to cross the last stretch of the Aegean during daylight on 21 May under the protection of the VIII Air Corps which was ready to attack any Royal Navy ship which showed itself, and reach the coast of Crete by nightfall; the caiques would use their sails as well as engines.

An Italian escort vessel was necessary since the German surface fleet could not pass the guns of Gibraltar. Mussolini had claimed the Mediterranean as *Mare Nostrum*, a point Hitler had to concede, yet when Operation Mercury was prepared, the Italian admiralty in Rome refused German requests for their capital ships to put to sea. The Battle of Cape Matapan was too fresh in their minds.

Admiral Cunningham's problems were the opposite. The British Mediterranean Fleet enjoyed supremacy on the surface of the sea, yet without aircraft carriers – HMS *Formidable* had lost most of its Fulmar fighters – his ships were vulnerable to bombing attacks from the Greek mainland and island bases. The only solution was to sweep the Aegean by night with 'light forces', mainly mixed groups of destroyers and cruisers, and withdraw them at dawn to less dangerous waters beyond the Kaso strait to the east of Crete and the Antikithera strait to the west.

Cunningham, determined to fulfil the Royal Navy's role of defence by sea, had first dispatched three task-forces to sweep the Aegean on the night of 16 May. A further force, the battleships *Queen Elizabeth* and *Barham* with five destroyers, stayed to the west of Crete in case the Italian fleet emerged. A relay was established over the next few days, with ships returning to Alexandria to replenish, while others took their place.

As soon as news of the airborne invasion reached Alexandria on 20 May, Cunningham ordered his task-forces to prepare to sweep the Aegean again that night. His heavy group, now based on the battleship *Warspite*, remained to the west of Crete. To the east of the island, the destroyers *Jervis*, *Nizam* and *Ilex* went to bombard Skarpanto airfield, which the VIII Air Corps used as a base for Dornier 17s and about fifty of its Stukas.

During the morning of 21 May, the groups of ships seeking safer waters after their night sweep in the Aegean found themselves heavily attacked. Rear-Admiral Glennie with the cruisers *Dido*, *Orion* and *Ajax* and four destroyers faced bombing attacks over four hours. They were extremely fortunate to escape with little damage. Admiral King's force to the east lost the destroyer *Juno* which was hit by three bombs at once. The ship listed and broke in half. The bow rose vertically then sank, all in less than two minutes. A petty officer suffered appalling burns as he swam into an expanse of hot oil to rescue a seaman. The destroyer *Nubian* picked up most of the survivors.

At dusk, three of Cunningham's task-forces steamed back into the Aegean. Signals intelligence had identified the convoy and its course from Milos to Maleme. Following the rules to protect 'most secret sources', Admiral Cunningham had sent a single Maryland aircraft out to make a 'chance sighting' of the flotilla, which it duly picked up in the afternoon. The two cruiser squadrons were greatly helped by a lower-grade version of signals interception than Ultra, each flagship having a 'Y officer' on board. Rear Admiral Glennie later claimed that his best way of keeping track of the other British squadron was through sightings reported in German wireless traffic.

Glennie's Force D, using radar, closed on the First Light Ships' Group some eighteen miles north of Canea. Glennie in HMS *Dido* had two other cruisers, *Orion* and *Ajax*, and four destroyers, *Janus*, *Kimberley*, *Hasty* and *Hereward*. At 11.30 p.m., *Janus* signalled a warning to the flagship. Captain H.W. McCall of HMS *Dido* gave the order 'On searchlights!' The beams revealed the Italian light destroyer *Lupo*, freshly painted and flying the Italian ensign. The *Lupo* did not abandon its charges, and steamed with great bravery past the cruisers firing torpedoes at them. The cruisers immediately turned to starboard 'to comb the tracks, and close and engage' the *Lupo*. *Dido* scored two hits, then *Ajax* blasted the *Lupo* with a broadside at close range.

For the mountain troops on the caiques, the sound of heavy marine engines, then the searchlights on the *Lupo* followed by the devastatingly brief fight, was a terrifying experience. Some soldiers had the presence of mind to haul down sails to reduce their profile. (They were still at sea during the dangerous hours of darkness because the wind had failed during the day.) Men hid irrationally below the level of the gunwales, as if planks of wood could protect them from the warships' guns. Yet it was the fingers of blinding white light which inspired the greatest fear.

The twenty-inch searchlights of the cruisers soon picked out the caiques. German soldiers stood up and began waving handkerchiefs and white towels in surrender. The captain of *Dido* gave the order to fire. According to one eyewitness (a yeoman of signals on the bridge), the commander protested that to open fire on unarmed caiques would be murder, but the captain pushed him aside to shout the order down the speaking-tube himself: 'Guns, open fire!' Perhaps he remembered the German dive-bombing of a hospital ship, to whose aid *Dido* had sailed during the evacuation from Greece. All the ship's light armament — Oerlikons, pom-poms and Hotchkiss's — opened up.

Using radar, the destroyers hunted down any caiques which tried to escape their searchlights. As the destroyers twisted and turned after their prey, like wolfhounds amongst dazed and helpless rabbits, this confusion nearly led to collisions. All this time gunnery officers

1. Greek troops on the Albanian front, winter 1940

2. John Pendlebury aiming with his glass eye

3. The German invasion of Greece, April 1941

4. Generals Blamey, Wilson and Freyberg in Greece, April 1941

Captain
Michael Forrester
M.C.

Crete, May 1941

5.   Captain Michael Forrester, drawn by Patrick Leigh Fermor
when staying with Prince Peter of Greece

6. Soldiers of the 5th Mountain Division emplaning in Greece before flying to Maleme

7. Mountain troops on a caique heading for Crete

8.   German paratroopers landed in a Cretan vineyard

9. The paratroop drop at Heraklion, taken by Lt Hope-Morley

10. Suda Bay after an air attack

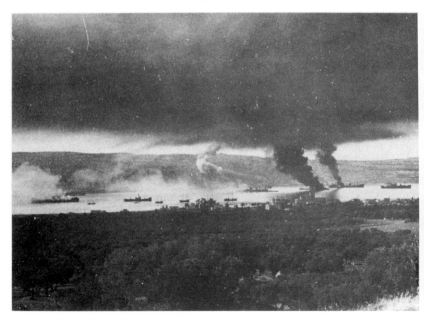

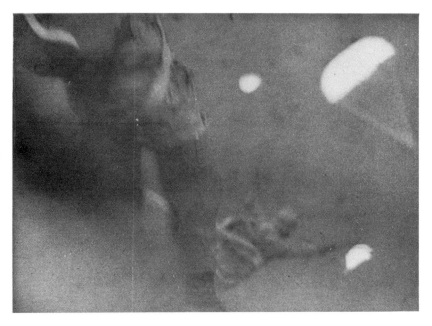

11. Jumping out in 'the crucifix' position
12. Leaping from a Junkers 52 over Crete

13. Colonel Bruno Bräuer with cigarette-holder at Heraklion

14. The HQ of the 14th Infantry Brigade on the last day
(by Patrick Leigh Fermor)

15. New Zealanders captured by Ramcke Group near Canea

16. General Student inspects Italian troops with General Carta

17. Manoli Bandouvas and bodyguards

18. Patrick Leigh Fermor in the Amari valley, spring 1943

19. Manoli Paterakis with his Marlin sub-machine gun

20. Taking General Kreipe *(second from the front)* over the top of
Mount Ida to avoid German patrols

screamed themselves hoarse with fire orders for the main armament. Machine guns and pom-poms fired ceaselessly at any target that presented itself whether caique, lifeboat, rubber dinghy or even, according to German sources, groups of men in their life-jackets either swimming in the water or clinging to spars. Cunningham's report states that the engagement lasted for two and a half hours. No mention is made of the depth-charges, which according to British rumour although not German accusation, were used to kill soldiers in the water with shock-waves. Despite all this gunfire only 327 men were killed: the rest were picked up by German vessels and Arado seaplanes in the morning well after Glennie's ships had left the area.

A single caique reached Crete unharmed. Early in the voyage, the Greek crew had abandoned ship, so the soldiers took over. This caique became separated from the rest and reached Cape Spatha to the west of Maleme with its full complement of 3 officers and 110 men. The only other soldiers from the convoy to reach the coast of Crete landed in a cutter on the unfriendly shore of the Akrotiri where a fighting patrol from the Northumberland Hussars soon cornered them.

At Creforce Headquarters, the tension leading up to the engagement had been intense. Just before 11.30 p.m., a runner arrived from Captain Micky Sandford, the Australian intelligence officer who decoded each Ultra signal, showing the message to Freyberg and then destroying it. That night Sandford's signals group above the quarry was listening in to radio traffic at sea. The Royal Navy had located the convoy and was about to engage. Coastal defence batteries were also ready to fire. The heaviest were the two pairs of 6-inch guns manned by the Sherwood Rangers Yeomanry, B Battery at Khelevis at the entrance to Suda Bay, and Y Battery on the top of St John's Hill, behind Canea. Their contribution was not needed.

'Suddenly', wrote Geoffrey Cox, 'on the horizon away to the north came the flash and thunder of guns, and the dull red glow of burning vessels.' Freyberg and his staff officers watched in great excitement. David Hunt remembers Freyberg 'bouncing up and down' at the destruction of the caiques with schoolboy enthusiasm, then addressing him by his Christian name for the first time.

Cox happened to notice Colonel Stewart make 'some remark to Freyberg which I did not hear. But I heard his reply. "It has been a great responsibility. A great responsibility." His tones conveyed the deep thankfulness of a man who had discharged well a nightmarishly difficult task. His comment indicated, I believe, that he felt now the island was reasonably safe.'

Freyberg and most of his staff then went to bed. 'I for one', added Cox, 'climbed into my sleeping bag with a feeling of profound thankfulness – indeed almost of disappointment that it had all been over so quickly.' Before going off to sleep, Freyberg did not even ask for news of progress on the counter-attack preparations for Maleme. He clearly thought the battle was as good as won.

General Freyberg's behaviour that night entirely contradicts the revisionist theory that although he knew that Maleme was the key to the battle, the secrecy rules surrounding Ultra frustrated him. Freyberg was a very brave and greatly liked man, but unimaginative. Having grasped the wrong idea about the 'seaborne invasion' he could not let go.

His fundamental misunderstanding still permeated defence orders even after the reality of the situation had become clear next morning. Officers and soldiers of the Sherwood Rangers manning the 6-inch guns on St John's Hill found it 'torture to watch the fat cluster of Germans on Maleme aerodrome enjoying comparative peace' over the next two days. The battery commander sought permission to traverse their guns and engage the airfield, but this was refused on the grounds that coastal artillery was strictly for defence against sea invasion. Only in the early hours of 24 May, two days after the destruction of the convoy, were they told that they could engage enemy concentrations to the west. By then Maleme was far behind enemy lines, and the Germans were within five kilometres of Canea.

14
Disaster by Land and by Sea
22 May

At one o'clock in the morning of 22 May, when the counter-attack on Maleme was due to cross its start-line, nobody at Creforce Headquarters seems to have been aware that the timetable of troop movements had already collapsed.

The plan for this counter-attack had first been discussed by field telephone towards the end of the morning of 21 May, before the first troop-carriers landed on the airfield. There were signs that the Germans intended to thrust north from Lake Ayia in Prison Valley to cut off Hargest's 5th Brigade round Platanias from Kippenberger's 10th Brigade at Galatas.

Little more was done until mid-afternoon, when Freyberg summoned a conference at Creforce Headquarters to ensure that the Australian 2/7th Battalion from Georgioupolis replaced the 20th Battalion guarding the coast. He also signalled Cairo to ask for a bombing raid on Maleme airfield that night, but his request must have arrived too late. A fairly ineffectual mission was flown the following night instead.

The final decision on the counter-attack was taken at about six o'clock in the evening. Nobody appears to have argued that two battalions were now insufficient against an enemy reinforced with troop-carriers landing every few minutes. Nor did anyone question the timetable or Freyberg's insistence that the 20th Battalion must not be allowed to move forward until the whole of the Australian battalion had arrived.

Vasey, the Australian brigade commander from Georgioupolis, was taken aback since he had planned to use the battalion to clear the road to Rethymno and join up with Campbell's force there. However, he felt he had no alternative but to obey the order, and said nothing either of the difficulty of assembling sufficient lorries in daylight under the eyes of enemy pilots, or of the hazards of a night move. The commanding officer of the 2/7th Battalion voiced his concern after the meeting, but Brigadier Inglis dismissed it with the ill-considered remark that 'a well-trained battalion could carry out such a relief in an hour.'

General Puttick returned to his divisional headquarters and, deciding that he should stay there ready for the seaborne assault on Canea, sent his chief of staff, Colonel Gentry, to brief Hargest at his headquarters. On the way Gentry collected Major Peck, who commanded the squadron from the 3rd Hussars, and Lieutenant Roy Farran, whose troop was also to take part in the action.

They reached the 5th Brigade's headquarters, a peasant farmhouse on the edge of Platanias. Farran later described Hargest as 'a red, open-faced man, who looked like a country farmer: it was obvious that he was suffering from acute fatigue. He asked us to wait half an hour while he had some sleep. Disgusted, intolerant, we sat on the steps until he was ready.'

Gentry recorded later that 'no doubts were expressed about the plan . . . It was clearly recognised that success depended on the attack being carried out under the mantle of darkness.' Yet though Creforce Headquarters had fixed the start of the advance for one o'clock in the morning, the attack was not due to begin until four. This left less than three hours of darkness in which to defeat a superior enemy force. If the Australians arrived late to replace the 20th Battalion, then the mantle of darkness would be scanty indeed.

Meanwhile, observation posts from 4th Brigade headquarters continued to watch seawards and detachments from the 18th and 20th Battalions continued to patrol the beaches to the west of Canea. The commanding officer of the 20th, understandably anxious about the delay to the counter-attack and having seen the convoy engaged by the Royal Navy at sea, rang twice to see if he had to wait any longer, but was firmly told to stay until the whole of the Australian battalion was in position before his men moved out.

The Australians made great efforts: their lead company drove along the twisting and badly maintained road from Georgioupolis as fast as possible while trying to ignore the Messerschmitts. Subsequent companies, however, had to wait longer for their vehicles to assemble, and they seem to have had less adventurous drivers. Confusion when trying to cross Canea led to long delays. The result was that the 20th Battalion was not finally relieved until after 11.30 p.m., when the battle at sea commenced. As a result, the 20th Battalion did not begin to join the Maoris on the start-line just beyond Platanias until nearly three o'clock in the morning. The advance from Platanias finally began at 3.30 a.m., two and a half hours late. The attack on Pirgos and the airfield could not now start until after dawn. This not only exposed them to air attack, it also lost them another advantage: throughout the battle the Germans had shown a marked dislike of night operations.

With the 20th Battalion spread between the coast road and the sea, Farran's tanks on the road itself and the 28th (Maori) Battalion to the left of the road, the main attack consisted of an advance up the coastal strip towards the airfield. (Farran later commented that Hargest's plan had 'the merits of simplicity if nothing else'.) At the same time, the 21st Battalion south-west of Kondomari was trying to punch round behind Hill 107.

However simple the plan, the advance was soon held up on the right when the 20th Battalion encountered in vineyards and isolated farmhouses pockets of paratroopers left over from the drop of the day before. To save time, and avoid further confusion in the dark, the New Zealanders charged head-on. Lieutenant Charles Upham, who won the first of his two Victoria Crosses during the battle, observed: 'The amount of MG fire was never equalled. Fortunately a lot of it was high and the tracer bullets enabled us to pick our way up and throw in grenades. We had heavy casualties but the Germans had much heavier. They were unprepared. Some were without trousers, some had no boots on.'

The Maoris on the left met less resistance to begin with, but then they ran into strongly held positions. Soon two of Farran's light tanks were out of action, one hit by a captured Bofors, the other with a broken sprocket. Farran refused to let the third one go on alone. It was by then after dawn and German fighters had already appeared to strafe the attackers. Except along the right-hand side closest to the beach, where D Company of the 20th Battalion pushed on, the attack ground to a halt in bitter fighting round Pirgos, two kilometres short of the airfield.

D Company, now commanded by Lieutenant Maxwell, the only unscathed subaltern, reached the eastern corner of the airfield. One private, frustrated at having carried an anti-tank rifle for such a distance without a chance to use it, fired twice at one of the damaged

Junkers which littered the perimeter. But with Colonel Ramcke's paratroopers concentrating their mortars and machine guns on his exposed survivors, Maxwell pulled them back into one of the cane-brakes of fifteen-foot high bamboo which swayed in the slipstream of strafing Messerschmitts. However, the limited cover gave too little protection and, misunderstanding a message brought by runner, Maxwell ordered his men all the way back to the start-line.

While the 20th Battalion and the Maori 28th Battalion were blocked, even after magnificently brave fighting, the 21st Battalion on the extreme southern flank made some headway against the mountain troops during the course of the morning, but it could not continue alone. By afternoon, failure had become all too clear. The New Zealanders were exhausted by their efforts.

The Germans, clearing wrecked Junkers 52 troop-carriers from the runway with frenetic energy, managed to land another two fresh battalions of mountain troops on the airfield at a rate of twenty troop-carriers an hour.*

Brigadier Hargest demonstrated an astonishing capacity for self-delusion, reporting to divisional headquarters: 'Steady flow of enemy planes landing and taking off. May be trying to take troops off. Investigating.' He then followed later with: 'From general quietness and because eleven fires have been lit on drome it appears as though enemy might be preparing evacuation.' These extraordinary reports, just the sort of rumour which soldiers long to believe after a heavy fight, slipped out. The New Zealanders would be cruelly undeceived.

The day also brought disaster at sea for the Royal Navy. Admiral Cunningham in Alexandria was still determined that no troop-transports should reach Crete. Well before dawn, Rear Admiral King's Force C steamed into the dangerous waters of the Aegean from the east through the Kaso strait. Cunningham was prepared to take this risk because signals intelligence had revealed the departure of the second flotilla from Milos, delayed by the late arrival of their escort, the *Sagittario*.

King's squadron of three cruisers and four destroyers first made for Heraklion, then turned north-north-east for Milos along the second flotilla's intended course. Soon after 8.30 a.m., a caique was

---

* The next day Ultra signal OL 20/424 reported, 'Yesterday, Thursday, one unit lost 14 aircraft out of 46. Another had at least 37 aircraft unserviceable out of 46'.

sighted with German soldiers on board. (How it had become entirely detached from the rest of the convoy is still not clear.) The Australian cruiser *Perth* sank the caique, temporarily saving itself from air attack. The pilots of the Junkers 88s overhead could not risk near misses which would kill German soldiers in the water with shock-waves. The cruiser HMS *Naiad* attracted their attention instead, but once the *Perth* was well clear of the swimmers, the bombers changed their aim again.

The cruiser *Calcutta* sighted a small merchant vessel half an hour later. After this had been dealt with by the destroyers, King's squadron steamed on towards Milos. Soon after ten o'clock, and less than twenty-five miles from the island, the *Sagittario* was sighted with a brood of caiques. They turned to escape and the *Sagittario* laid a smoke-screen. But King at this point came to the difficult decision to withdraw, not pursue. His ships were already low on anti-aircraft ammunition, they were under constant attack from the air, and the enemy had been scared off from the attempt to land troops.

Cunningham, having taken the risk, was exasperated by this missed opportunity. He later insisted that the safest place during an air attack would have been in among the flotilla of caiques. But this safety, as the *Perth* had discovered, was only temporary. A rash commander might well have led the whole squadron to disaster.

Despite Admiral King's caution, the squadron suffered. *Naiad* was damaged by near misses, her speed reduced to sixteen knots, and the cruiser *Carlisle* was hit. Force C, after three and half hours of attack, eventually met Rear Admiral Rawlings's Force A1, with the battleships *Warspite* and *Valiant*, coming through the Kithera channel to its assistance. This attempt to serve 'a useful purpose by attracting enemy aircraft' was gallant but ill-advised. A bomb struck *Warspite*, then fifty minutes later the destroyer *Greyhound*, which had just sunk a large caique, went down after a heavy air attack. Admiral King, now the senior officer in the area, ordered *Kandahar* and *Kingston* to pick up survivors. He then sent the cruisers *Gloucester* and *Fiji* to give them anti-aircraft support without realizing that they were very short of ammunition.

Such a concentration of virtually stationary ships brought wave after wave of German bombers and fighters whose pilots did not shrink from machine-gunning survivors in lifeboats or in the water. King, told of the shortage of ammunition, instructed the two cruisers to withdraw. On their way back, *Gloucester* was hit by several bombs within view of *Warspite*. On fire, with her superstructure twisted into grotesque shapes, *Gloucester* was doomed. King and Rawlings in *Warspite* agreed that the battle-fleet should not be put at risk any longer. *Fiji* too was forced to accept that she must leave *Gloucester*, which the Luftwaffe did not allow to sink in peace. Her crew was also machine-gunned and bombed in the water. Altogether 722 officers and ratings from the ship lost their lives.

Air attacks continued as Force C and Force A1 withdrew to the south-west. Two bombs hit the battleship *Valiant*, in which Sub-Lieutenant Prince Philip of Greece was serving. Then, two hours later, at 6.45 p.m., a Messerschmitt 110 suddenly appeared out of a cloud and dropped its bomb on *Fiji*. The damage brought the cruiser to a halt. Thirty minutes later at last light another aircraft appeared, a Junkers 88 flown by Lieutenant Gerhard Brenner on his fourth mission of the day. Brenner, who had taken part in the attack on the *Perth* south-east of Milos and, after skirting the *Warspite*, in an unsuccessful attack on the *Fiji*, had set out alone on her trail once more. He dropped three bombs and the *Fiji* capsized. Over five hundred of her crew, most of them clinging to life-rafts, spent several hours in the water that night. Eventually, two large shapes appeared, *Kandahar* and *Kingston*, and survivors were hauled aboard on scramble-nets.

In the course of a day, the Mediterranean Fleet had suffered two cruisers and one destroyer sunk, and two battleships, two cruisers and several destroyers damaged. Just after dark, Rawlings was ordered to dispatch two of his remaining destroyers, *Decoy* and *Hero*, to the south coast of Crete on a special mission.

The remark of General Wavell's ADC, Peter Coats, that King George of the Hellenes escaped from Crete 'like Jesus Christ, on a donkey though wearing a tin hat', was not strictly accurate. In full service dress with medal ribbons, Sam Browne and highly polished riding boots, but without a steel helmet, he had ridden a mule for much of the way across the mountains. Rather embarrassingly, his mule attracted the amorous interest of another, which caused some alarm since its abnormally pale coat risked catching the eye of a German pilot.

As the party toiled high into the White Mountains, out of touch with events while bombs and guns still detonated in the distance, the King's cheerful stoicism impressed both the New Zealanders guarding him and also his entourage – Prince Peter, Tsouderos and Levidis, whose city shoes were ill-suited to the journey.

On their first night, 20 May, the royal party had slept at Therisso, ironically Venizelos's headquarters in the revolt of 1905. Colonel Blunt had found a telephone line working to Suda Bay, and heard from the naval staff there that the Commander-in-Chief Mediterranean would arrange for a destroyer to collect the King's party and senior members of the British Legation from Ay Roumeli. (The King was given the rather obvious code-name of Timon.)

The night of 21 May, their second in the mountains, was very cold. They were above the snowline when dusk fell and only through sheer good luck found a shepherd's hut. The shepherd and his wife killed a sheep and milked some ewes for them, enough to sustain them during the freezing night which followed. The descent to Samaria the next day – the third of their journey – was hazardous, and they reached the village with relief. There, a boy handed them a note from Sir Michael Palairet, who was waiting for them five miles along the coast at Ay Roumeli. The young messenger returned at top speed to the Legation party, clearly relishing his role in the drama. 'The King is coming! The King is coming!' he cried out. Lady Palairet promptly organized a meal of potatoes.

After the King's arrival and the meal, the enlarged group moved down to the seafront. It was now nightfall and, looking back towards the north, they could see flashes in the sky over the mountains from the battle on the other side of the island.

On a rudimentary jetty, hardly more than a few rocks joined together, Admiral Turle self-importantly signalled seawards with a hand torch. An inter-service rivalry of sublime pettiness had been simmering between him and General Heywood over the proper command of the Legation party in a theatre of war. In the end, Heywood had retained this purely nominal command as far as Sphakia, but as soon as they had embarked in a dilapidated fishing launch to sail round to Ay Roumeli, the Senior Service had taken precedence.

Admiral Turle's attempts with the torch proved fruitless. The tantalizing lights far out in the Libyan Sea ignored his stream of Morse, and tempers became strained. Harold Caccia considered the torch hopelessly inadequate for the task. Eventually, as the youngest male non-combatant, he was told to take the launch out to sea to find the destroyer, but his diplomatic immunity was rather compromised when Heywood insisted that one of the New Zealanders armed with a Thompson sub-machine gun should accompany him.

As they left the shore far behind, the owner of the boat became increasingly alarmed. He warned Caccia that they would run out of fuel, but just as he insisted on turning back an unmistakable ward-room voice bellowed out of the darkness: 'Who the bloody hell are you?' HMS *Decoy* had found them. Her captain had not wanted to go closer in because the uncertain reports of the battle made him cautious of a German ambush. Within an hour, the party and the platoon of New Zealanders were embarked and bedded down as comfortably as the cramped space allowed. The destroyer turned round to head south-east.

Next morning, 23 May, the royal evacuees, with emotions straight out of Hornblower, looked through portholes to see the battle-fleet including the *Valiant* with Prince Philip of Greece on board. They were all returning to Alexandria together. Unknown to them, another relative, Prince Philip's 'Uncle Dicky', was at that time following on behind, his three destroyers under heavy air attack.

The 5th Destroyer Flotilla under Captain Lord Louis Mountbatten in HMS *Kelly* had left Malta on the night of 21 May just as Glennie's ships engaged the caiques north of Canea. Cunningham had realized from signals intelligence that the delay to the second group of caiques would impose a much greater strain on his forces. Mountbatten's destroyers were replenished and his crews fresh, and Malta was little further from Cretan waters than Alexandria.

Designated to join the battle-fleet, Mountbatten's flotilla was first diverted to pick up survivors from *Fiji* and *Gloucester*. But as they approached the areas of search, Cunningham ordered the five destroyers into the Bay of Canea where they engaged two caiques and shelled Maleme airfield. *Kipling* had had to turn back with steering problems, and *Kelvin* and *Jackal* were diverted on another search. Mountbatten, with only three destroyers, returned round the western coast of Crete in the early morning of 23 May. Cunningham, prompted by a mistaken message that the battleships had run out of anti-aircraft ammunition, but also reassured by signals intelligence that there would be no further attempt to transport troops, ordered the recall of all warships to Alexandria.

Just before eight o'clock, twenty-four Stukas attacked in series. Mountbatten's three destroyers began zigzagging at maximum speed. '*Kashmir* was hit and sank in two minutes,' ran Cunningham's dispatch. '*Kelly* was doing thirty knots, under full starboard rudder, when she was hit by a large bomb. The ship took up an ever-increasing list to port, finally turning turtle with considerable way on.'

The dive-bombers machine-gunned survivors in the water, then left. *Kipling* began rescue work, but twin-engined bombers arrived overhead and their attacks, although unsuccessful, made the task difficult. *Kipling* miraculously survived eighty-three bombs and managed to pick up from the water 279 officers and men. Fifty miles short of Alexandria, she ran out of fuel and had to be rescued.

In spite of the heroic aura surrounding this engagement – mainly inspired by Noël Coward's film, *In Which We Serve* – Mountbatten's performance as a destroyer commander has generally been regarded as indifferent, though he was later to prove an excellent commander-in-chief. In any case, Mountbatten appears to have recovered rapidly from his ordeal, to judge by the letter Crown Princess Frederica wrote to her aunt, the Crown Princess of Sweden, from Alexandria after they all met up: 'Palo and I met Dicky here after he had been sunk for the fourth time in this war. He seemed very well and cheerful.'

Although 22 May was a disastrous day for the defenders of Crete, an unusually heartening episode occurred at Galatas. After the furious attacks against Pink Hill on the first day of the battle, Colonel Heidrich held his 3rd Parachute Regiment in defensive positions along Prison Valley until they were resupplied by parachute – almost 300 containers altogether. There they rested and reorganized during 21 May. One of Heydte's platoons, dug in on a small hill across the valley from Daratsos, played dance music on a captured gramophone. And when one of the desultory exchanges of fire with the Australians opposite carried on for longer than usual, one of the paratroopers shouted from his trench, 'Wait a moment while I change the record!'

The 3rd Parachute Regiment, too weak to launch a major attack as Student hoped, expected a large-scale counter-attack at any moment: Colonel Heidrich later said that it would have put his formation 'completely in the cart'. But on 21 May there was only a small push by the New Zealanders to force an advance outpost off Cemetery Hill. Roy Farran, whose troop of light tanks had been sent to support the 19th Battalion for this action, went to report to the commanding officer only to find him trying to pot a sniper. After several shots the German tumbled from a tree, and the colonel handed the rifle to his adjutant. 'Well, that's that', he said. 'That joker has been causing trouble all morning.' He gave Farran his instructions: the tanks were there to keep the paratroopers' heads down while a company of infantry slipped in close. The attack began after midday, but although the infantry platoons killed several Germans in a fierce fight and chased the rest off the hill, they were exposed to mortar and machine-gun fire from paratroopers in the valley. Cemetery Hill, appropriately enough, became a no-man's land.

While the battle for Cemetery Hill went on, Michael Forrester had been training his two hundred Greeks – the remnants of the 6th Regiment rallied by Captain Bassett – in Galatas, protected by John Russell's Divisional Cavalry. Since few had any experience of military manoeuvres, instructions were kept simple, and to avoid any language difficulties he instituted a series of whistle signals – one blast: stand-by; two: move; three: deploy; four: charge. He suggested that when the moment of attack came, they should yell 'Aiera!', the battle-cry which he had heard the Evzones use on the Albanian front. When he instructed his Greek recruits, Forrester found that villagers would sidle up to learn what they could about basic fieldcraft and tactics.

By the morning of 22 May, Colonel Heidrich realized that the New Zealanders on the heights of Galatas and Daratsos were not going to launch an attack. He reorganized his much reduced III Battalion and the parachute engineers into fighting patrols, and sent them northwards towards the coast to probe behind Hargest's 5th Brigade at Platanias, as Hargest had begun to fear the day before.

Meanwhile, to test Hargest's theory that the Germans were bringing in troop-carriers to evacuate their troops rather than reinforce them, General Puttick told Kippenberger to send out fighting patrols along his front. Kippenberger took this as an excuse to order the 19th Battalion to advance right down and across the valley. A vigorous response, which forced Kippenberger's companies to withdraw, disproved Hargest's fancy, but the idea still lingered.

Colonel Heidrich, at his headquarters in the prison, now felt that with reinforcements soon to arrive from Maleme he must again attempt to push the New Zealanders off the heights of Galatas. He summoned Major Derpa, the commander of the II Battalion, and gave him the order to attack.

Derpa foresaw the unnecessary loss of life and expressed his doubts. This provoked Heidrich, 'whose nerves were stretched to breaking point', into a rage. He accused him of cowardice. Derpa was a 'sensitive and chivalrous' man according to Captain von der Heydte. He went pale with outrage, then drew himself up and saluted. 'It is not a question of my own life, sir,' protested Derpa. 'I am considering the lives of the soldiers for whom I am responsible. My own life I would give gladly.'

At about seven o'clock that evening, Derpa's paratroopers attacked the heights from Cemetery Hill to Pink Hill. One group of his men reached the summit of Pink Hill, forcing back the Petrol Company. Since Pink Hill was crucial to the whole of the 10th Brigade's position, this represented a dangerous situation. But before Kippenberger's reserves were in a position to help, he suddenly heard 'a most infernal uproar'. One of the drivers with Kippenberger described the scene. Out of an olive grove on the adjoining hill, 'came Captain Forrester, clad in shorts, a long yellow army jersey, brass polished and gleaming, web belt in place and waving his revolver in his right hand. He was tall, thin-faced, fair-haired, with no tin hat. It was a most inspiring sight. Forrester was at the head of a crowd of disorderly Greeks, including women; one Greek had a shot gun with a serrated-edge bread knife tied on like a bayonet.'

Forrester's commands blown on his service whistle inspired the brigade major, Captain Bassett, to describe him as 'tootling a tin whistle like a Pied Piper', a fanciful image taken literally in later years by war comics. 'Over an open space', continued Kippenberger, 'came running, bounding and yelling like Red Indians, Greeks and villagers including women and children, led by Michael Forrester twenty yards ahead. It was too much for the Germans. They turned and ran without hesitation.' In spite of orders to stand fast, members of the Petrol Company joined this sudden, exhilarating surge.

Forrester's leadership evoked great admiration amongst New Zealanders, who tended to depict British officers as characters out of P.G. Wodehouse. CSM James of the Petrol Company said 'he was one of the coolest men I have ever met'. And a captain described watching this charge as the most thrilling moment of his life.

Furious fighting also went on in front of the Divisional Cavalry's position. Among the German casualties was Major Derpa, mortally wounded. His men dug a grave for him next morning adjacent to a small Greek cemetery near the prison. Paratroopers in Heidrich's regiment believed that had Derpa survived 'he would have been summoned to court martial'.*

---

* Colonel Heidrich's war ended in Italy after a patrol from the 3rd Battalion of the Grenadier Guards surprised him in a bush with his trousers down. However, he nearly managed to turn the tables on his captors. When interrogated by Lieutenant Nigel Nicolson, the intelligence officer, he began a discussion about the relative merits of British and German weapons. Heidrich, apparently to illustrate a point, asked the sentry to pass him his Thompson sub-machine gun. The guardsman moved to obey until Nicolson shouted at him to stop. Heidrich smiled.

On that evening of 22 May, Freyberg came to the decision to withdraw Hargest's 5th Brigade from the front opposite Maleme to Galatas. Freyberg, influenced by Hargest's notion that the Germans were pulling out and also by unjustifiably optimistic accounts of the counter-attack on Maleme, had not fully appreciated the gravity of the situation until the afternoon. Hargest's fears that his brigade would be cut off by Colonel Heidrich's probing attacks up towards the coast road convinced him that withdrawal had now become inevitable.

Freyberg had gone to bed sixteen hours before in the belief that the battle had been won. He was now plunged into pessimism by what struck him as an unexpected turn-around. As a result he does not seem to have considered his options properly. Withdrawal to Galatas meant conceding Maleme airfield to the enemy, and thus ultimate defeat – either an early surrender, or a protracted fight involving unnecessary loss of life, or retreat over the mountains to the south, followed by an evacuation far riskier than that from Greece. Even without knowing the Royal Navy's losses of that day, Captain Morse would have advised him that the forces in the Suda–Canea sector were too numerous to evacuate from the north coast.

His only other alternative – and there was nothing to lose in strategic terms – was attack: but an all-out attack in superior strength, not another doomed gesture of too little too late. The convoy had been destroyed. He had three uncommitted battalions near Canea – the New Zealand 18th Battalion, the Australian 2/7th, and the Welch Regiment, the strongest of them all. Had they joined the 23rd Battalion and the apparently inexhaustible Maoris of Hargest's brigade, together with the remaining tanks, and had they attacked in the full knowledge that this was their last chance to hold Crete, the effect could have been electrifying. That they were capable of such a feat was demonstrated with astonishing bravery at Galatas three days later. But by then the Germans had landed the whole of the 5th Mountain Division.

Creforce Headquarters instead issued the order for withdrawal. Underneath a burly exterior, Freyberg was curiously soft-hearted, not at all the sort of First World War general who did not care about the 'butcher's bill'. He did not want to be remembered as the general who had thrown away the New Zealand Division. Next day, Friday, 23 May, mountain troops who had landed at Maleme made contact with patrols from Heidrich's force in the Ayia valley. A German victory was now assured.

15
Stalemate at Rethymno and Heraklion
21–26 May

If events at Maleme had followed the pattern at Rethymno and Heraklion, then the Germans would have lost the battle of Crete.

At Rethymno, where Campbell and Sandover demonstrated the necessary virtue of rapid counter-attack, the 2nd Parachute Regiment never had a chance to organize. To make matters worse, neither Kroh's group, barricaded in the olive oil factory at Stavromenos, nor Wiedemann's, dug in round Perivolia, had a wireless. Attempts to drop them one, then to land one by a Fieseler Storch light aircraft, all failed. They were also short of food. A goat unwise enough to show itself near the olive oil factory was soon butchered and cooked with sea water in ammunition boxes over a rapidly prepared fire.

The Australians had spent most of 21 May mopping up and reorganizing after the morning's successful counter-attack on Hill A. The 4th Greek Regiment advanced on the olive oil factory from the south, while the 5th Greek Regiment and Sandover's 2/11th Battalion turned on Wiedemann's group at Perivolia.

Sandover had not only benefited from the German operational order which he had translated in Colonel Sturm's presence; his men had also captured the instructions for ground-to-air communication with a quantity of the necessary flags and signal panels. His companies were therefore able to lay out the swastika flags and appropriate tapes to direct air strikes by German bombers and fighters on to their own troops, and call for resupply by parachute. The paratroopers, without any form of wireless contact with the mainland and reduced to writing messages in the sand, could do little to prevent this.

The olive oil factory with its thick walls proved a tougher fortress than Campbell had at first imagined. A co-ordinated attack on 22 May with the 2/1st Battalion and the 4th Greek Regiment failed because of linguistic confusion over the plan.

That night Sandover's 2/11th Battalion began to advance on Perivolia, with leap-frog attacks along the shore. But an unfortunate misunderstanding which had led to a clash between Greek and Australian troops on an earlier occasion prompted him to halt his companies short of the objective. The Greeks had swung round to the south, and with Cretan guerrillas, including the heavily armed monk, were harrassing Wiedemann's flank.

A virtual stalemate continued for several days at both Perivolia and Stavromenos until, on 25 May, Campbell's men suddenly captured the olive oil factory after a bombardment with the remaining shells from the field guns. But inside they found only German wounded. Major Kroh, and all men capable of walking, had escaped.

Meanwhile Sandover's men experienced some bloody fighting in attacks on Perivolia. They captured some of the outlying houses, but then the Germans blasted them with light anti-tank weapons. The two Matildas damaged in the early fighting near the airfield were repaired and, with improvised crews, driven back towards Perivolia for another night attack, but they were knocked out. Sandover came to the conclusion that, without heavy weapons, any more attacks would only lead to a waste of lives. In any case, the force at Rethymno had more than fulfilled their orders to deny the airfield and the port to the enemy.

At Heraklion, many of Colonel Bräuer's paratroopers were in a sorry state. Thirst on the first night led to dysentery from drinking stagnant water out of irrigation ditches. Some chewed vineleaves in a desperate attempt to find liquid. Many lost their lives in the search for water, picked off by Cretan irregulars who then armed themselves with their weapons. During the first forty-eight hours, the worst was reserved for those on their own, still lying wounded where they had fallen, dehydrated and at the mercy of armed Cretans, or in some cases British soldiers and officers.

Yet for the British and Australians, killing became less impersonal after the initial blood-letting. The faceless dangerous silhouettes who had descended from the sky began to take on human guise. A 17-year-old whimpering in fear, with a smashed leg, was no longer an aerial stormtrooper, but an overgrown child, even if he had come to kill. When soldiers were told to remove all papers from the dead, including poignant photographs of sweethearts and families, they felt curiously at one with their enemy, a long way from home on a foreign battlefield. By the nature of their profession, soldiers are apt to swing from violence to sentiment.

A tacit agreement became established between the opposing sides that, during the relative quiet of the night, rations, water and ammunition were distributed, the dead were buried, and casualties evacuated. But for the Cretans, this was not a foreign battlefield: it was their homeland, violated without justification. They were in no mood either for compassion or for surrender.

When Major Walther received orders from Colonel Bräuer to gather his men and march in from the east to relieve Blücher's men, cut off in the midst of the Black Watch on the hill south of the airfield, he discovered that one of his platoons, Lieutenant Lindenberg's, had been completely annihilated by Cretan civilians. Altogether he is said to have lost some 200 men from Cretan irregulars round Gournes where his battalion dropped.

The platoon of Lieutenant Count Wolfgang von Blücher began its final stand on 21 May, a drama which became a rich source of myth. For the rest of Walther's battalion, relieving their comrades in the midst of the Black Watch was more than just a point of honour. But the Scottish infantry was well dug in with unrestricted fields of fire.

In their small bowl in this rocky landscape south of the airfield, Blücher's platoon had tried to scrape trenches with helmets and fingers to escape the fire of Vickers machine guns, the odd mortar bomb and even a few shells from a Bofors firing from its sand-bagged position beside the end of the runway. Blücher and many of his men were wounded. The platoon, soon down to less than half its effective strength, ran out of field dressings and became very short of ammunition.

At that point, according to the story, a horseman was seen galloping towards them with ammunition boxes tied to his saddle. This spectacle caused amazement at first in Scottish ranks, then attracted their fire. But the rider and the horse were hit only as they reached the besieged platoon.

As the ammunition was passed rapidly around, the lieutenant asked how the rider was. He learned that the horseman was his 19-year-old brother, Leberecht, and that he was dead. Next morning, Wolfgang, the eldest of the three brothers, was killed along with the survivors of his platoon. The youngest brother, Hans-Joachim, was also killed, but his body was never found.*

Es starben den Heldentod auf Kreta unsere geliebten Söhne, Brüder, Enkel und Netten

der Ritterkreuzträger

Wolfgang Graf von Blücher
Oberleutnant in einem Fallschirmjägerregiment
im Alter von 24 Jahren

Leberecht Graf von Blücher
Gefreiter in einem Fallschirmjägerregiment
im Alter von 19 Jahren

Hans=Joachim Graf von Blücher
Jäger in einem Fallschirmjägerregiment
im Alter von 17 Jahren.

Darze, Post Stuer, in Mecklenburg
Posen und Altengottern, den 23. Juni 1941

Gertrud v. Nordheim, geb. Freiin Marschall,
    verw. Gräfin Blücher
Ludwig v. Nordheim, Gaulandwirt im
    Luftgau II
Elisabeth Gräfin v. Blücher
Adolf Graf v. Blücher, Leutnant zur See
Gertrud Gräfin v. Blücher
Richenza v. Nordheim
Wilhelmine Freifrau Marschall,
    geb. Gräfin Rittberg
Charlotte Freiin Marschall

The Blücher family's announcement of the three deaths

At Knossos, eight kilometres south of Heraklion, Manolaki Akoumianakis, who had been Sir Arthur Evans's chief assistant in the Minoan excavations, vowed to fight the parachutists after hearing that his eldest son Miki had been killed serving with the Cretan Division in Epirus. He sent his wife and other children to stay with relations in the mountains. And on receiving a message from John Pendlebury that the ridge opposite Knossos was vital, Manolaki Akoumianakis led a group of Greek soldiers and Cretans there. The Villa Ariadne, which had been turned into a British military hospital, came under mortar fire, but little damage was done either to the house or the site of Knossos itself.

Manolaki was the first killed in this attack against the paratroopers: he was about two hundred metres ahead of the Greek soldiers he had led there. Yet Miki, his son, was alive: the report had

---

* The most curious part of this story is that for many years poor families who lived in a shanty-village near the site, tending a few goats, claimed to have seen the ghost of a horse and rider, but they thought the ghost was that of a British officer.

been mistaken. Miki Akoumianakis returned to Crete not long afterwards and made a proper grave for his father in spite of the German edict forbidding the burial of any civilian killed bearing arms. Later, during the occupation, he took over the Allied intelligence network in Heraklion and became the key British agent in the region for the last three years of the war.

Jack Hamson, also on Pendlebury's orders and ignorant of his fate, continued to guard the small Plain of Nida on the eastern flank of Mount Ida against a landing by enemy gliders or troop-carriers. His hundred Cretan volunteers had grown restless on hearing the distant fighting round Heraklion. They wanted to go down to join the battle, yet Hamson felt obliged to exert what authority he had from Pendlebury to make them stay at their posts in case the Germans did try to land later in the battle. Starved of information as much as food, Hamson himself went down for supplies. He met Satanas at Kroussonas on the night of 24 May and heard of Pendlebury's death. Returning to the Plain of Nida, he felt less certain than ever that the Germans were going to land there but was still obliged to continue if only in memory of Pendlebury.

Major Schulz's battalion, after its withdrawal from within the city walls of Heraklion, remained hidden to the south and west. On 25 May they watched the heaviest bombing raid on the city. The destruction was terrible.

Schulz and his men received an order by wireless from Athens to swing on a long detour south-eastwards that night to join up with Colonel Bräuer. Schulz's men moved in small parties to avoid being seen, but this fragmented move inland risked attack. Several guerrilla groups belonging to Pendlebury's informal network, principally the bands of Petrakageorgis, Bandouvas and Satanas, inflicted heavy casualties. The Cretans were far better at night-fighting than either the British or the Germans.

The British and Australians at Heraklion had also watched the raid. Their feelings were divided between sorrow for the inhabitants and relief that they themselves were safely dispersed in their slit trenches. They had learned, like their counterparts at Rethymno, to confuse the pilots of the transport planes and bombers. They laid out captured swastika flags on their positions, stopped shooting and, when the Germans fired green Very lights, they did the same. On a number of occasions, captured recognition strips produced containers with weapons, ammunition, rations and medical supplies. Sets of surgical implements were parachuted, with true German practicality, in containers shaped like coffins to provide a second use. Two outstanding examples of this military manna from heaven were a pair of motor-cycles with side-cars, one dropped to Major Sir Keith Dick-Cunyngham's company of the Black Watch and the other to the Australian battalion on the Charlies. The Australians found themselves so well provided with German weapons that large quantities could be handed over to the less fortunate Greek troops.

The Black Watch had become used to seeing only German aircraft in the sky, and when a lone Hurricane had landed on the runway in the middle of an air raid on 23 May they were astonished. One historian compared its arrival to 'Noah's dove', but the pilot brought no promise of salvation. Six fighters had taken off from Egypt only to encounter heavy fire from Royal Navy vessels unused to finding friendly aircraft overhead. Two were shot down, and three more had to turn for home badly damaged. Another wave of six set out more successfully, but their long-range fuel tanks made them sluggish in combat. Only one aircraft out of the twelve survived. This belated attempt to provide air support was a thoroughly ill-considered gesture. Hurricanes had been needed earlier, operating from an airfield on the south coast properly established with fighter pens. The idea was not lacking, only the energy. On the day before this wasteful mission, Admiral Turle and General Heywood *en route* to Ay Roumeli had encountered a wing commander wandering in search of sites: as Turle pointed out, he was six months too late.

Despite the lack of air support, morale remained very high. Casualties equivalent to almost three parachute battalions had been inflicted on the first day and there was cockiness as well as bravery. During a dawn air raid Piper Macpherson from Lochgelly climbed out of his slit trench on the airfield to play reveille.

Brigadier Chappel has been criticized for not advancing against the severely reduced enemy to crush them, then marching to the aid of the New Zealand Division having cleared up Rethymno on the way. Chappel, although decisive on the first day, subsequently displayed little of the initiative Campbell and Sandover showed at Rethymno. Yet his caution is understandable: the 14th Infantry Brigade no longer had enough ammunition for a major engagement and Chappel had not had Sandover's stroke of luck in discovering how few reserves the Germans possessed.

Chappel had also overestimated the strength of Bräuer's force, because outer battalions sent in reports of large-scale reinforcements landing by parachute. These drops, which took place at too great a distance for their load to be identified, had consisted mainly of supplies. Since his orders had been to hold Heraklion and the airfield, he was reluctant to take risks by advancing outside his perimeter.

GHQ Middle East's plan to pass units along the coast was optimistic. The idea was for the Argylls on the south coast at Tymbaki to move to Heraklion, then a battalion from Heraklion to move to Rethymno and so on. This was all very well on a map back in Egypt (or in Creforce Headquarters, for Freyberg also favoured the plan), but it did not take into account the state of the roads, the possibility that harrassing attacks by German paratroopers might delay the Argylls' advance northwards — their leading company with two Matildas only arrived at midday on 23 May — or that the coast road remained firmly blocked at Rethymno by the parachute battalion strongly dug in at Perivolia. Freyberg had sent a company of the Rangers from Suda but, lacking heavy weapons, they had had no more success than Sandover's Australians. None of Chappel's force could ever have reached Canea in time to influence the course of events at Maleme. He sent the two newly arrived Matildas, another of his own and some field guns to Suda by lighter, but they arrived only in time to strengthen the rearguard during the withdrawal.

So stalemate set in at both Rethymno and Heraklion. Their garrisons, ignorant of the sequence of disasters at Maleme, assumed that they had only to hold on and the German invasion would die on its feet. Once again, the lack of wirelesses had proved a grave weakness.

16
The Battle of Galatas
23–25 May

When men of the New Zealand 5th Brigade were shaken awake by their NCOs early on the early morning of 23 May and told to prepare to withdraw, most refused to believe what they heard. Those not on sentry had dossed down the night before, certain that things were still going well. Even if they did not fully believe the rumour of the Germans pulling out the New Zealanders still thought they had given them such a bloody nose that they could not prevail.

'They all felt the same,' wrote Sandy Thomas, a young platoon commander with the 23rd Battalion. 'They had seen so many of the enemy dead that their morale was quite unshaken by the terrific air attacks by day. Man for man they considered that they could lick the German despite his superior weapons and equipment.'

Although less than five kilometres, the retreat from positions in front of Dhaskalania and Kondomari to Platanias was hard. Without any ambulances the wounded had to be brought back by tired men stumbling over rough ground. Some casualties were carried on doors, or crudely fashioned ladders found by farmhouses, others on improvised stretchers made out of a pair of rifles and two battledress jackets. Those too ill to move were left behind with the last medical officer in the brigade, Captain R.S. Stewart, and a chaplain to ensure that they were treated correctly by the enemy. Due to a growing shortage of ammunition on the island, ammunition boxes and spare grenades had to be taken as well as personal weapons and kit. Some companies had acquired a donkey to carry heavy equipment and weapons, but soldiers remained the main beasts of burden.

The Germans were quick to spot the retreat which was covered by a company of Maoris under Major H.G. Dyer. The Maoris could not have been a better choice. Their unconventional and alarming tactics of suddenly turning round for an unexpected bayonet charge would send the pursuing paratroopers back in a rush. Largely thanks to them, the withdrawal was completed that morning with very few casualties.

When Major General Ringel arrived, field command of all German troops passed to him. Ramcke's paratroopers, the reconstituted Storm Regiment, pushed along the coast using to great effect the mobile Bofors guns captured at Maleme. Two battalions of the 100th Mountain Regiment advanced in the centre over the coastal hills between the Ayia valley and the sea, while a battalion of the 85th Mountain Regiment swung round on the right. This unit of mountain troops, commanded by Major Treck, was intended to encircle the New Zealand Division from the south through the foothills of the White Mountains. Instead it encountered fierce resistance from the undervalued 8th Greek Regiment and indefatigably brave Cretan irregulars. It is probably no exaggeration to say that their sacrifice saved the New Zealand Division.

The Germans, in their advance along the coast and along the coastal hills, came across sights and smells they would never forget. For much of the way the terraces of vineyards and olive groves retained their classic Mediterranean beauty, but periodically the advancing troops would find pockets fouled by military occupation — slit trenches, latrines, ration tins and empty ammunition boxes.

As the sun rose, it strengthened the stench from black and swollen corpses covered by swarms of blow-flies. Corpses of fellow paratroopers from the first day still hung from their olive tree gibbets, shockingly macabre in the dappled light under the leaves. Some bodies, free of their harnesses, appeared from single bullet wounds in the head to have been shot after surrender. In almost all cases, the pockets of jumpsuits had been ripped open in the search for papers, or items such as flat metal boxes of Dextrosan energy tablets. Finally, a passing Cretan might have stripped the body of useful apparel, especially the boots since leather was already in short supply on the island. The paratroopers, eager for revenge, pressed on.

Not long after Hargest's 5th Brigade had established a new line west of Platanias, a duel of counter-battery fire broke out between the 95th Mountain Artillery Regiment and the surviving 75mm guns of various field troops, Australian, British and New Zealand. At the same time there were some fierce infantry skirmishes in the area of the Platanias bridge and north of the coast road along the beach where Ramcke's paratroopers pushed forward at every opportunity.

During the afternoon four RAF bombers appeared overhead on their way to bomb Maleme airfield. This raised morale but the attack, according to German sources, did only slight damage. There had been little contact with the enemy to the south of the coast road until late afternoon when it became clear that the II Battalion of the 85th Mountain Regiment was outflanking the severely reduced New Zealand battalions to cut them off from the Galatas position behind. Hargest and Puttick, who had long expected this to happen, prepared to pull the exhausted 5th Brigade back that night into reserve beyond Galatas and Daratsos.

By the next morning, when the 5th Brigade had made their second consecutive night withdrawal, the front line ran from Galatas to the sea. The tired and demoralized Composite Battalion of drivers, gunners, cooks and service corps personnel who had been manning this sector since the first day also had to be pulled back into reserve.

The 18th Battalion from Inglis's brigade took over the line. Kippenberger was heartened 'to see them come in – looking very efficient and battle-worthy – in painful contrast' to his 'unfortunate quasi-infantry'. But the 18th, only four hundred strong, had a two-kilometre front to hold. Russell Force, the survivors of the Divisional Cavalry and a group of the Petrol Company, all under the engaging John Russell, still held the southern exit from Galatas facing down towards Ayia prison.

Prison Valley had been relatively peaceful on 23 May, but clearly the lull was not to last. On the New Zealand side Kippenberger found the morning of Saturday, 24 May, 'ominously quiet', while on the German side, Heydte found it 'almost oppressive'. The men of his battalion were virtually out of ammunition, dehydrated – many suffering from dysentery – and severely under-nourished. 'The faces of some of them had grown taut, almost shrunken, their eyes lay deep in their sockets, and their beards, unshaven now for five days, accentuated the hollowness of their cheeks.' The members of one platoon, which had stood to arms when a sentry gave warning of noises in the bushes to their front, found themselves face to face with a stray donkey. The poor beast was shot as quickly as if it had been the enemy; its carcase was hauled in for butchering and roasting.

General Freyberg, meanwhile, learned from an Ultra signal that south of Maleme German motor-cycle detachments had advanced at least two-thirds of the way across the island. This force, the 55th Motor-Cycle Battalion armed with Spandau machine guns mounted on their side-cars, was advancing towards Paleokhora on the south coast to prevent reinforcements from Alexandria being landed there. An intercept reported them six miles north of Kandanos at midnight on 23 May, then the following day Ultra reported the same detachments held up by 'increasing British resistance'. Since there were no British troops in the area, the resistance was purely Cretan, and presumably included Father Stylianos Frantzekakis and those of his parishioners who were still alive after such savage fighting. They held this German force for two days; their success could be sadly measured later by the scale of reprisals at Kandanos.

Another German column, the 95th Mountain Engineer Battalion strengthened by a weak company of paratroopers, was sent on 24 May to Kastelli Kissamou where the unfortunate detachment of paratroopers under Lieutenant Mürbe had been dropped on the first day. The Germans could not possibly land their light tanks, a company from the 5th Panzer Division, anywhere along the Gulf of Canea, so Kastelli Kissamou, far from ideal because of the shallowness of the bay, offered the only hope.

Kastelli itself was defended by the 1st Greek Regiment and an advisory detachment of New Zealand officers and NCOs. They had wiped out Mürbe's men, except for twenty-eight survivors who had been taken prisoner. But on 24 May a Stuka attack to soften up the town as the mountain engineers arrived enabled a number of these prisoners to escape and rearm themselves. After some confused and bloody fighting – the Germans were convinced that Mürbe's men had been tortured and mutilated by civilians – the town was occupied by the following day. But the guerrilla resistance which continued was so fierce that tanks could not begin to land until 27 May. This delay of two days, achieved at a considerable cost in Cretan lives, was of inestimable help to Freyberg's force during its subsequent withdrawal when it had barely any anti-tank weapons left.*

In the afternoon of 24 May, following that oppressive morning described both by Kippenberger and Heydte, squadrons of the VIII Air Corps in relentless rotation carpet-bombed Canea. This technique had been developed by the Condor Legion under Richthofen in the

* Ultra signal OL 27/464 on the morning of 26 May reported the German intention to use it for disembarkation the next day.

Spanish Civil War, first outside Oviedo, then for the destruction of Durango and Guernica. It had a dual objective – to terrorize soldier and civilian alike and to block the roads of a communications centre behind the front line with masonry and debris. In Canea only the harbour front was left unharmed, because it would soon be useful. Thirteen Venetian palaces from the fifteenth and sixteenth centuries were destroyed.

Stephanides saw villagers 'gathered in stunned silence watching the holocaust, and I could sense that to them it was like the end of the world. Canea was the only town that many of them had ever known.' 'Like the end of the world', was the same comparison made by eye-witnesses to the destruction of Guernica. Although the bombing of Canea lacked the nightmare images of frenzied livestock depicted in Picasso's painting, it produced surreal sights of its own. Against a background of the blazing town, Geoffrey Cox observed a Cretan diving into the water of the harbour, then hurling to three women fish stunned by the bombs. He also saw a drunken Australian deserter magnanimously offering goods he had looted from shops.

The attack on Canea was perhaps Richthofen's envoi before the VIII Air Corps withdrew to prepare to deploy for Operation Barbarossa. If the Cretans needed a memory to rekindle their anger when the German authorities later tried to make friends during the occupation, that afternoon had provided it. The population fled to the surrounding villages where, with true Cretan generosity, they were taken in and cared for without question.

A few hours after the departure of the bombers, Freyberg and his staff at Creforce Headquarters abandoned their quarry and moved round to the south side of Suda Bay. Everyone lent a hand. The Welch Regiment, still in immaculate order, directed traffic, and an Australian artillery colonel steered a fifteen-hundred-weight truck through the outskirts of the burning town.

Early on the morning of Sunday, 25 May, General Student landed at Maleme.* Those who knew him found him aged by the last week: his creation, the Parachute Division, had been half destroyed.

The same morning, with the stench of Canea's burnt-out buildings in the air, the men of the 3rd Parachute Regiment in Prison Valley

---

* Student arrived in Crete much later than expected. As early as the morning of 22 May Ultra (OL 17/411) noted 'advance headquarters Eleventh Air Corps' at the Tavronitis bridge.

listened as Radio Berlin at last announced Germany's invasion of Crete. For Heydte's men, it was the first sign of official confidence in victory. As if to confirm this in the best style of historical drama, a runner arrived to say that contact had been made with a patrol of mountain troops advancing from Maleme. The patrol's lieutenant possessed the rather improbable title of Count Bullion. He was, according to the keen genealogist Heydte, a descendant of 'the Burgundian knight who had marched eastwards as a crusader some eight hundred and fifty years ago and received the crown of Jerusalem'.

The mountain troops were concentrating to assault Galatas from the southern as well as the western flank. On the western flank between Galatas and the sea, the New Zealand 18th Battalion came under mortar fire and strafing attacks from Messerschmitts. By midday German troops could be seen manoeuvring for attack, then at four in the afternoon a dozen Stukas began to dive-bomb Galatas. Soon afterwards, Ramcke's paratroopers and part of Colonel Utz's 100th Mountain Regiment suddenly attacked the 18th Battalion. The crackle of rifle-shots 'swelled to a roar'. Mortar fire also increased, with up to six rounds a minute dropping on one company. All round the village spent bullets whipped through the leaves of the olive trees, bringing down twigs and small branches.

Kippenberger went forward to observe the battle: he seems to have been the only senior officer on Crete to have done so. 'In a hollow, nearly covered by undergrowth,' he wrote, 'I came upon a party of women and children huddled together like little birds. They looked at me silently, with black, terrified eyes.' Galatas was threatened from both directions. The attack on John Russell's group on the south side of Galatas was also heavy, but the 18th Battalion's line up to the coast was the first to crack. At about six o'clock, the right-hand company was overwhelmed by Colonel Ramcke's men. A counter-attack with the battalion reserve — 'padre, clerks, batmen, everyone who could carry a rifle' — was led by their commanding officer, Lieutenant Colonel Gray, but it failed.

The Composite Battalion had meanwhile disintegrated in panic, although in the second line. 'Back, back!' some of its members shouted. 'They're coming through in thousands.' Once again the wounded, two hundred of them this time, had to be carried back. A German breakthrough down the coast road to Canea was prevented by part of the 20th Battalion, fortunately sent forward by Inglis. But the collapse spread to the other end of the line. On Wheat Hill, the corner of the whole Galatas pocket, the company there broke after Kippenberger had refused two requests to withdraw. The 18th Battalion's line then disintegrated along its whole length. Kippenberger strode round yelling 'Stand for New Zealand!' and seizing men who retreated through the village, but his efforts were in vain. The only hope of preventing a complete rout was to fall back to the hill between Galatas and Daratsos.

Brigadier Inglis, guessing the situation more by noise than from hard information, sent reinforcements forward. The 4th Brigade band arrived first, followed by a Pioneer platoon and the Kiwi concert party. They were distributed down a long dry-stone wall running north–south.

Not all the defenders had retreated. Russell Force remained cut off on the south-west corner of Galatas. Kippenberger, not wanting to abandon them, and convinced that the New Zealanders had to hit the Germans hard and unexpectedly to gain the respite they needed, decided to mount an immediate counter-attack. His basic force would be two companies of New Zealanders from the 23rd Battalion, 'tired, but fit to fight and resolute.'

Pipe in mouth, he told the two company commanders that they were going to attack to knock the Germans back, otherwise the whole front would collapse. The two companies fixed bayonets and waited. The young subaltern Sandy Thomas eyed his platoon. 'Everyone looked tense and grim and I wondered if they were feeling as afraid as I, whether their throats were as dry, their stomachs feeling now frozen, now fluid. I hoped, as I sensed the glances thrown in my direction, that I appeared as cool as they. It occurred to me suddenly that this was going to be the biggest moment of my life.'

'There was Kip', remembered another officer present, 'walking up and down steadying everyone.' By then dusk was falling fast. Two of the light tanks of the 3rd Hussars came up the road. Roy Farran, the troop leader, asked if they could help. Kippenberger welcomed their arrival and told him to go into Galatas to have a look round. The two antiquated and battered machines clattered off into the village, each spraying the windows on opposite sides of the street with machine-gun fire. On reaching the village square, dominated by an unusually tall church, the second tank was hit in the turret by an anti-tank rifle: its commander and driver were wounded.

The two tanks returned to Kippenberger. Farran's head appeared out of the top of the turret. 'The place is stiff with Jerries,' he shouted over the noise of the engine. Kippenberger asked him if he would go in again leading the infantry. Farran agreed, but first he had to extricate the driver and the corporal who had been wounded in the second tank. Once this was done, two New Zealanders volunteered to take their place and Farran took them off down the road for some basic instruction.

Captain Michael Forrester, whose Greeks were by then dead or scattered, had taken a rifle and bayonet and, easily recognizable by his fair hair − he had lost his service dress cap on Pink Hill − joined the ranks of the 23rd. He noticed how Kippenberger's force continued to increase. Men had begun to appear from nowhere as news spread of this come-as-you-are attack. Stragglers from a variety of units who had run away less than an hour before turned back, proving that bravery could be as infectious as fear. Walking wounded limped up requesting permission to join in as well. And the force would not have been complete without a group of those tireless fighters, the Maoris.

This most composite of composite units assembled behind the start-line, a track running roughly from north to south, with one company on each side of the road. Farran's two tanks reappeared, the improvised crew ready to go. Kippenberger and Farran spoke together, then Farran yelled to the second tank to follow. He disappeared inside his turret and closed the hatch as his tank lurched forward. 'The Maoris', recorded Forrester, 'began their harka war-chant and everyone took it up. The noise was incredible.' Those who listened from a distance compared the sound to the baying of hounds. The remnants of the 18th Battalion under Lieutenant Colonel Gray promptly joined in from another direction.

'The effect was terrific,' wrote Thomas. 'One felt one's blood rising swiftly above fear and uncertainty until only inexplicable exhilaration, quite beyond description, remained.' They charged up the hill, a lane with one- and two-storey white houses either side, unable to keep pace with the tanks.

As they disappeared from view, there was an eruption of noise. Kippenberger recalled 'scores of automatics and rifles being fired at once, the crunch of grenades, screams and yells − the uproar swelled and sank, swelled again to a terrifying crescendo.' Women and children, finding their village a battlefield once again, fled down the road.

Almost as soon as Farran's tank reached the village square on the summit of the hill, an anti-tank grenade struck the side. Having ensured that the others in his crew escaped, Farran, who was badly wounded, just managed to drag himself out. From the lee side, he shouted encouragement: 'Come on New Zealand, clean them out!'

According to Sandy Thomas's account, after Farran's tank was hit the new commander of the second tank panicked and ordered the driver to turn round and drive out of the village. But a little way down the road his flight was blocked by Thomas's platoon advancing to the village square. The commander screamed at them to let him through. Thomas refused and ordered the driver to turn back, which he did.

Their attack hardly delayed, the New Zealanders charged on up towards the square, their eighteen-inch bayonets fixed. Some threw grenades into the windows of the houses held by the Germans. Others rushed any defender who emerged. In the square, firing was still frenetic. Bullets ricocheted off the useless dented hulk of Farran's 'armoured perambulator'. To break the danger of immobility in the open, Thomas brought his men to charge across the square. Whether prompted by the sight of the bayonets or the desperation on the New Zealanders' faces, most of the Germans in the houses opposite panicked and fled. Only one resolute group remained.

Several men, Farran amongst them, shouted a warning when the silhouette of a German helmet showed above the line of a roof. The German threw a grenade, and at the same time another opened fire with a Spandau. Thomas, his back lacerated with shrapnel from the grenade, was hit in the thigh. One of his men tried to bandage the wound, but the opening was too large for a field dressing.

Soon the order to withdraw arrived from Kippenberger. The attack had achieved its aim and he did not want to waste any men unnecessarily, for as soon as the Germans had retreated, their mortars began to shell the village. The more seriously wounded, Farran and Thomas among them, had to be left behind. One of Thomas's soldiers, also badly hit in the leg, managed to pull him into a ditch which offered some protection. The mortar bomb explosions did not deter the women of the village. They slipped out of their cellars to bring water to the wounded. A 12-year-old girl appeared beside Sandy Thomas with a mug of fresh goat's milk.

Kippenberger gave the order for withdrawal back to a line on Daratsos. Russell's survivors from the Divisional Cavalry and Captain Rowe's last members of the Petrol Company on Pink Hill had been able to extricate themselves. They were all that remained of Kippenberger's 10th Brigade.

Those who took part in the counter-attack on Galatas will never forget the astonishing resurgence of spirit it engendered. Perhaps it is best explained as a gesture of anger at retreat − at the gut certainty that they should have won the whole battle. The New Zealanders had shown in a spectacular manner what could have been achieved had they been given the chance and the leadership at the crucial moment four days before.

Kippenberger, 'more tired than ever before in my life, or since', stumbled around in the dark trying to find Inglis's make-shift command post, 'a tarpaulin-covered hole in the ground'. Most of the battalion commanders were assembled there already. Inglis raised the subject of another counter-attack to gauge reactions. Then Colonel Gentry, Puttick's chief of staff, and Colonel Dittmer, the commanding officer of the 28th (Maori) Battalion, arrived. Dittmer volunteered to attack again, but after discussion Inglis came to the conclusion that it was too late, and Dittmer's battalion was one of the last New Zealand units to remain reasonably intact. There was no alternative but to fall back to a line linking up with Vasey's two Australian battalions at the end of Prison Valley. Although nobody voiced the inevitability of defeat, they all knew that their escape would depend once again on the Royal Navy.

17
Laycock's Commandos and Force Reserve
26 and 27 May

After the last deceptive flash of hope had died away at Galatas, General Freyberg knew that he must warn Wavell that Crete could no longer be held. He postponed writing his signal until the next morning, 26 May. It began 'I regret to have to report'. This must have been one of the most unpleasant duties he had ever faced.

The task cannot have been made easier by stirring exhortations still arriving from Churchill in London, or by the simplistic mathematics of military intelligence in Cairo which estimated that he still enjoyed numerical superiority. But this was partly his own fault: he had not clearly told Cairo or London how rapidly Maleme had fallen. A circuitous phrasing of reports gave the impression that the airfield was still hotly contested for some time after the Germans had established their air bridge.

Efforts were then made by GHQ Middle East to send Blenheims and Wellingtons to bomb the runway, but they were far too late and too few to make a difference. In spite of a short lift in morale caused by a raid on 25 May, the RAF had once again become a target for abuse with their initials converted to crude epithets.

During Monday, 26 May, the new line west of Canea held, albeit shakily and by a stroke of luck. Shortly after 1 p.m., the Luftwaffe bombed and strafed a battalion of the 85th Mountain Regiment by mistake for fifty minutes; this severely demoralized German troops across the whole front and induced caution in their commanders. The unlucky battalion had been advancing in the foothills towards Perivolia where the 2nd Greek Regiment, Freyberg heard, was in the process of disintegration. This was one of the factors which convinced him that Suda Bay would soon be under fire.

Next to the Greeks, and barring the end of Prison Valley, were the two Australian battalions, the 2/8th and the 2/7th, back under the command of Brigadier Vasey as the 19th Australian Brigade. Then, stretching to the coast, forming a line in front of Canea, were three reduced and semi-amalgamated New Zealand battalions starting with the Maoris west of Daratsos. Holding the enemy at this line was especially important to allow warships to land essential stores and reinforcements in Suda Bay that night.

Behind this insecure and scarcely dug-in force, the remnants of other battalions tried to recuperate and reorganize. Round Suda, the unarmed rear echelon, nearly twelve thousand men at the start of the battle, lay scattered in their makeshift camps: dock operating companies, ordnance corps fitters and supply personnel — what the fighting troops called the odds and sods and what Churchill called the *'bouches inutiles'*.

Often unfairly derided and left in even greater ignorance of events than the average soldier, these 'base wallahs' had suffered from continual bombing without an *esprit de corps* to sustain them or the capacity to strike back at the enemy. A number of those who had been able to grab a rifle to stalk paratroopers in the olive groves proved themselves natural guerrilla fighters, despite or perhaps because of their lack of formal infantry training. But the nerves of the majority were badly strained by air attack. When someone dropped his tin mug with a clatter in Stephanides's casualty clearing station, everyone threw themselves on the floor, including the man who had dropped it.

Many of the rear echelon had been evacuated just before the battle in ships bringing supplies and equipment to the island. But now no merchantman stood a chance of running the gauntlet of Stuka attacks through the Kaso strait. And after the disasters at sea of 22 May, Admiral Cunningham would allow only the fastest warships to make the round trip from Alexandria, restricting their presence in the dangerous waters of the Aegean to the hours of darkness. He had, contrary to Admiralty instructions, ordered a convoy bringing a battalion of the Queen's Royal Regiment to return to Alexandria. And an attempt to land commando reinforcements at Paleokhora in the south-west by destroyer to attack the German flank had to be aborted because of heavy seas. If they had managed to land, they would soon have come up against the German 55th Motor-Cycle Battalion, which had by then begun to break through the brave Cretan defenders round Kandanos.

A party of two hundred men from this commando force had, however, arrived in Suda Bay on the night of 24 May by the fast minelaying cruiser, HMS *Abdiel*. The main body, having returned to Alexandria after failing to land at Paleokhora, finally reached Suda Bay two nights later in the destroyers *Hero* and *Nizam* and the *Abdiel* on its second run.

These two commando battalions, lightly armed and only five hundred strong, were commanded by Colonel Robert Laycock, an officer from the Royal Horse Guards with considerable qualities of leadership and the face of a gentleman boxer. His brigade major was Freddie Graham, and his intelligence officer Captain Evelyn Waugh. 'A' Battalion was commanded by Lieutenant Colonel F.B. Colvin, who had already arrived with the advance party, and 'D' Battalion by Lieutenant Colonel George Young of the Royal Engineers, the sapper officer who had originally been flown out in 1939 by MI(R) to sabotage the Ploesti oilfields.

Also on the quay at Suda that night was Peter Wilkinson of SOE who had gone there earlier in the evening to see if some sabotage equipment had arrived for Bill Barbrook. 'We were busy', Wilkinson reported to Gubbins, 'burning 25 German uniforms which DH/A [Ian Pirie] had brought with him from Greece at a time when the nearest parachutist was only about 300 yards away. The inefficiency and lack of preparedness in DH/A's office was not too good!' But a surprise awaited him. Captain Morse, the Naval Officer-in-Charge, had received a 'Top Secret – Decode Yourself' from the Admiralty ordering him to get Wilkinson off the island. Somebody in London had wrongly assumed that he knew all about 'most secret sources', and the capture of anyone who was 'Ultra-indoctrinated' had to be avoided at all costs. 'You're to be put on the next ship back,' Morse told him. The ship turned out to be the *Abdiel*, and one of the first members of Layforce Wilkinson spotted in the light from a burning tanker was George Young.

Evelyn Waugh commented that Young 'was unimpressive in appearance but proved to be a good officer.' Young was indeed a good officer, and D Battalion, an amalgamation of the two Middle East Commandos, was its best unit thanks to his training. Waugh's depiction of the débâcle on Crete, both in his diaries and in his novel, *Officers and Gentlemen*, is more vivid than anything else written about those last few days, but the novel in particular must be seen more as a projection of a personal sense of disillusionment than as an objective depiction of events.

His feelings about the commando force which Laycock had raised in Britain the previous year were very mixed. The commando, which he joined at Largs in Scotland, was recruited from the Household Cavalry, the Foot Guards and line cavalry regiments, especially the Royal Scots Greys. Although he loved being with 'the smart set' who 'drink a very great deal, play cards for high figures, dine nightly in Glasgow, and telephone to their trainers endlessly,' he disapproved because they did not take their responsibilities as officers seriously. 'I saw few symptoms of their later decay,' he wrote. 'They had a gaiety and independence which I thought would prove valuable in action.'

Layforce, since its arrival in the Middle East, had not been fortunate. So many operations were cancelled that it became known as Belayforce, and in the troopdecks of their assault ship, HMS *Glengyle*, someone had scrawled: 'Never in the history of human endeavour have so few been buggered about by so many.' They had set out for Crete in the belief that their objective was to 'raid enemy aerodromes and seaports etc., from which bombers were sent out to bomb our troops on the island'. They were also given a completely false idea of the state of affairs they would find on arrival. Randolph Churchill had been telling them that the battle was as good as won. And their orders issued in Alexandria had 'stated that the situation in Crete was "well in hand", only that "the Maleme aerodrome garrison was hard-pressed", suggesting wrongly that the aerodrome was in our hands and was being attacked from outside'.

Their arrival, an introduction to what the brigade major described as 'a nightmare of unreality and unexpectedness', dramatically disabused them of the idea that things were well in hand.

No sooner had the ship anchored [wrote Graham in 1948] than boats from the shore began to come alongside and, just as the Brigade Commander, myself and other officers were bidding farewell to the captain of the minelayer, the door of the latter's cabin was flung open and a bedraggled and apparently slightly hysterical Naval officer burst in. In a voice trembling with emotion he said 'The Army's in full retreat. Everything is chaos. I've just had my best friend killed beside me. Crete is being evacuated!' Cheerful to say the least of it and something of a shock to the little party of Commando officers, armed to the teeth and loaded up like Christmas trees, who stared open-mouthed at this bearer of bad news.

'But we are just going ashore,' I faltered.

'My God,' he cried. 'I didn't know that. Perhaps I shouldn't have said anything.'

'Too late now, old boy,' I said. 'You can at least tell us what the password is.' But he had forgotten it.

From the deck they saw lighters coming out from the mole loaded with wounded. The scene became chaotic with commandos pushing forward trying to disembark as they arrived. Somebody gave the order to throw all equipment except personal weapons, ammunition and food over the side. Several wireless sets, desperately needed only a week before, were dropped in Suda Bay. Crates of food and ammunition boxes were broken open. Men filled the pockets of their battledress with loose clips of .303 rounds and stuffed tins of bully beef inside their shirts. Ammunition boxes for the Thompson sub-machine guns and Brens were piled on to stretchers, which pairs of men carried away from the quayside. Once ashore on the Canea–Georgioupolis road, Laycock 'noticed that all the troops we met seemed to be going the wrong way.'

The troops going the wrong way were mostly stragglers from the rear echelon and dispirited elements from the second line round Canea who had broken away prematurely. Defeat could not be concealed and word of the decision to evacuate troops from Sphakia on the south coast had somehow got out. Confusion had increased throughout that night of 26–27 May. A German breakthrough was expected at any moment from the foothills round Perivolia where the 2nd Greek Regiment had disintegrated. To emphasize the danger, tracer bullets from the mountain troops' Spandau machine guns on the southern flank were curving over Puttick's headquarters.

Inglis had been appointed to command the 1,200-strong Force Reserve – 1st Welch, the Rangers and the Northumberland Hussars – which was to relieve the exhausted New Zealanders on the coastal strip west of Canea. But General Weston kept control for himself, and Inglis, to avoid confusion, did not attempt to intervene. Nobody seemed to know which formation came under which headquarters. Brigade commanders, without wireless or field telephones, resorted to walking around in the dark in search of one another.*

* Freyberg had the best means of transport. Despite his huge figure, he rode pillion behind Second Lieutenant M.B. Payne of the Northumberland Hussars, an amateur trick motor-cyclist who had performed at Olympia.

At first, nobody could find General Weston who had established his headquarters in a peasant's house near '42nd Street', which was a sunken track running south from the Canea end of Suda Bay. Named after the 42nd Field Squadron, Royal Engineers, based there before the invasion, 42nd Street was to be the next line of defence. Having ordered Force Reserve forward to replace the 5th New Zealand Brigade in front of Canea, Weston fell asleep on the earth floor of his 'hovel in an olive grove', as Laycock described it. He had sent no orders to the New Zealanders to withdraw when replaced, and does not appear to have known that the Australian Brigade to their south was by then outflanked, and so would have to fall back.

Puttick and Hargest became exasperated by the lack of orders. During the crucial part of that night, Freyberg was away from his headquarters and could not be contacted. For some of this time he had been on the quay at Suda Bay, not to meet Layforce, although he spoke to one of their officers, but to check that a landing craft carrying supplies and, most important of all, a message warning about the imminent evacuation reached Campbell's force at Rethymno. It says much for Freyberg's humanity, although less for his generalship, that at such a critical point of the battle he should have spent a considerable time walking up and down with a young lieutenant of the RASC, Jack Smith-Hughes, agonizing over the chances of the craft getting through safely. Unfortunately, the message had already gone astray, and the commander of the landing craft had left without knowing of its existence.

Puttick sent Captain Robin Bell, one of Freyberg's intelligence officers, to explain in person to Weston the gravity of the situation, but Weston's staff officers prevented Bell from disturbing their chief. Puttick, with uncharacteristic decisiveness, countermanded Freyberg's order that the Australians should stand firm come what may and told both Vasey and Hargest to withdraw to 42nd Street while they still had the cover of darkness. Thus Force Reserve was left to advance unsupported against a vastly superior enemy.

When Weston was woken at about one in the morning (possibly by the arrival of Laycock and Waugh) he finally learned of the disaster about to befall the Welch Regiment, the Rangers and the Northumberland Hussars. Orders to Colonel Duncan of the Welch Regiment to turn back were sent by two dispatch-riders. Weston then went back to sleep on the floor, but he was soon woken again, this time by Puttick in search of an explanation of what was going on. But Weston appears to have been almost incoherent from exhaustion.

Force Reserve meanwhile advanced towards the enemy through a deserted and devastated Canea. In the early hours of the morning, it fanned out beyond in an eerily empty countryside. More than one Welsh wag remarked 'Here we go for Custer's last stand.' A group with the quartermaster came upon a New Zealander fast asleep. 'We told him to hop it. His lot had pulled out long ago.' They also found a young sapper who had been left to blow a bridge, something he had never done before. 'He was a brave boy to have stayed there,' remarked a Welshman who helped him detonate the charge with the battery from their fifteen-hundred-weight truck.

Towards dawn, patrols were sent out to the south to make contact with the Royal Perivolians of the recently formed 'Suda Brigade', but both they and the Australians on the left flank had withdrawn the evening before. The patrols never returned. Soon after dawn on 27 May, Force Reserve heard firing well to their rear on the road to Suda. The implication was plain.

To their front were ranged Ramcke's paratroopers still following the coast and the 100th Mountain Regiment advancing over the Galatas–Daratsos hills. The majority of the German mortars and light artillery were concentrated on them. Heidrich's 3rd Parachute Regiment, although down to battalion strength, was at last able to advance out of Prison Valley and encircle them from the south, and the firing on the Canea–Suda road to their rear had come from the advance of the 141st Mountain Regiment.

When the German attack began at 8.30 a.m. with a heavy mortar bombardment, Force Reserve was already cut off. Part of it managed to fight a desperate rearguard action on to the neck of the Akrotiri, but most of it was trapped in front of Canea, with even the Welch Regiment's commanding officer, Colonel Duncan, manning a Bren gun. Their bitter resistance continued in pockets until the afternoon, in one case until the next morning. Seven officers and about two hundred and fifty men managed to fight through in small parties to rejoin the main force to the east: one group charged a road block in a lorry.

This sorry blunder had thrown away nearly a thousand of the fittest troops left. Perhaps the greatest tragedy of the Force Reserve was to have had its moment of action preserved until this futile hour, and not to have been sent into the counter-attack five days earlier. The squabbling of senior officers afterwards over who was to blame is reminiscent of the unseemly wrangles that followed the Charge of the Light Brigade at the Battle of Balaclava. Puttick strongly believed that Weston was at fault, Weston found Puttick's countermanding of orders unbelievably cavalier, and Freyberg was convinced that Inglis had evaded his responsibility to command Force Reserve. Once again, orders which had not been thought out, bad communications and in this case complicated alterations to the chain of command had made chaos virtually certain.

The remnants of the 3rd Parachute Regiment swung round Canea with orders to advance on the Akrotiri. With Heydte's men leading, they passed empty trenches behind barbed wire, deserted command posts, abandoned equipment and field guns with their breech-blocks removed, still pointing westwards. They advanced through orange plantations, vineyards and olive groves to the Canea–Suda road.

Fearing that his men were too tired to deal with pockets of resistance on the rocky peninsula, Heydte switched his line of advance to enter Canea through Halepa from the east. He ordered them to display every recognition flag they had to avoid another accidental attack by German aircraft. 'Anyone watching us on this march', he wrote of his unshaven and tattered band, 'might well have taken us for a band of medieval mercenaries rather than a modern military formation.'

In the deserted, rubble-strewn streets rats dived out of sight at their approach. The odd fire still burned and beams smouldered from the air raid of three days before. The smell of olive oil drained from smashed vats and wine run from broken casks mingled with that of decomposing corpses. Venetian façades in the narrow alleys stood with the guts of the houses destroyed and the upper windows showing only blue sky.

On reaching a square, the paratroopers were greeted by wounded comrades, captured at the beginning of the battle then left behind in a makeshift hospital by the retreating British. The Mayor of Canea arrived, wanting to surrender the town to ensure there would be no further civilian casualties. Captain von der Heydte was much amused when he refused to believe that this filthy and unshaven scarecrow, with only a knotted handkerchief for headgear, was a battalion commander in the conquering army.

The swastika flag was hoisted on the minaret of the old Turkish mosque in the centre of Canea. Heydte then set up his headquarters in the British Consulate in the suburb of Halepa beyond the east wall of the town. Meanwhile General Ringel's mountain troops marched on in pursuit of Freyberg's retreating force.

Ringel assumed that Freyberg was withdrawing along the coast, first to Rethymno, then to join up with the strong garrison at Heraklion. This misapprehension was fortunate for the retreating troops, otherwise he might have made a more determined effort on the southern flank. As it was, Freyberg's force had already been saved from almost certain encirclement and a humiliating surrender by that astonishing feat of resistance near Alikianou by the 8th Greek Regiment and Cretan irregulars.

In the early hours of 27 May while Force Reserve was still advancing to its undeserved fate, Laycock and Waugh went first to see General Weston, then to the headquarters of Colonel Colvin who commanded the advance guard, and then to General Freyberg whom Waugh described in his diary as 'composed but obtuse'. He was ruder about General Weston the next evening: 'General Weston popped out of the hedge; he seemed to have lost his staff and his head'. (This cannot be attributed merely to Waugh's aggravation: his 19-year-old soldier servant, Private Tanner, was taken aback by the sight of a general 'flapping about on his own'.)* Even an air attack did not escape Waugh's scathing flippancy: 'it was like everything German — overdone.'

While Laycock and Waugh visited the generals in search of instructions, Graham organized a rudimentary deployment of the two commando battalions. He was appalled at the image of retreat which greeted them: 'the road was jammed with troops in no formed bodies shambling along in desperate haste. Dirty, weary and hungry — a rabble, one could call them nothing else. It was a sight I was to become only too familiar with in the next days, and I shall never forget it.'

Yet, as the Germans found to their cost, not all units were in a state of collapse. At about eleven in the morning of 27 May, the 141st Mountain Regiment, having bypassed Force Reserve, came up against the Australians and Maoris on the 42nd Street line. The mountain troops advanced, never expecting an attack from exhausted troops. When the Australians and Maoris charged, they scattered most of the regiment's I Battalion. In this action the Germans admitted to losing 121 men killed, over half their casualties for a day

---

* Tanner, who described himself as Waugh's 'cushion-bearer' since he carried his pillow for him throughout the battle, found Waugh most considerate. Regular officers, disconcerted by Waugh's irony, seem to have harboured a strong dislike.

which saw a total of 220 men killed, 50 more than on 25 May, the day of the Battle of Galatas.

That afternoon, nearly thirty hours after his original signal declaring the inevitability of defeat, Freyberg finally received agreement from Wavell to a withdrawal over the White Mountains to Sphakia, a small fishing harbour on the south coast. Wavell had wanted him to withdraw to Rethymno and link up with the Heraklion brigade, just as General Ringel had expected, but Freyberg had been right in his original assessment and Wavell was forced to agree. He gave his consent without waiting any longer for confirmation from the War Cabinet. That evening, Creforce Headquarters set off southwards by car and truck over the mountain road towards Sphakia.

18
South from Suda Bay
28–30 May

After Freyberg's departure to Sphakia, command of the withdrawal was left to General Weston. But Weston's unreliable leadership, not helped by false rumours and bad communications, prompted Hargest and Vasey to formulate their own orders. Having seen mountain troops moving round to their south, well beyond the Malaxa escarpment, they withdrew their New Zealanders and Australians from the 42nd Street line on the evening of 27 May. They marched through the night to Stylos, which lay to the south-east on the route to Sphakia. Fortunately, the mountain troops stopped for the night, and only resumed their eastward advance shortly before dawn.

Hargest's men reached Stylos just in time. At daybreak on 28 May, two companies of the 23rd Battalion were roused from where they had lain down to sleep. Two of their officers, on a tour of inspection before lying down themselves, had spotted the renewed advance of the 85th Mountain Regiment. The exhausted New Zealanders rushed forward to a dry-stone wall curving over the top of a hill. The leading Germans, advancing up the other side, were within twenty metres when the New Zealanders' helmets appeared above them. Sergeant Hulme, who sat on the wall firing, won a Victoria Cross in the brief but highly successful action which followed.

To the north of them at Megala Khorion above the turn-off from the Canea–Rethymno road, a troop of Spanish Republicans from George Young's battalion became engaged in Layforce's first rearguard action. Laycock had rightly objected that it was a bad position to defend, but he was overruled. They were joined by two companies of Maoris. Soon an impressive procession of vehicles led by motor-cycle troops came in view advancing east from Suda towards

Rethymno. Only a small proportion of this force turned south to attack and, in the scrub and broken terrain, the Maoris managed to delay them until midday.

Most of the Spanish Republicans, regarding their mission as unnecessarily suicidal when everyone was in retreat, fell back to Babali Hani where the rest of George Young's battalion had been sent ahead to prepare another stop line. Meanwhile Colonel Colvin's battalion of commandos, left behind to delay the enemy at Suda, was in some disarray after two confused engagements in which many men were captured. Waugh describes Colvin's conduct in scathing terms in his memorandum on Layforce; in fact he had started to crack up so obviously that Laycock relieved him of his command and amalgamated the two battalions under George Young.

Laycock and his brigade major, Freddy Graham, were nearly captured by mountain troops who had cut the road between Stylos and Babali Hani. The arrival of two of the Matilda tanks brought round from Heraklion saved them. These tanks also helped stiffen the resistance at Babali Hani where George Young's battalion backed by the remainder of the Australian 2/8th Battalion faced two battalions of mountain troops later that day. Laycock set up his brigade headquarters in a house on the edge of the village so that he could stay close to the fighting.

The tactics of the mountain troops were to advance to contact then, once the enemy positions had been identified, to send machine-gun and mortar groups off to climb prominent features on each flank. This took time and effort, but 'Sweat saves blood!' was General Ringel's maxim.

Young's battalion and the Australians fought back until dusk, when it was clear they were being outflanked to the west. The two tanks had run out of petrol and were destroyed. A third Matilda was fixed across the road in a crater, prematurely blown by a party of sappers, the oil and water were drained and the engine set racing until it seized completely. The commandos and Australians pulled out after nightfall, marching as fast as they could southwards to the Askifou plain where the Australians set up another defence line.

All this time, ahead of the rearguard, a mass of soldiers trudged forward, first across the Apokoronas foothills then, after Vrysses, up into the White Mountains. Olive groves became rarer as the ground became rockier, with ilex and scrub oak or pine and gorse, and the 'treadmill' of the climb began under the strong sun. Higher still, there were only prickly little bushes to break the sterile expanse of shale and limestone outcrops. For fresh, well-nourished troops with good boots, the worst part of the journey — the twenty-four kilometres from Stylos up to the Askifou plain — would not have caused great hardship. But most of those on this retreat were exhausted before they started, they had little food and water, and their boots were falling to pieces.

'I found it hard to realize', wrote Theodore Stephanides of the early stage, 'that I was taking part in what would probably be a historical event. It seemed somehow more like a crowd leaving a football match and finding the trains were not running, than a retreat.'

During this retreat, a number of curious sights and encounters took place. One of the RAF officers who remembered Nicki Demertzi from the Argentina night-club in Athens suddenly spotted her in khaki uniform. So did Geoffrey Cox who had run the newspaper *Crete News* from the SOE base at Fernleaf House. Her long blonde hair looked very fetching against this informal attempt at camouflage. Ian Pirie was wearing a major's crowns: he apparently had a habit of producing different badges of rank out of a pocket. On arrival in Cairo he became one of SOE's political advisers. His colleague in subterfuge, Bill Barbrook, escaped from Canea with a young English schoolteacher from the Dodecanese who had been helping him as an interpreter. Barbrook told him to put on uniform just in case the Germans took him for a spy. Others in borrowed battledress and steel helmets included a couple of Greek hospital nurses adopted by a company of New Zealanders: they tramped along with them joking in broken English.

Two encounters involving Bob Laycock, one by night and one by day, seemed somehow typical of the British abroad in unusual circumstances. Myles Hildyard, a subaltern from the Sherwood Rangers, heard Laycock's voice in the dark and recognized it immediately: he knew him from parties in Nottinghamshire. Laycock's brother was serving in the Sherwood Rangers, the local yeomanry regiment. They had a brief chat about him and mutual friends at home, then went on their way. On another occasion, Monty Woodhouse and Colonel Guy Salisbury-Jones, while resting by the roadside, saw Laycock in a staff car. Laycock stopped to chat to Salisbury-Jones, who had been in the Coldstream Guards. After he had driven on, Salisbury-Jones turned back to his companion. 'Funny thing,' he said. 'Last time I saw him he was riding up the Mall at the head of a Sovereign's escort of the Household Cavalry.' Woodhouse agreed that it was indeed a funny thing.

Lighter moments such as these were rare. At Stylos, the rows of wounded on stretchers at the dressing station reminded a New Zealand colonel of a scene from the film *Gone with the Wind*. Signs of stress and demoralization were almost everywhere. Kippenberger noticed one of his officers 'walking very fast with odd automaton-like steps and quivering incessantly'.

Whenever a Messerschmitt roared over, strafing at low altitude, its tracer bullets liable to start brushwood fires, there would be some hysterical cries of 'Take cover!' as well as the more relaxed 'Here comes Jerry!' Everyone froze face down. Evelyn Waugh's batman, Private Tanner, remembered an Australian voice screaming, 'If anybody moves, I'll shoot them!' Yet although the fighter sorties unnerved those severely strained by exhaustion as much as battle shock, they were far less intense than earlier in the battle. Tuesday, 27 May, had been the last day of heavy air attacks before most of the VIII Air Corps was pulled back to prepare for Operation Barbarossa.

Members of the rearguard suffered more than most from lack of food simply because they came last. Creforce was retreating away from its depots, and there had not been enough time or transport to prepare proper dumps along the route. Those which had been established were raided by the *bouches inutiles* who had set off for Sphakia well ahead of the fighting troops. This mixture of British, Cypriot and Palestinian servicemen had few officers and little discipline. Many lived like outlaws, sheltering in caves along the way and raiding the food stockpiles for cigarettes and luxuries such as tinned salmon and pineapple chunks which made such a change from the salty monotony of bully beef.

As a result, the daily ration was soon down to a quarter of a tin of bully beef with one and a half hard tack biscuits each. In Layforce, those lucky enough to get a tin of thirteen sausages had to share it among twenty-seven men. That they received anything was largely thanks to the efforts of Freddie Graham, the brigade major. At the end of the hardest stretch of the march, Sergeant Stewart's troop of A Battalion found Graham and two men waiting for them with tins of M & V (a mess of meat and vegetable) and Army hard tack biscuits. 'After drawing water with the help of some Staff officers, we ate our rations as quietly as a female pig after suckling her young.'

The shortfall could only be made up by foraging, a skill at which the Spanish Republicans proved themselves the most experienced. Waugh's Catholic prejudices evaporated when they invited him and Laycock to a meal of roast sucking pig and rice. The Cretans were remarkably forgiving as the passing of thousands of desperate troops emptied their wells and stole eggs, chickens and even sheep. Thirst led to terrible scrambles round wells as soldiers lowered water-bottles or steel helmets on webbing equipment. Those without either lowered a field dressing, then sucked the water from it as from a sponge. Some men found wine on the way and drank themselves into oblivion.

British troops were small and scrawny-chested in comparison to the Australians and New Zealanders. Wiry was the best that could be said for many of them, and they could not keep up. In contrast to the unshaven and dishevelled rabble, infantry battalions, although down to company strength, marched in a body, forcing their way through the crowd and halting for the regulation ten minutes every hour.

By day the litter of retreat marked the way: abandoned vehicles pushed over the side, gas-masks, rifles, webbing equipment, kitbags, blankets, cartridge boxes, even officers' suitcases, the few remaining contents strewn about by passers-by rummaging for anything useful or valuable. The instinct to scrounge for its own sake, Stephanides observed, was astonishingly deep-rooted.

By night the pale dusty road was easily visible in the starlight, and on either side the lighted tips of cigarettes brightened and dimmed as resting men smoked. At other times, the scene was less relaxed. Colonel Kippenberger, halting his men at one point, took out a torch to study the map. This provoked threats and curses from stragglers afraid of air attack. One man leaped at him and kicked the torch from his hand. Kippenberger grabbed him by the throat and nearly throttled him, then warned the audience in the surrounding dark that he was going to use the torch again and if anyone objected he would shoot.

'It was pitiful', wrote Sergeant Charles Stewart of Layforce, 'to see the state and marching of the British soldiers, some lacking rifles, or equipment; discipline seemed to have left them, (I do not blame the men altogether), and they had sore feet through sweat and marching, the skin peeling off their shoulders with carrying extra ammunition and their comrades' rifles.'

Even the recently arrived commandos were soon tired, as Stewart found. ' "Keep moving lads, change over those Brens and keep closed up" were the orders given out. But physical endurance can reach its

limit, and within the next hour I was forced by the appeals of the
men to ask my captain to give them a rest every twenty minutes. The
halt was passed along the line, some of the lads lay down on the road
and were asleep in a few minutes. Twenty minutes up, it was nigh
impossible to waken some.' Often during night halts men fell instantly
asleep, or rather into a state of exhausted unconsciousness, and could
not be woken even by prods and kicks from their sergeants. Others,
unnoticed, woke up several hours later and found their comrades
gone.

When the order to withdraw over the mountains to Sphakia had
finally been issued on 27 May, Kippenberger, as he later admitted,
was 'unashamedly pleased'. The New Zealand Division, after the
withdrawal from Galatas, had no further illusions about the outcome
of the battle. Yet at Heraklion the troops had scant idea of the state
of affairs to the west. They still thought the Germans were as good
as beaten.

Soon after dawn on 28 May, commanding officers were summoned
to Brigadier Chappel's headquarters. There they heard that a
squadron of the Royal Navy would take them off from Heraklion
harbour that night. Secrecy must be preserved at all costs. Battalion
orders groups were held at midday, but the men were not to be told
until the last moment in case anyone in the forward positions or on
patrol was taken prisoner. For Colonel Pitcairn of the Black Watch
the news that morning was particularly bitter. One of his most
popular company commanders, Major Alastair Hamilton, who had
dramatically promised that 'the Black Watch leaves Crete when the
snow leaves Mount Ida', was killed by a mortar bomb.

The feeling in the 14th Infantry Brigade's headquarters was that
'the other end had let the side down'. They also felt that they had
been forced to let down the Cretans who had fought with such
astonishing bravery. On that last evening, Pendlebury's friend Satanas,
the guerrilla kapitan from Kroussonas, suddenly appeared in the cave
as soldiers destroyed equipment and officers burned documents. Word
of the evacuation had somehow reached the guerrillas, but not Greek
army units for whom, it was decided in Alexandria, there was not
enough room on the warships.

The white-haired Satanas, a dramatic and impressive figure in his
Cretan dress, was taken to Brigadier Chappel. Paddy Leigh Fermor
described the scene years later: ' "My son," he said, placing his hand

on the Brigadier's shoulder, "we know you are going away tonight. Never mind! You will come back when the right time comes. But leave us as many guns as you can, to carry on the fight till then." Deeply moved, the Brigadier told us to hand over all the arms we could collect.'

Platoon commanders in the York and Lancaster Regiment did not tell their men until eight o'clock in the evening, as instructed. The news caused an 'astonished silence as to them the whole battle of the last ten days had seemed to have been eminently successful'.

There was little time to prepare for the withdrawal. No heavy equipment could be taken on the ships. Breech-blocks from the field guns and unspent ammunition had to be buried, vehicle engines were ruined by being run at full speed after sand had been put in their sumps, signals equipment was smashed and petrol poured into rum jars. The rest of the kit was booby-trapped with grenades, and explosive charges set for early the following morning were placed in the fuel dumps.

Officers in the Leicesters contributed to this denial of stores to the enemy by retiring to their mess in a cave where a farewell dinner had been prepared. Each was rationed to 'one glass of sherry, one whisky and one liqueur', then they smashed the remaining bottles and the crockery.

The withdrawal was carried out perfectly, largely due to the experience and competence of NCOs in these regular battalions. Colonel Bräuer's paratroopers had no idea of what was afoot. At 9.30 p.m., the two companies on the airfield moved in the dark along the road to the harbour. Officers could not help thinking of the burial of Sir John Moore at Corunna. The Black Watch's covering party, the platoon watching the gorge beyond the airfield, would have to run to the mole when their turn to pull out finally came at one in the morning.

'It was an eerie business', recorded one regimental account, 'trailing down in the darkness past the well-known landmarks: past the airfield, the Greek Barracks, and the Club, where many a good party had been enjoyed with the hospitable people of Heraklion.' But the darkness concealed the state of the city. After the air raids, parts of Heraklion were as badly wrecked as Canea. Sewers had burst, and there was a stench of unburied bodies which had attracted the attention of starving dogs.

When the troops lined up on the mole ready to embark, Paddy Leigh Fermor noticed a very small soldier in ill-fitting battledress and steel helmet tilted forward. He took a closer look. A nervous giggle revealed a Cretan girl illicitly trying to accompany a corporal to Egypt. He did not have the heart to give them away, so hurried on to where brigade headquarters had been told to assemble. She was not alone. That night, four women managed to get aboard HMS *Orion*, the flagship of the rescuing force, as well as twelve Greek soldiers and six civilians.

At 11.30 p.m. Rear Admiral Rawlings's force reached Heraklion with only two cruisers. Rawlings had ordered the *Ajax* to turn back to Alexandria after she suffered damage during a heavy air attack. While the cruisers *Orion* and *Dido* remained offshore, their six accompanying destroyers ferried troops out to them from the mole of the New Harbour in pairs. One of these destroyers, HMS *Imperial*, had also suffered a near miss, but the extent of the damage to her steering gear did not emerge until later.

When the cruisers had been loaded with over a thousand men each, the destroyers then returned for their passengers. Finally, Brigadier Chappel, his headquarters and the rearguard went on board HMS *Kimberley* and HMS *Imperial*. Every man assembled had embarked − 3,486 in all − by the deadline of 2.45 a.m. on 29 May.

In retrospect, it seems almost as if the operation had gone too well. An hour and a half after the squadron sailed, the steering gear on HMS *Imperial* jammed. She slewed round, nearly ramming a caique with Mike Cumberlege and Nicholas Hammond on board; they were escaping in a similar direction.* *Hotspur* turned back on Admiral Rawlings's instruction to take off the crew and soldiers, a mixture mainly of Black Watch and Australians. Orders were given on the *Imperial* to line the side at once and jump from one ship to the other as the *Hotspur* came level. A group of Australian soldiers, semi-insensible from drink, had to be left below. As soon as everyone capable of jumping was aboard, *Hotspur* pulled away and fired torpedoes into *Imperial*, leaving her to sink. The Australians left on board went down with her.

---

* The engine of the *Dolphin* had failed completely, so Cumberlege and Hammond had pirated a replacement in Canea harbour just before the town fell to the Germans, then sailed her eastwards to Heraklion. Two days later in the Libyan Sea, a Messerschmitt attacked them. Cumberlege was wounded, his cousin Cle and Able Seaman Saunders were killed. On their landfall in the bay of Sollum, Hammond saw from puffs of smoke that they were heading for the front line, so, turning eastwards, they carried on to Mersa Matruh where they were fêted by the Navy.

The rest of the force in the meantime had reduced speed to fifteen knots, waiting for the overloaded *Hotspur* to catch up. By then Rawlings's ships were over an hour late. They were still well short of the Kaso strait and the island of Skarpanto with its enemy airfield. 'So it was', wrote an officer on the flagship, 'that when daylight came we were still inside the Aegean, turning to the southward as the sun rose at six o'clock. Against the dawn was silhouetted the first wave of attackers.'

The bombing, which began with five Stukas, continued in waves for six hours. The *Hereward* was hit first. She had to turn in to try and beach on Crete. The *Orion* was attacked twice that morning. She received two direct hits and underwater damage from six or seven near misses. The two bombs penetrated three levels of decks where most of the thousand soldiers were crammed in conditions akin to the Black Hole of Calcutta. The devastation formed a vision of military hell: 260 men were killed and 280 seriously wounded. The NCOs who had elected to stay on deck, bravely manning eighteen Bren guns to increase the ship's anti-aircraft fire, had made a fortunate choice. 'Since I was a boy', wrote the same officer in the *Orion*, 'I had always wondered what it must have felt like to take part in the Charge of the Light Brigade. Now I know.'

Dido was also singled out for attack. Two bombs fell in sequence, one destroying a gun turret and the other breaking right through to explode in the canteen packed with troops. Over a hundred soldiers were killed, either by the blast, or by burns, or by drowning when water had to be pumped in to prevent the fire spreading to the magazine.

As the severely damaged ships limped into Alexandria harbour that evening, a Black Watch piper lit by a searchlight played a lament from the bridge. Men wept unashamedly. Over a fifth of the force at Heraklion had been lost, the majority at sea, not in combat with the paratroopers.

Small groups out of contact, such as standing patrols, as well as the wounded lying in the military hospital at Knossos, had to be left behind. Some, hearing from Cretan irregulars of the withdrawal, arrived too late. Others crossed the island to join up with the rear party of the Argylls on the south coast.

Jack Hamson with his hundred men on the flank of Mount Ida first heard of defeat when stragglers from a Greek militia group posted near Knossos streamed past his position. Hamson did not believe them. On 30 May, a messenger arrived on the Plain of Nida exhausted from the climb: 'They've fled, the English, from Heraklion. They've gone. Ships came and took them off in the night, two nights ago. The fighting's finished. You must go now.' The news was confirmed by Satanas, who also added that a large Italian force had landed at the eastern end of the island near Siteia on 28 May. Mussolini, true to form, had waited until the Germans had won the battle before sending troops from the Dodecanese to the eastern and least warlike part of the island. Italian torpedo bombers had taken part in a number of generally unsuccessful attacks on British warships over the previous week, and high-level bombers had raided the port of Hierapetra on 25 May.

At Rethymno, Colonel Campbell and his two Australian battalions had no idea of these events. The small landing craft sent from Suda with supplies reached them in the early morning of 28 May. The young naval officer commanding it, Lieutenant Haig, had not brought Freyberg's message with instructions for evacuation due to confusion at Suda and Creforce Headquarters on the night Layforce arrived. All Haig could tell Campbell was that he had been told to head for Sphakia on the south coast. Campbell, burdened with a regular officer's consciousness of responsibility, would not contemplate abandoning his mission at Rethymno until officially relieved of it. Unfortunately, several attempts to drop messages by aircraft failed.

Haig had arrived a few hours after the Australians' two tanks had been finally destroyed in an attack on the German strongpoints round Perivolia. Both Campbell and Sandover finally had to accept that they could not break the German grip on the coast road. An idea to attack towards Suda was discarded, and Campbell insisted on continuing to deny the airfield to the enemy as ordered.

The same morning, General Ringel ordered the bulk of his force in their direction. Lieutenant Colonel Wittmann's 95th Mountain Artillery Regiment with the 5th Mountain Division's motor-cycle, reconnaissance and anti-tank detachments were to lead the way followed by the 85th and 141st Mountain Regiments. Tanks from the 31st Armoured Regiment, landing that day at Kastelli Kissamou having been delayed by guerrilla action, would be hurried forward to support them. Wittmann's orders were 'to pursue the enemy eastwards through Rethymno to Heraklion without a pause. First objective Rethymno and the relief of the paratroops fighting there.' Although disastrous for Campbell's force, Ringel's misapprehension — German intelligence was still astonishingly inept — resulted in his sending only the 100th Mountain Regiment southwards on the pursuit towards Sphakia. Thus the bulk of the British and Dominion forces on the island escaped.

On the evening of the following day, 29 May, a Greek officer warned Campbell that the British had left Heraklion and that a German force from there was advancing towards Rethymno from the east. Meanwhile Ringel's mountain artillery advancing from the west had begun ranging and motor-cycle troops had entered Rethymno. Food and ammunition were in short supply. All that night Australian soldiers took turns on the beach flashing the morse letter 'A' seawards in case Royal Navy warships were coming to save them. Next morning, the Germans renewed their advance from Rethymno towards the airfield, which Campbell held with the survivors of the 2/1st Battalion. Sandover's battalion, the 2/11th, soon spotted the procession of tanks and motor-cycles. The two commanders conferred by field telephone. Already the company on the coast road had been forced into leap-frog withdrawals, but accurate fire delayed the Germans very effectively. 'The game's up, Aussies!' the Germans yelled forward.

Severe warnings of reprisals against civilians if resistance continued had been dropped by German aircraft, and Campbell rightly rejected the idea of futile casualties. As a regular soldier, however, his view of the hopeless situation followed the rules of war to negotiated surrender. Sandover, an accountant and businessman, believed that every man should be given the chance to get away, and he proposed to lead those of his men who wanted to try their luck over the hills. The two men in this final conversation agreed to differ and wished each other luck. Campbell became a prisoner of war, while Sandover, with thirteen officers and thirty-nine NCOs and soldiers, escaped to Egypt by submarine after several months in the mountains.

The true measure of the Cretan spirit was its even greater generosity in defeat. On their departure, Ray Sandover received a message from one of the many volunteers who had helped them in the battle. 'Major, my greatest wish is that you will take a glass of wine in my house the day we are free. That is all I wish to live for.'

19
Surrender
31 May and 1 June

On the night of the large operation at Heraklion, the Royal Navy embarked the first thousand evacuees at Sphakia in four destroyers. Fear of being left behind was the best spur to the weary troops. Feet burning, they slogged up the mountain road from Vrysses. One false ridge followed another as the route twisted up above the line at which the hardier vegetation gave way to grey shale. To the west, the view was dominated by the snow-capped peaks of the White Mountains, including Mount Venizelos.

Finally, their efforts were rewarded by an unexpected sight beyond the pass. Below them lay the Askifou plain, a fertile flat-bottomed bowl (troops dubbed it 'the saucer') of meadows, orchards, small tilled fields and streams. Stephanides thought this haven, only a few kilometres across, too idyllic for war. 'The Luftwaffe', he noted, 'even went out of its way to shoot up a derelict and dilapidated farm tractor.'

The two Australian battalions under Brigadier Vasey and the last three light tanks of the 3rd Hussars took up position round Askifou itself. The New Zealand 23rd Battalion manned the pass. Next morning, mountain troops came into view again. But when they found that the position was well defended their advance slowed. The action at Babali Hani the previous day had discouraged them from taking risks.

With the end of the battle in sight, these Bavarians and Tyroleans from the 100th Mountain Regiment of Bad Reichenhall had adopted a light-hearted approach. Their dress had become very informal. Many, jettisoning their winter-weight jackets and trousers, wore oddments of captured British tropical uniform; this inevitably caused some confusion. The most bizarre variation occurred after they had taken the village of Askifou. There they looted the richest house, which belonged to a newly married couple, and seized the wife's trousseau. The Tyrolean soldiers decided to wear her delicately embroidered knickers and petticoats on their heads like the neckcloths of Foreign Legion képis as protection against the sun. They looked, with their shorts, muscular thighs and boots, more like a chorus-line in a regimental concert than fighting troops.

At the southern end of the Askifou plain lay the Imbros gorge, a deep ravine of great beauty. Waugh compared its natural rock terraces, with Aleppo pines growing precariously, to a seventeenth-century baroque landscape. The first-comers had not realized that this ravine offered a much safer and easier descent to the coast.

The road from the north continued on a few kilometres more, then came to an abrupt end on a massive bluff overlooking the Libyan Sea. There, amidst the heady scent of pine and wild thyme, the sight of the sea evoked powerful yet mixed emotions: relief that the journey was over, fear that after such a purgatorial experience they might still not get off, and dismay at the last precipitous stretch of the way, little more than a goat track down a steeply sloping rockface. Abandoned vehicles lay wrecked all around. Never was the failure of the military authorities to connect the road to the port so bitterly felt.

The Australians made the descent to Komithades, the village next to Sphakia, into a 'sheep-race', so that 'once a man got into the flow of traffic he just could not (and was not allowed to) stop'. But for the wounded and the lame, or even just the bootless, the descent was alarming and painful. One party of wounded descending by daylight were surprised by an air raid. Fortunately, they had been told to discard their helmets to look less like a fighting unit, and a brave Royal Army Medical Corps corporal advanced in front waving a red cross flag. The Messerschmitt pilots spotted the flag in time, waggled their wings in recognition or waved from the cockpit, and turned away.

Creforce Headquarters, from where Captain Morse communicated with Alexandria while organizing the evacuation, was established in the rockface below the end of the road in a cave which Geoffrey Cox described as 'like a setting for the legend of Cyclops'. There, Freyberg summoned Puttick to tell him to leave the island, since Weston's command of the rearguard made a divisional headquarters redundant. Puttick arrived with his officers at last light on Thursday, 29 May. He saluted Freyberg and said 'We did our best. We did all we could.'

Freyberg had also decided to send off his own staff. But that morning, a messenger with orders for Brigadier Vasey commanding the Australian rearguard had to be found, so junior officers in Creforce Headquarters drew lots. The loser, Geoffrey Cox, felt certain he was doomed to a prisoner-of-war camp, but thanks to a helpful Australian on the 'top storey', as the escarpment was known, he found a vehicle which still worked. He was therefore able to make the return trip to the Askifou plain, hand over the orders and obtain a receipt, and return just in time to embark with his colleagues and members of the British Military Mission on the Australian cruiser HMAS *Perth*.

That night, 29 May, saw the largest evacuation. Rear Admiral King had arrived in HMS *Phoebe* with the cruisers *Perth*, *Calcutta* and *Coventry*, three destroyers and the commando troopship HMS *Glengyle*, whose landing craft were invaluable. Over 6,000 men were embarked.

Among others who boarded the *Perth* that night were Stephanides and Michael Forrester. Six months later, they heard of its destruction with all hands off Java after an attack by Japanese bombers. Below decks, the New Zealand officers found to their disgust some of the commandos who were supposed to be forming the rearguard. But the issue of who had been ordered to stay and who had been authorized to leave became very complicated and muddy.

Freyberg himself with the remaining staff officers from the different headquarters were taken off in two Sunderland flying-boats the following night.

When the 5th New Zealand Brigade descended the escarpment on the morning of 30 May, Brigadier Hargest, who like Puttick and Freyberg himself had shown more determination and sound judgement during the retreat than during the battle, was appalled by the wretched state of the stragglers below. Starving and thirsty base-area personnel still several thousand strong were living without any pretence at military order in the ravines in rows of caves like colonies of sand martins. They were panic-ridden by day, especially at the approach of aircraft, and raided the dwindling food dumps and water supply by night. When the wounded were evacuated on the first night,

28 May, some of these men tried to join them, having tied field
dressings round uninjured heads, but the genuine casualties shouted
at them and most were shamed away. The order had gone out that
only formed bodies of men would be embarked, so stragglers begged
any spare officer passing by to form them into a group and march
them in for embarkation. The New Zealanders had set up a cordon
with fixed bayonets to ensure that fighting troops left first. 'My mind
was fixed,' wrote Hargest later. 'We had borne the burden and were
going aboard as a brigade and none would stop us.'

In spite of Hargest's determination, the choice of who was to stay
and who was to go was not so simple. Priority would be given to
officers on the grounds that they were needed to re-form battalions
on their return to Egypt. And an order was issued early in the
afternoon that the 'HQ of each unit must be embarked tonight'.
Numbers of NCOs and soldiers were then allocated by battalion.

Later in the afternoon, there was a sudden outbreak of firing. A
detachment of mountain troops, twenty-two strong, had penetrated
the Sphakia gorge on the west side of the escarpment. A company of
New Zealanders pinned them down while Charles Upham, although
seriously weakened by dysentery, worked his way up with his platoon
round the feature opposite, then annihilated the enemy below.

When night fell, stragglers tried to slip down in the dark past the
armed pickets posted to prevent attempts to rush the boats. And
when the formed bodies of men authorized to embark were marched
down, the last part of the route was lined with the unsuccessful.
'Some begged and implored,' wrote Kippenberger, 'most simply
watched stonily, so that we felt bitterly ashamed.' A few tried to force
or infiltrate their way into a column but were pushed away with
rough outrage. The Maori detachment had a rearguard armed with
Thompson sub-machine guns and a Luger ready to shoot if necessary.
A number of officers behaved little better, even if their tactics were
more sophisticated. Myles Hildyard heard the unmistakable voice of
a contemporary from Eton claiming to be an 'embarkation officer'
and demanding to be let through.

In contrast to the self-serving, some soldiers defied an order that
stretcher cases must be left behind and went to great lengths to
smuggle wounded comrades past the cordon.*

* On the first night, 28 May, HMAS Napier reported her 'haul' as 36 officers, 260
other ranks, 3 women, 1 Greek, 1 Chinaman, 10 distressed merchant seamen, 2
children and 1 dog.

From the beach next to the little harbour of Sphakia, the queue for the landing craft stretched back a considerable way. Hopes and fears rose and fell as the thick shuffling line advanced or halted in the dark. Two of the destroyers had been forced to turn back, so fewer men could be taken off. One New Zealand officer described the welcome sound of 'Navy voices in cultured Dartmouth accents' shouting in the darkness, 'Come on, come on! Get a move on!' But only 1,500 men were embarked that night.

After the chaos on land, everyone greeted the efficiency of the Navy with profound relief. Calm orders from naval officers instilled a forgotten confidence, and for many, the Army suddenly appeared amateur alongside. Exhausted and famished soldiers had great difficulty climbing the scrambling nets, so sailors lent over to grab their shirts to haul them up.

Some found themselves on board the same ship on which they had gone to Greece or left it. Ratings handed out mugs of cocoa and bully beef sandwiches just as they had in the earlier evacuation. Kippenberger, on HMAS *Napier*, noted that an Australian commanding officer and his adjutant came aboard, but on discovering that their battalion had not embarked, they hurried ashore again.

But for those who left, the danger was not entirely over. Michael Forrester, who was on board HMAS *Perth* when she was hit on 30 May, suddenly understood what aerial attack meant to those in a ship at sea. 'My God, the faces of those sailors down below,' he remarked later. And Kippenberger 'formed the opinion that it is nicer on land than aboard ship'.

At dawn on 31 May, Rear Admiral King sailed again from Alexandria with two cruisers, *Phoebe* and *Abdiel*, and two destroyers. After a meeting with Wavell, Cunningham had decided to risk another sortie to Crete even though the Mediterranean Fleet had already been severely diminished while helping to defend the island. 'It takes the Navy three years to build a new ship,' he had declared. 'It will take three hundred years to build a new tradition. The evacuation will continue.'

The Royal Navy was justifiably proud of its work. A favourite toast in the wardrooms of the Mediterranean Fleet was 'To the three Services, the Royal Navy, the Royal Advertising Federation and the Evacuees.' In that last effort, Admiral King's force left at three o'clock on the morning of 1 June with nearly 4,000 men. They returned safely, but the anti-aircraft cruiser HMS *Calcutta*, sent out to cover them, was sunk within a hundred miles of Alexandria.

On arrival in Egypt, most of the men shambled down the gangways of their ships, still exhausted from their ordeal over the mountains. But some battalions fell in on the quayside, right markers and all, then marched off refusing to look like a defeated army.

More troops probably could have been taken off, but that is apparent only with hindsight. The Navy had thought that, under a strong moon, ships would be vulnerable to dive-bombers at night as well as during the long days approaching mid-summer. But Cunningham, in spite of Ultra, did not know that the risk to his ships had decreased sharply in this the last stage of the VIII Air Corps's withdrawal for Operation Barbarossa.

Much has been made of the facts that out of 5,000 troops left behind, there was no officer above the rank of lieutenant colonel, and that a far higher proportion of officers got away than men.

Jack Hamson, captured with a party of the Argylls near Tymbaki, vented the understandable frustration of a prisoner of war. 'One of the worst episodes in that affair', he wrote, 'was the notion that superior officers were specially valuable, that there was an obligation upon them to save themselves, that they were not finally and personally committed in the issue of the operations they were conducting, that they were merely to do their best and would have an opportunity to try again another day. Although the cases are not wholly comparable, the naval tradition that the commander is the last person to be saved out of the catastrophe is, I think, perhaps the sounder one. There were some honourable exceptions, much too conspicuous in their rarity, but for the most part we witnessed not so much a *sauve qui peut* as a damnable and disgraceful scramble for priority, a claim to the privilege of escape based on rank and seniority.'

Freyberg, the general who had stayed until the last in Greece to make sure his men got away, again remained as long as he could. His return to Egypt was essential if only because he was Ultra-indoctrinated. And to have left a figure of his renown in German hands would have added an unnecessary propaganda defeat. Brigadier Inglis offered to stay but Freyberg 'sharply overruled' that idea. Whether Weston or Laycock should have stayed is a difficult question. There was clearly little point in giving the enemy the satisfaction of capturing senior officers; and the British Army's equivalent of a ship's captain is the commanding officer of a battalion or regiment, not a formation commander. But the moral question still hangs unanswered, especially since the self-centred actions of some were thrown into contrast by the selflessness of those regimental officers, NCOs or soldiers who volunteered to stay behind in the place of others.

Mainly due to the diaries of Evelyn Waugh (Layforce's intelligence officer) and his novel *Officers and Gentlemen*, interest in this issue has tended to focus on Colonel Laycock as commander of the rearguard. On the evening of 30 May, just before he left the island, Freyberg told Laycock, 'You were the last to come so you will be the last to go'. At the final conference held by General Weston on the afternoon of 31 May this was reaffirmed. Evelyn Waugh recorded this meeting in Layforce's war diary: 'Final orders from CREFORCE for evacuation (a) LAYFORCE positions not to be held to last man and last round but only as long as was necessary to cover withdrawal of other fighting forces. (b) No withdrawal before order from H.Q. (c) LAYFORCE to embark after other fighting forces but before stragglers.' But later that day Laycock told Freddie Graham, his brigade major, that General Weston had said to him: 'You and your staff and as many of your troops as you can get away must go tonight – my staff will see to it.' He claimed that this had come after a staff officer had intervened to point out that 'Laycock still had two battalions of his brigade in Egypt.' One can hardly imagine one of Weston's staff speaking up to give priority to Layforce when they had their own Marine battalion to get off.

A more likely version is that Laycock collared Weston some time in the early evening, long after the conference in the cave, and persuaded him to allow Layforce Brigade Headquarters to leave. Waugh in his private account wrote, '[Weston] first charged Bob with the task [of surrender] but later realized that it was foolish to sacrifice a first-class man for this and chose instead [Colvin].'

Soon after dusk, Graham reported to Creforce cave on Laycock's instructions. There he found General Weston and Colonel Colvin.

General Weston asked me if I had paper, pencil and carbon paper – quite remarkably I was able to reply in the affirmative thanks to that old friend Army Book 153 which was in my haversack. On my reply General Weston said 'Sit down on that suitcase and take this letter to my dictation. Make three copies.' He then proceeded to dictate the capitulation of Crete! The letter was written in the form of a short operational instruction addressed to the officer whom I have

already said shall remain unidentifiable [i.e. Colvin] instructing
him to go forward at first light to capitulate to the enemy.
General Weston took two of the copies I had made, handed
one to the officer concerned, put the other in his pocket and
with the words: 'Well gentlemen, there are one million
drachmae in that suitcase, there's a bottle of gin in the corner,
goodbye and good luck.' He walked out of the cave and down
the hill into the darkness. Later he was flown out by a flying-
boat which had been sent to fetch him.

Graham was left despondently gazing 'at the miserable little piece of
paper'. It confirmed his worst fears that there was to be no further
evacuation after that night. He roused himself and called the brigade
sergeant major. They would secure one of the landing craft and try
to escape in it later.

Laycock and Waugh must have arrived soon after. They swept
Graham and any other Layforce personnel they could find down to
the beach at Sphakia to join the queue for landing craft out to the
destroyers. Evelyn Waugh made the following entry in the war diary
for 2200 hours.

On finding that entire staff of Creforce had embarked, in view
of fact that all fighting forces were now in position for
embarkation and that there was no enemy contact, Col.
Laycock on own authority, issued orders to Lt. Col. Young to
lead troops to Sphakion by route avoiding the crowded main
approach to town and to use his own personality to obtain
priority laid down in Div. orders.

This version, although closer to the truth than Laycock's, was still
disingenuous. Laycock knew perfectly well from the afternoon
conference that Weston and the rest of Creforce Headquarters were
leaving. There was no enemy contact at that moment only because
the Germans did not fight at night: detachments of mountain troops
had by then surrounded the beachhead and Waugh himself had
recorded firing at dusk. The key point – the claim that all fighting
troops were in position for embarkation – was definitely false. The
Marines and the 2/7th Australian Battalion had not arrived, and
Layforce's orders were to stay in position until they were safely away.
Laycock did not send the message to Young until about 11 p.m.,
by which time he was waiting on the beach with brigade headquarters

staff for a landing craft to take them out to one of the warships. He called for a volunteer, but most of the soldiers present muttered that their boots were not up to the journey. Private Ralph Tanner, Evelyn Waugh's batman, was chosen for the job because he did not object. Nobody could tell him where George Young's headquarters were, so he scrambled up towards the start of the Sphakia ravine. Although only about a mile away the ground was very difficult in the dark, and he wandered about shouting for Layforce. Eventually a member of D Battalion led him to their headquarters cave, where Young gave him some sherry to drink which he gulped down after delivering his message. Young said he would try to bring in his men, but he must have guessed that there was not enough time for those in forward positions to reach the beach. Tanner left bearing this reply for Laycock. Outside the cave, he thought better of the sherry he had consumed on an empty stomach and forced his fingers down his throat. When he got to the beach there was no sign of Laycock. Tanner was so weak that when he was taken out on the last landing craft to a destroyer, he could not climb the scramble net. A sailor reached down to grab the waistband of the unusually tall Tanner, saying, 'Come on, Lofty, for fuck's sake,' and heaved him over the bulwarks on to the deck. Laycock later awarded Tanner a Mention in Dispatches for his efforts.

There is no question of cowardice in the behaviour of Laycock and Waugh. Both men amply demonstrated their fearlessness – in Waugh's case virtually a death wish – during the retreat. But in another context Graham suggested that Waugh perhaps 'had a personal horror of being captured'. This seems highly possible and is perfectly compatible with the degree of courage, astonishing to others yet matter-of-fact to himself, which Waugh displayed on Crete.

Laycock, too, had every reason to believe that he would be of more use to the war effort in Egypt than staying to be captured, but his own words on the subject of the surrender do not help his case. 'My orders were to go with the men, but I am not sure that in cases like that the Commanding Officer should behave in the same way as the captain of a ship and be the last to leave. I attribute the fact that so many were left behind to bad beach organisation, or rather to the entire lack of organisation.' In this account of events on Crete, Laycock was right when he argued that the commandos were not suitable troops for a rearguard. Yet they had been given the job because they were the only fresh troops available, and a lack of suitability is a poor excuse for arrogantly disregarding orders.

In the end Colvin did not carry out the surrender. He seems to have left that night with Laycock, Graham and Waugh although they make no mention of him. At the last moment, Laycock somehow managed to send Weston's surrender instruction back to George Young. He had crossed out Colvin's name and inserted 'Senior officer left on the island' in its place.

Young, who stoically accepted his fate as a prisoner of war, never blamed Laycock. And the suggestion of another officer that Young was left behind because he 'wasn't one of the White's Club gang' is mistaken. Few members of 'the smart set' or 'dandies' as Waugh called them were on Crete: they were mostly in B Battalion, formerly 8 Commando, then in an advanced state of decay at Sidi-Bishr camp near Alexandria.

Evelyn Waugh depicted the collapse in Crete as symbolic of the collapse of the British ruling class. In a letter to Diana Cooper some months afterwards, he wrote: 'The English are a very base people. I did not know this, living as I did. Now I know them through and through and they disgust me.' A dozen years later, when writing *Officers and Gentlemen*, Waugh made Ivor Claire, the Household Cavalry officer who deserts his soldiers in Crete, the personification of this betrayal. When the book was published in June 1955, the dedication read: 'To Major General Sir Robert Laycock KCMG CB DSO. That every man in arms should wish to be.' On seeing this, Ann Fleming sent Waugh a telegram which read: 'Presume Ivor Claire based Laycock dedication ironical.' Waugh's reply she thought 'violent indeed but not wholly simulated'.

'Your telegram horrifies me,' he wrote. 'Of course there is no possible connexion between Bob and Claire. If you suggest such a thing anywhere it will be the end of our beautiful friendship . . . For Christ's sake lay off the idea of Bob=Claire . . . Just shut up about Laycock, Fuck You, E Waugh.' In his diary, he wrote: 'I replied that if she breathes a suspicion of this cruel fact it will be the end of our friendship.'

The term 'cruel fact' does not exactly dispel the suspicion. And even if the character of Ivor Claire represents not an individual, but Waugh's sense that his myth of their gallant company had been betrayed from the start, he and Laycock were the only officers from the original band in 8 Commando who went to Crete. In *Officers and Gentlemen*, Waugh saves Tommy Backhouse (the character bearing the closest resemblance to Laycock) from the moral mess by making him fall down a ship's companionway on the voyage to Crete. Waugh subsequently claimed that officers had behaved disgracefully in Crete, with many of them taking places in the motor transport and leaving the wounded to walk. The degree of disgrace is, of course, hard to assess. In the almost total disintegration of the retreat there were undoubtedly pathetic and shameful spectacles, but the proportion probably remained small, especially amongst regimental officers. In Layforce, although Colonel Colvin went to pieces, and according to Sergeant Stewart's account a subaltern in his battalion cracked up with 'a severe recurrence of chronic neurasthenia', many more officers appear to have performed well, especially George Young and his adjutant, Michael Borwick of the Greys, and Colvin's second-in-command, Ken Wylie, who in Waugh's own words had 'redeemed the Commandos' honour by leading a vigorous and successful counter-attack'. (Both Young and Wylie received the DSO.) Freddie Graham clearly made great efforts for the men and Laycock's leadership during the battle had been admirable. But the passing on of the surrender order and the departure of brigade headquarters raised more than a doubt in Waugh's mind. His cataclysmic view of the débâcle on Crete certainly seems to contain a streak of self-loathing.

Out of all of those left behind, the Australians of Lieutenant Colonel Theo Walker's battalion, the 2/7th, had the right to feel the most bitter. Assured places on the ships, they had marched down to the beach having maintained the perimeter on 'the top storey' until the last moment. They had the longest and most difficult route in the dark of all the troops due to embark that night. On the way, they were delayed by bolshie stragglers refusing to clear a path and by resentful officers who, pretending to be in charge of movement control, demanded that they identify themselves and their authority. It is curious that the Australians showed none of the ruthless determination of the New Zealanders the night before.

Unaware that over two hundred men from Layforce had slipped in ahead of them, they waited patiently in line on the beach. 'Then came the greatest disappointment of all,' wrote their second-in-command later in prison camp. 'The sound of anchor chains through the hawse.'

Many of the others left behind believed the Navy would return again the next night. They did not realize that surrender was imminent. Some were misled during the night. An embarkation officer on the beach told Jack Smith-Hughes not to worry because 'they're coming back tomorrow'. When Smith-Hughes finally escaped from the island several months later by submarine, he happened to see this major again in a restaurant in Cairo and achieved a measure of satisfaction in expressing what he thought of him.

Some of Walker's Australians would not accept the idea of surrender. When they saw soldiers displaying white flags next morning, they asked him whether they should shoot them. But already orders were being shouted from the beach for all troops to remove magazines and bolts from their rifles. The men were told that there would be no further evacuation and were advised to display as much white cloth as possible. Most wandered off in search of food and water. A group of Australians killed a donkey, and began to roast hunks of meat on the fire.

George Young refused his adjutant's offer to accompany him on the surrender. He told Borwick to tell the men. But when Borwick assembled them, his voice broke, he was so close to tears. 'It's all right, sir,' a corporal said, putting a hand on his arm. 'We know it's not your fault.' Young set off alone in search of a German officer to whom he could offer the surrender. Instead, he encountered Colonel Walker and, discovering him to be senior, handed over the order addressed in Laycock's correction to 'Senior officer left on the island'. Walker followed the track up to the village of Komithades and found an Austrian officer of the 100th Mountain Regiment there.

'What are you doing here, Australia?' the Austrian said in English.
'One might ask what are you doing here, Austria?' Walker replied.
'We are all Germans,' he said.

After the surrender had taken place, many of those left climbed back up the hill from the beach. 'There', Myles Hildyard of the Sherwood Rangers recorded in his diary, 'they proceeded to cook the little food they had, and they were sitting around doing this, thinking themselves prisoners and perfectly safe, when German planes came over and machine-gunned them. One of our men was killed outright. The wounded were in a little church, and among them was our sergeant-major Fountain with twelve bullets in him. We heard later that he died. Three Germans who ran out shouting and waving to the planes to clear off were also killed.'

Before the mountain troops began rounding up their captives, commando officers warned their men to get rid of their 'fannies' (a knuckle-duster cum knife which had become the emblem of the Middle East Commandos) in case the Germans felt like executing members of special forces. Most were thrown down a well.

For the Spanish Republicans, the prospect of capture was especially grim. The Germans would almost certainly return them to Franco's Spain where they would be shot like all the other Republicans they had handed over, from militiamen to former ministers in the Popular Front government. Fortunately, the battalion medical officer, Captain Cochrane, who had served in Spain with the International Brigades, had the idea that they should pretend to be Gibraltarians when interrogated.

Some soldiers, horrified by the prospect of imprisonment, tried to escape inland up the gorges. Several died in the attempt. Years later, the skeleton of a soldier who had attempted to scale a cliff was discovered in an inaccessible spot by one of the most famous guerrillas of the resistance, Manoli Paterakis, when illegally hunting an ibex. Others, with equally desperate courage but more success, set off across the Libyan Sea in unsuitable boats. A landing craft moored inside a grotto all day after the surrender left soon after dark with sixty-three men on board. Mountain troops opened fire from the escarpment but missed.

From Rethymno and then Heraklion the advance of General Ringel's mountain regiments, led by tanks and motor-cycle troops, continued across the island. Beyond Ayios Nikolaos at Pahia Ammos the point detachment sighted some light tanks ahead. These vehicles appeared to be abandoned, so a German officer went forward to investigate. He claimed to have found their Italian crews crouched behind them trembling with fear, but German stories about their allies must always be treated with caution.

This Italian force had taken part in the unopposed landings at Siteia starting on 28 May. The Italian occupation of the eastern provinces of Siteia and Lasithi was made the responsibility of General Angelo Carta's Siena Division, which had fought rather unsuccessfully against the Cretan V Division on the Albanian front.

For those captured at Sphakia nothing was crueller than the march back to Canea over the same painful route, a double ration of the 'via Dolorosa'. The only consolation for the Welch Regiment captured on the north coast was that they were spared this return journey.

A German propaganda photograph shows a millipede of men in single file snaking as far as the eye can see. Many of those whose boots had given out had nothing more than soles of cardboard tied to their feet with strips of cloth. There was little food to eat except

what Cretan villagers offered along the way. Many men had eaten no
more than a tin of bully beef and a few biscuits in the course of a
whole week.

On the way, outbursts of firing in the distance gave heart to those
who had been with the 50th Middle East Commando in Heraklion
the year before and had worked with John Pendlebury. Not knowing
of his death they were certain that this must be his work, but it was
probably German execution squads carrying out reprisals against
Cretan *francs-tireurs*.

Prison camp conditions on the site of the field hospital west of
Canea were deplorable, mainly due to the German authorities' lack
of interest. The paratroopers detailed to guard the prisoners, while
their officers toiled over casualty returns and letters of condolence to
next-of-kin, preferred to spend their time on the beach sunbathing,
their bodies glistening with olive oil. Their naked bathing scandalized
the socially conservative Cretans, for whom the display of nudity was
insult piled on injury. Fortunately for British prisoners, the guards'
insouciance allowed them to slip out of the camp to forage for food
with the help of villagers, and in some cases recover their belongings
abandoned at the start of the retreat.

Among the wounded, survival depended on the speed with which
they were flown back to Athens for treatment. Sandy Thomas, who
was hit at Galatas, had to be moved away from the other patients
because of the gangrenous stench from his leg. To everyone's
astonishment, he never lost it. Thomas reached Athens in time for it
to be saved because the shuttle of Junkers 52 transport aircraft
worked so well from Maleme.

Many prisoners escaped, swelling the number of stragglers
sheltered in mountain villages by Cretan families. Myles Hildyard and
a brother officer from the Sherwood Rangers, Michael Parrish,
decided instead to make their way by caique across the Aegean to
Turkey. By an extraordinary coincidence they came to the uninhabited
island where the *Kalanthe* sank, arriving the day after fishermen had
recovered two bodies and a tin box containing the correspondence
between Sir Michael Palairet and King George II. Hildyard buried the
two skeletons, one of which wore the remnants of British uniform and
a signet ring. Nearly fifty years later he met Harold and Nancy
Caccia, and they concluded that he had indeed buried Nancy's
brother Oliver Barstow, whose body was never found after the
explosion. When Hildyard and Parrish finally reached Turkey, they
delivered the box of papers to the Embassy.

20
Cairo and London

After Crete, to return to Egypt was to return to an unreal normality. It took many forms, both personal and official. Michael Forrester, arriving on the embattled *Perth* at Alexandria, caught a train to Cairo and that afternoon, surrounded by the well-tailored uniforms of GHQ staff officers known as the gaberdine swine, he had tea at the Gezira club. 'There was Cairo, just as I had left it.'

Stephanides soon found that the wheels of mindless military bureaucracy ran in the same grooves. Those who had served in the expeditionary force in Greece and subsequently in Crete received notification that Colonial Allowance was to be docked from their pay for the full period of their absence from Egypt. Not surprisingly, there was a spate of black humour. The word went round that a special evacuation medal would be presented with the inscription EX CRETA.

In London, humour while dark was more flippant. The fashionable new word for coming unstuck was *'dégommage'*, and wits claimed that BEF, the initials for British Expeditionary Force, really meant Back Every Fortnight. But levity could not conceal a profound unease, even a fear that the war might be lost after all. Apart from the fall of Greece, London had been heavily bombed in April, the House of Commons hit on 10 May, and now Rommel threatened the whole of Libya. The popular press was full of scare stories that Hitler would attempt an airborne invasion of Britain. And the sinking of the *Bismarck* in the Atlantic by no means effaced the shock of the loss of the British battleship HMS *Hood*.

The débâcle on Crete had an effect out of proportion to the number of troops involved. And if one of Churchill's main objectives in supporting Greece was to appeal to American opinion, his attempt seems to have been counter-productive. 'The reaction of the US to our naval losses round Crete, and of the *Hood* has been very bad,' wrote David Eccles in Washington to his wife, Sybil. 'Why do they fear death more than the consequences of defeat?' She replied that the Crete episode had 'instilled a horrid doubt as to whether we've really got the hang of the thing'.

For Churchill, the most passionate believer in the defence of Crete, its fall was a bitter and personal blow. He also came in for a good deal of criticism. Harold Nicolson, then in the Ministry of Information, wrote in his diary: 'The public are in a trough of depression over . . . Crete feeling that we shall probably be turned out again. I must say that this 200-mile jump is terrifying. No wonder people say that if they can take Crete from 200 miles away, what will happen to Great Britain.' Churchill, to Nicolson's irritation, believed this mood to be 'purely a House of Commons anxiety'.

In Cairo, the British Ambassador Sir Miles Lampson, after talking to Wavell while the evacuation was in progress, wrote in his diary: 'I don't think I have ever seen our Archie quite so gloomy.' Wavell was especially saddened by the appalling casualties inflicted on his old battalion of the Black Watch during the return from Heraklion. And Wavell's ADC, Peter Coats, recorded Freyberg's desolation. 'As I write, General Freyberg is in my office, sitting opposite me. A crushed Goliath, and almost in tears. His stepson, Guy McLaren, has been reported killed in the desert. What a home-coming the poor man has had.'

One of Freyberg's most admirable qualities was his refusal to pass blame on to others. For him, the post-catastrophe atmosphere in Cairo was doubly unpleasant. The RAF attracted much of the obloquy. It was a repeat, or rather an extension, of the recriminations which had followed the fall of Greece, when accusations flew back and forth between RAF and Army at all levels, and soldiers and airmen fought each other in the bars and streets of Alexandria. An air marshal described GHQ as 'a hum of splenetic activity, reminiscent of an overturned beehive'. 'Everyone', commented Peter Wilkinson more succinctly, 'was pouring shit all over each other.'

But for Freyberg worse was to come. Since he never attempted to shift any blame on to subordinates, he felt especially betrayed by Brigadier Inglis, who had returned to London immediately after the evacuation and had seen Churchill on 13 June. Most of Brigadier Inglis's verbal report to the Prime Minister was directed against the lack of preparation and hard thinking on the part of GHQ Middle East. But he also expressed his views on the handling of the battle.

I am far from reassured [wrote Churchill the following day to General Ismay for the Chiefs of Staff committee] about the tactical conduct of the defence by General Freyberg, although full allowance must be made for the many deficiencies noted above. There appears to have been no counter-attack of any kind in the Western sector until more than 36 hours after the airborne descents had begun. There was no attempt to form a mobile reserve of the best troops, be it only a couple of battalions. There was no attempt to obstruct the Maleme aerodrome, although General Freyberg knew he would have no Air in the battle. The whole conception seems to have been of static defence of positions, instead of the rapid extirpations at all costs of the airborne landing parties.

No mention was made at that stage of Freyberg's fundamental misunderstanding over the seaborne invasion that-never-was, although this was the main reason why he, Puttick and Hargest had held back. Churchill later realized that Freyberg's view of the airborne and seaborne threats had been reversed, but he never understood the extent or the exact consequences of this misunderstanding. And the enquiry set up under Brigadier Salisbury-Jones in Cairo, on Churchill's insistence, did not have access to the Ultra signals. Thus it was never aware of the futile defence of Canea on the crucial night of 21 May.

Inglis's 'betrayal' obsessed Freyberg for the rest of his life, no doubt partly because the criticisms had been delivered to Churchill, his own friend and patron. And when both coded and open criticisms of his handling of the battle appeared later, especially in Alan Clark's *The Fall of Crete*, Freyberg seems to have convinced himself that Inglis, virtually single-handed, had distorted posterity's view of his role in the battle.

For General Student, his 'disastrous victory' on Crete also led to a painful anti-climax. Along with his leading officers he was invited to Hitler's headquarters, the Wolfschanze, where congratulations were made with presentations of the Knight's Cross of the Iron Cross. Then, during coffee after lunch, the Führer abruptly turned to him. 'Of course, you know. General,' he said, 'we shall never do another airborne operation. Crete proved that the days of parachute troops are over. The parachute arm is one that relies entirely on surprise. In the meantime the surprise factor has exhausted itself.' Most of his men were then sent to Russia as ground troops. The irony of this outcome when London was panic-ridden at the idea of a parachute invasion and the British and Americans were developing their own airborne formations needs no underlining, except perhaps to add that Student was the general commanding the Arnhem front in the autumn of 1944 when the great Allied airborne operation failed.

Every paratrooper who survived the battle received an Iron Cross, but for Student himself Crete always remained 'a bitter memory'. The Germans had lost 3,986 killed and missing and 2,594 wounded between 20 May and 2 June: paratroopers killed on the first day made up half of this total. These heavy losses, 'particularly in missing', were 'attributed by the German Command to the considerable activity of Cretan *francs-tireurs*.'

The loss of 350 aircraft, especially the 151 Junkers transport planes, nearly a third of Student's fleet, was even more serious for the Nazi war effort. If Crete had an effect on the Russian campaign, it was that German production of transport aircraft never caught up in time for the Stalingrad airlift. As mentioned earlier, the notion that the battles of Greece and Crete delayed Barbarossa with fatal effect was nothing more than wishful consolation.

Freyberg was not the only one to acquire *idées fixes* during his time in Crete. On the beach at Alexandria, shortly after his return to Egypt, Evelyn Waugh began an argument with Gerry de Winton and Randolph Churchill about the withdrawal. 'His attitude', de Winton recalled, 'was that everyone there had behaved in the most cowardly way.' He answered Waugh by pointing out that in Greece 'everybody kept their heads really to the last moment', because they had not suffered the combined effect of continuous bombing and extreme fatigue which eventually saps any courage. Waugh refused to take the point, and insisted that in Crete the lack of courage was shameful. 'I thought he was quite childish about it,' de Winton commented.

Waugh had arrived fresh with Layforce, while others had been fighting with little sleep for seven days and nights. Nor was he able to judge the full force of air attack, since it was much reduced in the last few days as the VIII Air Corps started to withdraw for Operation Barbarossa. And although Layforce's welcome to Crete had been demoralizing, it was still not as devastating a disappointment as that suffered by soldiers who, after a week of fighting, were convinced that they had beaten the enemy.

Laycock, rather surprisingly in the circumstances, argued: 'In my view the island should never have been evacuated at all, since the loss of shipping and of sailors' lives could not be balanced by the advantage of withdrawing some 15,000 soldiers who were already considerably demoralized after the evacuation of Greece.' But this advantage, the equivalent of a couple of divisions when the battle-experienced cadres were brought up to strength, was in crude terms worth far more at that moment of the war than all the cruisers and the destroyers lost, if only because warships alone could not stop Rommel's advance.

Hamson passionately argued that only will had been lacking. 'Our case was indeed not desperate; and a resounding victory over the Germans in the spring of 1941 was militarily of very great value.' His thesis, although wild at times due to the frustration of the prison camp, is more convincing than that of Chips Channon, for example, who dismissed the battle as a waste from the start.

Determination had not been lacking amongst the troops. Nor had it really been lacking amongst the commanders on the island, although one cannot help suspecting that the preoccupation with a seaborne assault also offered an excuse to postpone difficult decisions. What the commanders lacked, Freyberg above all, was clarity of thinking. The consequence of this failing was to be enchained by his own misconceptions. Every German account of the battle emphasizes that in spite of the handicaps, of which communication was the greatest, Freyberg undoubtedly had the means to win the battle during the critical period of the first forty-eight hours. But he did not win it, he could not win it, because his fatal misreading directed him in entirely the wrong direction.

Whether or not winning the battle would necessarily have been a good thing in the long term has stimulated a lively hypothetical debate. Many people more militarily expert than Chips Channon have argued that it would have been impossible to maintain a garrison on the island and supply it. But no British troops would have been needed. Raising a second Cretan division combined with other Greek troops escaped from the mainland and arming them with captured German weaponry would have been sufficient.

An unexpected argument has, however, been advanced against this. It runs roughly as follows. If Crete had been held, the King of the Hellenes, George II, would have insisted on retaining command in this the last corner of his kingdom. But the combination of his intransigence, Cretan anti-monarchism and political unrest in the Greek armed forces which led to the mutinies in Egypt in 1944 would have brought on the Greek civil war even more rapidly, and reduced any British influence either on the mainland or on Crete. A victory for the Anglo-Greek forces in May 1941 would thus have led to Communist control of the whole country on the German withdrawal in 1944.

Leaving aside the unpredictability of Greek politics, if the Allies had won the Battle of Crete Hitler would not have switched his attention from Barbarossa for another attempt to invade the island. He had always been sceptical of Student's plan and had no personal stake in it. He would only have been provoked into a second invasion of Crete if long-range bomber bases had been established there in late 1942 or early 1943 to attack the Ploesti oilfields with Liberators. Then he would have been forced to divert badly needed resources from the Russian front. Britain had no idea that spring quite how important Crete could have become to the war effort, and many preferred to overlook it afterwards simply because the battle had been lost. American influence subsequently ensured that attention was concentrated on Italy, not the Balkans, so the whole weight of the war shifted away from the Eastern Mediterranean.

Yet for the Cretans themselves, and a handful of British, the battle for Crete was far from over.

PART THREE
The Resistance

21
Reprisal, Evasion and Resistance

In the short period of silence after the fighting was over, many Cretans felt a bewildered exasperation with British incompetence and the refusal to give them arms. This mood did not last long. Hatred of the invader, and thus affinity with their allies, was soon resuscitated by German reprisals.

German resentment was strong, especially among the rear echelon as is so often the case. The Wehrmacht had just suffered its heaviest losses so far during the war. Hurt pride was fuelled by anger that so many of their finest troops had been killed before they even touched the ground. They somehow felt that the British should have allowed them to land first. But that was nothing beside their anger at the resistance of armed Cretan civilians, whom they regarded with dread and loathing.

Every paratrooper on joining his regiment received a copy of General Student's 'Ten Commandments of the Parachute Division'. The ninth read: 'Against a regular enemy fight with chivalry, but give no quarter to guerrillas.' This dictum reflected a very Germanic attitude to the rules of war: no one but professional warriors should be allowed to fight. And in Crete paratroopers had encountered a popular resistance unprecedented in the Wehrmacht's experience.

The excessively high casualties of the Parachute Division were soon being explained away by outraged stories in which Cretan crones with kitchen knives cut the throats of paratroopers caught in trees, and roving bands of civilians tortured wounded German soldiers lying helpless on the field of battle. As soon as these accounts reached Berlin, Goering ordered Student to instigate an immediate judicial enquiry and carry out reprisals. In typical Nazi fashion, the reprisals took place before the twelve military judges had had time to report their findings.

The first affidavits were taken on 26 May and the whole process continued for three months. Judge Schölz, in a preliminary report on 4 June, wrote that: 'Many parachutists were subjected to inhuman treatment or mutilated', and that 'Greek civilians participated in the fight as *francs-tireurs*.' Later on, after a more careful study, Judge Rüdel could only account for about twenty-five cases of mutilation on the entire island, and almost all of those had almost certainly been inflicted after death. But General Student had already issued the following order on 31 May:

> It is certain that the civilian population including women and boys have taken part in the fighting, committed sabotage, mutilated and killed wounded soldiers. It is therefore high time to combat all cases of this kind, to undertake reprisals and punitive expeditions which must be carried through with exemplary terror.
>
> The harshest measures must indeed be taken and I order the following: shooting for all cases of proven cruelty, and I wish this to be done by the same units who have suffered such atrocities. The following reprisals will be taken:
> 1. Shooting
> 2. Fines
> 3. Total destruction of villages by burning
> 4. Extermination of the male population of the territory in question
>
> My authority will be necessary for measures under 3 and 4. All these measures must, however, be taken rapidly and omitting all formalities. In view of the circumstances the troops have a right to this and there is no need for military tribunals to judge beasts and assassins.

When this order was issued, a number of officers protested against the indiscriminate execution of civilians. Major Count von Uxküll, the Parachute Division's chief of staff, was fearless in his denunciation of the plan and when it was announced, he is said to have stormed out of the conference followed by several other officers.* Colonel Bruno

* There is some doubt, however, whether such a meeting took place, and Baron von der Heydte, who was a friend of Uxküll's, does not remember it.

Bräuer, who later became the General commanding the garrison of Crete, derided the stories of torture as fabrications.

Inevitably there were a few officers prepared to lead the execution squads. At Kondomari, where about sixty civilians were shot, the firing party was commanded by Lieutenant Horst Trebes who had taken part in Dr Neumann's occupation of Hill 107. Trebes, a former member of the Hitler Youth, was in a merciless mood: he was the only officer of his battalion to have come through unscathed. (Trebes met his death in Normandy three years later when commanding a paratroop battalion.) But Franz-Peter Weixler, the journalist who survived the glider crash, was court martialled and jailed for helping a Cretan to escape and for having taken photographs of the executions.

A German military doctor sent to investigate the charges of mutilation in Kastelli Kissamou, where Lieutenant Mürbe's detachment had been almost wiped out, reported that German troops had executed 200 male civilians because of the mutilation stories. (According to Judge Rüdel there had been six to eight cases there, the highest number on the island.) The villages of Kakopetro, Floria and Prasses also suffered. The later, and more open, German Command under General Bräuer recorded the execution of a total of 698 alleged *francs-tireurs*, and 180 men who came under General Student's heading 'Extermination of the male population of the territory in question'.

On 3 June Kandanos paid the price for resisting the advance of the motor-cycle detachments to the south coast. 'This is the site of Kandanos', began the German proclamation displayed at the blackened site. 'It was destroyed as a reprisal for the killing of twenty-five German soldiers.' And on 1 August a punitive drive south of Canea – 'Special Action No. 1' – destroyed more villages, including Alikianou, Fournès and Skenès. A further 145 men and 2 women were shot, the majority of them from Fournès. But most of the executions had already been carried out before 10 June, when the State Department in Washington informed the British Embassy of Berlin's intention to try British and Cretan prisoners for atrocities committed against German paratroopers. The message said that 'certain punitive measures, at least with respect to the Cretans, appear to be necessary for the parachute troops'.

Agathángelos Xirouhakis, Bishop of Kydonia and Apokoronas, tried to persuade General Waldemar Andrae, the general who replaced Student as commander on the island, that his policy would only generate further bloodshed on both sides. Andrae 'was inclined to agree', recorded the report compiled under his successor General Bräuer, 'but wished that a demonstration of force should take place first so that the gesture might not be taken for a sign of weakness. This demonstration of force was termed "League of Nations Undertaking".'

However, this bizarrely misnamed operation took the form of another punitive expedition rather than a display of strength. On 1 September 'a reinforced regiment [presumably about two thousand strong] of German mountain troops surrounded the Omalos plain in the White Mountains having approached from several directions. Sporadic resistance was encountered, but no proper guerrilla organization. German losses were one dead and two wounded. The population had to submit to the inquest of the Expedition Tribunals. The Tribunals found 110 men guilty, including 39 civilians and 6 British military personnel; all faced summary execution for attempted resistance.* The German Command considered the expedition a complete success, having given the population the impression that even in the most distant areas it was impossible to escape the discipline of the conquerors.'

General Ringel, the commander of the mountain troops, was in the White Mountains for other purposes. He was a keen chamois hunter at home in the Alps, and longed to bag one of the rare Cretan ibex. Manoussos Manoussakis, a young Cretan reserve officer who had gone to the Askifou plain to buy lentils because of the food shortage in Canea, found himself drafted as Ringel's guide, but he managed to avoid finding him an ibex.

The German propaganda machine soon changed direction. The English-language edition of *Signal* magazine showed photographs of paratroopers with local children entitled: 'Despite the tough battle no resentiments [*sic*] on Crete.'

For the Cretans, however, hatred of the enemy was so great that it sometimes went to irrational lengths. Even after the war, tractors and a steam-roller used on the Omalos plain to build an airfield were destroyed simply because they were German.

Occupied Crete was divided between the main German zone and a subsidiary Italian zone. The Italian forces, for the most part consisting

---

* Of the 1,135 Cretans executed from the start of the invasion until 9 September 1941, only 224 were sentenced by military tribunal.

of the Siena Division commanded by General Angelo Carta, were based in the two eastern provinces of Siteia and Lasithi. General Carta had his headquarters in Neapolis and ran his zone, admittedly a more pacific part of the island, with an easy-going attitude of which the Germans disapproved. Wanted men like the Communist leader Miltiades Porphyroyennis, on whom Harold Caccia had taken pity, were to hide in the Italian zone.

The three German-occupied provinces of Canea, Rethymno and Heraklion were controlled by garrisons in the major towns and a network of smaller outposts commanded by a sergeant or sergeant major. Along the southern coast, which became a prohibited area once British assistance to the Cretan resistance began in earnest, a line of linked guardposts was established in a vain attempt to prevent clandestine landings.

Predictably, the mountain villages with their warlike traditions and spirit of resistance represented the greatest threat to the Germans. Troops were most reluctant to venture out in highland areas. Often on approaching likely ambush points they would spray bushes with sub-machine gun fire as a precaution. The large towns which were heavily garrisoned proved much easier to cow. But the Germans' comparative lack of success in recruiting informers made it far harder to infiltrate nascent resistance networks, whether Nationalist or Communist, than in the rest of occupied Europe.

The German commander of the *Festung*, the Fortress of Crete, had his headquarters in Canea. His residence was the Venizelos family house in Halepa, built early in the century by a German architect. The first *Festung* commander was General Andrae. He was succeeded by the more enlightened Bräuer in the autumn of 1942, and Bräuer was succeeded by the most hated of them all, General Müller, in the spring of 1944.

In addition, there was a divisional commander who had his headquarters south of Heraklion at Arkhanes and his residence at the Villa Ariadne. Müller made his reputation for brutality while holding this position before his promotion to commander of the *Festung*. His replacement, General Kreipe, abducted in a joint Anglo-Cretan operation in April 1944, was the last. The total of the Axis forces fluctuated greatly, according to the fortunes of the North African campaign, the situation on the Eastern Front, or the perceived threat of invasion: it ranged from around 75,000 in 1943 to just over 10,000 at the time of the surrender in 1945.

Conditions in Crete deteriorated drastically under the occupation.

The threat of starvation ebbed and flowed, but fortunately famine never took hold as it did on the mainland where many thousands died. For example, in Asi Gonia – an area where sheep-stealing was endemic and even the priest overlooked the provenance of his meat – only the high-principled schoolmaster died of hunger. But basic materials were very hard to find. Leather became virtually unobtainable, so soles were cut from old car tyres. A skilled cutter could get up to a dozen pairs from each tyre.

Life was most difficult in the big towns, especially for anyone without peasant relatives. But those with easy access to produce could do more than deal in the local black market. German officers and NCOs proved surprisingly easy to corrupt as the occupation continued. One family in Heraklion obtained the release of a relative by supplying the Cretan mistress of a German officer with food. Relations with local women constituted a disciplinary offence, and since official army brothels were provided for the garrison the penalties could be severe. A German sergeant in Canea who made a cleaning woman pregnant forced her to marry a drunken layabout in the port to avoid retribution.

Trade with the mainland did not cease entirely despite the confiscation of caiques to prevent escaped prisoners of war and stragglers leaving the island. Enough boats evaded the German round-up to take olive oil and assorted British, New Zealanders and Australians to the mainland, providing they could pay, and bring back cigarettes and members of the Cretan Division on the return journey. Myles Hildyard's family only knew that he was alive – he had been posted missing – when their bank in Newark rang up to enquire about a personal cheque he had written for £50 to pay his passage.

Some of the confiscated caiques were thought to have been put to a dreadful purpose. About two hundred Cretan Jews, mainly from Canea and Heraklion, were taken away in the night. 'One day they were there,' an old woman in Canea remembered of their neighbours, 'the next morning they were gone.' The exact fate of Cretan Jews is still unclear. A few Jews from Heraklion were amongst those shot in reprisal for a British raid in June 1942. Many more were held in Ayia prison before being shipped to the mainland and thence to the death camps of Northern Europe, but SOE Cairo heard that most of the Jews were put on a vessel sunk by an Allied submarine. This might explain why many Cretans think the majority were embarked in caiques which were then sunk, like the *noyades* of the French Revolution.

On 26 July, nearly two months after the conquest of Crete, the submarine HMS *Thrasher* put Commander Francis Pool RNR ashore on the south coast near the monastery of Preveli. 'Skipper' Pool, invariably described as 'a colourful character', knew Cretan waters well. Before the war he had run the Imperial Airways flying-boat station on the island of Spinalonga, a former leper colony.

In Turkish times messages had been rapidly transmitted by trumpet along the string of small forts built between Canea and Sphakia. News of Pool's arrival seemed to spread across the island even faster. Cretan optimism surged. The British had promised to return with weapons for them, they told each other. But Skipper Pool's mission was far less dramatic.

He had come, initially only for one trip, to organize the evacuation of the stragglers and escaped prisoners who had gravitated towards Preveli. It was a huge task, and one which the Cretans must have privately appreciated. Their compulsive generosity – housing and feeding those who had come to fight on their side – had developed into an immense burden during that famine-haunted year.

Cretans seldom complained even when a small minority of British and Dominion soldiers proved both a trial and a danger to those who risked execution by sheltering them. Drunken singing, both 'Tipperary' and 'Waltzing Matilda', could occasionally be heard from some distance outside villages, as khaki-clad figures lurched about drowning their sorrows. A year after the invasion there were still so many stragglers sheltered on the island that when Tom Dunbabin took over command of the SOE mission and cautiously admitted to some villagers that he was English, the laconic reply was: 'Ah yes, we have plenty of those.'

Skipper Pool was taken to see the Abbot of Preveli, Father Agathángelos Langouvardos, a fearless and enchanting old man of enormous size who agreed to the monastery's use as a marshalling yard for escapees. Deciding to stay to round up more, Pool set out into the interior of the island to make contact with other groups. Rather optimistic news of a ferry service to Egypt even reached the badly guarded prison camp at Galatas and encouraged more to escape.

The dignified and discreet 'Uncle' Niko Vandoulakis at Vaphé sheltered so many on their way south-eastwards that he became known as the British Consul. One of the most important junctions of the overland network of escape routes was the large village of Asi Gonia, situated at the eastern end of the White Mountains where the island narrows. Like other villages which began by helping stragglers, it later proved itself among the most valiant centres of resistance in Crete under the leadership of its kapitan, Petro Petrakas. Petrakas, a friend and bodyguard of Venizelos, was given the code-name Beowulf because of his Nordic blue eyes and his fair hair and whiskers.

In the mountains above Asi Gonia, Lieutenant Colonel Papadakis, a reserve officer invalided out of the Greek army in 1922, also took escaped prisoners of war into his house. One of them, an unusual subaltern in the Royal Army Service Corps called Jack Smith-Hughes, was to be the first officer sent to Crete by SOE to help organize resistance.

The open secret of submarines off Preveli could not be kept from the ears of 'bad Greeks' and from the Germans. In fact British officers later dubbed this rapid spread of supposedly secret information 'the Cretan wireless'. The Germans sent out spies in battledress posing as escaped British soldiers to discover the escape routes and the villages involved. Very few Cretans were fooled. When villagers discovered these imposters, they would 'thrash them like donkeys', all the while declaring their loyalty to the great German Reich, then drag them to the nearest garrison where the senior officer, no doubt with an acid smile, was obliged to thank them.

Because of the danger, the old Abbot of Preveli had to go into hiding before his eventual evacuation to Cairo. His disappearance enabled his equally helpful monks to transfer all the blame when the Germans surrounded the monastery one morning. No escapers were discovered, but the Germans, convinced that guilt was collective, stripped the monastery farm of livestock and supplies. Then, to ensure that no further submarine visits took place on that stretch of coast, they established a post nearby.

Skipper Pool, having rounded up another 130 men, left on 22 August aboard HMS *Torbay*, establishing a record for the number of people ever jammed into one submarine. The *Torbay* was famous for the eccentricity of its subsequently controversial captain, Commander 'Crap' Miers VC. One of Miers's passengers, Major Ray Sandover, the Australian battalion commander from Rethymno, felt slightly self-conscious in his disintegrating uniform when invited to join the captain on the conning tower for their entry into Alexandria harbour. 'Usual drill, Number One,' ordered Miers, as the crew prepared to pay compliments. For the *Torbay*, compliments to the Vichy French ships interned in the harbour consisted of a row of bared bottoms.

The first British mission with the task of developing and assisting a local resistance movement landed in Crete on 9 October. It consisted of two men: Jack Smith-Hughes of SOE and Ralph Stockbridge of ISLD – Inter Services Liaison Department, the cover-name for MI6. Stockbridge, at that time a signals NCO not long down from Cambridge, knew little about wirelesses. He had transferred to ISLD from the Field Security Police, with whom he had served in Heraklion from December 1940 until the evacuation.

Of all the British officers who were to serve in Crete, Jack Smith-Hughes – a barrister with a brilliant mind and a strong sense of the ridiculous – was the most obviously English. A tall, pink-cheeked and rather portly young man, he looked conspicuously incongruous in Cretan dress.

Smith-Hughes and Stockbridge crossed from Egypt in the submarine HMS *Thunderbolt*. Smith-Hughes did not tell his companion that their vessel was really the old *Thetis* which had sunk with all hands and had later been recovered. (The change of name was no protection, for *Thunderbolt* was lost for good later in the war.) After landing in the south-west near Tsoutsouro, where they were feasted by the whole village, they set off for Colonel Papadakis's house at Vourvouré. Papadakis was the only Cretan officer whom Smith-Hughes had encountered during his escape from the prison camp, and his orders from Cairo – a model of imprecision – were 'to feel out the country to see who had influence'.

In this superannuated colonel he could hardly have stumbled upon a more unsuitable candidate. Papadakis, a man of great egotism, wasted no time in proclaiming himself head of 'The Higher Committee of Cretan Freedom', much to the embarrassment and subsequent tribulation of British officers. Yet Papadakis, although impossible himself, had assembled a handful of remarkable men who were to make major contributions to the resistance later, especially in the field of intelligence. Perhaps his greatest coup was to recruit George Halkiadakis, the chief of police in Rethymno. One lasting benefit to come out of this re-encounter was the appointment of George Psychoundakis (Smith-Hughes's guide during his earlier escape to Preveli) as their permanent runner.

Psychoundakis – a jester in the true sense of the term since his wit was based on a disconcerting honesty – proved one of the most outstanding characters to emerge during the Cretan resistance. Although little more than a shepherd boy with the most rudimentary education, his juvenilia included precocious poems such as 'Ode to an

Inkspot on a Schoolmistress's Skirt'. His natural talent finally achieved international fame with *The Cretan Runner*, an unrivalled account of the occupation years and the resistance. In 1988 he was fêted by the Greek Academy for his translation of *The Odyssey* into the Cretan dialect.

Although Smith-Hughes and Stockbridge could do little to help resistance at such an early stage, some Cretans were already fighting back against the Germans. That sweep in the White Mountains during the first week of September had produced minor clashes in which four soldiers were killed. The Germans offered an amnesty on 9 September and, though there were relatively few respondents, they regarded it as a success. But in the second week of November about seven soldiers were killed during another sweep.

On 23 November, Monty Woodhouse reached Crete on Mike Cumberlege's latest caique, the *Escampador*, and landed at Treis Ekklisies – Three Churches – to take over from Jack Smith-Hughes who returned to Cairo to run SOE's Cretan desk. Woodhouse came with four of his prize students from the SOE training school at Haifa, one of whom later turned traitor and was executed by Tom Dunbabin, the senior British officer.

Expecting a clandestine landing, Woodhouse found a reception committee of bewildering size. Apart from Jack Smith-Hughes, there were the three main guerrilla kapitans of central Crete: Manoli Bandouvas, his *frère ennemi* Petrakageorgis and Satanas, together with scores of British and Anzac soldiers clamouring for evacuation. A number had acquired Cretan girlfriends and wanted to take them to Egypt.

Jack Smith-Hughes left Crete a week before Christmas with three abbots, including the twenty-two-stone Abbot of Preveli, who before he died swore in the new Greek government-in-exile. Woodhouse, then a 24-year-old captain, was left in sole charge. Woodhouse had trouble dealing with Bandouvas, whom Smith-Hughes had awarded the code-name of Bo-Peep because he owned so many sheep.

Bandouvas was a complex man. Illiterate, undeniably patriotic, crafty yet headstrong – Smith-Hughes said that he had 'the restless, furtive eyes of the rich peasant' – he was a ruthless chieftain who was all too conscious of his considerable following in the villages of central Crete and disliked the idea of receiving instructions from a young Englishman, irrespective of their provenance. He later demanded unsuccessfully that he should have his own wireless link with Cairo and control arms drops. German propaganda circulated the rumour that Woodhouse had tried to persuade Bandouvas to make Crete part of the British Empire, a fabrication which the Communists later disseminated as proven.*

Petrakageorgis, on the other hand, received the code-name Selfridge because his olive-crushing enterprise was Crete's closest approximation to big business. Petrakageorgis was one of the most pro-British of the guerrilla kapitans, but even he could not conceal his disappointment that SOE in Cairo had nothing more to offer than a handful of Italian rifles from the booty captured in Cyrenaica.

Woodhouse was reinforced some seven weeks after his arrival. The submarine *Torbay* arrived off the beach at Tsoutsouros on the night of 11 January and put ashore two officers who could hardly have been more different. Xan Fielding was slim, energetic and not inclined to suffer fools gladly. His stinging signals on the subject of SOE Cairo's incompetence became famous. Sandy Rendel, a later member of the British Military Mission, described his reports as 'fruity, flippant and bloodthirsty'. The Cretans took to Fielding's robust sense of humour immediately and respected both his bravery and his judgement.

His companion, whose selection for special operations was never satisfactorily explained, was the brave but lumbering Captain Guy Turrall, who if he was not Evelyn Waugh's model for the unfortunate Apthorpe certainly should have been. An old Africa hand from Abyssinia, he apparently said in all seriousness on the beach: 'Are the natives friendly?' Turrall refused to abandon his uniform for local dress, and had even brought his pyjamas and an enamel wash basin which amazed the Cretans. Only the thunder-box was missing.

The Cretan impression of English eccentricity was greatly increased as they saw more of him. Guy Turrall was a keen amateur geologist and botanist. His collection of wild-flower specimens – one plant was no different from any other in Cretan eyes – did not concern them. But a young Cretan who found himself having to carry Turrall's pack at one stage discovered it to be loaded with rock specimens. These he drastically reduced.

Fielding and Turrall followed Jack Smith-Hughes's tracks to Colonel Papadakis above Asi Gonia. Xan Fielding quickly saw that little would be achieved with this self-proclaimed leader of the pan-

---

* Bandouvas, as his long and very unreliable memoir dictated in old age shows, had great difficulty distinguishing any truth other than his own.

Cretan resistance: nobody outside Papadakis's immediate circle acknowledged him. Competent and dedicated officers such as Major Tsiphakis, who had brought together an intelligence network round Rethymno, refused to take him seriously. Evenings with Papadakis were excruciating. The lugubrious conversation was not helped by Turrall's inability to speak Greek. He attempted to converse in French. 'I say, *mon colonel, vous ne m'avez pas mis dans le tableau*', was but one of his classics.

Fielding soon moved closer to Canea and Suda Bay. He based himself at Vaphé with the 'British Consul', Niko Vandoulakis, and began to transmit intelligence on air and sea movements to Cairo with the help of a small group of exceptionally able and courageous young men known as 'the Quins', led by Marko Spanoudakis.

British and Cretans alike were thinking of the future, and the need for an organization, both political and military, to co-ordinate activities. On 1 April, Fielding slipped into the centre of Canea to the town hall. He entered the Mayor's office, brushing past some German officers on their way out. The Mayor, Nikolaos Skoulas, an elderly, patriarchal figure, was at first appalled, then roared with laughter. During this meeting they discussed the establishment of what became EOK, the Cretan nationalist resistance movement.

Turrall meanwhile had set off in search of the Communist leader, General Mandakas. He stumped about the island in his British uniform, a row of medal ribbons on his chest, asking villagers in English if they knew where he was. Such an improbable secret agent was lucky not to have been handed over to the Germans in the belief that he was one of their spies. Turrall never made contact so alas we will never know how Mandakas would have reacted to his stock request for enlightenment: to be *'mis dans le tableau'*. When Monty Woodhouse was recalled in April, Guy Turrall left with him.

Woodhouse's replacement, Tom Dunbabin – 'O Tom' the Cretans called him – arrived on 15 April 1942. There was only time, he recorded later, for 'a few hasty words with Monty, who left in the ship which brought me, and I was left in my new kingdom'.

Dunbabin, a Tasmanian and a fellow of All Souls College, Oxford, was a distinguished archaeologist and the author of *The Western Greeks*. He had enjoyed a friendly Oxford–Cambridge rivalry with John Pendlebury. At odd moments over the next three years, Dunbabin returned to the search for undiscovered Minoan sites, but found few. 'It is ill-gleaning after Pendlebury,' he wrote.

Dunbabin had a strong-featured face with a straggling moustache which he would absent-mindedly twirl round a finger. Engagingly paradoxical in several ways, Dunbabin was a shy man yet possessed a very determined character. He was large, and could be ferocious when necessary, yet had a voice whose pitch rose at unexpected moments. Junior officers sent out later were a little in awe of his exploits which included spending a whole day in a tree overlooking the airfield at Tymbaki. One described him as 'immensely brave and immensely modest'. Yet he had moral as well as physical courage, a rare combination. Paddy Leigh Fermor wrote: 'One of Tom's most valuable qualities, like pre-Borodino Koutouzow in *War and Peace*, was never to hinder anything helpful, always to bar anything harmful, a sort of traffic policeman to the flow of events.'

Dunbabin based himself just above the Amari valley, with his main hideout on the western flank of Mount Ida. The Amari valley, especially the village of Yerakari, soon became known to British officers as 'Lotus Land' because of its abundance of food and drink and welcome. 'The villagers were so hospitable', Dunbabin wrote after the war, 'that they plucked you by the sleeve as you walked down the narrow street, to come in and drink a glass of wine with them.' There they enjoyed vine-covered arbours and cherry orchards and the cheeses of Ida and Kedros, and watched 'the last rays fade on the bare summit of Ida which rose immediately opposite'.

Yerakari lay on the 'high spy route' across the western and central cordilleras – the White Mountains, the Kedros range and the Mount Ida range – with villages organized like post-houses to help with the transport of wirelesses, the distribution of arms and the concealment of fugitives. The village also became the focal point for the Amari valley resistance movement. The Germans obliterated it in 1944 and shot many of those who had plucked at Dunbabin's sleeve.

Cretan resistance, starting with isolated acts of revenge and minor skirmishes (twenty Germans were killed during December 1941 and January 1942), gradually became more coherent. Cretans welcomed British officers, certain that another Allied army would return to help throw out the German occupiers. 'Everything depended throughout on their magnificent loyalty,' wrote Ralph Stockbridge. 'Without their help as guides, informants, suppliers of food and so on, not a single one of us would have lasted twenty-four hours.'

22
Into the Field

'SOE', wrote Monty Woodhouse in his memoirs, 'was a strange organization, whose only consistent feature was that it was drastically purged every August.' The purge which began this phenomenon took place in the summer of 1941.

In the heady days of amateurism just before the German invasion of Jugoslavia and Greece, this world of schoolboy heroics was upset from an unexpected quarter. On 24 March 1941, Hermione Ranfurly, the rather grand secretary of George Pollock, then head of SOE in Cairo, decided to take matters into her own hands. Her husband the Earl of Ranfurly had just been captured in the desert, and she felt so strongly about the war effort that she did not flinch from going behind her chief's back.

Peter Fleming happened to be sitting on the veranda at the British Embassy after lunch with Sir Miles Lampson and Anthony Eden when a message was brought to say that Lady Ranfurly was extremely anxious to see Eden on 'a matter of importance to do with the war'. 'This rather surprised us,' Lampson wrote in his diary, 'and Peter Fleming let out that she is working in the same secret organisation as he is. This as it subsequently transpired was rather awkward. She arrived in due course and insisted on seeing AE alone. To him she imparted her feeling that the whole of this hush-hush organisation is not only in a state of chaos, but that any amount of public money is being wasted thereon. This, in point of fact, only confirmed what AE (as he subsequently told me) had already long suspected.'

George Pollock, beleaguered by conventional military distrust of his organization spiced with large measures of jealousy, eventually fell victim to this first purge after repeated calls from GHQ Middle East to Dr Hugh Dalton, the minister responsible for SOE in London. A committee of enquiry found little evidence of wrong-doing, but the demand that heads should roll overcame any question of natural justice. The organization was reformed under Colonel Terence Maxwell, a banker with Glyn Mills before the war, and moved to a large and cheerless block of flats on Sharia Kasr-el-Aini called Rustum Buildings. Notwithstanding elaborate, yet rather obvious, security precautions, Cairene taxi drivers soon knew it as 'secret building'. In spite of the summer setback, SOE Cairo was about to embark on an extraordinary growth by sending military missions to the Balkans.*

The Greek section, B6, and the Cretan section, B5, were separated administratively and physically: Jack Smith-Hughes and his assistants operated from an 'outhouse over the road'. This illogicality, which made Crete as different from Greece in bureaucratic terms as it was from Albania or Jugoslavia, turned out to be extremely fortunate since it helped the Cretan section distance itself from the minefield of mainland politics.

A far greater divide existed between the Cretan sections of SOE and ISLD (Inter Services Liaison Department), a military branch of the Secret Intelligence Service. The Earl of Selborne, who in February 1942 replaced Dr Hugh Dalton as Minister of Economic Warfare and thus political master of SOE, later wrote: 'SOE and SIS were separated by War Cabinet decision in June 1940. In my opinion their functions are quite distinct and as SOE work inevitably comes more into the limelight (e.g. Greece and Jugoslavia), the desirability of keeping the organisations separate increases.'

In Cairo, ISLD was run by Captain Bowlby RN (known as 'the beautiful Bowlby'), Colonel Teague and Wing Commander Smith-Rose based in the GHQ complex. The two headquarters loathed each other with fanatical suspicion, but fortunately in Crete the personnel in the field co-operated amicably. 'SOE', said Ralph Stockbridge, 'was basically a bunch of adventurers while ISLD was a very mixed bag.

* Special Operations Executive had a variety of cover names, allegedly to confuse its rivals as much as the enemy. From its early origins as MI(R) and Section D, the para-military branch became known as SO(2) — SO(1) was black propaganda under the Political Warfare Executive — then MO1(SP) which prompted the nickname Muddled Operations in Secret Places, then MO4, its denomination within GHQ Middle East; and finally Force 133. For the sake of simplicity, it will always be referred to as SOE.

SOE personnel were always treated as officers and gentlemen, not as agents.' This even seemed to extend to a bizarre disparity in the field. SOE officers, who later received sovereigns in generous quantities from their cashier, Lieutenant Shread RNVR (inevitably known as 'Golden Shred' after the marmalade), sometimes had to help out their poor relations. In the early days, however, Xan Fielding landed with a wad of drachma banknotes which turned out to be worth only £16, so great was the rate of inflation.

After the battle for Crete had been lost, Monty Woodhouse and Paddy Leigh Fermor landed at Alexandria like thousands of other evacuees. A few days later they moved to Cairo where they were 'held in a kind of limbo against the possibility of further operations in Crete or Greece, but months passed without anything happening.' Woodhouse, recruited into SOE by Bill Barbrook, went into the field first. He returned to Crete in late November 1941 to take over from Jack Smith-Hughes and was replaced in turn by Tom Dunbabin less than five months later.

For Paddy Leigh Fermor, transfer to SOE brought a life of virtually enforced pleasure in Cairo while the organization sorted itself out following the summer purge. Officers without an apartment in the city lived in a mess at Heliopolis, known to some as Hangover Hall. Leigh Fermor decided to move instead into the Continental Hotel. Two years later an even better solution presented itself as a base when on leave from Crete. He and a few friends also engaged in special operations set up house in a rambling Zamalek mansion discovered by Billy Moss of the Coldstream Guards, with whom he abducted General Kreipe in the spring of 1944. The others included Billy Maclean of the Greys, David Smiley of the Blues, and Rowland Winn (later Lord St Oswald) of the 8th Hussars; and Countess Sophie Tarnowska, Moss's future wife. Tara, as the house was called after the legendary castle of the Kings of Ireland and the even more mythical home of Scarlett O'Hara, had a ballroom and soon became the centre for the best and wildest parties in Cairo when its occupants were on leave.

Motives for volunteering for special operations varied enormously. Curiosity or boredom with routine could play as large a part as a yearning for adventure. Apart from the thrill of escaping military predictability, one of the more satisfying by-products of special operations was the opportunity to break rules, often with the help of influential friends, and outrage stuffy 'dug-outs' or regulars. Xan Fielding, who was to become Paddy Leigh Fermor's great companion-in-arms, had an instinctive loathing for the institutional claustrophobia of normal army life and both had a deep-rooted passion for Greece.

Volunteers seldom forgot their initial interview, a formula of circumlocution which made its way into cinematic cliché. 'I can't tell you what you've come here for', said Colonel Guy Tamplin to one captain, 'except to say that it's very secret and it involves a good deal of danger and isolation. If on reflection you have second thoughts, nobody will think the worse of you, and you can go back to your regiment as if nothing had happened.'

In theory, as soon as an officer had been accepted, he was sent off to SOE's own training school in Palestine for a course in 'resistance warfare'. The camp, based on Mount Carmel overlooking Haifa, also trained Greeks, Jugoslavs and Albanians for infiltration into their own countries. Although the official designation of this establishment was ME 102, it became known both in conversation and in signals as 'Narkover' after J.B. Morton's *louche* public school in the Beachcomber column.* Various individuals received corresponding nicknames, such as Dr Smart-Allick and Captain Foulenough. The engagingly eccentric commandant of Narkover was Colonel Harry Cator of the Royal Scots Greys, a relative of the Queen by marriage and a hero of the First World War.

Monty Woodhouse and Paddy Leigh Fermor were thrown straight in as uninstructed instructors, the former in charge of map-reading and the latter in charge of weapon-training – British, German and Italian models – even though his knowledge was limited to the Bren gun from Guards Depot lessons. The young Cretans needed little guidance. Stripping Spandaus, blindfold if necessary, they showed the natural aptitude of a race proud of its relationship with firearms. They were also the most zealous students. A place on a Narkover course became highly prized. Manoussos Manoussakis, who played an important part in the Canea intelligence network, remarked that for a Cretan to be sent to ME 102 had the sort of cachet that graduating from Harvard Business School has today.

The third main member of the training staff in the spring of 1942 was Nick Hammond, whose reputation for demolition work had already been well established in the field. Hammond grew an outsize

---

* Examples of other SOE nicknames include Bakerstrasse for SOE headquarters in London, Jugland for Jugoslavia, and Never-Never Land for Crete.

moustache and acquired the nickname of Captain Vamvakopyrites – Captain Guncotton.

One day King George of the Hellenes visited the camp to see groups of Greek commandos in training. A big demonstration was prepared in which the climax was an attack on a blockhouse using live ammunition. A German flag was fixed to the wall, and after all the commotion and shooting was over the flag, its swastika heart shot out, was dramatically presented to the King who was most impressed by the marksmanship displayed. Only later did Paddy Leigh Fermor admit to Nick Hammond that he had shot it out himself the day before. (Perhaps the most effective demonstration of a guerrilla operation was put on by non-students, when young Jews raided the camp to strip the armoury for the benefit of the Haganah.)

Other subjects taught included unarmed combat and demolition – 'a subject', observed an officer destined for Crete, 'which anyone with an ounce of the schoolboy left in him is bound to enjoy'. Blowing up steel girders to practise sabotaging railway lines may have been fun, but it was not very useful for those going to Crete where railway targets were rarer than the over-hunted ibex. Students also went down to the Crusader castle of Athlit, where the Special Boat Squadron later set up its headquarters, to practise marine sabotage: swimming out to caiques to attach limpet mines.

For those to be dropped into enemy territory, the parachute course took place at Ramat David. One of the Cretans to qualify was Father Ioannis Skoulas, the priest of Anoyia, who had been given permission by the Orthodox church to shave off his beard and cut his hair as a warrior for the duration. The British called him Friar Tuck or the Parachute Priest.

Some students, especially those destined for intelligence gathering, would do another course afterwards on secret procedures – they included disguises, codes and dead-letter drops – at the American School of Archaeology in the valley of Megiddo.

In the summer and autumn of 1942 the instructors at Narkover began to return to enemy-occupied territory to practise what they had taught. After Crete, Monty Woodhouse parachuted into Greece for Operation Harling, the destruction of the Gorgopotamos bridge, which was probably SOE's greatest achievement in the war. Nick Hammond soon followed him as a British liaison officer with the Greek guerrillas; theirs was to be a thankless task coping more with political intrigue than with the enemy. Paddy Leigh Fermor went back to Crete to work with Tom Dunbabin.

On his return to Cairo from Palestine, an SOE 'new boy' usually started by helping for a time on the Cretan desk, which was run for much of the war by Jack Smith-Hughes. His first foray would be as 'conducting officer' which meant he had responsibility for stores and personnel on a run into Crete by submarine, caique or Fairmile motor launch. He would help with the handover and landing and come out again with any Cretans evacuated for their own safety.

When the time came for a tour of duty on the island, preparation for departure was an elaborate and often lengthy procedure. A series of letters or cards to next-of-kin had to be written with anodyne news saying 'I'm fine' and dated for dispatch by headquarters staff at regular intervals. But this system was notoriously unreliable. One staff officer from Rustum Buildings acknowledged that 'the personnel people were rather accident prone'. The worst example of callous incompetence occurred after the great success at Gorgopotamos. 'Four months after the first party of British parachutists had been dropped in Greece, SOE Cairo could not even trace any record of their names.'

Kitting up in second-hand Greek clothes also took time, as did the preparation of identity documents which were forged by Professor Wace's department in ISLD for both services. Suicide pills, known as 'cough drops', encased in grey rubber were issued. Most people had them sewn into the points of collars, from where they could be bitten out in a hurry. 'This part of our farewell', wrote Sandy Rendel, 'seemed all too like a third-rate thriller and therefore faintly bogus.' But Rendel, who kept a couple of the pills in a pocket of his jacket, once allowed them to become mixed up with some raisins thrust into his hand by a peasant woman. When later he began absent-mindedly to eat the raisins he realized, with understandable alarm, that one in his mouth had rather a rubbery texture.

Finally, depending on the advances or retreats of the desert war, embarkation would take place at either Bardia, Derna, Mersa Matruh or Alexandria. In the early days – late 1941 until the spring of 1943 – infiltration and exfiltration was done by caique or submarine. The armed caiques *Escampador*, *Porcupine* and *Hedgehog* were captained by sailors of extraordinary skill and courage such as John Campbell or Mike Cumberlege of *Dolphin* fame who in late 1942 was captured in a raid on the Corinth Canal and shot at Flossenburg concentration camp in the last days of the war.

Royal Navy submarines were only used in the early days. After a disastrous episode at Antiparos, Admiral Cunningham withdrew them from special operations. By mid-1942 the Greek submarine *Papanikolis* and a flotilla of Fairmile motor launches operating from Derna took on responsibility for almost all runs. These Royal Navy vessels had young lieutenants in command – most of them with tanned faces and beards like the sailor on the pack of Player's cigarettes. Their achievements, particularly those of the Canadian Bob Young, were no less remarkable than those of the old salts.

British liaison officers or wireless operators who served on Crete never forgot their first arrival. Shortly before sunset they might just distinguish Mount Ida or the White Mountains above the horizon. The motor launch would continue, all hands moving and talking more cautiously now that they had entered enemy waters. There was always the chance, albeit a very slim one, of an encounter with an armed caique manned by the Kriegsmarine. The night would be moonless, so only when quite close in could the island mass be distinguished. On summer nights, the smell of wild thyme would greet them several miles out to sea.

For the last stretch the launch would creep in on low throttle, the crew communicating in whispers as eyes strained ahead for the recognition signal of two letters in Morse. Everyone would exclaim at once in an excited whisper when it finally came. The launch would be brought to a stop some thirty yards offshore, then the landing party and stores would be ferried to the beach in rubber dinghies. A slight swell could cause serious upsets, with tommy guns, oilskin-covered maps and documents, and other equipment tumbling into the surf. The supplies landed were both bulky and heavy: a new wireless set with charging engine and batteries; a *sakouli* – an embroidered woollen knapsack – laden with gold sovereigns; ammunition boxes; and sacks of food and of boots, which were probably the most highly prized commodity on the island. Anyone coming out on the launch would leave theirs behind on the beach for others to use.

Scenes on arrival were astonishing to the newcomer. Cretans, wearing their black *sariki* headcloths with tiny tassels and 'crap-catcher' breeches, greeted friends and cousins and god-brothers with shouts and embraces. Suddenly the most villainous-looking one would address the newcomer in an English public school accent. Rendel on first arrival could not help feeling that the whole thing was 'more like a practical joke played on the Germans in fancy dress'. Few seemed to notice when the motor launch turned about with a bubbling putter from its engine and the brief link with that outside world of normality and safety was broken. Ironically, it was more dangerous to leave on the boat than to stay. If the Germans became aware of a landing, they could plot the launch's likely course back to Derna. Next morning at dawn, one of the Arado seaplanes based at Canea would be out hunting.

From the beach, the party would often move to a typical smugglers' cave with a fire and grotesque shadow-figures cast on the walls. Then, shouldering heavy loads, Cretans and Britons would trudge upwards into the mountains so as to be off the coastal strip by dawn. At first the scent of wild thyme may have made their route seem 'like marching through a cloud of incense', but soon the strain on shoulder and leg muscles while trying to keep up left little room in the mind for poetic thoughts.

The Cretan guides, mostly shepherds used to leaping from rock to rock like goats, often had to pause and wait while their charges stumbled on behind, cursing impotently each time they barked their shins or twisted an ankle. British officers did not always make life easy for themselves. George Psychoundakis remembered how on one occasion 'Michali' – Paddy Leigh Fermor – leaped for the top of a dry-stone wall with great panache, then toppled over backwards, much to the amusement of the Cretans who had walked round it.

The British were often difficult to disguise because of their fair or ruddy colouring, but other little things gave them away, above all their gait, which the Cretans found most comical. They could easily betray themselves too by their ignorance of custom: Xan Fielding, well-disguised in Cretan costume, was dismayed at being spotted as an Englishman when he greeted an old woman approaching. She instantly blessed him with a prayer for a safe return home. George Psychoundakis, who was with him, explained that the person on the move must always greet the other first. And a British officer soon found that to offer to pay for food was regarded as insulting. Even out on high pastures a shepherd, however poor, would regard himself as the host, for the mountain was his home.

Food often consisted of little more than sour milk and cheese provided by shepherds, or snails collected after rain, and a chewy mountain grass known as *khorta* soaked in oil, perhaps with ground acorns or chestnuts. From time to time a sheep or goat would be bought and killed to roast the meat as kebabs on an open fire. There were no delicate lamb chops, but hunks off the bone, entrails, eyes, brains and all.

Whatever privations the Cretans underwent during the war, *tsikoudia* – the local raki – never seemed to be in short supply, nor was locally grown tobacco which helped to dull the pangs of hunger. For the British, Cretan hospitality could be daunting in its alcoholic generosity. But in drinking contests SOE could often hold its own, and sometimes win. The legendary New Zealander, Sergeant Perkins, is said to have been able to consume three and a half tins of *tsikoudia* (large salmon tins from Cairo, or more often Player's cigarette tins, provided the British Military Mission's standard drinking vessels) without losing consciousness.

Outlaw life had its exhilarating and romantic moments, especially in retrospect, but life in the mountains was harsh and most uncomfortable. On the high ground men lived either in caves or in cheese huts, conical limestone constructions smelling of sheep and goat's milk, but snug.

Choosing the right cave was essential. Apart from tactical considerations, such as escape routes and a good view of the surrounding terrain, it had to be close to a spring. If the ceiling were too low the inhabitants would be suffocated by smoke, and if too high the cold could be numbing, especially if water dripped or even ran down walls. Brush, covered with blankets or parachutes, served as bedding. Often, to the surprise of the cave-dwellers, they would become attached to a place, and leaving was akin to moving home.

The mountain air was both invigorating and clean but the insect life proved formidable. John Pendlebury composed the following verse on the martial qualities of the Cretan flea (to be sung to the tune of the British Grenadiers):

Some talk of being bitten and some of being bit
By wasp or bee or hornet, or by the humble nit,
But of all the world's best biters you can commend to me
The best of all is what we call the homely little flea.

Perhaps even worse than the flea was the ubiquitous louse, whose colonies rapidly infested even the cleanest individual. When one ISLD newcomer enquired rather ingenuously what a louse looked like, the fastidious Leigh Fermor exclaimed: 'What, never seen a louse, old boy?' and reached inside his shirt. 'Here you are.'

Lice were the biggest curse for the wireless operators. Corporal Matthew White, who spent months cramped in a tiny cave known as 'Matthew's hermitage' on the western side of Mount Ida, took his revenge by collecting the largest specimens from his body and putting them in a Player's cigarette tin to starve.

The wireless operators had to put up with loneliness and appalling conditions – few of them spoke enough Greek to converse with their Cretan guards and they usually lived in rocky holes with a groundsheet over them to protect them against the drips. They also suffered the continual frustration of running radio sets off very unreliable batteries. These required a heavy charging engine, sometimes concealed in a wicker-covered demijohn with a detachable top which could be filled with wine or olive oil. This cumbersome gadget was designed for transport by mule or donkey, but in panic moves following the betrayal of a hideout human beasts of burden usually bore the load instead. Whenever a wireless went wrong – a depressingly frequent occurrence – and there was an urgent message to send to Cairo, a runner would have to travel for two or three days over mountainous terrain to reach another set.

The troglodyte existence could be boring for everyone. When Paddy Leigh Fermor was questioned whilst on leave by Lawrence Durrell about life on Crete, and the strain of living in enemy-occupied territory, he complained in jest that the conversation was probably about as limited as in the Guards' Club: everyone seemed able to talk only about their guns and their boots.

Without diversion, nerves became frayed. The best distractions were story-telling and singing. Cretans were taught English folk songs and they taught the British *mantinadas*: rhyming couplets with a sting in the tail. Fortunately, Cretan and British humour, especially a sense of the ridiculous, was entirely compatible. This important link helped get over any minor irritations and differences in national character.

In a moment of exasperation, one officer complained to Cairo about 'having to deal with some of the most un-team-spirited and undisciplined personnel in the world'. The British also joked that in Crete nobody had any sense of timing: even the nightingales used to sing during the day. And the compulsion of some Cretans to boast never failed to amaze, since nobody doubted their real courage. Xan Fielding called it the '*pallikari*-complex', a *pallikari* being a heroic and chivalrous fighter.

Cretans are the first to tell stories against this vice. A member of the resistance recounted the following incident about the great battle celebrated by one village. Apparently, a German patrol in the mountains not far from this village set off a rock slide and three soldiers were killed. The local kapitan and all his followers promptly claimed throughout the region that they had wiped out the whole patrol in twelve hours of bitter hand-to-hand fighting.

Since caution and reticence were alien to the Cretan character, good security did not come naturally to many. Some, however, displayed remarkable discretion. And the women were often outstanding. A number played a dangerous double game, working as interpreters or secretaries for the Germans and all the time passing on to the resistance details of those denounced by traitors. Women left at home showed no less resourcefulness. Wives and sisters, with an inspired presence of mind, often managed to conceal incriminating papers during a German search.

While the battle against the paratroopers had shown the true degree of Cretan courage, their warlike style had an engaging element of theatre. Old men, unflinching under fire, fiddled with their ancient 'gra' muskets in the tradition of the Cretan joke: 'Stand still Turk while I reload.' It also had a roguish quality. In Crete the outlaw had a historic nobility, rather as the *contrabandista* in Andalucia was seen as a heroic knight-errant figure ready to slay a local tyrant. Even sheep-stealing had acquired a patriotic tinge since that was the way the resistance fighters against the Turks had survived. They were called the klephts: a name synonymous with robber. And Theodore Stephanides recorded how he had met a Cretan in the First World War who proudly put down his profession as brigand. When asked what the dividing line was between thief and brigand, the man had replied that a thief finding a wallet full of money on the ground would take it. A brigand would first return it to the owner, then take it from him face to face.

The Cretan senses of honour and justice were firmly interwoven. Those who offended village society found themselves effectively banished. Such outcasts were the ones most likely to become traitors, a tiny minority. The Germans offered them their liberty on condition that they infiltrated communities suspected of aiding the British. They would pretend to have fled a German round-up in their own neighbourhood and, Cretan generosity being what it was, they would be taken in and fed. The only risk arose when someone who knew them of old passed through the area.

Almost all the British liaison officers sent to Crete adapted themselves to this strange existence with enthusiasm. When they first arrived, the idea of enemy-occupied territory conjured up visions of German sentries every few hundred yards. Yet most of Crete, especially its mountainous regions, saw little of the occupying power in the early days. German troops were reluctant to venture into the mountain ranges, and moved only in daylight.

The two principal dangers in the hills were either betrayal or bumping into a German patrol quite by chance. A sudden dawn cordon and search was seldom a threat since, although the British often had an evening meal with friends in a village, they would always spend the night well outside. And on most occasions news of troop movements would be brought by a boy running from the next village to warn them.

After living in the mountains almost as if the Germans did not exist, to enter a town in disguise and pass among the enemy quite naturally produced a curious sensation. The first time was always the worst. 'Your knees began knocking as soon as you met your first German,' said Stephen Verney, who was based in Canea from August 1944. 'You assumed he knew immediately that you were an English officer.' On one occasion, Tom Dunbabin had to brush past a German officer he recognized, an archaeologist like himself from pre-war days. The German looked straight at him, but Dunbabin's disguise proved sufficient protection in such an improbable encounter.

A narrow escape, whether from a patrol in the countryside or from accidental discovery in a town, produced a surge of fearful excitement later followed by what Paddy Leigh Fermor described as 'a sort of post-coitum-triste feeling'.

British officers with the Cretan resistance have left an impression of a rather dashing and eccentric amateurism — what might be expected from a mixture of romantics and archaeologists. Yet in spite of the occasional unmilitary image in intelligence reports, such as 'mines cylindrically the size of a jeroboam of champagne', the information collected and collated was most impressive in its detail. It covered: telephone systems; the state of every gun position, whether machine-gun nest, flak battery or heavy coastal artillery; satellite airfields; military roads; and the grid reference and defence details of each garrison and guard post with their strengths and armaments. Every aircraft in and out of the main airfields was logged with its direction of departure. Every ship or caique, loading and unloading in the harbours of Heraklion, Rethymno and Canea, was noted with its cargo. Landing beaches and dropping zones were reconnoitred.

Most of the credit, of course, must go to the Cretans who assembled so much of this information for the Allied cause knowing it was of little immediate use to themselves. Almost from the beginning their information networks, especially those in the main towns of the north coast, worked ceaselessly at great risk. Often the

information would take a long time to filter in through the arteries
– the work usually had to be carried out and delivered on foot – but
the bank of intelligence built up comprised the most comprehensive
survey of enemy dispositions and communications in any part of
Europe. If Allied Forces Headquarters had decided to invade Crete
rather than Sicily in 1943, they could not have had a better basis for
planning, nor a more willing resistance organization to attack and
disrupt the German communication system behind the lines. The main
danger on Crete was of premature attacks caused by overeagerness.

In theory, intelligence work was the responsibility not of SOE, but
of ISLD, and in 1943 Ralph Stockbridge and another officer returned
to help with this task and with the running of the networks. SOE
field officers had more than enough to do already. They had to travel
constantly from village to village to develop their contacts and help
the preparation of resistance groups while persuading them not to
act on sudden impulse, a very difficult balance to achieve. They also
had to organize the evacuation of those identified by the Germans,
or candidates for training at 'Narkover'. Lists of their nominees were
signalled back to Cairo well in advance of each trip by motor launch.

Parachute drops were time-consuming and often frustrating, both
in preparation and waiting. To attract attention to one's movements
could be disastrous. Half the population of the valley, perhaps tipped
off by the cousin of one member of the group, would assemble for
the spectacle or the pickings. Brushwood to make the signal fires had
to be gathered with great discretion, otherwise local shepherds might
light their own fires to see what came drifting down for them.

On several occasions, officers had to hang around at some bleak
spot in the mountains for anything up to sixteen consecutive nights.
And once the drop was made successfully, the collection of canisters
and parachutes before German search parties reached the scene often
become a nightmare, especially if shepherds made off with several
containers. Such appropriations could be dangerous. Xan Fielding
came across one group smashing a tin containing an anti-personnel
grenade: they thought they were about to feast on pineapple chunks.

The yellow silk parachutes were also in great demand. SOE
personnel and their Cretan helpers used them as sleeping bags, or as
a commodity for barter. By the end of the war when almost half the
women of the central massifs must have had yellow silk underwear,
courtesy of the British government, parachute drops had lost their
novelty. But in 1942, when Rommel's advance on Egypt threatened
the whole of the Middle East, they had a semi-miraculous quality.

23
The Peak of German Power

In the late spring of 1942, Cretan airfields became important staging posts for reinforcing the Afrika Korps' advance on the Nile Delta. Three teams from the Special Boat Squadron and one from the Special Air Service were sent to the island in an attempt to disrupt this traffic.

Tom Dunbabin met the SBS advance party on 23 May and provided guides. The SAS seaborne group included four members of the Free French squadron under Commandant Bergé, a very tough Gascon, with Captain the Earl Jellicoe as British liaison officer and Lieutenant Petrakis, a Cretan, from the Royal Hellenic Army. The SAS had allocated itself the prize target of Heraklion aerodrome while the three SBS teams planned to attack the airfields at Maleme, Kastelli Pediados and Tymbaki.

David Sutherland of the Black Watch, who led the Tymbaki team, was exasperated to find on arrival that the airfield had been temporarily abandoned. Tymbaki on the south coast was the most vulnerable to air raids from Egypt. The Maleme group met with a different sort of frustration. Their target, with its recently installed electrified fences, was too strongly guarded to penetrate.

Kastelli Pediados airfield on the other hand offered a textbook sabotage operation. Five aircraft together with nearly 200 tons of aviation fuel and other stores were destroyed on 9 June with delayed action bombs.

The Heraklion operation ran into difficulties at the start and at the end. Landing in dinghies from the Greek submarine *Triton* then crossing the terrain to the target took much longer than expected. They arrived too late on 12 June to mount an effective operation, but the delay proved an unexpected blessing: many aircraft had been away on a night raid. The attack took place the next night, 13 June. Bergé's group, having cut their way through the wire, managed to fix explosive charges to twenty Junkers 88 bombers, most of which were severely damaged or destroyed. In the confusion, the group got away and set off across the island towards the south coast, jubilant at their success.

Next day, the Germans executed fifty Cretan hostages including Tito Georgiadis (a former Governor-General), a 70-year-old priest, and a number of Jews still held in prison. The initial euphoria aroused by the raids rapidly turned to anger, some of it directed against the British even though Cretan groups never ceased to demand arms to attack the Germans. Morale, as one might expect under the occupation, could be very mercurial.

The French SAS group was horrified when Lieutenant Petrakis brought back news of the reprisals from a foraging expedition to a nearby village. At one point near the end of the march to the south coast, Jellicoe and Petrakis left the four Frenchmen to cook and rest while they went on to make arrangements for the evacuation. On returning to collect them, Jellicoe learned that a Cretan had betrayed their hiding place to the nearest German garrison. One French chasseur had been killed, and Bergé and the two others captured when their ammunition ran out. The three Frenchmen apparently escaped execution because Bergé convinced their captors that if they were shot, German officers held prisoner in Cairo would share a similar fate. Bergé ended up in Colditz Castle with David Stirling, the founder of the SAS, captured in the desert.

The attacks on Kastelli Pediados and Heraklion accounted for twenty-six aircraft, a number of vehicles and considerable quantities of stores. Altogether ten Germans died as a result of these raids. They did not, as one account claims, cause 'the deaths of over 100 enemy soldiers'. The survivors of the raiding force left from the beach near Trypiti on the caique *Porcupine,* together with Satanas, seriously ill and soon to die of cancer in Alexandria, and other Cretan evacuees. They reached Mersa Matruh only just in time. A few hours later the town fell to Rommel's advance.

The *Porcupine*, on its outward journey, had brought Paddy Leigh Fermor for his first clandestine tour of duty. On that evening of 23 June, he had arrived with his wireless operator, Sergeant Matthew White, to a scene of dismay. German troops were closing in on the area, having just lost four men in clashes near Vassilika Anoyia, and there had not been enough room on the caique for the two other kapitans, Bandouvas and Petrakageorgis, waiting on the beach with their families. News of the retreat in Egypt, which threatened to sever the sea link completely, did not improve their mood.

This was the most difficult time for all British officers in Crete. Xan Fielding, whose wireless set was broken, had no contact with Cairo and did not know whether the British defence of the Nile Delta had collapsed. For all he knew Alexandria might have fallen to the Afrika Korps. 'To be out of wireless communication, as I had been for the last fortnight and more,' he later wrote, 'always produced a sense of panic and loss, as though God had ceased to exist. For the invisible and distant Headquarters which were responsible for my fate had assumed in my eyes a quasi-divine power.'

Even those with a set that worked managed to extract little information from headquarters. This was the time of the 'Great Flap' in Cairo, which reached its crescendo on 'Ash Wednesday', when the city was overcast by the smoke from bonfires of documents. All secret organizations had been evacuated, and the submarine base moved to Beirut. As a result all the intelligence gathered on Crete about the concentration of troop-carriers ferrying reinforcements to Rommel was never received.

To make matters worse, mischievous rumours that the British liaison officers on Crete were about to flee or even surrender to the Germans caused great confusion and alarm amongst the resistance groups and outrage amongst the officers themselves when they heard.

The Germans, perhaps guessing at the decline of morale in resistance circles, stepped up offensive sweeps in the Heraklion area. On 9 July Petrakageorgis's group, attacked near Temeneli, managed to kill seven of the enemy. A more insidious, and therefore more alarming development, was the German attempt to recruit more traitors. Six, most of whom were German-appointed mayors, had been assassinated in May by Cretan loyalists, and an attempt was made on Polioudakis, the hated police chief in Heraklion.

The officer in charge of 'counter-espionage' at this time was called Hartmann. Levantine by blood, Hartmann had been adopted by a German family in Salonika and, with the rise of Nazism, had tried to become more German than the Germans. His superiors clearly regarded him as ideal for such an unpleasant job. Hartmann first used amnestied criminals as spies, then in the summer of 1942 he managed to recruit a number of the Tsouliadakis clan in Kroussonas by exploiting a family feud and an inter-village feud. The Tsouliadakis clan, to whom one of the assassinated mayors had belonged, loathed the young relatives of Satanas as well as the strongly pro-British inhabitants of the rival town of Anoyia.

Xan Fielding's troubles with Colonel Andreas Papadakis came to a head soon afterwards. Not content with proclaiming himself the head of all Cretan resistance, Papadakis began to behave like a South American dictator. He regarded all parachute drops as his private property and hoarded urgently needed supplies such as boots when George Psychoundakis, running between Xan Fielding at Vaphé and the Colonel above Asi Gonia, was virtually barefoot. After a stormy meeting with Papadakis, Fielding decided that there was no other course but to evacuate the Colonel at the first opportunity.

Handing over his responsibilities for western Crete to Paddy Leigh Fermor in July, he escorted Papadakis and his family to the south coast. The atmosphere of suspicion and injured *amour propre* did not improve. After confusion and delay over the arrival of the boat, Papadakis's paranoia was even further aroused and Fielding could not help visualizing the muzzles of his henchmen's guns pointed at his back. Eventually, on the night of 5 August, the Royal Hellenic Navy submarine, *Papanikolis*, arrived to take them all to Beirut. Colonel Papadakis later became commandant of the Greek forces in the Jerusalem garrison.

The havoc caused by Papadakis's delusions did not end with his departure. The worst legacy was his rash enrolment of a traitor by the name of Komnas. Komnas produced what appeared to be very accurate figures – supposedly taken from ration returns made by a clerk in the German headquarters. His figures, impressive both in detail and in size, were finally questioned by GHQ Cairo's intelligence branch, much to SOE's exasperation at the time: some of the units identified did not tally with any other information.*

Even the Colonel's dedicated chief of staff, Andreas Polentas, who had finally come to see through Papadakis, never suspected Komnas. He and the wireless operator Apostolos Evangelou, a schoolmaster and poet from the Dodecanese, were arrested on 18 November.

---

* For example, an SS battalion commanded by a Major von Teitzen based at Perama was described in great detail, but Dr Helmut Fichtenthal, who was interpreter to the commander of the Fortress of Crete, has confirmed that there were never any SS troops on the island.

Polentas's mistake cost them appalling tortures and eventually their lives in Ayia prison. But they did not go unavenged for long. Although Komnas was moved for his own protection into a house in Canea surrounded by German billets, his body was discovered in the kitchen one afternoon with seventeen stab wounds, the blood still uncongealed. Nobody had heard a sound. The deed was carried out by Polentas's cousin Pavlo aided by an execution squad run by George Alevizakis of Argyroupolis.

Paddy Leigh Fermor, responsible for the western end of the island during Xan Fielding's absence in Egypt, got to know the main characters in the Canea region. His first task was to sabotage shipping in Suda Bay. He and his guide, Yanni Tsangarakis, helped by the Vandoulakis family and the Karkanis clan at Askiphou, received a parachute drop in the White Mountains on the night of 8 September. The limpet mines – commonly known as 'toys' – were all present, but the dispatchers in Egypt had omitted to include wire cutters.

Leigh Fermor and Tsangarakis hurried down with their loads, only to find that the petrol tanker, the chief target, had left, and that the Suda wire defences and sentry system were too formidable to penetrate. Tsangarakis crossed round through Canea to reconnoitre from the Akrotiri side, but any attack from that direction would have required a three-mile swim. Apart from Leigh Fermor, who in much later life swam the Hellespont in emulation of Lord Byron, there were no strong swimmers available at that moment.

Xan Fielding had often complained about the cancellations and inaccuracies of parachute drops. Now on leave in Cairo, he was challenged by the RAF to accompany one of their flights and see for himself. After a long and cold round trip, he had to confess he had no idea how anyone could distinguish any given spot in the mountains.

His time in Cairo coincided with news of the spectacular success of Operation Harling, the destruction of the Gorgopotamos railway bridge led by Eddie Myers and Monty Woodhouse. This gave him his first glimpse of the new SOE following the purge of August 1942, after which Lord Glenconner replaced Colonel Maxwell. Glenconner, frequently absent due to other responsibilities, was known simply as 'God'.

Glenconner's absences provided a good opportunity for the officer

in charge of military operations, Brigadier Mervyn Keble. Keble, who
at one stage in his career had commanded a prison in Palestine,
came from GHQ's intelligence department, where Enoch Powell did
all the work for which he claimed credit. Monty Woodhouse
remembered him from the intelligence school at Swanage as 'a
dynamic tubby little major whose eyes almost popped out of his head
with lust for killing'. He first learned of Keble's promotion to Colonel
and transfer to SOE on seeing, with astonishment, his name at the
bottom of a set of orders for the Gorgopotamos operation. This
document, phrased in all the right jargon, was clearly designed more
to impress his superiors than to guide the men sent on the mission.

Keble, although a regular officer from the most regular of county
regiments – the Wiltshires – proved himself a formidable bureaucratic
in-fighter, both shameless and ruthless. The success of Operation
Harling, which he promptly appropriated for himself, provided the
springboard for an ambition which could only have stemmed from a
deep resentment.

Keble may well have had a complex about his unattractive
appearance which he felt curiously compelled to flaunt. Although
known in the Army as Bolo (apparently to signify bolshiness) he was
called the Panda in SOE – his girlfriends were called Panderenes –
because he was so uncuddly. His tubby figure was often clad in no
more than a singlet and a pair of shorts, and his wiry hair was cut *en
brosse*.

Rustum Buildings was not a happy place. 'Nobody who did not
experience it', wrote Bickham Sweet-Escott, 'can possibly imagine the
atmosphere of jealousy, suspicion, and intrigue which embittered the
relations between the various secret and semi-secret departments in
Cairo.' Almost all the stories of tapping colleagues' telephones, poison
pen letters and anonymous telephone calls, libellous verses, even
suspicion of murder have been well chronicled both in historical
accounts and lightly-veiled fiction.*

The Cretan section was unusually fortunate. There were no
serious disagreements as to which groups on the island to back, so
Cretan resistance, unlike its mainland equivalent, never became a
political morass in which the logical military strategy was anathema
to Whitehall. And Jack Smith-Hughes, who ran the Cretan desk, was

* See Artemis Cooper's *Cairo in the War*, Hamish Hamilton, 1989, and Christopher
Sykes's *High Minded Murder*, Home & Van Thal, 1944.

both clever and robust enough to defend his patch. He was of course helped by Keble's relative lack of interest in the island. Crete, with its small population and relatively small German garrison, could not at that stage justify a British Military Mission large enough to be commanded by a Brigadier, and Keble's strategy of self-advancement was to create a swelling pyramid of stars and crowns to bear him aloft to the rank of major general.

There was one man whom neither Jack Smith-Hughes nor any of the officers in the field were able to protect. Keble had conceived a venomous dislike for Captain Arthur Reade, a lawyer of great gentleness and goodness with a love for Crete based on his passionate admiration of Venizelos. Tall and much older than his colleagues, he presented a slightly eccentric figure. According to Paddy Leigh Fermor, 'The reddish beard and moustache he grew made him look exactly like Henri IV with a dash of Verdi.'

Reade, who had longed to be sent to the island, was granted his wish but with a sting in the tail. He would go in on the same run as Xan Fielding in November, but after that, with only the most rudimentary training, he was expected to blow up HMS *York*, the cruiser partially submerged in Suda Bay, to prevent the Germans refloating her. Friends warned Reade, but he was determined to go ahead.

Reade landed from the submarine *Papanikolis* on 27 November with Fielding and an ISLD mission led by Lieutenant Stelio Papaderos who were to set up a radio station in the southern part of the White Mountains.

As Reade's colleagues had predicted, the operation against the cruiser proved impossible. He would have thrown away his life for nothing. Arthur Reade was based at Kyriakosellia in the foothills above the exit to Suda Bay. He acted as liaison officer with the resistance organization, an ideal post since all Cretans took to him immediately. But Keble, determined to destroy him, ordered his return a few months later. Reade was heart-broken at leaving, and this gave Keble the chance to concoct a report that he was too unstable for special operations.

For Xan Fielding, the arrival by submarine had begun with catastrophe when almost all his equipment went into the sea after a rubber dinghy capsized. But three Australian soldiers who turned up in hope of a passage to Egypt dived and dived again in the icy waters until almost everything was saved. These Australians were to prove very useful a few months later.

On his way north across the White Mountains to his old base at Vaphé, Fielding had another chance encounter on 3 December, this time with the left-wing leader General Mandakas.

Mandakas, a native of Lakkoi just to the north of the Omalo plain where they met, was clearly frustrated that his personal support was limited at that time to the western part of the island and that his band of followers was small: in George Psychoundakis's words, 'Mandakas wanted to be a great leader, but few joined.' A shortage of men did not restrain his demands that he should control arms drops and have his own wireless link with Cairo.

Xan Fielding also heard from Mandakas for the first time about the German offensive against groups linked to the British, and the arrests on 18 November of Polentas and Evangelou at Vaphé. It was an unpleasant shock, not softened by Mandakas's brutal manner of announcement.

His last encounter of the journey took place on arrival in Vaphé where he ran into Paddy Leigh Fermor, who had not heard of his return to the island. Fielding was at last able to hear the full story of the arrests and discuss the future. Jo Bradley, an RAF sergeant shot down during a raid on Kastelli airfield early in September, became the new wireless operator. In the language of military bureaucracy, he was thus defined as 'locally recruited'. Bradley, a Welshman with a beautiful singing voice, thought this a curious euphemism in the circumstances.

That November also saw a change in the German command: General Bruno Bräuer succeeded General Andrae as commander of the Fortress of Crete. Bräuer, the commander of the 1st Parachute Regiment in the invasion, was the officer brave enough to belittle the mutilation stories. He also proved the most humane German general on the island during the war. He tried to make his officers understand the Cretan attitude towards the occupying power, and why they had fought as *francs-tireurs* in the battle. On the other hand, he made it clear that he would not tolerate resistance activities or collaboration with the British.

A curious incident a year and a half later showed how, unusually for a soldier, he looked forward to the post-war world. In honour of the Greek national day, 25 March, he released from prison a hundred Cretan prisoners. They included Constantinos Mitsotakis, the present Prime Minister of Greece, who was then a lieutenant in the Royal Hellenic Army and, more importantly, a member of the intelligence network known as the Quins. Not long after his release, Mitsotakis was walking through the fashionable suburb of Halepa with his friend Manoussos Manoussakis, when Manoussakis, spotting Bräuer, suggested that he should thank the General personally. Bräuer invited them into his official residence, the Venizelos house, for coffee. 'Young man,' he said, 'I released you because from what I have heard, you will one day play an important part in your country's affairs. Keep out of trouble.'

Bräuer had no illusions about the Cretans supposedly under his command. Addressing officer reservists who had to report to the authorities once a week in an attempt to keep them from resistance activity, he acknowledged that Britain was Greece's ally, but added: 'Why don't you keep your bravery in reserve?' 'Nearly the whole population remains hostile towards the forces of occupation, and is still pro-British' stated a report he commissioned. 'In fact a reconquest of the island by the British is expected in the near future. Account must also be taken of the assistance which the civilian population is giving to the two British organizations whose activity on the island has been ascertained, i.e. the espionage organization of Captain Huse [Jack Smith-Hughes] and the sabotage organization of Captain Jellicoe.' The inaccuracies are significant, considering the efforts to which the Germans had gone to infiltrate resistance groups connected with the British.

By Christmas the news from North Africa and Stalingrad warranted a double celebration. Paddy Leigh Fermor and Xan Fielding joined Tom Dunbabin and their friends at the Kokonas house in Yerakari. But elsewhere during the celebrations to see in the New Year of 1943, minor scuffles between those who cried 'Long Live Britain!' and those who replied 'Long Live Russia!' pointed to other difficulties to come.

Apart from odd encounters with General Mandakas, the British liaison officers operating out in the generally more conservative mountain regions had had little contact with left-wing groups. As on the mainland, the Greek Communist Party had set up a resistance coalition called EAM (Ethnikon Apeleftherotikon Metopon) or the National Liberation Front which they controlled from behind the scenes. On the mainland, but very rarely on Crete, the political right was tainted by passive and active collaboration with the enemy, and many distinguished men of liberal ideals joined EAM, unaware of Communist machinations. EAM, the political wing, had set up ELAS (Ethnikos Laikos Apeleftherotikos Stratos) or the National Popular

Liberation Army as its guerrilla army, and the two together were known as EAM–ELAS. (See Appendix D for a glossary of the main Greek political movements.)

Although EAM–ELAS enjoyed nothing like the following it achieved on the mainland, as much through coercion as conviction, on Crete it grew surreptitiously in the larger towns and in several isolated and impoverished areas of the countryside. Crete would be spared the worst ravages of the Greek civil war largely because EOK (the National Organization of Crete), which Xan Fielding had encouraged Nikolaos Skoulas and others to set up, succeeded in bringing together the various non-Communist resistance groups into a surprisingly effective alliance. On Crete, the Communists never managed to employ 'the salami tactic' of slicing off one rival after another.

24
The Year of Change

After the great advances of 1942 to the Volga and deep into Egypt, German self-confidence suddenly flagged following the reverses of Alamein and Stalingrad. A fear that Greece and Crete would be invaded arose in January 1943, some five months before the final surrender of Army Group Afrika in May. The island was reinforced with tanks, motor transport and men at a time when the Russian front was in desperate need of them. Lieutenant Tavana, the Italian counter-espionage officer who later defected to the British, put the figures at 45,000 Germans and 32,000 Italians.

The German command on Crete ordered the mining of bridges and the construction of underground command bunkers. Ammunition stocks were increased. The defences to Suda Bay were further improved. Units were put through street-fighting courses combining infantry, tanks and artillery. The Askifou garrison was trebled to defend the passes from Sphakia. Counter-invasion manoeuvres were practised with mobile columns ready to reinforce threatened sectors. General Bräuer announced: 'We will in the event of an invasion defend Crete to the last man and the last round.'

Bräuer's clichés did little to rouse his men. The innermost German terror was of a Cretan rising in their rear. 'They know the Cretans hate them', wrote one British officer in his report to Cairo, 'and are living for the moment to dig up their rifles and say it with bullets.' And yet at the same time 'the Germans are hurt and puzzled at not being loved, and are constantly asking why'. This accurate observation is astonishing when one reads German regulations for requisitioning and forced labour. They paid 700 drachma for a day's work, a sum insufficient to buy two eggs, and most scandalously of all,

120 drachma for a cow, just enough to buy a couple of cigarettes. They also resorted to sheep-stealing on a massive scale. No basic provisions came from Germany, so they lived off the captive population.

General Müller, the young and brutal commander of the 22nd Bremen-Sebastopol Division, established a policy of aggressive patrolling to intimidate the population, but German patrols were more frightened than ever in the mountains.

In one village a Cretan who had a German lieutenant billeted on him for the night brought some washing water at dawn, as he had been instructed the night before. When he tried the door there was a clatter as a mug and an enamel basin fell off a chair propped against the door as an alarm. The lieutenant was sitting bolt upright in bed, 'clutching his submachine gun, his eyes popping out of his head'.

Apart from snap arms searches carried out by detachments 50 strong, the Germans mounted cordon and search operations using between 200 and 500 men. They would surround a village during the night, then move in at dawn. The population would be locked in the church or school while floors and gardens were dug up. Many of these raids followed tip-offs from spies, but with merciful frequency their information was not sufficiently detailed or fresh.

In a raid on Alones during the first week of January 1943, they found a wireless battery in the garden of its priest, Father John Alevizakis, a much-loved figure in the resistance. He escaped into the mountains, following the example of the two British wireless operators, but his son was arrested with two compromising letters on him. Meanwhile, Father John's parishioners wasted no time in hiding the charging engine and all the other equipment which the Germans had missed on their first search.

A few days later the Germans raided Asi Gonia in search of George Psychoundakis. This time they brought their informer to the edge of the village hidden in a raincoat.

Another denunciation triggered a German drive in the Apokoronas region round Gournes. Troops surrounded the cheese-hut known as the Beehive which a large group — Paddy Leigh Fermor; Arthur Reade; Sergeant Alec Tarves, the wireless operator; and the two guides, Yanni Tsangarakis and George Psychoundakis — had abandoned only the day before.

From the opposite mountain, the British and Cretans spied the detachments, altogether around two hundred men, searching the area. They decided to split up. Later that morning, Leigh Fermor, Arthur Reade and Yanni Tsangarakis climbed a large snow-laden cypress tree to escape a patrol and had to remain hidden in its branches almost until nightfall, such was the activity of mountain troops around them. This day, 25 January, became known as 'oak apple day' in memory of King Charles II's rather similar experience, although he had not suffered from such intense cold.

One of the most serious betrayals occurred in the south-west of the island in March. The Germans received word of a caique carrying Cretan officers on their way to join the Greek forces in the Middle East. A patrol craft intercepted and sank it with gunfire some distance off the coast.

With German morale so vulnerable in the early spring of 1943, Dunbabin, Leigh Fermor and Fielding did not let the opportunity to undermine it further slip past. They prepared flysheets to play upon the homesickness and sense of isolation of soldiers.

A particularly ingenious touch was to have these German-language leaflets stamped with swastika-bearing eagles, and messages in Greek asking anyone who found them to hand them immediately to a German soldier. This ensured distribution, protected the local population and enraged officers, who knew they were being made to look foolish.

A graffiti campaign was also mounted. Slogans in German suggestive of a discontented soldiery were painted at night around barracks and guard-posts: 'Scheiss Hitler!'; 'Heil Stalin!' accompanied by a hammer and sickle; 'We Want to Go Home!'; and 'The Führer is a swine!'

Leigh Fermor proposed another leaflet:

Germans!
    You have now been two years in our island and your rule has been the blackest stain on the pages of your already besmirched history. You have proved yourselves unfit to be considered as a civilized race, and infinitely worse than the Turks, who were noble enemies and men of honour.
    You have proved yourselves savages, and as such you will be treated.
    But not yet.

Wherever you go, Cretan eyes follow you. Unseen watchers dog your footsteps. When you eat and when you drink, when you wake and when you sleep, we are watching you.

Remember!

The long Cretan knife makes no sound when it strikes between the shoulder blades. Your time is running out. The hour of vengeance is drawing near.

Very near.

Black Dimitiri
Archegos of Central Crete

The Germans, on the other hand, realizing that propaganda could not win Cretans over, tried at least to achieve a degree of neutrality in the event of a British landing. Diatribes were aimed less at the British and concentrated instead on Communists as the enemy of all true Cretans.

The German command, influenced by events in Russia, may well have seen ELAS as the greater long-term threat; it must also have realized that to try to turn the Cretans against the British was a waste of time. In any case, it clearly hoped to create a split in the resistance movement.

After the war, a conspiracy theory developed in left-wing circles that the British officers in Crete had set out to destroy the Communists from the beginning. In fact British officers on numerous occasions had done their best to prevent an open breach between Venizelist groups and EAM–ELAS. They did not really dislike General Mandakas, the most senior Cretan officer to throw in his lot with the Left. One British officer thought Mandakas, whose character combined great caution and great ambition, 'a nice old boy': his great problem was that he thought he could bend ELAS to his own will.

Nick Hammond, who later encountered him on the mainland when he became 'minister of war' in the stalking-horse government set up by the Communists, described him as 'large, bluff and ponderous in conversation'. Mandakas was almost certainly telling the truth when he said he was not a Communist himself, although he collaborated closely with the Party. (The Greek Communist Party's surprisingly effective fiction on the mainland that EAM and ELAS were independent coalitions was never repeated very seriously on Crete.)

The Communists, realizing that General Mandakas, although a valuable prize, would never make a sufficiently charismatic leader, decided to win over to their cause Manoli Bandouvas. Bandouvas already had a large popular following in the mountain villages of Heraklion province and amongst those peasants most likely to distrust EAM–ELAS.

On the surface his recruitment appeared a likely way of increasing Communist influence, but outsiders picked and promoted in this way tended to turn against the Party later with embarrassing results. The British Military Mission was, nevertheless, disturbed at this development.

'By dint of hard work, clever guidance and unscrupulous methods, the LOLLARDS [informal code for Communists] have succeeded in playing a far larger part in Cretan affairs than their numbers entitle them to. They have succeeded in hooking a General and Crete's one guerrilla leader – both of them large fish – and have thrown up a smokescreen of high military sponsorship in the one and patriotic peasant support in the other.'

The British, ironically, were then wrong-footed by Bandouvas, not by the Communists. Hoping to appeal to his vanity, they said that GHQ Middle East wished to consult with him. This, it was thought, would give him a breather away from Communist influence, and in any case he had requested a break in Egypt not long before. But Bandouvas smelt a rat: he had quarrelled bitterly with Dunbabin the previous year over the distribution of weapons, and he no doubt sensed that Leigh Fermor was about the only British officer who had a soft spot for him. (The jealousy of Petrakageorgis, his rival kapitan in the region, is said to have caused a good deal of the trouble.)

Bandouvas accordingly set up a meeting to ensure that this proposal was repeated in front of key witnesses. He then refused the offer with a grand declaration that his place was with his men in the field. He turned to the Cretan officers present and asked whether they did not think so too. They had no alternative but to agree. Bandouvas, who made sure that the story spread rapidly, no doubt with a few dramatic embellishments, secured himself a triumph in the eyes of his peasant supporters: the British generals in Cairo waited upon his every word, yet he preferred to stay on the island with his fellow Cretans.

But the British Military Mission did not give up. To wean Bandouvas away from Communist influence, they then bestowed upon him the grandiloquent title 'Chief of *Francs-Tireurs* of the Province of

Heraklion'. (Bandouvas dropped the last part to make it sound pan-Cretan.)

This new nomenclature appealed to him so much that when King George of the Hellenes, the Communists' favourite figure of hate, sent a message of greeting to the Cretan resistance on the prompting of SOE Cairo, Bandouvas (the Communists' great hope) immediately prepared a loyal reply in his new dignity. 'As Chief of *Francs-Tireurs*, I ask you to forward our thanks by telegraph and say that we are inseparably bound to him, grouped spiritually and materially at his side with all our might to strike the satanic wolf.'

In April, the Communists committed their greatest political blunder of the whole occupation. They summoned a pan-Cretan conference at Karines to which they invited representatives of all the Cretan groups, but no British officers.

On discovering this exclusion, Major Christos Tsiphakis, the Cretan officer who had directed the defence of Rethymno, promptly refused to take part and left. None of the other groups boycotted the meeting, which was fortunate for the British as things turned out: otherwise they might have missed the Communists' greatest political gaffe of the war.

Amongst the resolutions to be debated, two in particular were ill-chosen. The first was roundly anti-British; the second read: 'That Greece renounces all claims to Northern Epirus, Thrace and certain parts of Macedonia as they are not ethnically Greek.'

For patriots, this avowal of the international Communist policy of a separate state of Macedonia (something EAM on the mainland wisely did not mention) was outrageous treason. The meeting ended in uproar, and Communist hopes of an alliance with the Nationalist EOK – which they presumably intended to manipulate and one day dominate – were irretrievably broken.

After the Communist débâcle, the Nationalist EOK was able to hold its first pan-Cretan meeting at Prines on 15 June in an optimistic mood. Political representatives and military commanders were appointed for the four main provinces – Canea, Rethymno, Heraklion and Lasithi.

The resistance in the Canea area lacked a military leader but had an administrative structure. Many of its members already held official positions under the German authorities while secretly assisting the Allies. This made them a sort of local government-in-waiting. Their most prominent figure was Nikolaos Skoulas, the Mayor of Canea: he would soon have to flee into the mountains despite his advanced age. And amongst the younger generation, Constantinos Mitsotakis, Manoussos Manoussakis and Mikhaili Botonakis worked with the Quins' intelligence network run by Marko Spanoudakis.

At that time, there were no guerrilla groups operating in the immediate vicinity of Canea – a deliberate policy to avoid reprisals – and the bands soon to form in the south of the province would be too far away for any form of effective liaison.

In the province of Rethymno, Major Tsiphakis had set up a resistance network, bringing together very different political tendencies – Venizelist, Communist and monarchist – almost immediately after the fall of Crete. But the Communists' blunder at Karines led to their exclusion.

Crete's most important monarchist was Emmanuel Papadoyannis, a minister after the war. His slightly self-important manner went well with his pepper-and-salt beard and upturned moustache.

British officers, amongst whom he seems to have inspired both affection and respect, gave him the codename 'Pooh Bah' because of all the posts he had held up to acting governor-general. As a monarchist, albeit not a Metaxist, he was one of the few Cretans acceptable to the King and the Greek government-in-exile, and thus represented a vital link in such a republican stronghold.*

Major Tsiphakis had more of an academic than a soldierly air: one British officer remarked that he possessed 'none of that Cretan swagger'. And in spite of a certain taste for intrigue, he was an honest man with little apparent ambition for 'captaincy'.

The province of Rethymno also included the best example of resistance organization on the whole island, the council of the Amari valley. British liaison officers gave it the codename of Lotusland County Council. Alexandros Kokonas, the widely loved schoolmaster of Yerakari, was its very effective co-ordinator.

The military commander for the province of Lasithi, Colonel Nikolaos Plevres, was a former brigade commander in Albania and had many veterans of the Cretan V Division amongst his followers. But Tom Dunbabin and Sandy Rendel, who later became the British officer in the region, were suspicious when the Germans rapidly released Plevres after a round-up of the Neapolis network. Eighteen

* King George II's unfortunate manner with his subjects was well illustrated when Papadoyannis was presented to him as the former governor-general of Crete. He immediately said 'you mean former *acting* governor-general.'

months later Plevres, a right-wing Nationalist, received weapons from the Germans who were hoping he would fight the Communists.

The province of Heraklion had appointed a unifying council – the Committee of Civil Advisers – with prominent figures such as church dignitaries and educationalists. Some were wise, but a few were highly unpredictable. Colonel Beteinakis, the military leader for the whole province, was an officer whose bravery greatly exceeded his judgement.

The most important asset in Heraklion was the information service run by two very clever young students: first George Doundoulakis and then Miki Akoumianakis, the son of Sir Arthur Evans's overseer at Knossos – hence his codename of Minoan Mike. The responsibility for the purely intelligence side of this network was handed over to the ISLD mission which arrived on 12 May.

Ralph Stockbridge, who had been Jack Smith-Hughes's wireless operator on the first mission, was now a captain, and returned with John Stanley, an old school-friend, officially as his wireless operator. He had recruited Stanley – a bimbashi with the Sudan Defence Force – for this mission to Crete 'rather as one would suggest coming to a day at the races'.

The submarine *Papanikolis* brought them to the north coast of Crete, a unique occurrence since every other landing took place on the other side of the island. Stockbridge described this submarine as an alarmingly ancient vessel that had to surface to charge batteries. Commanded by Captain Athanasios Spanidis, the crew of the *Papanikolis* had a reputation for mad bravery, dating from earlier in the war when they sank Italian ships in the Adriatic at point-blank range.

Dropped between Rethymno and Heraklion, but rather a long way out, Stockbridge and Stanley had to ferry themselves to shore in a round rubber dinghy which, like a coracle inexpertly propelled, spun in circles and advanced little. The experience must have been most unpleasant for the two carrier pigeons that ISLD Cairo had insisted they bring.

As they came in, they made out some figures in a small boat, so they called the password agreed in advance: 'We've come for the bees.' These Cretans, fishing illegally, disappeared in panic thinking they had been discovered by the Germans. Stockbridge and Stanley finally reached shore, but their relief was cut short on discovering that they had landed in a minefield. Eventually, they made their way out safely and a bit further down the coast discovered their contact, who turned out to be Paddy Leigh Fermor.

Leigh Fermor took them first to the tiny monastery of Vossákou and then up to his base at that time, a stone sheepfold belonging to the Dramoundanis family on the northern slopes of the Mount Ida range above Anoyia.

A great number of people had collected there, prior to a trek to the south coast for the evacuation to Egypt of several *andartes* and intelligence agents. On 25 May, one of those tragic accidents, so common in war, took place. Seated in a circle outside the sheepfold were Ralph Stockbridge, John Stanley, Paddy Leigh Fermor and Yanni Tsangarakis, the guide of great courage and reliability whom Leigh Fermor had already recommended for a British decoration.

A sentry appeared to warn them that a German patrol had moved into Anoyia below. There was no panic at such a relatively common event, but Leigh Fermor, like the others, reached for his rifle. He pulled back the bolt to check the working parts were well oiled. The chamber was clear, but he did not spot a live round which had been left in the magazine. After closing the bolt, an action which automatically forced the round into the chamber, he pulled the trigger to ease the spring. There was a shot, and Tsangarakis squatting opposite received a wound in the thigh.

At first this wound did not look serious. They bandaged him carefully, while a runner dashed off to fetch a doctor in spite of the Germans below. But Tsangarakis died not long afterwards. They buried him under two ilex trees and camouflaged the grave with brambles and rocks in case another German patrol came that way.

Leigh Fermor was grief-stricken. He had been devoted to Yanni Tsangarakis, and Tsangarakis's few words to absolve him before he died only made the sense of guilt more excruciating. But worse was to follow.

Ill-disposed people, hearing of the accident, promptly spread the story that Yanni Tsangarakis's death had been planned and tried to convince the family of it. This led to years of bitter estrangement on one side and lasting regret and distress on the other. Many years were to pass before all were convinced of the true story by common friends, especially George Psychoundakis.

Although the story could not end happily, the bitterness was finally effaced over thirty years later when Paddy Leigh Fermor and his wife, Joan were invited to be godparents to Yanni's great-niece, a bond of considerable significance in Crete. She was named Joanna after Joan Leigh Fermor.

Petrakageorgis returned from Cairo on 7 June. During his stay in the Egyptian capital he had been contacted by the Organization of Strategic Services, the American equivalent of SOE. They offered a better service in weapons, equipment and cash. Petrakageorgis came back full of importance – visits to Cairo often seemed to produce that effect – but the promises of support from OSS were not fulfilled (perhaps SOE put a stop to this behind the scenes) and he had to continue, a little out of spirits, in the rather less glamorous British routine.

As soon as the Germans heard of his return – the news was over two months old – they mounted an attack on his band above Vorizia. The Germans, for some reason, seem to have harboured an especially personal enmity for Petrakageorgis, more than for any other kapitan. Heavily outnumbered, he escaped with only seven of his men after a fierce battle lasting all day in which the attackers lost thirteen men killed. In revenge, the Germans drove out the villagers, then destroyed Vorizia with Stukas on practice dive-bomb attacks.

In Xan Fielding's area of Western Crete, meanwhile, the final evacuation of stragglers from 1941 had been taking place. The boat on which Tom Dunbabin and George Psychoundakis left for a break in Cairo in February had brought in a New Zealander, Sergeant Tom Moir of 'A Force'. This was a cover name for MI9, the organization responsible for bringing escaped prisoners or evaders out of enemy-occupied territory.

Moir, a member of the 'infantillery' at Galatas and an escapee after the battle, had been trained and sent back to bring off the remainder still on the island. He made contact with many groups, prior to organizing a motor launch shuttle back to Egypt. One difficulty lay in moving a paralysed Australian, who was hidden in a cave nursed devotedly by the inhabitants of Kyriakosellia. Xan Fielding was particularly keen to relieve them of this burden and danger, but to his dismay, Sergeant Moir was captured on 6 May. Although in civilian clothes, Moir managed to convince the Germans that he had never left the island. He thus escaped execution and was flown to Greece to an ordinary prisoner-of-war camp.

Fielding immediately took over the work. He luckily encountered the three resourceful Australian soldiers who had saved his equipment from the sea the previous November and was able to delegate much of the task to them. In a remarkably short space of time they brought outlying groups to a hide in the woods above Koustoyérako, a spot which soon began to look like a brigand's lair.

Fielding used the nearby ISLD wireless station for his communications with Cairo to organize the evacuation by Royal Navy motor launch for the night of 7 May. Everything was prepared to transport the paralysed Australian from the cave at Kyriakosellia: disguised as a sick old woman, he would be moved on the back of a donkey. But at the last moment, certain that he would not survive the journey, and not wanting to put others at risk, he refused to go. He died soon afterwards.

At the beginning of June, Schubert, the counter-espionage chief who took over from Hartmann, decided to play the role of free-roving stool pigeon himself. He went to Koumara, above Asi Gonia, with four of his renegade Cretans, and pretended to be an English officer newly arrived from Cairo.

A trusting boy told them all about the English in the area but at the last moment, when they asked to be led to the English base, he became suspicious. They seized him as he tried to run away and shot him on the spot. Neighbours heard the report and began to appear. Schubert and his accomplices, although armed, fled to fetch reinforcements, such was their fear of the villagers' anger.

At the end of July, George Psychoundakis returned to the island from his stay in the Middle East. He was accompanied by one of the several remarkable figures of those years: Sergeant Dudley Perkins, a New Zealander known to the British as 'Kiwi' and to the Cretans as 'Vasili'.

Perkins, another member of the 'infantillery' at Galatas, had escaped from the prison camp with Moir. He proved a natural guerrilla leader with a great flair for tactics. His outstanding bravery led Xan Fielding to recommend him for the Victoria Cross, but the award was refused because no officer had been present to witness his deeds. The caution of the British authorities did not deter the Cretans who entered him in their own heroic folklore.

Perkins, like Moir, had picked up some Greek during his time as a straggler. In spite of his university education, he had been rejected during an officer training course which seemed to expect mindless discipline, but he appeared perfectly content as an NCO. Impressions of him vary. Sandy Rendel who was on the same course at 'Narkover' remembered him as 'a fox-terrier quivering with eagerness'. This gives an impression of a humourless, almost over-dedicated fighter. Yet George Psychoundakis, who had spent nearly a month improving Kiwi's Greek in Egypt, found him an engaging companion.

One evening in Vaphé, during his introductory tour, the two of them visited a woman teacher 'devoted to the resistance'. In the ill-lit room, she accepted a cigarette, and joked in Greek out of the side of her mouth to George Psychoundakis: 'I'm only lighting a cigarette to see how good looking he is'. Perkins, having concealed his knowledge of the language, had to grab a cigarette for himself to conceal his laughter.

After this round of key villages with Psychoundakis, Xan Fielding sent Perkins back to the Selino area to work with Alec Tarves — known as 'the Tinker' — the radio operator in the area, and to train the Selino band based on the Paterakis family. Fielding had quickly recognized Perkins's qualities, and had no qualms about leaving him to operate independently. Less than twenty strong, the Seliniots, with his guidance, soon proved themselves one of the most effective fighting groups on the island.

A month after Perkins's arrival, Fielding organized a parachute drop. The Paterakis band and another in the area were armed with Sten guns, Bren guns and Thompson sub-machine guns. And as the resistance on Crete was moving into a different phase, Fielding had requested a sort of uniform for them: Australian slouch hats and British Army riding breeches which were the nearest thing to Cretan crap-catchers. The breeches were a bonus from the mechanization of the Cavalry Division in Palestine.

Xan Fielding's attention was rather diverted that summer by another concern. General Mandakas had begun to demand weapons because GHQ Middle East had recently recognized EAM and its military wing, ELAS. Colonel Kondekas, Mandakas's chief of staff (a rather grandiose description considering their shortage of followers) issued an ultimatum that if Fielding did not accept Mandakas as the leader of the Cretan resistance, EAM would declare that he was not an official Allied representative.

Fielding also found to his dismay that the Greeks left to run the ISLD wireless station in the Selino area were all EAM–ELAS supporters. They had put their set at General Mandakas's disposal, thus enabling him to claim that he was in regular touch with Cairo. Even more provokingly, he had sent a signal to Cairo protesting that

Fielding's refusal to supply arms was a scandalous interference in the internal affairs of his country, now that GHQ Middle East had recognized EAM–ELAS. (Monty Woodhouse on the mainland had arranged the signing of the 'National Bands Agreement' on 5 July in an attempt to bind the Communists to a command structure and prevent their attacks on the non-Communist group EDES led by General Napoleon Zervas.)

Fielding, who knew nothing of this new arrangement, refused to give in to Mandakas's blackmail. He said that he would provide weapons only when Mandakas fully accepted the Allied – and thus British – chain of command in the Eastern Mediterranean. This fortunately turned out to be one of the provisions of the National Bands Agreement, so Mandakas could only huff and puff. But Fielding found it galling in the extreme to hear of this new arrangement from the Communists.

25
The Italian Armistice

The invasion of Sicily in July 1943 and the ensuing downfall of the
Fascist regime in Italy brought a marked increase in the scale and
tempo of resistance in Crete. Until that summer there had been little
more than isolated skirmishes and attacks on lone soldiers. From then
on, actions resulting in the death of up to twenty Germans were not
uncommon, and on a couple of occasions in the following year, up to
forty were killed in battles involving a hundred or more *andartes*.

Preparations for the Sicilian landings, Operation Husky, had begun
several months in advance with a major deception campaign to
convince the Germans that the Allied invasion of southern Europe
would come via Crete and Greece. A series of raids across Greece,
including the destruction of another railway bridge, was launched
under the code-name Animals.

A dummy fleet was assembled at Tobruk but a storm smashed it
back into its constituent pieces of canvas and plywood. Perhaps the
best-known ingredient of the campaign was that brilliant confidence
trick Operation Mincemeat.

A Royal Navy submarine dropped a body dressed and identified
as a British staff officer off the Spanish coast. Documents with him
'revealed' that Sardinia and Greece were the real objectives, and that
the attack on Sicily (the first landings took place on 10 July) was
simply a diversion. Berlin, largely thanks to Hitler's obsession with the
Balkan flank, swallowed the deception whole.* Two fighter groups, a

* Sir William Deakin wrote that Hitler developed a 'chiromantic belief that the
ultimate Allied assault would come from the south-east — the personal revenge of
Churchill for the Dardanelles failure in 1915'.

bomber wing and the 1st Panzer Division were immediately ordered to Greece.

Four weeks before the Sicilian landings, another round of Special Boat Squadron raids took place against German airfields on Crete. They had a dual purpose: to destroy German aircraft in the region which might be used against the invasion fleet, and to keep up the impression that Crete and Greece were the main targets for invasion. At their training base in Palestine, Athlit Castle, the SBS teams had become bored with constant practice, so this new operation was eagerly accepted. David Sutherland, who had commanded one of the raiding parties the summer before, controlled three groups led by Lieutenants Lassen, Lamonby and Rowe.

Rowe, who arrived on 27 June, four days after the others, had the closest objective, Tymbaki airfield, but once again it was found to be out of use. Lamonby set off towards Heraklion, but the guide provided by Dunbabin warned him that the airfield there was hardly used any more. A much better target would be the fuel dump at Peza. This Lamonby destroyed with spectacular success.

The third group under Andy Lassen found Kastelli Pediados heavily guarded after the attack of the year before. The only solution was a diversionary attack to allow the bomb-placers the chance to flit from one group of aircraft to another under cover of the confusion. Lassen, a legendary Dane who won the Military Cross and two bars and later received a posthumous Victoria Cross, was known for his cry 'Vork before Vomen!' when weapons and kit needed cleaning on return to base.

They all reached Sutherland's hideout in the coastal hills above Treis Ekklisies by 11 July, but so did a number of Cretans who also wanted to be taken off to avoid retribution. A small German patrol discovered the gorge in which they had hidden to wait until night had fallen before going down to the beach. Two of the Germans were captured without a shot, but the other two retreated rapidly when fired upon by the Cretans. Lamonby went after them alone, a brave but foolhardy course. The motor launch which picked up the rest of the party pulled in close to the shore near where he had last been sighted, but there was no sign of him. He had underestimated the two soldiers he tried to stalk. His body was discovered much later.

To coincide with the other attacks, Paddy Leigh Fermor had entered Heraklion with Manoli Paterakis. A donkey brought their load of limpet mines into the centre of the city, where they were hidden by

Yanni Androulakis. They planned to attack shipping in the harbour, but having managed to get through the wire they were spotted and had to escape before the general alarm was raised.

At the end of July, staying in Yerakari with Alexandros Kokonas, Leigh Fermor received a message from Miki Akoumianakis which brought him back to Heraklion at speed. Mussolini had been overthrown, following the invasion of Sicily, and the Italian commander of the division occupying the east of the island, General Angelo Carta, wanted to speak to a British officer.

A very indirect approach had been made via Bandouvas at the beginning of the year to suggest that if the British invaded Crete, the Italians would surrender immediately, but nothing more had been heard. This time Lieutenant Franco Tavana, General Carta's counter-espionage officer, offered to send a staff car and Italian uniform to bring Paddy Leigh Fermor to their headquarters.

Tavana, formerly a customs official on Lake Como and now an officer in the Alpini, had already proved himself unorthodox and brave. The year before, he had arrived at the house of the Communist leader Miltiades Porphyroyennis, the unusual passenger on the *Kalanthe* and later a member of the Party's central committee on the mainland. Porphyroyennis, seeing the chief of counter-espionage, assumed the worst, but as an alternative to arrest and execution he was told to move to the area controlled by the Germans and stay there.

Stories of friction between the Axis allies were not new. There had been fights between Italian and German soldiers: on one occasion an Italian threw a grenade at a group of Germans killing one and wounding two others. The Italian military authorities had to arrest him, but then released him a few days later to the fury of the Germans. Cretans sentenced to death in the provinces of Lasithi and Siteia on German insistence were smuggled away, in some cases to the Dodecanese. Meanwhile executions were faked, and graves dug and then filled in again.

Every precaution for Leigh Fermor's journey had to be taken. General Carta was very nervous. Schubert's recruitment of informers had not slackened. But nor had Bandouvas's squads. They had recently accounted for fourteen traitors. Their tactics were simple: a couple of men dressed in gendarmerie uniforms accompanied by a fair-haired Cretan in German uniform would 'arrest' their suspect, claiming he had been denounced as a member of the resistance. The man, if really working for the Germans, would then promptly show them proof, usually a piece of paper from the German authorities.

Mussolini's fall prompted great jubilation in Italian barracks: black shirts were torn up and his portrait ripped down. But General Carta became uneasy. Leigh Fermor tried 'a lot of flattery laid on with a trowel', his letters beginning *'Mon général, j'ai l'honneur de communiquer à votre Excellence . . .'* Yet Carta continued to vacillate even after General Bräuer flew in from the other end of the island to reassure him that the Germans would not attack providing the Italians behaved.

The crucial question for the Italians was whether the British would invade and effectively decide the matter for them. In the wake of the Sicily landings and the cover-plan, great confusion still surrounded Allied plans. Rumours of an offensive in the Eastern Mediterranean against islands 'so long the object of strategic desire' were not baseless.

On 2 August Churchill told General Ismay: 'Should the Italian troops in Crete and Rhodes resist the Germans and a deadlock ensue, we must help the Italians at the earliest moment, engaging thereby also the support of the populations.' But although Leigh Fermor was asked to provide Cairo with bombing targets in the event of Italian resistance – news of the request may have leaked out in resistance circles during the assembly of this information – Crete was soon dropped from contingency planning. Middle East Command then focused solely on the Dodecanese islands of Rhodes, Cos and Leros.

Churchill had a dangerously impractical vision of securing a route through the Dardanelles to Russia as an alternative to the Arctic convoys. 'This is a time', he signalled to General Wilson, 'to think of Clive and Peterborough and of Rooke's men taking Gibraltar.' But the Germans occupied Rhodes with great speed and plans had to be scaled down drastically after a decision at the Quebec conference to divert available shipping from the Eastern Mediterranean. Only one brigade, some very unsuitable craft and a handful of fighters remained for the operation. British troops landed on the islands of Cos and Leros on 14 September, but stood little chance against strong German counter-attacks, first against Cos, then Leros.

General Carta was a short, plump officer with a monocle and a mistress conveniently installed near his headquarters in Neapolis. A friend of the Italian royal family, he was 'a Palace man', not a Fascist, and his administration of the eastern part of Crete had been unusually humane. Carta's lack of boldness during the month of August stemmed mainly from a desire to avoid useless bloodshed. Tavana, his counter-espionage officer, was a much more daring and more resolute man. He raised the prospect of Italian forces, in alliance with Cretan *andartes*, holding the eastern part of the island against the Germans.

Since Bandouvas, the only guerrilla leader with a large following, was encamped not far to the south-west at Psari Phoráda on the Viannos plateau, Leigh Fermor set off there on 12 August. He was accompanied by his wireless operator, Staff Sergeant Harry Brooke, and Niko Souris. Souris, Dunbabin's right-hand man, was an Alexandrian of great intelligence and tact, and one of the very few Greeks from outside whom the Cretans really trusted.

Bandouvas's highland lair was impressive. This plateau, well above the sheepfolds and far from any other trace of habitation, had views over the whole province. Sentries of wonderfully dramatic appearance accompanied Leigh Fermor up to their camp which had rows of huts made of woven branches. A baker, a tailor's shop, a cobbler and an armourer helped to make them self-sufficient.

Most striking of all was the composition of Bandouvas's force. Apart from shepherds and mountain villagers, there were students, army officers, two heavily armed monks, a priest, some policemen, a few stranded Greeks from the mainland, a huge Cossack called Piotr who had escaped from the camp for Russian prisoners at Ay Galini, an Australian and a New Zealander, both stragglers from the battle of over two years before, a group of Royalists led by Athanasios Bourdzalis, and lastly a handful of Communists, recruited mainly by Bandouvas's secretary, Yanni Bodias. Bodias, a good-looking and intelligent young Greek from Asia Minor with a certain charm, had been in prison when the parachute invasion occurred. His crime was attempted murder: having indecently assaulted a boy, he had dropped him down a well. Now that Bodias's influence over the Chief of *Francs-Tireurs* had waned, a split between them was perhaps bound to develop.

Volatile shifts of mood amongst such a heterogeneous group were inevitable. One day, when Leigh Fermor and Bandouvas were out of the camp, one of the anti-traitor squads brought in a suspect by the name of Loukakis. He was strung up by his ankles for torture, but Niko Souris, backed by Sergeant Harry Brooke, intervened, and when Bandouvas and Leigh Fermor returned, a brigand court martial assembled and he was shot. The following day, the traitor Syngelakis who had betrayed the officers escaping by caique from the south-west was captured. He too confessed and was shot.

Bandouvas's curious but effective force was increasing every day as men arrived from near and far. Leigh Fermor estimated its strength at around 160 men, and Bandouvas, probably without much exaggeration, reckoned he could call to arms 2,000 more. On 20 August, a week after Leigh Fermor's arrival, the eagerly anticipated arms drop took place. Everything worked perfectly. Sergeant Paddy Fortune, the pilot, flew in low, waggled his wing tips in greeting and the parachute containers came out in an impressive stream.

Everything was borne back to camp in triumphal procession with *feux de joie*. Apart from weapons and ammunition, the containers held cap comforters, bush shirts, web belts and bayonet frogs. Bandouvas wanted his men freshly kitted out so as to be accepted as a regular unit of the British Army. Yet although Leigh Fermor explained to Bandouvas in the clearest terms that the role of his band was to help the Italians, should they decide to resist the Germans, and take over their surplus arms to distribute to the Cretan resistance as a whole, the Chief of *Francs-Tireurs* was secretly convinced that something greater was afoot. The idea of a British invasion lingered long after a call by King George II to help Allied forces. This broadcast, which had preceded the Sicilian landings, referred to raiding rather than invading forces, but the ambiguity had been part of the overall deception plan.

With Bandouvas's men equipped, Leigh Fermor left for Neapolis, where he stayed in Lieutenant Tavana's house. Tavana supplied him with all the German defence plans for the island, confidential reports, orders and assessments of Cretan resistance organizations.

Hitler had ordered contingency plans to be drawn up two days after Mussolini's fall from power. Measures which included the German occupation of Italy were gradually put into effect during the month of August. Hitler was correct in his suspicion that the new government of Marshal Badoglio would seek an armistice, and an operation code-named ACHSE to disarm Italian troops was prepared for the moment this happened.

On the morning of 9 September Leigh Fermor, suffering from a bad leg, was resting at a goatfold above Kastelli Pediados when Miki Akoumianakis arrived in great excitement with news of the Italian armistice announced the day before. About midday Tom Dunbabin appeared with Niko Souris, who had met him at the beach at Tsoutsouro the day before on his return from Egypt. Dunbabin finally

confirmed that there was no hope of an Allied landing in Crete. 'If
there had been', he joked to Leigh Fermor, 'we'd have both become
brigadiers.'

Very soon afterwards, a runner arrived from Bandouvas with a
message so badly written that it was passed round. While Miki
Akoumianakis was studying the scrawl, Dunbabin asked Leigh Fermor
in English who this young man was and whether he could be trusted.
When told, he could hardly believe it. There were great greetings and
memories of Knossos in the days of Sir Arthur Evans. Eventually
Akoumianakis returned to the note and, to their horror, deciphered
the key phrase: 'When are the English landing to help us fight the
Germans?'

Bandouvas had ignored his instructions to prepare to help the
Italians and await further orders. He had already moved to attack the
Germans in the area of Viannos on the south coast. The runner was
sent back with the strongest possible message telling him to stop
immediately and withdraw. Leigh Fermor had to leave Dunbabin to
cope with the Bandouvas problem as best he could, while he and
Miki Akoumianakis left to confer with Tavana in response to the
momentous news of the armistice. But their hopes of Italian
resistance to the Germans soon evaporated.

When word of the armistice arrived, a large number of Italian
soldiers had promptly drunk themselves into a stupor of celebration:
they naïvely assumed that the war was over and they could go home.
And the only two battalions of infantry who were prepared to fight,
and had gone up into the mountains, came down again a couple of
days later because the local population, in spite of its readiness to
help, could not feed so many men.

General Bräuer ordered German troops into the province of
Lasithi and the dispersal of Italian forces to new locations chosen for
them. General Müller, the divisional commander, issued a 'General
Order to All Italian Troops in Crete' which was in effect an
ultimatum.

'The Commander of the Fortress of Crete', he began, 'has charged
me with the defence of the province of Lasithi.' He then offered
three choices. Italian soldiers could continue to fight under the
command of the German armed forces, thereby adhering to
Mussolini's new government – the puppet show which became the
Republic of Salo. Or they could assist the Germans in non-combatant
duties on the island after having been disarmed – a euphemism for
working in labour gangs. If they refused these two alternatives then

they would be interned. 'Whosoever', he finished, 'sells or destroys arms of the Italian forces, or whosoever deserts from his unit, will be considered a *franc-tireur* and as such shot.'

General Carta, resigned to the idea that resistance was impossible without a British landing, circulated Müller's order to all Italian units with his own recommendation attached. 'The above is a natural consequence of the situation resulting from the armistice. We are in a besieged fortress. It is therefore essential to follow the orders of the German command with a sense of realism.' Tragically, the Italians who refused to work for the Germans were embarked in a ship which was then sunk by an Allied submarine.

Paddy Leigh Fermor made plans for General Carta's escape to Egypt. The details were arranged by Miki Akoumianakis and the two brothers, Stelios and Roussos Koundouros. A signal was sent to Cairo to arrange a rendezvous for a motor launch on the beach near Treis Ekklisies. Meanwhile, to the despair of all British officers on the island, and contrary to all instructions, Bandouvas had allowed his men to attack German soldiers in the Viannos region. A group of them began on Friday, 10 September, by killing two privates who were collecting potatoes at Kato Simi. The bodies, wrapped in sacks, were dropped down a hole, but a Cretan 'Gestapite' ran off to warn the nearest garrison.

Still convinced that an Allied invasion was heading for this portion of the coast, Bandouvas, compounding his own rashness, sent runners northwards calling for a general mobilization in the whole province of Heraklion. The impetuous Colonel Beteinakis rushed to support it. Dunbabin could only issue furious countermands.

Two days after the attack at Kato Simi, a force nearly 2,000 strong reached the area. Bandouvas's men stood little chance. They killed just under twenty soldiers (according to German figures) then scattered. One account from a reliable source says that they also took prisoner thirteen Germans. Local citizens, including an Archimandrite and the Mayor of Kalami, urged Bandouvas to release the prisoners. Added to similar advice from within his band, he agreed, but this had to be carried out secretly since others wanted them executed. The soldiers were freed on the evening of 19 September, but next morning they ran into another group of Bandouvas's men who promptly killed them.

The German military authorities, already paranoid about the defection of Italy and the possibility of Carta's troops fighting alongside the resistance, reacted with murderous resolution. General

Müller gave orders for the immediate destruction of six villages in the Viannos area and about five hundred civilians were shot.*

Bandouvas and his band had to run from the nest of hornets they had provoked. The German retaliatory drive in the region forced them westwards. Bandouvas again demanded help from the kapitans around the Mount Ida range, and sent a peremptory request to Tom Dunbabin that he urgently organize their evacuation. Dunbabin's temper was sorely tried.

Paddy Leigh Fermor, meanwhile, had smuggled General Carta and a few members of his staff out of their headquarters at Neapolis on 16 September, and across the Lasithi mountains. Fieseler Storch spotter planes flew overhead searching for them and dropped hurriedly printed leaflets offering a reward of thirty thousand drachma for General Carta's capture. One of them fell virtually at Carta's feet. He bent down, picked it up and waved it at Leigh Fermor. *'Ah, ah, mon capitaine!'* he exclaimed. *'Trente pièces d'argent! Un contrat de Judas!'*

The small party managed to evade the German patrols and they reached the beach near Treis Ekklisies on 23 September. There Leigh Fermor found Dunbabin and the other British officers, all of whom had been dragged into the Viannos débâcle, and also Bandouvas who, with impermeable self-assurance, tried to shift the blame demanding that he and his men should be evacuated first. Despite everything, Leigh Fermor could not help feeling a certain pity at the almost total destruction of his band.

The Royal Navy motor launch which was coming to take off General Carta brought Sandy Rendel, his wireless operator and Father Skoulas, 'the parachute priest'. They arrived to a scene of chaos on the beach that night. To make matters worse, the sea was choppy. Rendel's attaché case and the charging engine for his wireless went over the side as the rubber dinghy was loaded.

Rendel only had time to catch a glimpse of an elderly man in a felt hat – General Carta – and Paddy Leigh Fermor, who had come aboard to hand over important German documents provided by Tavana to Bob Young, the commander of the launch, without Carta's knowledge. But Young became concerned at the deterioration in the weather and turned his craft out to sea. Leigh Fermor with Manoli

---

* Although not kinsmen of the kapitan, many seem to have suffered simply because they bore the name of Bandouvas — a name dating from the Venetian occupation which signified a native of Padua.

Paterakis thus made an unplanned exit from Crete. The next time he returned would not be by sea but by parachute.

On the beach, Tom Dunbabin had to exert all his authority to deal with Bandouvas's demands that another boat be sent from Egypt immediately. The newly arrived Rendel was also deeply impressed by Dunbabin's stream of Cretan curses when a young Greek officer — a nephew of the Prime Minister — chucked away an empty sardine tin with British markings.

The German troops still searching for Bandouvas and his band forced them and the British further westward. A week later the fugitives were on the flank of a hill called Tsilívdika near the Rodakino beach which was used for clandestine landings.

There, in a bowl in the hills with a network of caves, the company, by now almost a hundred strong, settled to rest and wait. Sheep were taken from nearby flocks, slaughtered and roasted on blazing fires in the caves.

Sentries from Bandouvas's band posted on surrounding hills kept watch, and Sandy Rendel later remembered gazing out over the Libyan Sea while bees hummed in the thyme all around them. But the British officers and their Cretan associates — Tom Dunbabin, Xan Fielding, Sandy Rendel, Ralph Stockbridge, John Stanley, George Psychoundakis, Niko Souris and various detachments from bands in the central region — felt ill at ease in the unnatural calm. Events seemed to have overtaken them. Bewildered and exasperated, they wondered whether a motor launch would ever arrive to solve the impasse.

Dunbabin's runner returned from the wireless set on Mount Ida to relay the message from Cairo that no craft was available. In case Bandouvas might react unpleasantly to this news — it was hard to forget that he had threatened to seize parachute stores by force of arms the autumn before — Tom Dunbabin warned his officers to keep their revolvers to hand. But by then Bandouvas was preoccupied with another matter.

One of the local *andartes* happened to mention to him that a man from his region had recently turned up in their area. Bandouvas asked his name and, when told, declared that he was in league with the Germans. Men were sent off to seize him, and Bandouvas conducted a trial which lasted most of the night. British officers kept dropping off to sleep, then waking up again to this strange scene. The accused, one Georgiou Ergazakis, finally confessed. Polioudakis, the collaborationist police chief in Heraklion, had recruited him. He went on to give the names of other agents working for the Germans, but this did not save him.

At dawn – it was now 4 October – he was taken off to be shot. His body was then dropped down a pothole. Very soon afterwards firing broke out. A reconnaissance patrol of Feldgendarmerie and Italian carabinieri was spotted by Bandouvas's lookouts who, without waiting for them to come closer, blazed away at maximum range. After a confused and scattered skirmish, most of the enemy force were either killed or captured. Amongst the prisoners was a Cretan who claimed he had been forced into German uniform.

This Cretan was put under guard with what he thought was a captured German soldier. But 'Gussie', as the British and Cretans called him, was Ralph Stockbridge's 'tame German' who had fled his Wehrmacht barracks. Gussie murmured to the Greek collaborator in German that they would both be shot.

The traitor whispered back, also in German, that he should not give up hope. He and the others had been the advance guard of a much larger force which had the whole area surrounded. He went on to boast of how long and successfully he had worked for the Germans. Once he had truly condemned himself, Gussie stood up and told the *andartes* all that he had said. A second traitor met his fate.

This successful ruse had also provided a warning of their dangerous position. But later towards evening, the weather changed. They were saved by a heavy mist covering the hills and coast. That night, splitting into small groups, the curious assembly at Mount Tsilívdika broke up. Bandouvas was directed further westwards along the coast; Dunbabin sent Niko Souris with him to provide sound advice.

Hoping for another boat, Bandouvas and his men hid near Kalo Lakko in the province of Sphakia. But the villagers in that area became worried by his presence, so he and his men were prevailed upon to return to the Mount Ida range. Eventually, he left Crete on the last day of October.

Dunbabin meanwhile had returned to the Amari having wasted nearly a month. The ISLD team of Ralph Stockbridge and John Stanley, after breaking through the German cordon round Tsilívdika, ended up completing a clockwise circuit of the western half of the island. Sandy Rendel went to the mountains of Lasithi to take over the wireless station there. Dunbabin told him to take Franco Tavana,

General Carta's counter-espionage officer. But Tavana's intention to set up a resistance group of Italians and local Cretans petered out for lack of local support.

After the Viannos catastrophe the trail of misery ran to more than the six villages. Schubert's newly formed battalion of Greek-speaking Italians from the Dodecanese began to terrorize the southern coast.* Rodakino, Kallikrati and Kali-Sykia close to Mount Tsilívdika were also destroyed. In Kali-Sykia, old women are said to have been burned alive in their houses and thirty villagers were shot in Kallikrati.

The remains of Bandouvas's band split up on the departure of their leader. In his brother's absence, Yanni Bandouvas assumed a very diminished mantle of leadership. Bodias, assisted by Niko Samaritis, left with the Communist group to operate with ELAS – Bodias in the province of Heraklion and Samaritis in Lasithi. In spite of Tavana's failure to raise support, Lasithi was attractive to the Communists because of the quantities of Italian arms available there.

The Selino area in the south-west of the island also witnessed fighting and reprisals at this time. On 25 September, a German detachment surrounded the village of Koustoyérako, the home of the Paterakis family. They had presumably heard of the arms drop made only a week before to Kiwi Perkins and the Seliniot band.

Finding no men, the German patrol lined the women and children up in the square and demanded to know where they were hiding. Infuriated by the women's silence they set up a machine gun for an execution. The menfolk, notably Costi Paterakis, had in fact crept on to a bluff above the village. Their rifles were trained on the German firing party. At a range of four hundred yards, Paterakis's shot felled the machine gunner, and a fusillade from his fellow villagers brought down several others. The surviving Germans fled.

Since the fate of the village was clear, the women and children took their most treasured possessions and tramped up into the mountains to hide, while many of the men joined the Selino bands. The German reaction was as swift as they had expected. Between 30 September and 3 October German detachments burned the villages of Koustoyérako, Moni and Leivada. But the resistance was

---

* His unit in Wehrmacht uniform was designated the Jagdkommando Schubert: the Cretans nicknamed its members the Schuberaios.

fierce. In the same period, twenty-four of their soldiers were killed.

Perkins by now had a very effective guerrilla force. They were well armed after three parachute drops, and strengthened by men from the destroyed villages: the Selino district became dangerous for the Germans that autumn. Skirmishes, following the ambush of patrols, continued into the second week of October. They culminated on 18 October with a battle at Akhlada.

Akhlada is a tiny plain in the mountains two hours above Koustoyérako. The shepherds from the village had cheese-making huts there, solidly built in stone and without windows. The place had been used for some of the parachute drops and so German patrols visited it frequently.

Kiwi Perkins had an inspired idea for an ambush. Having picked his ground with great care, he and the Seliniots waited in position for an approaching patrol to enter their trap. Antoni Paterakis manned the Bren gun, a weapon with which he achieved fame, and on Kiwi's signal opened fire as the patrol of nineteen Germans and three Italians reached the cheese huts.

The immediate reaction of soldiers coming under fire is to seek cover first and fight back later. Since the cheese huts offered the only protection from the bursts of fire, they threw themselves inside, forgetting that these huts had no windows. Perkins, while the rest of the band took aim on the entrances, slipped from hut to hut rolling a grenade into each. He waited after pulling out each pin, so that the Germans inside would not have time to throw them back, and any who tried to escape were cut down by the Seliniots. Only two members of the band were wounded: Perkins, who had a bullet lodged beside a shoulder-blade, and another member of the band, Manolis Tzatzimakis, more seriously hurt.

The soldiers who surrendered fared no better than their dead comrades. They were taken to the band's hideout. There was no chance of sending this batch of prisoners out by sea to Egypt: after such a large engagement the Seliniots expected the whole area to be sealed off. Next morning the band drew lots. It fell to Antoni Paterakis and one other to deal with them.

They took the prisoners further up the mountain to a pothole at a place called Tafkos. Antoni Paterakis steeled himself with memories of how ruthless the Germans had been to captured *andartes*. The prisoners tied together in a line realized what their fate was as they shuffled forward to the edge of the drop. Paterakis intended to shoot them there, then roll the bodies in afterwards, but the first German to be shot staggered backwards and fell into the hole. He dragged the next man with him, and so on until all had disappeared.

Although the hole was well over a hundred feet deep, some of the Germans survived the fall. Perkins, in spite of the wound received the day before, volunteered to go down to finish them off, but Antoni Paterakis insisted on doing it himself. He was lowered down on a rope improvised out of parachute tapes, but it broke and he too fell. Paterakis's fate appalled all those at the top. His father broke into lamentations until it became clear that he was still alive, albeit with a damaged back. Trapped in this human snakepit of his own making, he heard one of the Germans whisper to him: 'And now, Greco, we will die together.'

Perkins finally persuaded the others to lower him down. He reached the bottom safely, finished off the surviving Germans and, with Paterakis strapped across his own wounded back, had himself hauled to the surface. Afterwards the bullet was removed from Perkins's back with a large Cretan knife. This act of rescue made him a national hero. From then on he was known as 'the unforgettable Vasili'. Antoni Paterakis survived his injuries. He was evacuated by motor launch and treated in a Cairo hospital. But Manolis Tzatzimakis had to be smuggled into Canea for treatment where he was betrayed to the Germans and shot.*

During the course of the year the military hierarchy on Crete was formalized. Tom Dunbabin became a lieutenant colonel commanding the British Military Mission. Xan Fielding, responsible for the west of the island, was promoted to major at the age of 25. Not long afterwards, Paddy Leigh Fermor, who was in charge of eastern Crete, was also promoted to major; he was 28. This was part of Keble's ambitious plan which created almost eighty SOE missions in the Balkans by October 1943.

The original SOE officers scattered around the Balkans thus found themselves reshuffled and upgraded. Their only consolation was rapid promotion. This rank inflation was intended mainly to give them weight in dealing with local guerrilla groups, and partly to increase the rank pyramid from below, thus raising Keble on the freshly crowned and pipped shoulders of others.

The over-rapid growth in British Military Missions had not been

* Another action, carried out by another band, must have taken place at about the same time because forty-two Germans died between 18 and 22 October.

matched by a similar increase in the number of cypherenes. Only the Cretan section managed to cope because Jack Smith-Hughes and his officers took over the decoding work when the quantity of messages increased. For the Greek section, on the other hand, the situation became disastrous. Officers in the field were furious. They found it almost impossible to extract replies, and they suspected that any attempt to pass back information was a waste of time. The cypherenes, mainly South Africans renowned for their glamour – this was not just the fantasy of men too long in the field, staff officers in Cairo admitted that they were picked for their looks – bore the brunt of the outraged and often obscene messages.

Nobody with any experience of Keble could trust a distant headquarters run by such a man. Anyone who stood in his way or objected to his methods was either bullied into submission or, in one or two cases, such as Arthur Reade, subjected to a campaign of vilification. Eventually Bolo Keble picked on the wrong man. Furious that Churchill had appointed Fitzroy Maclean to head the British Military Mission to Tito without reporting to him, he resorted to a campaign of lies that Maclean was an untrustworthy, drunken homosexual. When news of this attempt to blacken Maclean's character reached General Wilson, Keble's extraordinary career with SOE came to an abrupt end.

The other contribution to that year's annual upheaval was the political row building up with the Foreign Office over mainland Greece. This burst upon a remarkably ill-informed and unimaginative officialdom when Brigadier Myers, the leader of the British Military Mission in Greece, brought a delegation of *andartes* back to Cairo. EAM–ELAS and non-Communist representatives alike emphasized in blunt terms that King George II should not consider returning to Greece without a plebiscite on the future of the monarchy. The Foreign Office and the Greek government-in-exile were furious that such an embarrassing revelation should have been allowed to take place.

Myers was made the scapegoat for this contradiction between ossified assumptions and the political reality within Greece. The story on the mainland that the British had parachuted left-footed boots to the left-wing groups of ELAS and the right foot to EDES to cause trouble is appropriate, however apocryphal. British policy towards Greece was less a Machiavellian conspiracy than a sequence of blunders resulting from ignorance, arrogance, muddled thinking, lack of imagination and refusal to listen.

The head of SOE Cairo, Lord Glenconner, also suffered from the effects of Myers's unwelcome honesty and Keble's flagrant dishonesty, when General 'Jumbo' Wilson decided that SOE Cairo was 'rotten to the core'. Keble was returned to 'routine duties' and after a short interregnum under Major General W.A.M. Stawell, Brigadier Karl Barker-Benfield took Keble's place.

The new military director, a decent and guileless man with a quiet manner, could hardly have been more different from his predecessor. The Greek Communists on the mainland identified his character with hawk-like accuracy when he made a tour of inspection the following year and they played him accordingly. In Crete there was less of a political trap, so section officers regarded him more with amusement than exasperation.

Barker-Benfield, who had in Monty Woodhouse's description 'a shiny round head, almost completely bald, and a strangely Teutonic accent', inspired in Jack Smith-Hughes the whim that his real name was Barcke von Bohnenfeld. This later developed into a running joke based on the notion that the German Colonel Barge (pronounced Barcke) who took command of Festungsdivision 133 in Canea was really the long-lost twin brother of Brigadier Karl Barker-Benfield, the commander of Force 133.

In Crete, British officers were determined to maintain a *modus vivendi* with EAM–ELAS which would prevent civil war. On the night of 7 November, Xan Fielding set up the first major meeting between representatives of EAM and EOK since the row at Karines in the spring. This took place in the hills behind Canea near Therisso, where Venizelos had set up his revolutionary headquarters in the rebellion of 1905. Fielding arrived escorted by his guide and valued counsellor, Pavlo Vernadakis. The Mayor of Canea, Nikolaos Skoulas, led the EOK delegation and General Mandakas and Miltiades Porphyroyennis were the EAM–ELAS representatives.

Fielding, having set the agenda, claims to have drifted off to sleep from exhaustion after the march across the mountains, but he has always played down his role in the non-aggression pact which was eventually reached. Skoulas, who had made a dramatic scene before the meeting demanding 'What will history say if I sign an agreement with the Communists?', then told the colonel of gendarmerie to sign on his behalf along with Constantinos Mitsotakis. The agreement, once signed, was generally kept, unlike on the mainland. And many Cretans believe that this first step helped save the island from the worst effects of civil war.

After fourteen months in the field Xan Fielding went back to Cairo. During his time in Egypt, he came to the conclusion that there would now never be an Allied invasion of Crete. Since he was bilingual in French, having been brought up in France, he would be of more use there.

Fielding's replacement, Dennis Ciclitira, a captain in the South Staffords, arrived just before Christmas. Ciclitira had been Jack Smith-Hughes's very competent staff officer on the Cretan desk since October 1942, but so far the nearest he had come to work in the field was as conducting officer on clandestine crossings from Derna. Tired of the sneers which Cairo-bound officers tended to receive from their operational counterparts, Ciclitira had volunteered to take over from Xan Fielding when he next came out for a rest. A short time after the handover, his appointment was made permanent by Fielding's transfer.

Although his family was of Greek origin, Ciclitira played it down mainly because Cretans instinctively distrusted Greeks from outside. But Ciclitira did not warm to the Cretans, and his rather scathing tongue did little to conceal the fact.

The western area of Crete which he took over had two radio sets: one down in the Selino area with Kiwi Perkins, and the other at Asi Gonia, which was to be his base for the first few months. Ciclitira's relationship with Perkins was not an easy one. He was amazed that the Cretans should regard the New Zealander as a hero, mainly as a result of his rescue of Antoni Paterakis from the pothole, and he found it difficult to accept that they should consider a sergeant as their natural leader.

A clash of wills followed. Ciclitira believed that Perkins was causing 'more trouble than it was worth' down in the south-west, and gave orders for his return to Cairo. Perkins, determined to fight on until the end with the Seliniots, refused to leave the island. The dispute was resolved in a tragic manner at the end of February 1944. Perkins, on his way to see Ciclitira near Asi Gonia, met his death in a German ambush.

26
The Abduction of General Kreipe

Just before the end of 1943, Sandy Rendel in the Lasithi mountains received a message from Tom Dunbabin that Paddy Leigh Fermor would be dropping by parachute into his area with a team. They were coming from Brindisi to kidnap a German general.

The idea had first been raised in June 1942 when General Andrae, the Commander of the Fortress of Crete, following the example of General Ringel, had ordered Manoussos Manoussakis to take him on an ibex hunt in the White Mountains. Manoussakis had tipped off Marko Spanoudakis, the leader of the Quins network, and he had discussed plans with Xan Fielding. SOE Cairo had approved the project, but even with Manoussakis's help it was virtually impossible to organize. In any case the expedition was called off halfway through when news of Jellicoe's raid arrived and Andrae's authority was required for the execution of the prisoners in Heraklion. Now the kidnap idea was raised again.

After several postponements, the drop was fixed for the night of 4 February 1944 on to the Katharo plateau. Leigh Fermor was the first to jump, but then as the aeroplane made a wide circuit – the dropping zone was too small for more than one at a time and Leigh Fermor was to signal the all clear with a torch for the second run – heavy clouds, already closing in, suddenly covered the sky. The watchers below could hear the aeroplane continuing to circle. Finally, it had to fly away southwards over the sea.

Paddy Leigh Fermor holed up with Sandy Rendel in his cave above Tapais. The next few weeks became an infuriating sequence of confused signals to and from Cairo. Seven drops were aborted at the last moment. Inevitably, this activity and the overflights soon attracted

German attention. On the assumption that a strong raiding force had landed in the area, the fifty-strong garrison at Kritsa was doubled. It was some consolation when two German patrols encountered each other in the dark and fought it out, leaving two of their number dead and several wounded.

Soon after Leigh Fermor's arrival, an anti-traitor squad from Bandouvas's gang – the one with the fair-haired young Cretan in German uniform – turned up very pleased with themselves. They had caught a notorious traitor with the same old tactic, and flourished the paper from the German authorities which their prisoner had promptly handed over. In the absence of their kapitan in Cairo, they sought out Rendel and Leigh Fermor, who consented to the execution but sent some of their own men along to ensure that there was no unnecessary suffering. This was a bad time for traitors in Crete. At Meskla, an ELAS group cornered and killed eight 'Schuberaios'. The Germans decided to disband the Jagdkommando Schubert.

On 24 March, when Sandy Rendel was away on his rounds, Paddy Leigh Fermor was startled by the arrival of more figures muffled against the cold. He again recognized characters from his time with Bandouvas the year before. These were the three leading Communists who all now led their own bands: Yanni Bodias in Heraklion; Samaritis, the ELAS leader in Lasithi, 'a bitter, sneering man'; and Mitsos O Papas, a most likeable and brave individual, famous for having sunk a ship single-handed.

They had come to discuss the National Bands Agreement, which Monty Woodhouse had arranged on the mainland between ELAS and the non-Communist group EDES (see Appendix D). They wanted arms for their men, and Leigh Fermor said that he would make a recommendation to Cairo. He acknowledged that their demand was justified, but privately he feared that an unrestricted supply of arms would be dangerous if relations between ELAS and EOK deteriorated.

Finally, after all attempts at a parachute drop had been abandoned in mid-March, the rest of the team arrived from Egypt at Tsoutsouro on the night of 4 April. As soon as their gear had been rowed ashore from the motor launch by dinghy, four Luftwaffe deserters were sent on board together with a typist from the German headquarters at Hierapetra called Antonia, who had provided the resistance with vital information.

Leigh Fermor and Rendel were on the beach to welcome the late arrivals: Captain William Stanley Moss, a very good-looking young captain in the Coldstream Guards, Manoli Paterakis, that formidable fighter and ex-gendarme from the Selino district, and George Tyrakis, a Cretan from the Amari valley who had worked closely with SOE from the start. Both Paterakis and Tyrakis had done the Ramat David parachute course with Paddy Leigh Fermor. Also at the rendezvous were Gregori Khnarakis, who in September 1942 rescued Sergeant Jo Bradley when his aeroplane was shot down, and Antoni Papaleonidas. Two goats were slaughtered for breakfast once everyone had trudged inland to a safe spot.

Leigh Fermor, after a total of exactly seventeen months on the island, now felt almost Cretan himself. He had been saddened by the Viannos disaster of the previous September and wanted to mount a bloodless coup against the Germans which might unify rival factions in an operation that was at least as much Cretan as British – despite the fiction to avoid reprisals that it was mounted entirely from Egypt.

When he briefed the group later, he told them that their target, Major General Müller, the commander of the Sebastopol Division responsible for so much blood and misery, had been replaced by Major General Heinrich Kreipe, an officer from the Russian front about whom little was known. 'As far as the ultimate effect of our plan was concerned', Moss wrote later, 'we supposed that one general was as good a catch as any other.' SOE at that time thought that Müller had been transferred to the Dodecanese, when he had in fact replaced General Bräuer in Canea as Commander of the Fortress of Crete. In any case the plan was based on carrying out the abduction in the relatively open country of the headquarters at Arkhanes, or at his residence, the Villa Ariadne at Knossos, John Pendlebury's pre-war base.

Two days after the landing, Leigh Fermor and his party met up with Athanasios Bourdzalis, an old-fashioned kapitan from Asia Minor who despite his years was an irregular fighter of great strength. They discussed the possibility of using his *andartes* as a defence force during the abduction in case of mishap.

The party from Egypt had settled themselves at Kastomonitza, to which Miki Akoumianakis came from Heraklion by bus. Although his town clothes may have looked out of place in a mountain village of Cretans in boots and baggy breeches, Akoumianakis was in many ways the most important member of the team. Not only did he know the area round Knossos better than anyone, having been brought up there, but he had even managed to cultivate the General's driver and spend a night in the Villa Ariadne. Akoumianakis was very collected when faced with sudden danger. On one of the reconnaissances for this operation he found that he had offered a German sergeant an English cigarette from the supplies which came in by launch. As the German stared at the packet in amazement, Akoumianakis casually apologized for offering him English cigarettes, and added that they came from the black market, so they were no doubt captured stock.

The main party had to hide in a cave for a week while Paddy Leigh Fermor and Miki Akoumianakis went off to study the route between the German headquarters at Arkhanes and the Villa Ariadne at Knossos – 'Theseus House' in the very insecure code of the British Military Mission. Leigh Fermor wanted to seize Kreipe in the Villa Ariadne itself, but Akoumianakis persuaded him against the idea. The house and grounds were heavily guarded and surrounded by double apron wire. During their tour of inspection of the district, they saw General Kreipe drive past and could not resist waving. He looked astonished and waved back. This gave them the idea of carrying the general off in his own car.

Having agreed upon the ambush site – where the Arkhanes road joins the Heraklion–Kastelli road – Miki Akoumianakis then left to collect a pair of German uniforms for the two Englishmen. Leigh Fermor returned to the cave on 19 April, Easter Sunday, with Akoumianakis's lieutenant, Elias Athanassakis, a student, who then went back to Knossos to watch the Villa Ariadne. In Leigh Fermor's absence, the party had been joined by some Russian prisoners escaped from a road-gang. Billy Moss, whose mother was a White Russian, was entranced with the idea of creating a force out of Red Army deserters, but the Russians were later sent off to another hideout. Three other Cretans who would be of much greater use in the circumstances – Nikos Komis, Dmitiri Tzatzas and lastly Pavlos Zographistos, who owned a vineyard conveniently near the vital road junction – were recruited at about this time.

Leigh Fermor and Moss decided that they did need Bourdzalis and his *andartes* as a blocking force in case reinforcements arrived. A runner left with a message, and two days later Bourdzalis and his fourteen *andartes* arrived at the rendezvous having completed a fast day's march. But three days later, after the operation was postponed for the second time, local peasants spotted Bourdzalis's men who were strangers in the neighbourhood, and the *andartes* had to be sent home. At the last moment, two more Cretans were recruited: Antoni Zoïdakis, an old friend of Leigh Fermor's, and Stratis Saviolakis, both gendarmes. This brought the group to eleven in all. But even with their Marlin sub-machine guns they could only have put up a brief resistance if a truckload of soldiers had arrived at the wrong moment.

On three consecutive days they waited until evening, then had to stand down because the General returned to the Villa Ariadne before dusk. On the fourth day, 25 April, waiting for nightfall, rain began to fall. This forced them to move from their hiding place in the old river-bed, because villagers came in search of snails. But on 26 April the General had not appeared by the time it grew dark, so they swallowed their benzedrine tablets and took up position near the road junction.

After numerous false alarms, the General's car came in sight at 9.30. Elias Athanassakis, the student, had spent days and nights studying the car and the shape of its headlights. He gave the signal, and several hundred yards down the road an electric bell connected by wire rang near where Leigh Fermor and Moss waited in their German uniforms.

They stepped out into the middle of the road to wave the car to a halt. They went up to it, one on each side. Leigh Fermor flashed his torch on the General inside and demanded to see his papers. The driver protested impatiently, whereupon they wrenched open the doors. Moss coshed the driver with a life-preserver, then the Cretans behind dragged him out on to the road. On the other side, while Leigh Fermor covered General Kreipe with his Colt and pulled him out, Manoli Paterakis and two of the others grabbed and handcuffed him. Miki Akoumianakis, carried away by the intensity of the moment, yelled into the face of this senior representative of the men who had killed his father: *'Was wollen sie in Kreta?'*

Moss took the wheel, and the General was bundled back in on the floor at the rear, where he was sat on by Tyrakis, Paterakis and Saviolakis. The whole operation had taken less than a minute. Paddy Leigh Fermor, having put on the General's forage hat, sat in front and, bidding goodbye to the rest of the group with whom they would rendezvous on Mount Ida, they drove off towards Heraklion. As they approached the Villa Ariadne, the sentries on the gate presented arms, only to see the staff car sweep past.

Miki Akoumianakis had kept away from the driver's side, because he did not want to be recognized by the man he had befriended. Afterwards, however, when two of the band were about to lead the driver off – the plan was to meet on Mount Ida – he sensed they might disobey Leigh Fermor's strict instructions not to kill him. The objective of the operation was to achieve a dramatic, yet bloodless, coup which could not justify any reprisals against Cretan civilians. Akoumianakis reminded them of this and also emphasized that the man had helped them, even if unwittingly. Later, he discovered that they had taken the driver a few kilometres and found a spot where his body could be hidden. They had allowed him a last quick look at a snapshot of his family by the light of a shaded torch, then cut his throat because of the need for silence.

Not long after passing the astonished sentries outside the Villa Ariadne, they reached the heavily guarded gates of Heraklion. Moss slowed down to give the sentries time to see the pennants on the front of the car, then Leigh Fermor in front wearing Kreipe's cap shouted 'Generals Wagen!' from the window. Inside Heraklion the evening crowds in the streets prevented them from advancing at much more than walking pace. All the time they were afraid that an off-duty soldier would stare in through the windows. And they still had to leave by the Canea Gate, the most heavily guarded of all. But thanks to the pennants on the car, the General's hat and the German soldier's automatic respect for authority, they passed through with Leigh Fermor acknowledging the salutes.

On the Rethymno road at Yeni Gavé (now called Drosia) the car stopped and the party split. Moss and two Cretans escorting the General, now unbound, set off on foot towards Anoyia on the northern slope of Mount Ida. Paddy Leigh Fermor carried on with George Tyrakis to dump the car as close to the coast as possible to suggest that the party had already left by submarine. On the front seat he placed a sealed letter addressed to the German command announcing that the operation had been carried out entirely from Cairo with British officers and members of His Hellenic Majesty's forces based there, so no form of reprisal against the local population would be justified. For good measure, various articles of British manufacture were also left in the car. Leigh Fermor and Tyrakis then snapped off the car's pennants and carried them off as souvenirs.

Moss and his party escorting the General walked up to a hideout near Anoyia, where they spent the rest of the night. The General was greatly preoccupied by the loss of his Knight's Cross which must have come off during the struggle. Next morning they had to hide in a cave when warned that German search parties had already arrived in the area. Fieseler Storch reconnaissance planes flew with an exasperating slowness round and round the flanks of Mount Ida, from

time to time dropping hastily printed leaflets threatening the
destruction of villages if the General were not handed over.

Paddy Leigh Fermor and George Tyrakis only reached Anoyia at
dawn. Leigh Fermor's German uniform provoked looks of intense
hatred. Men turned their backs, women spat and slammed windows
shut, and the Cretan call to warn of the presence of the enemy —
'The Black Cattle have strayed into the wheatfield' — heralded his
progress up the street. For both men it was a strange sensation. They
went to the priest's house, where the wife of Father Skoulas, the
parachute priest, vigorously refused to admit them until finally
convinced that this figure in the hated uniform was indeed her
husband's friend.

That night, fed and cared for in every way, the two of them set
off into the mountains to join up with the rest of the party. Then
together they went on to the hideout of Mikhali Xylouris's band
where a British trio of Tom Dunbabin's group led by a cavalry
subaltern, John Houseman, awaited them eagerly.* The next day, 28
April, the party trudged up and over the snowcap of Mount Ida, a
gruelling climb. On the way, an escort from Petrakageorgis's band
turned up to take over from Xylouris's men. Scouts went on ahead
because large German detachments were said to have moved into the
Amari valley ahead of them.

That night, as they hid in a huge labyrinthine cave used by the
klephts fighting the Turks, it seemed as if everything had begun to
go wrong. Dunbabin had gone to ground with a bad bout of malaria,
and could not be contacted. The wireless set at his hideout failed to
work, so they could not confirm the rendezvous on the coast at
Saktouria with a motor launch. Runners were sent off in different
directions — to Sandy Rendel in the east; to Dick Barnes, the officer
in charge of the Rethymno area, on the north coast; and to Ralph
Stockbridge of ISLD who was also near Rethymno — with copies of
the message for Cairo.

Kreipe became increasingly depressed. He could imagine only too
well the jokes likely to be made at his expense in officers' messes.
(With dreadful irony, his promotion to Lieutenant General, for which
he had waited so long, came through the day after his
disappearance.)

Uncertain about the state of the German cordon round the Mount

* Xylouris had taken over the leadership of the Anoyian band in the previous
winter after the Germans had shot their kapitan, Stephanoyannis Dramoudanis.

Ida region, the party moved down the mountain. A fortunate misreading of a note advising them not to move led them to break through the German line at night during a downpour. They spent several days in a thicket of saplings dripping from intermittent rain. The only consolation at the time was to hear that there had been no reprisals, despite the threatening leaflets.

They moved in the direction of the beach near Saktouria, but bad news awaited them at Ayia Paraskevi. German troops had swamped the area and a strong force occupied the exit beach. Paddy Leigh Fermor immediately headed for Dick Barnes's hideout to the north to arrange another spot. But that this was a 'hideous coincidence' did not become clear until next day. The Germans had only just heard that an arms run had been made by caique on the night of 20 April, and that thirty mule-loads of weapons had reached bands in the interior of the island. German anger had also been roused by Petrakageorgis's attack over Easter, which killed eight of their men.

In horror, the party listened to the dull explosions of dynamite and watched the palls of black smoke as four villages were destroyed during those first four days of May 1944. These reprisals were not in fact connected with the Kreipe operation, as the proclamation published on 5 May in the German-dominated newspaper *Paratiritis* makes clear. Kreipe's abduction was only mentioned in another article as part of a catalogue of crimes committed against the occupation forces.

NOTIFICATION

The villages of Kamares, Lokhria, Margarikari and Saktouria and the neighbouring parts of the Nome of Heraklion have been destroyed and extinguished. The men have been taken prisoner and the women and children moved to other villages.

These villagers had offered shelter and protection for months to Communist bands under the leadership of mercenary individuals. At the same time the peaceable part of the population is equally guilty because they failed to report these treasonable practices.

Bandits frequented the Saktouria region with the support of the population and transported arms, supplies and terrorists, and concealed them there. Kamares and Lokhria gave refuge and food to the bandits. At Margarikari, which also supplied them with shelter and supplies, the traitor and agitator Petrakageorgis celebrated Easter without any interference from the inhabitants.

Cretans listen carefully! Know your real enemies! Defend yourselves against the murderers of your compatriots and the robbers of your flocks. For some time the German Armed Forces have been aware of these rebellious acts, and the population has always been warned and informed of this.

But our patience is exhausted. The blade of the German sword now strikes the guilty ones, and in future will smite each and every person who is guilty of links with the bandits and their English instigators.

According to another statement German troops had searched the village of Lokhria on 14 March and found weapons including an American machine gun. Kamares had been 'the refuge and shelter for hundreds of armed men', while Margarikari, 'the home of the arch-bandit Petrakageorgis', had demonstrated its anti-German sentiments by turning out *en masse* when 'the funeral of the arch-bandit's mother, conducted by five priests, took place with great pomp'.

The unfortunate coincidences had been more extensive than Leigh Fermor and his companions realized. On 29 April, a German patrol from the small coastal garrison of Plakias (less than twenty-five kilometres west of Saktouria) arrested three shepherds for grazing their flocks within the forbidden coastal strip. The local band of *andartes* from Rodakino ambushed the Germans escorting the three shepherds, two of whom were immediately shot by their captors. In this short, but bloody action, the *andartes* killed five soldiers and captured the other two. German records show that these two soldiers were shot the next day. A Cretan source claims that they were sent to Egypt as prisoners by boat two days later, but this seems most unlikely when it was impossible to get General Kreipe off the island.

The Kreipe party had to strike back inland away from such commotions, so they took the General to a sheepfold above Yerakari. It was here, looking across at dawn breaking on Mount Ida, that General Kreipe recited the first two lines of Horace's ninth ode, *Ad Thaliarchum*. Leigh Fermor completed the remaining five stanzas, thus creating a bond between captor and captive outside the war.

The party then set off westwards across the waist of Crete, moving from one mountain hideout to the next. The going was slow, for the General fell from his mule down a rock-face and hurt his shoulder.

On 7 May contact was finally made with Barnes and Stockbridge. Signals were sent to Cairo, and next morning a runner brought a message back from one of the wireless sets to say that a covering force from the Special Boat Squadron led by George Jellicoe would land to cover their evacuation.

The very last stretch of the journey almost resembled a triumphal procession. *Andartes* and villagers alike lined the sheep path to see the General. Literally hundreds knew of his whereabouts, yet the Germans never received word through their spies. An eleventh-hour complication occurred when a detachment of soldiers occupied the beach at Limni chosen for the embarkation. Fortunately, Dennis Ciclitira had moved closer with his wireless set, and details were rearranged for the beach near Rodakino.

Finally, at eleven o'clock on the night of 14 May, a motor launch commanded by Brian Coleman nosed its way in towards the beach in answer to their Morse recognition signal. The SBS covering force commanded by Lieutenant Bob Bury sprang into action, ready to take up defensive positions, and were crestfallen when told there was little prospect of a rearguard battle. And since a large number of *andartes*, including Petrakas's band from Asi Gonia, had gathered to see the party off, any German detachment in the area would have encountered a fierce reception. Following the usual practice, before embarking, everyone left behind their weapons and boots and spare rations, all of which were quickly shared amongst the large crowd on the beach.

The party, including Miki Akoumianakis and Elias Athanassakis, and joined by Dennis Ciclitira, went on board where they were greeted with lobster sandwiches and Navy rum. At Mersa Matruh a reception committee headed by Brigadier Barker-Benfield waited with a guard of honour ready to pay compliments before the General was taken into dignified captivity. Kreipe, at last accepting his fate, became almost jaunty. Paddy Leigh Fermor, on the other hand, felt the opposite of jaunty. During the last few days, he had begun to suffer attacks of stiffness. On arrival in Cairo, he collapsed with an almost fatal and temporarily paralysing bout of rheumatic fever. The immediate Distinguished Service Order which he received for his leadership of the operation had to be pinned to his pyjama jacket in hospital.

The Kreipe operation has often been criticized on the grounds that it caused unnecessary suffering to the Cretan population, but Professor Gottfried Schramm's study of the German Command's files would indicate that this is a canard. There was no connection with the destruction of Kamares, Lokhria, Margarikari and Saktouria, as has been shown. And the most serious wave of reprisals, the destruction of the Amari valley villages, took place in late August. Since they were intended to teach the local population a lesson, the essence of German reprisals lay in their rapidity: a delay of nearly four months is therefore highly improbable, whatever the catalogue of crimes listed by the military authorities in their proclamations. The Amari operation was essentially a campaign of pre-emptive terror just before the German forces withdrew westwards from Heraklion, with their flank exposed to this centre of Cretan resistance.*

The other argument that General Kreipe's removal was of little military significance is of course true. But the blow was aimed not at German strength but at German morale and their claim to mastery of the island. German officers may have made a show of jokes about Kreipe afterwards, but the audacity of the coup clearly rattled them. The effect was increased quite fortuitously when, within a few days of the abduction, a German garrison commander was killed in a train blown up near Patras.

The boost for the Cretans was very important at a time when the Eastern Mediterranean had been entirely bypassed. 'Everybody felt taller by two centimetres the next day,' observed Manoussos Manoussakis, who had been in Canea. And even if morale fluctuated in between, as was inevitable in those times, his joke that 'out of 450,000 Cretans, 449,000 claimed to have taken part in the Kreipe operation', indicates the immense pride aroused.

Afterwards, as a final propaganda twist, Dunbabin's team began a whispering campaign that Kreipe had planned his own escape. Handbills were stuck up round barracks with the words: *'Kreipe Befehl: Wir Folgen!'* − 'Kreipe give us the order: we are following!' a skit on the Nazi slogan of *'Führer Befehl: Wir Folgen!'*

* When Tom Dunbabin and Patrick Leigh Fermor were made honorary citizens of Heraklion in 1948, Leigh Fermor's 'care and foresight' to avoid giving 'the conqueror any excuse to carry out reprisals' were specially mentioned in regard to the Kreipe operation.

27
The German Withdrawal

Three days before the Allies landed in Normandy, a small party from the Organization of Strategic Services – the American equivalent of SOE – reached Crete. They came on the same boat which brought in another British officer to join Dunbabin's command: Lieutenant Hugh Fraser of the 7th Hussars. The purpose of this three-man mission led by Colonel MacGlasson was to 'gather political and military intelligence'. They insisted on being independent of the British and spent only a few weeks in the western end of the island.

A more lasting form of co-operation followed with the arrival of another American, Major Bill Royce. He landed on 13 July, and Dunbabin's organization became the Allied Military Mission.

Summer also brought the annual visit from the SBS. Sandy Rendel received a warning order in June to assist a raiding force due to arrive by sea. The main difference from previous attacks was that this time petrol dumps formed the SBS's primary target, not airfields. The idea was to force the Germans to send a tanker, by then in desperately short supply, into an ambush by submarine. These attacks were timed to coincide with others all over the mainland.

On their arrival at the beginning of July, the SBS advance party led by Ian Patterson found not just Sandy, but a crowd of helpers (Vassili Konios and a group of cousins) with twenty-three mules to carry their kit. The SBS never quite got used to the Cretan contempt for security precautions. The main party landed some ten days later and the different groups headed off towards their objectives – Kastelli airfield, Heraklion, a dump south of Neapolis and another near Armenoi.

The Armenoi group, led by Dick Hardman of the SBS and guided by Hugh Fraser and George Psychoundakis, then heard from their main informant, one Psaroudakis, that the fuel reserves had been evacuated. Psaroudakis in fact misled them: he is said to have wanted to avoid trouble with the Germans. So instead of a dump, the group blew up a bridge near Kouphi and ambushed a truck, killing five soldiers of whom a couple may have been Italians. In an attempt to avoid reprisals, Fraser allowed no Cretans to accompany them and left a note and items of kit, such as a beret, to convince the Germans that it was a purely British operation.

A number of other actions took place that night, 22 July, to increase the effect. Mikhali Xylouris, the sturdily pro-British kapitan from the Anoyia region, took his relatively untried band to take on a German outpost near Daphnes and they succeeded in killing fifteen soldiers. The main attacks are said to have destroyed 165,000 gallons of fuel, but two SBS members were captured. Both men, Captain John Lodwick and Bombardier Nixon, later escaped when the train taking them to Germany was ambushed by Jugoslav partisans. When they returned after numerous adventures, their commanding officer Lord Jellicoe remarked: 'Ah, you're back. Damned slow about it, weren't you?'

With news of Russian advances on the eastern front, and the opening of the second front in Normandy, the bands in the mountains and the numbers of reserve *andartes* in the towns greatly increased. Everybody wanted to become a member of the resistance before it was too late.

Attempts were made by both sides to keep the Nationalist EOK and the Communist-dominated ELAS from fighting each other. ELAS knew that it did not have the strength or popular support to take on EOK with any hope of survival. And fortunately EOK had received no news of events in mainland Greece where ELAS had set about eliminating its rivals one by one with a crude version of the 'salami-tactic', otherwise its groups might have attacked ELAS pre-emptively.

An attempt to foster ELAS–EOK friendship was organized in the region of Viannos. As might be expected, this gathering, which took place in a bowl in oak-covered hills, was a curious affair. The Communists were led by a local doctor. A small group of German deserters formed another delegation. Bandouvas's younger brother Yanni had brought his band; so had Colonel Plevres from Neapolis, the EOK leader for the province of Lasithi.

Altogether groups numbering nearly 300 men collected there that day. First, a priest provided by the Communists – a paradox typical of ELAS – blessed their cause, then goats were slaughtered for a meagre feast, which was followed by speeches of interminable rhetoric.

Billy Moss had returned to Crete on 6 July. His official mission was to mount a diversionary action with a force of escaped Russian prisoners to help the SBS in their co-ordinated attacks of 22 July. But Moss harboured a private scheme which he had not disclosed to Brigadier Barker-Benfield or anyone else. He had hatched a madcap plan to kidnap General Kreipe's replacement.

For this Moss attempted to reassemble the Kreipe abduction gang. He based himself with Mikhali Xylouris on the northern slopes of the Ida range above Anoyia. He may have deliberately kept away from Tom Dunbabin, who landed on 13 July, because Dunbabin would have vetoed the plan if he had known what was afoot.

Moss's idea proved impossible quite simply because General Kreipe had not been replaced: the only general on the island was Müller, the Commander of the Fortress of Crete. Time was wasted and the important night of 22 July came and went. Moss returned to Xylouris's hideout, having augmented his force with a handful of escaped Russian prisoners whom he armed with Sten guns. There was little to do but await a suitable opportunity for action.

Not to be outdone by the British raiding forces, one of the ELAS Rethymno groups cordoned off the village of Margarites in the early hours of 1 August to trap two German motor-cycle crews spending the night there. Having blocked the road by felling a tree across it, they moved in to capture the four men, whom they later shot. A German force intent on reprisals reached the area, between Perama and the monastery of Arkadi, and the ELAS band withdrew losing two men. At first they claimed to have killed forty Germans, then reduced the number to twenty and finally to five, which was still a slight exaggeration, since German records show that only four of their men died between 2 and 4 August. The scorn with which their diminishing claims were treated must have rankled, and this may help to explain their rash behaviour in the weeks to come.

An insurrectionary momentum was in any case building up as Cretans sensed the beginning of the end, now that the advance of the Red Army into Roumania threatened German lines of communication. Revolt took many forms, the most common the sudden attack on a lone soldier or a small detachment. And a slight incident could easily escalate into an unplanned battle.

On the morning of 7 August, Feldwebel Olenhauer, accompanied by seven men from the small garrison at Yení Gavé, came up to the town of Anoyia, Xylouris's home and a deep reservoir of anti-German sentiment. Olenhauer, although apparently liked by the villagers near his post, was loathed by their enemies at Anoyia. In the main street he began waving his whip and demanding labourers. There were few volunteers, so he ordered his detachment to round up any men they found as well as some women and children. These prisoners were then made to march off along the road towards Rethymno.

A group of seven ELAS 'reserve *andartes*' – locals with a gun hidden away as opposed to members of a permanent band in the mountains – ambushed this column. They were joined by another five non-ELAS locals. They began by firing in the air to warn the hostages to throw themselves flat. The Germans made no attempt to resist. Two men escaped, and Olenhauer, his dog, and the rest of his detachment were taken up into the Mount Ida range. The ELAS *andartes* had some idea of proposing to exchange their captives for a large number of Cretan prisoners in Ayia jail. Not surprisingly, this came to nothing, and the *andartes* shot all their captives, including Olenhauer's dog.

After the confrontation on the road, the townspeople of Anoyia feared the worst and, having packed a few valuables and some food, abandoned their houses. The men armed themselves with ancient guns and talked of resistance. A number of them had come to the Xylouris hideout, and Billy Moss decided that 'the stage was patently set for action'. If the Germans were about to destroy Anoyia, then he and his band could ambush their column on its approach.

Moss set out with his own nucleus of Cretans, the Russians and half a dozen of Xylouris's band, altogether about fifteen men armed with automatic weapons. They passed through the abandoned streets of Anoyia and pushed on over the hills and down to the main Rethymno–Heraklion road along which the Germans would come. A good ambush site was chosen near Damastas at a point where the road curved over a small bridge which they mined with Hawkins grenades.

Preparations for the ambush became chaotic. First they had to hustle local villagers and their flocks out of the way. Then they shot up a single German truck carrying labourers, then a larger army lorry which the trigger-happy members of Xylouris's band fired at out of range, necessitating a wild chase across country to catch the occupants, and then several other vehicles. At last the real force sent out to deal with Anoyia was sighted. It consisted of a truck full of infantrymen backed up by an armoured car. Fifteen Sten guns soon dealt with the soldiers, but the armoured car struck down both an Anoyian guide with an ancient rifle who stood in its path methodically reloading, and one of the Russians. More would have fallen had not Moss made his way round and, climbing on from the rear, dropped a grenade down the hatch. Altogether nearly thirty Germans were killed, including the dozen prisoners killed later by Xylouris's men. In the usual Cretan practice, their bodies were dropped down a pothole.

Moss's hopes that the attack at Damastas might have saved Anoyia were vain. The Germans simply waited five days until they had assembled a much larger force. 'Since the town of Anoyia', ran the proclamation of its destruction, 'is a centre of English espionage in Crete, since the Anoyians carried out the murder of the sergeant of the Yení Gavé garrison, since the Anoyians carried out the sabotage at Damastas, since the *andartes* of various resistance bands find asylum and protection in Anoyia, and since the abductors of General Kreipe passed through Anoyia, using Anoyia as a stopping place when transporting him, we order its razing to the ground and the execution of every male Anoyian who is found within the village and within an area of one kilometre round it. Müller, Commander of the Garrison of Crete. Canea, 13 August 1944.'

Virtually the whole town was burnt, and thirty inhabitants were shot together with another fifteen men caught nearby. Another account claims that over a hundred houses in Damastas were destroyed and thirty people shot there, but that only fifteen died in Anoyia.

The same day that Moss was fighting at Damastas, Tom Dunbabin, accompanied by Antoni Zoïdakis and two others, set out for Kyparisses to meet Group Captain Kelaïdis, the representative of the government-in-exile. But as the party emerged from a vineyard and crossed the Armenoi–Rethymno road, two Germans, their suspicions aroused, opened fire without warning. Zoïdakis, the last to cross, fell badly wounded. Dunbabin, turning back, killed one of the Germans with his revolver and hit the other. The almost instantaneous arrival of German reinforcements left the three survivors with little alternative but to run for cover. The Germans tied Zoïdakis to their vehicle. They drove off, dragging him along the road until he was dead. At Armenoi, orders were given that his body should be left there unburied for several days as a warning. But his horrific fate, especially since he was 'a true pallikari' in the Cretan phrase, only hardened hearts.

The purpose of Dunbabin's meeting with Group Captain Kelaïdis was to prepare for their discussions with the leaders of EAM. This took place at Melidoni on 17 August. The intention was to find some sort of common policy between the Nationalist EOK bands and the Communist-led ELAS groups which followed EAM's political direction, but mutual suspicion put paid to any agreement. The Communist-controlled EAM distrusted the British government, and above all its commitment to reimpose the King without a plebiscite, while Dunbabin knew better than most Cretans of the Communists' ruthless attempts to monopolize power on the mainland. Dunbabin's unease at the threat of civil war can only have been heightened during his trek south from Melidoni afterwards. An ELAS detachment surrounded his party and menacingly demanded news of the conference.

Even a successful agreement at Melidoni could have done little to prevent the next phase of destruction and slaughter. Five days after the meeting, several battalions of German infantry moved into the Amari valley. The Amariots were taken utterly by surprise. Over the next eight days – from 22 until 30 August – the Germans destroyed 9 villages and shot 164 of their inhabitants, 43 of them from Yerakari alone. The houses were stripped of valuables, which were piled on army lorries and taken to Rethymno, then set on fire. Livestock was also confiscated for German use.

Local bands and the ELAS group from the province of Rethymno offered little resistance. The size of the German forces deployed throughout the area would have made any attempt to intervene suicidal. Petrakageorgis later complained bitterly to Colonel Tsiphakis that the ELAS detachment led by Limonias and Veloudakis had failed to warn or help him when a German column passed them on its way to attack his position. But resistance flared again during the last few days of the operation when a dozen Germans were killed.

A number of cases were influenced by chance, or perhaps the whim of a German commander. Some villages were destroyed without reason and some were inexplicably spared. How Asi Gonia, of all the centres of resistance, escaped remains one of the mysteries of the occupation. Villagers believed that their patron saint, St. George, who had saved them from the Turks, must have interceded once again.

An element of revenge must certainly have influenced the German operation, but in military terms its purpose was clear in spite of declarations similar to those at Anoyia – to cow the main area of guerrilla activity on the flank of the planned line of withdrawal from Heraklion. That it failed in this purpose was demonstrated recklessly soon.

Prompted by the news that the Germans were sending their nurses home and starting to bring in outlying garrisons, Tom Dunbabin called a conference of liaison officers at the monastery of Arkadi on 8 September. An instruction arrived from Cairo to 'cease sabotage or any act which might bring harm to the civilian population'. Dunbabin circulated this message to all guerrilla bands, but ELAS had no intention of following British orders, and even some of the Nationalist bands linked to EOK chose to ignore it.

The ELAS group, which called itself the 44th Battalion although only some fifty strong, moved to the Amari valley within two weeks of the Germans' passage. Their plan was for a small operation which might win support in this generally Nationalist area. They would capture the German outpost of only three men controlling the agricultural school at Asomaton, and distribute the produce and livestock amongst the neighbouring villages.

On the morning of 11 September, the ELAS detachment took the place without bloodshed. This move infuriated the local Nationalist kapitans. Having heard of ELAS's intention, they had specifically warned against any action in the area. Their men surrounded the building and forced the ELAS group to release their prisoners and withdraw.

But the incident could not be effaced so simply. A few hours later, a large part of the '44th Battalion' saw two lorries full of soldiers sent from Rethymno on the road which snakes up the valley towards the watershed ridge on which the village of Apostoloi stands. Whether they were coming in response to the incident or to evacuate the soldiers as part of the general withdrawal of isolated outposts is uncertain.

At a point now marked by a bas-relief of a moustachioed *andarte*, the ELAS group ambushed these vehicles. The sound of firing drew almost every armed Cretan within earshot whatever his political loyalties. (Later, when Colonel Tsiphakis heard details of the action, he was beside himself with exasperation at such irresponsibility.) Nationalist *andartes* carried off Germans wounded in the ambush and they were well treated. The other prisoners seem to have been taken off by ELAS and shot later.

The battle escalated as German reinforcements arrived up the valley from Rethymno, only twenty-five kilometres away. They even brought a couple of field guns which were used to bombard the Amari valley and the village of Pandanassa over the ridge where some of the *andartes* had withdrawn. One of the shells killed Dr Alexandros Generales who had been tending the German wounded. Once again, grossly inflated figures of enemy dead were claimed by the *andartes*: one source says that the Germans lost around a hundred men. In fact German figures show that only sixteen or seventeen died as a result of this action. The ELAS execution of prisoners increased the figure of German dead to about twenty-six.

A far more efficient ambush, although mounted in even more flagrant disregard of Cairo's order, took place a few days later when, on 15 September, the Xylouris band of Anoyians wiped out a German patrol of fourteen men on the Heraklion side of Psiloriti.*

To the Amariots' surprise and relief, the Germans announced that they would not exact reprisals for the Apostoloi ambush. (And yet the execution of fifteen hostages in Ayia jail on 16 September has been linked to this fighting in the Amari.) Nationalist sources claim that their villages were spared a second wave of destruction because of the good care given to the German wounded. But the real reason may well have been more down to earth. German officers did not want to stir up any more hornets' nests at such a moment. The withdrawal from outlying posts prior to the complete evacuation of Heraklion had started, and German troops were becoming severely demoralized.

The rate of desertion alarmed German commanding officers. (Soldiers who received a posting to the mainland were apparently the most likely to desert: a flight across the Aegean in the face of Allied air power was by then regarded as almost a death sentence.) As an indication of the scale of the German command's problem, out of five hundred prisoners in Ayia jail, approximately one hundred and fifty were Italians and one hundred and fifty Germans, together double the number of Cretans. The balance consisted of about fifty Russian prisoners of war undergoing punishment. There would have

---

* Altogether 23 Germans are recorded as having died on 15 September. The balance presumably consists of the prisoners taken by ELAS near Apostoloi and executed later.

been even more desertions if German soldiers had felt more confident of becoming prisoners of the British. They knew that Cretans had killed a number of genuine deserters out of hand following Schubert's attempts to trick information out of villagers with his roving stool-pigeons.

The Allied Military Mission's campaign of propaganda on Crete was more extensive and elaborate than is generally realized. Both the American Bill Royce in the region of Heraklion, and his counterpart in Canea, Stephen Verney (later Bishop of Repton), were attached to the Political Warfare Executive, SOE's sister organization. Verney, at first a conscientious objector with the Friends' Ambulance Unit, later joined the Royal Army Service Corps as a private in Cairo. But his former headmaster at Harrow, Paul Vellacott, the Director of Political Warfare Middle East, met him at a party. Not wanting to waste a promising Balliol classicist, Vellacott promptly recruited him.

Verney was trained and sent into Crete on 20 August with a German Jew, Corporal Cohen, to act as interpreter. His mission was to cause disaffection in the German army. The heads of PWE had their eyes set on the mutinies of November 1918 in Wilhelmshaven, Kiel and Munich which caused the abrupt collapse of German resistance and shortened the First World War by up to six months.

Verney, guided by his Cretan guardian angel, Marko Drakakis, concentrated on three categories: Germans who disliked the Nazi regime; 'Nationals' such as Poles or Austrians in Wehrmacht uniform; and Germans in love with Cretan girls. Costa Mitsotakis, his first contact in Canea, was an invaluable guide to which Germans he should approach. One of the anti-Nazi officers, a former member of the Reichstag, said that he hated himself for talking to one of his country's enemies, but Hitler's regime left no alternative. Corporal Cohen meanwhile tried to identify secret Communists and socialists to recruit from German ranks, a hazardous operation which later led to the arrest of many in the network.

One of the 'Nationals' was Kurt Schlauer, a Pole drafted into the Wehrmacht because he was Protestant. He helped Verney and his EOK associates with translations. In the hills above Canea, they had set up a printing press in a cave. It was run by a Cretan journalist, Xenophon Hadjigrigorakis, who produced two news-sheets, one in Greek and the other, *Kreta Post*, in German. More help was provided by a German sergeant major in love with a Cretan school teacher. He deserted with his motor-cycle, which proved very useful.

Kreta Post, largely based on BBC broadcasts, offered a carrot of idealism with the idea that a new Germany would arise with the end of Hitler. Meanwhile the rest of the campaign set out to produce 'the impression that the whole system was cracking up'. Tasso Ninolakis, a brave and quick-witted young man working with the Verney-Mitsotakis network, kept passing the Germans false or grossly exaggerated information about resistance activities. He was also involved in a plan to infiltrate lumps of plastic explosive made to look like coal into the fuel stocks of the German officers' mess. Verney regularly wrote to General Benthag to remind him how hopeless his situation was and to insist that the time had come for *Kapitulation*. This single word and its initial letter became a campaign theme. Boys in Canea were recruited for a graffiti offensive. Acid was used to engrave the letter K on the windscreens of German vehicles. The letter was painted on sentry-boxes, posts and barrack walls.

Early in October, Verney suggested another ploy to Cairo: that the BBC broadcast rumours of a British landing in the west of the island. This was done, and it must have been one of the very few times the BBC agreed to transmit false information: presumably honour was saved by the word 'rumours'. In any event the ploy worked. A German officer in a staff car was hurriedly dispatched to make contact with this Allied force. At Kandanos, evidently convinced he was close to the invaders, he drove round waving a white flag and shouting '*Nicht boom-boom! Nicht boom-boom!*' through a loudhailer.

Cairo did not always respond to requests. Just before the infamous General Müller left Crete on 26 September, Verney's cell received details of the aircraft on which he would be travelling to Athens and its time of take-off. In the middle of the night, Verney signalled Cairo requesting interception by long-range fighters. He prefixed his message with four x's to denote highest priority and immediate action so that senior officers would be woken for a decision. To his exasperation, the only acknowledgement was: 'Keep Calm. Use Less X's.' Nothing was done.

Dunbabin's conference at the monastery of Arkadi on 7 September had decided the general strategy to be followed when the Germans carried out the second and major stage of their withdrawal to the west of the island. Looking around at all the faces, Dunbabin must have marvelled at the change from the days when he first took over. There were now eight officers on the island under his command: Rendel; Barnes; Ciclitira; Terence Bruce-Mitford, who had worked with Pendlebury on the island before the invasion; Barkham; Houseman; Fraser; and Matthew White, the long-suffering radio operator, now commissioned. There were also four attached officers: Eaton; Royce (Organization of Strategic Services); Verney (Political Warfare Executive); and Lukas (Polish Army) – and fourteen NCOs, many of whom had recently arrived as part of Bruce-Mitford's training team in heavy weapons.

Five days after the conference at Arkadi, Sandy Rendel and the Anoyian band, seventy strong, met with Miki Akoumianakis in the ruins of the Palace of Knossos. There, within sight of the German general's residence at the Villa Ariadne, they made their plans to infiltrate Heraklion. It would not be long before Tom Dunbabin was able to take over the villa, which he knew so well from before the war, and make it the Military Mission's headquarters. He later reported to the British School of Archaeology that the site of Knossos had been slightly knocked about by mortar fire in May 1941; perhaps in the battle which killed Miki Akoumianakis's father. But during the occupation the German authorities had done their best to prevent damage.

The Germans knew that Miki Akoumianakis was the chief British agent in the city, but they had not arrested him. Normal rules of counter-insurgency were suspended more frequently now that their position on the island began to look increasingly isolated. Negotiation was preferable to a blood-bath for which German officers would be held responsible by the victorious Allied powers. Corruption also appears to have infected the German garrison to a much higher level than might have been expected. One senior officer promised, in return for eighty gold sovereigns, to prevent the destruction of the harbour and town. But there were so many factors and factions at work during the next few weeks, while the various *andarte* groups closed in eager for the kill or the spoils, that a peaceful outcome was far from certain.

Colonel Andreas Nathenas, the new military representative of the government-in-exile, was officially governor of the prefecture of Heraklion, but his authority was recognized only by the Allied Military Mission and two EOK bands: Xylouris's Anoyians infiltrated in the city and Petrakageorgis's men on the western side. South of the town, Bodias had taken up position with his ELAS group. And the other two major bands in the region, those of Bandouvas and Plevres, were on the east side near the aerodrome. They had rearmed their men with German weapons after the British refused to supply them. Bandouvas, by now back from Egypt, proved even more unpredictable than before. The Germans had obtained his quiescence from time to time with various favours and his relationship with Bodias was hard to define. In spite of Bodias's betrayal – leaving him after the Viannos episode the year before – the two men clearly maintained some sort of understanding, as an unpleasant event soon showed.

For ten days from 1 October, German troops and *andartes* uncertainly sized each other up, each waiting for the other to make the first move. With German artillery positioned to shell the city in the event of attack, and several battalions of well-armed infantry in position, it would have been madness for the *andartes* to start a battle. The EOK groups of Petrakageorgis and Xylouris were however prepared to fight if the Germans attempted to destroy the port. Meanwhile, Plevres's men had begun to enter the city, apparently with the consent of the Germans, who had even given them some weapons because they were Nationalists, not Communists.

Eventually, the Germans became a little more reassured that hordes of Cretan civilians, knives clenched in teeth, would not throw themselves upon their retreating troops, and Heraklion's day of liberation came on 11 October. It was a curious carnival. Bill Royce, the American officer, and Sandy Rendel stood wearing uniform within sight of Germans at the New Gate. Soon the ELAS detachment appeared, led incongruously by Bodias mounted on a pony with a daisy chain round its neck. Rendel then saw Petrakageorgis 'seated in a captured German vehicle, with a broad and confident smile, and looking like some nineteenth century South American general about to lead a revolution. After three years in the mountains he was clearly going to have his day and enjoy it.'

There were several tense moments as the Germans, barracked with catcalls, nervously fingered the triggers of their rifles. But the bloodless departure of German troops was finally accomplished when Royce escorted their rearguard out of the Canea Gate – the route Pendlebury had taken on the second day of the battle three years before. As the last vehicle disappeared, the crowds erupted in joy with singing and cheers. In a mood only slightly more solemn, Evgenios, the Metropolitan of Heraklion and All Crete, held a service of thanksgiving in the Cathedral.

But it was not long before ugly scenes developed as crowds demanded vengeance on collaborators, especially on the hated police chief Polioudakis. Polioudakis, who had been abandoned by the Germans, was brought up from the cells to the balcony where Petrakageorgis, a large man, pretended to agree to throw him to the crowd. But he only dangled Polioudakis by the feet then pulled him in again. Most people believed that Polioudakis was executed shortly afterwards, but other, more reliable sources say that he somehow escaped to Athens where he worked as a scribe for illiterates outside government offices.

Before Colonel Nathenas imposed martial law, a number of women's heads were shaved and homes of collaborators looted. Most feared was a clash between the rival *andarte* groups. In an attempt to calm the situation and foster goodwill amongst the rival factions, General Nikolaos Papadakis, the newly appointed military governor of Crete, ordered a gathering of all the bands who had taken part in the liberation of the city to acknowledge him and their own kapitans together. Papadakis, a cousin of the difficult colonel, had arrived on 6 October with Major Jack Smith-Hughes as his liaison officer.

The military governor and the kapitans, EOK and Communist alike, assembled on the balcony of the Prefecture to wave to the *andarte* bands below. Suddenly a muffled shot was heard and Yanni Bodias, the ELAS leader, staggered shot through his arm. Athanasios Bourdzalis, the old-fashioned kapitan called in to help with the Kreipe abduction, had shot Bodias on the balcony from behind. He claimed that Bodias, with his degenerate reputation, had insulted his daughter.

Bodias was taken to hospital where he was successfully treated by the Nationalist leader and surgeon Dr Giamalakis. The incident provoked outbreaks of shooting between the bands which continued until Dunbabin and Smith-Hughes had driven round the town in a jeep to reassure both sides. Bourdzalis, who had been seized immediately, faced a summary court martial convened by General Papadakis. Bandouvas was one of the members. Bourdzalis was condemned to death and Papadakis confirmed the sentence, even though Bodias's wound was not grave. Battle-lines had hardened to such a degree that Tom Dunbabin became convinced that he should support Papadakis in confirmation of the sentence: the risk of civil war was too great.

As one of his closest colleagues later observed, Dunbabin firmly believed that he should never shirk unpleasant decisions, nor ask others to carry out his dirty work. The year before, when two traitors from the village of Kroussonas (one of them was Monty Woodhouse's pupil from Haifa) had come to his headquarters with a false offer of help, Dunbabin not only took the decision that they had to die, but felt obliged to do the deed himself. He gave each man some wine containing one of SOE's suicide pills but, disquietingly reminiscent of Rasputin in the Yusupov palace (and unreassuring for SOE officers), neither showed the slightest ill effect. They were then taken outside the cave and Dunbabin fired the first shot.

The tension between Nationalists and the supporters of EAM–ELAS was not restricted to Heraklion. All of the larger towns were affected. In certain cafés, a British officer entering might be greeted by an anti-British song current at the time. Stephen Verney in Canea was taken aback when youths asked to take part in the graffiti campaign against the Germans retorted that they would do no such thing without specific orders from the Party.

After the German departure from Heraklion, Rendel motored round the eastern part of the island to celebrate with friends and helpers, only to find that EAM–ELAS had been carrying out an intimidatory campaign since September. At Neapolis, the local bishop was under house arrest for having preached an anti-Communist sermon. In Ayios Nikolaos, although he was greeted by left-wing leaders in a show of allied celebration, Rendel found that they had imprisoned political opponents including those who had supported the British. And in Hierapetra the local EAM committee had locked up Brigadier Karandinos, a Nationalist, but had then been forced by protests to release him. Only in Siteia, where Nationalists were strongly in the majority, did the ELAS groups maintain a careful neutrality. Civil war was in the air, and both sides were certain that the British would intervene. But this was an overestimate of British power, as events in Athens would soon prove.

The last German troops left Rethymno on 13 October for the final and relatively unharrassed leg of their withdrawal to Canea. On the same day their forces on the mainland abandoned Athens.

On the ground, the only incidents occurred when an ELAS group became caught up in an inconclusive skirmish following an ambush, and Hugh Fraser could not resist trying out SOE's secret weapon: plastic explosive moulded and coloured to resemble donkey droppings. He carefully placed them on a sharp corner with a cliff beyond. The idea was to explode the tyres of a military vehicle at a dangerous spot, thus causing a fatal accident which the Germans would not attribute to sabotage. To his great horror, the first vehicle was a civilian lorry packed with Cretans. By a miracle its tyres did not touch the donkey droppings, but Fraser, determined not to put Cretan lives at risk, rushed down and removed his unusual mines. No sooner had he done this than a stream of German lorries went past.

Dunbabin had made other plans with Cairo. The columns of German vehicles moving along a single road presented a perfect target for fighter-bombers, and air strikes avoided the risk of reprisals. Spitfires equipped with long-range fuel tanks and flown mainly by South African pilots took part in a number of sorties. The first attackers tearing into the positions round Heraklion received a nasty shock. All the flak batteries withdrawn from airfields and other outposts had been concentrated there. A couple of aircraft were brought down, but the pilots were able to bale out. As soon as they had extricated themselves from the exuberance of Cretan hospitality, they were shipped out on one of the Royal Navy motor launches. Yet however effective the air strikes, the most permanent damage was done by the retreating Germans. They relentlessly destroyed every bridge behind them, including a Venetian masterpiece near Rethymno.

Shortly before the centre of attention in Crete moved westward from Heraklion, attempts were made in Canea to curtail the occupation. In September, Constantinos Mitsotakis had approached Captain Wildhage, the Abwehr officer on General Benthag's staff, to discuss a formula for surrender. Wildhage firmly rejected this advance and, referring to Verney's stream of letters to General Benthag on the same subject, added: 'tell Major Stephens [Verney's *nom de guerre*] that if he continues to send subversive letters, he will be arrested.'

Wildhage, presumably deciding that enough was enough, set out to trap the Mitsotakis-Verney cell with the stool-pigeon technique. A soldier pretending to be a secret Communist got in touch with Corporal Cohen and, against all rules of procedure, was brought to the house. Wildhage's men pounced on 22 October. They seized Mitsotakis, his friend Manoussos Manoussakis and Cohen.

The arrests of 22 October were the second serious blow in a week. British officers had been embarrassed by the arrest of Lieutenant Geoffrey Barkham on 17 October. Barkham, who had always been reckless, seems to have been affected by a sort of 'end-of-termitis' as the war wound down. He had bought a car with the help of Major Papayannakis (the commander of a German-formed gendarmerie battalion, who was secretly in contact with the British) and drove into Canea to flirt and thump away at a piano. Barkham's vigorous version of 'Roll Out the Barrel' could be heard a considerable way down the street. Dennis Ciclitira had also been in Canea that day and encountering Barkham had ordered him to leave. Ciclitira, wearing a gendarmerie uniform provided by Major Papayannakis, had then himself left the city on the road to Kastelli Kissamou. He was nearly caught when the vehicle he was in broke down at Maleme just by the heavily guarded aerodrome.

Barkham had meanwhile driven off in the car with Perikles Vandoulakis (of the family of the 'British consul' in Vaphé) but the two of them were stopped at a road-block. Barkham's red hair and round face did little to help him pass as a Cretan; and his Greek was not good enough to fool an alert sentry. Caught out, Barkham swore in English and admitted his nationality. He and Vandoulakis were taken off under guard and separated for questioning. After the war, Barkham admitted to a colleague that he had tried but failed to kill himself in his cell, fearing what the Gestapo might force out of him. But his luck was extraordinary.

The decision on his fate – to be sent to a concentration camp in Germany – was processed by a certain Captain Kurt Waldheim on the mainland. Barkham and John Lodwick, the SBS officer captured in July, were sent northwards, but the train was ambushed by Jugoslav partisans. Barkham later recounted how the partisans cut the throat of the elderly German sergeant major in charge of them. A prisoner of the British in the First World War, he had treated them with great kindness on the journey.

Verney's fears for the fate of his comrades were mercifully belied. With great psychological shrewdness, Mitsotakis berated his captors for violating the ancient traditions of the flag of truce. This was hardly an exact picture of events, since the cell had continued subversive activities for nearly a month after his peace-making approach. Mitsotakis even made great play of the fact that the German officer who had driven around Kandanos with a white flag had not been fired upon.

In Canea, his sister Kaite quickly made contact with the German authorities. And although the death penalty for captured enemy agents and members of the resistance was supposed to be mandatory, she found that German officers in Canea were reluctant to carry out executions: the war was lost, and they were beleaguered on the island. She met Dennis Ciclitira in the mountains and he addressed a strong letter to General Benthag's headquarters via the Bishop of Kydonia. Pressure was increased by Tom Dunbabin who also passed a letter to the German authorities through Bishop Xirouhakis. He threatened that if any executions were carried out, German prisoners of war would be treated in a similar fashion.

The Germans, it appeared, were willing to consider an exchange of prisoners and a meeting took place in a neutral area late in January 1945. Ciclitira, accompanied by Captain Lassen of the SBS then on the island, and with the Bishop to act as mediator, began the discussions with a German major on Benthag's staff and a lieutenant of Feldgendarmerie. After a time Lassen became exasperated with the excessive caution and suggested that a lot of time might be saved if his men played the Germans at football on the basis of winner takes all. The German interpreter at first refused to translate such a frivolous interjection, but then the Bishop started shaking with laughter and offered to be referee.

In the end, an agreement was reached. Ciclitira went to Athens by caique and persuaded the staff of General Scobie, the commander of British forces in Greece, to let him have twelve German officers and twenty-four other ranks – a lengthy process since this was contrary to regulations – and bring them back to Crete. He wanted well-nourished specimens, who had enjoyed fifty cigarettes a week, to persuade the garrison on the island that life as a prisoner of the British was better. The Germans selected were not pleased by the prospect of release on Crete. Crossing the Aegean was dangerous, and they feared the vengeance of the civilian population when the war ended.

The exchange, ten Cretans for thirty-six Germans, finally took place at Georgioupolis on 31 March 1945.* Perikles Vandoulakis, who had managed to maintain a false identity – he had assumed the name of Palakis – since his arrest with Geoffrey Barkham, waved back exultantly to Glembin, the head of the Feldgendarmerie, as they drove off and called: 'Yassou, Herr Glembin, I'm Perikles Vandoulakis, not Palakis.'

---

* After the war Dr Herbert Glembin told Mitsotakis that Hitler himself had had to sign the authorization for the exchange since such a procedure was formally forbidden. Although not impossible, this seems improbable.

28
The Last Days of
the Occupation

As the end of the war came in sight in the autumn of 1944, authorities from outside the island began to take precedence over those in the field. It was the inevitable triumph of the staff officer over the fighting man.

Instead of the rank inflation of Bolo Keble's day, there was rank escalation. On the Greek side, Colonel Nathenas had been superseded by General Papadakis, and Tom Dunbabin had to welcome Brigadier Barker-Benfield in his new guise as the commander of Creteforce. Barker-Benfield, an over-optimistic man whom ELAS had managed to impress, really could have come straight from the pages of Evelyn Waugh. His refusal to listen to the warnings from both Woodhouse and Hammond in Greece about Communist ruthlessness was almost as disastrous as the obstinate support of Churchill and the Foreign Office for the widely unpopular King.

Attempts to prevent a breach between ELAS and the Nationalist forces continued. On 25 October, a meeting took place between the senior Greek officer on the island, General Papadakis, and the commander of the rather optimistically designated ELAS 5th Division, Colonel Kondekas. Dunbabin also sent one of his most experienced officers, Terence Bruce-Mitford, as liaison officer to ELAS now that his work in heavy weapon training was done. Bruce-Mitford, with his red hair and new appointment, rather predictably was nicknamed the 'red Major'. His job was not only difficult from a political point of view. On 12 November a German force attacked ELAS headquarters at Panayia, directly inland from Canea. After fierce fighting, they withdrew having lost about twenty men.

In theory, the ELAS troops were under the Allied command of General Papadakis, a fiction which the Communists hardly bothered to acknowledge. They had a wireless set in direct contact with EAM–ELAS headquarters on the mainland, where General Mandakas was now supposedly in charge. And since the Communists had managed to infiltrate National Army headquarters in Athens, Colonel Kondekas in Crete learned of decisions made by the Greek government and by General Scobie on the mainland before Dunbabin received any notification. Kondekas used this advantage without scruple.

The idea began to set in that the war was as good as over. On 19 November the RAF arrived to take over the airfield at Kastelli Pediados, and soon afterwards Hugh Fraser was sent down to Sphakia where, from 3 December, Royal Navy launches began a regular daylight service, shipping in stores and taking off prisoners – one of whom was shot dead by a Cretan quite casually in front of him. On 15 December, Allied Forces Headquarters declared Crete a 'liberated area'. But with a fully armed German division still holding the island's capital city, this was rather premature. Only a week before, as if to remind everyone that things were not quite over, the Germans had launched a dawn attack on the British headquarters.

The German pocket ran from Georgioupolis, in the east, to the end of the coastal plain at the far end of the Gulf of Canea. Its depth varied; curiously it was at its shallowest behind Canea. Six main bands of *andartes*, whose combined maximum strength was less than 3,200 men, contained 11,000 German and Italian soldiers within a perimeter some 70 kilometres in length.* With a no man's land between them about five kilometres deep, both sides had settled down to a waiting game.

British headquarters at this time was most appropriately based in Vaphé at that refuge of 1941 and 1942 known as 'the British Consulate' – in other words the house of Niko Vandoulakis. George Psychoundakis records arriving one day to find Dunbabin, Smith-Hughes, Ciclitira and 'the high-spirited Mr Leigh Fermor' all drinking

---

* The besieging bands from east to west consisted of: Apokoronas (EOK) under Major Liodis, up to 600 men; Sphakia (EOK) under Major Voloudakis, up to 240 men; 5th ELAS Division under Colonel Kondekas, up to 1,250 strong; Lakkoi (EOK) under Colonel Antoni Papadakis, up to 300 strong; Selino under Major Marketakis, up to 500 strong; Kissamou under Colonel Kaisakis, up to 500 strong.

and singing round a table. 'Mr Mikhali', Psychoundakis explained, 'was in an exceptionally happy mood for he had just returned to Crete after six months.'

During his long recovery from the paralysis brought on by rheumatic fever, Leigh Fermor spent some of his sick leave in Beirut staying at the Mission with General and Lady Spears. Billy Moss joined him there a few weeks after the Damastas episode until recalled to Cairo to be sent into Macedonia, not back to Crete as he had hoped. Leigh Fermor, frustrated by his weakness, returned to see him off. Still convalescent, he then hung around in Cairo until the medical authorities agreed that he had recovered enough to return to Crete. He had finally reached the island on 28 October.

In Heraklion with Sandy Rendel, Paddy Leigh Fermor embarked on a lengthy round of meetings with Colonel Nathenas, the military governor of the province, and Petrakageorgis, the town commandant, and an even lengthier round with old friends who wanted to celebrate his return and his recovery.

He then went to Vaphé as Tom Dunbabin's second-in-command. Their curious existence there besieging the Germans could have led to a lack of watchfulness. Fortunately, Vaphé was exceptionally well-sited with its magnificent view across the Apokoronas plain south-east of Suda. At eight o'clock in the morning on 8 December, a German force led by several armoured vehicles smashed through the barricade across the road below the village. Perhaps most fortunately of all, Antoni Paterakis was on hand with his famous Bren gun. This gave the *andartes* in the village time to gather for a rearguard action.

Someone stuck their head round the door to yell to Paddy Leigh Fermor that the Germans had attacked, and that everyone was pulling back to the heights behind known as Vothonas. Leigh Fermor grabbed the supply of sovereigns and all the secret papers he could find, and ran as directed. But the retreat was by no means a rout, largely thanks to Antoni Paterakis and his Bren gun. The *andartes* fought back so well from the heights round the village that the Germans withdrew late in the afternoon, having lost about five men and many wounded.

Shortly afterwards, following a visit to Asi Gonia, Leigh Fermor was walking back along the hills inland from Lake Kourna when he saw a slim young man who looked familiar. Xan Fielding had returned to the island almost without warning. The resistance work in France for which he had sought a transfer at the beginning of the year had soon turned into a nightmare. He had been travelling by car with a fellow SOE officer Francis Cammaerts and a French officer when they were stopped at a road-block near Digne. They were arrested and taken to the local prison. A few hours before they were due to face a firing squad, he and his companions were rescued by a fellow agent in one of the greatest acts of nerve and courage in the war. Christine Granville, the Polish Countess Skarbeck, who had operated behind enemy lines longer than any other member of SOE, approached a Gestapo liaison officer, told him that she too was a British agent, and offered both money and a safe-conduct from the advancing Allies if he helped his prisoners to escape.

Paddy Leigh Fermor left Heraklion on 23 December aboard HMS *Catterick*. He reached Cairo just in time to join the others for a last Christmas back at Tara. Xan Fielding, who stayed on the island another month, missed an extraordinary celebration: somebody had even crumbled benzedrine tablets into the stuffing of the turkey to make the party last longer. It was the last one. Most of Tara's inhabitants went off to the jungles of South East Asia, still under the command of SOE, there known as Force 136. Fielding, after leaving Crete on 1 February, was sent first to Saigon and then to Phnom Penh. When the fighting came to an end, he set off on a journey he had longed to undertake to Kalimpong and the Tibetan border.

Leigh Fermor returned to England where he joined SAARF – Special Allied Airborne Reconnaissance Force. Mainly a group of SOE veterans rapidly recruited and based at Sunningdale golf course, they stood by to drop on Oflag IV C at Colditz Castle to rescue important prisoners – *Prominenten* – liable to be made hostages in the closing phase of the war. Fortunately, the recently repatriated Miles Reid who had commanded the Phantom Reconnaissance Group in Greece, warned SAARF command that such an operation would end in disaster. The whole plan was cancelled. So too was a project to rescue the inmates of Flossenburg concentration camp: time had run out. An idea that Mike Cumberlege, the gold-earringed commander of the *Dolphin* and the *Escampador*, might have been saved became one of many retrospective reproaches which can do little good. He and the others captured with him in 1943 in a raid on the Corinth Canal were taken out and shot two days before the German surrender.

The liberation of Greece and the increasing traffic between Crete and the outside world meant that events on the mainland at last began to have an influence. Yet Cretan politics were by no means an automatic reflection. Their pattern, balance and nature were all different. Perhaps one of the most significant contrasts to emerge was an ethical one. On the mainland, the government in its struggle with the Communists resorted to the hated Security Battalions formed by the Germans, and to the extreme right-wing 'X' forces, which were little better than death squads. In Crete, there had been hardly any collaboration in an organized form, only individual acts.

Five days after the Germans left Athens and an advance party of British troops arrived, the 'Government of National Unity' led by George Papandreou but paid for by the British was rather unconvincingly installed. George Seferis, the poet and diplomat attached to Papandreou's administration, said its ministers 'looked like boarders of an orphanage in their new winter outfits'. The government survived mainly because the Communists suffered from internal splits and uncertainty. Moderates believed that they could win power peacefully, and so should not alienate support, while hardliners such as Aris Velouchiotis argued that they should use ELAS to seize power before the British imperialists crushed them and handed everything to the 'monarcho-fascists'.

The question of guerrilla bands surrendering their arms to the National Army brought a crisis in late November. Mutual suspicion had led inevitably to a vicious circle of pre-emptive bad faith. But in a curious way, the worst example of bad faith was Stalin's towards the Greek Communist Party. He never told them of his 'percentage' agreement with Churchill, discussed in May and confirmed in October, dividing up the Balkans into spheres of influence. He had even given his blessing to the deployment of General Scobie's force – Operation Manna – more than three weeks before its arrival. Much bloodshed and misery over the next few years might have been avoided on both sides if the Greek Communists had known where they stood from the beginning.

Siantos, one of the ELAS leaders, began moving *andarte* divisions towards Athens on 1 December. Other Communist leaders, having at first agreed with this offensive, then began to have second thoughts. The Party's uncharacteristic indecisiveness proved fatal. When the Communist-inspired demonstration which triggered the preliminary phase of the Greek civil war took place in Constitution Square on 3 December, Communist and ELAS leaders still hesitated over the best course to follow. Although 'the Greek gendarmerie on the corner lost their heads and fired into the crowd' and thus technically started the bloodshed, the demonstration had been clearly 'aimed at a political solution': the Party euphemism for a putsch.

Communist disarray gave General Scobie's troops and their Greek allies, both honourable and dishonourable, a chance to recover. On 12 December, an advance party of the British 4th Division arrived crammed into Wellington and Liberator bombers. And by 7 January 1945, after a month of sporadic fighting, ELAS was forced to flee Athens and sue for peace. This was formalized with the Varkiza agreement, but the struggle was far from over.

In Crete, the main unrest in 1945 perversely followed the peace moves on the mainland. ELAS bands took up position round Rethymno on 17 January and cut the main Canea–Heraklion road on both sides. They refused entry to anyone they suspected of supporting EOK. Lieutenant Colonel Pavlos Gyparis, the Nationalist commander and an old Balkan War guerrilla fighter in Macedonia, sent them warnings to disperse. ELAS commanders agreed to discussions, but none took place and Gyparis, suspecting stonewall tactics, sent in some men. There were several outbreaks of firing and a number of casualties. By next day ELAS groups were in flight and the town had returned to normal. EOK *andartes* who captured some Communists wanted to kill them on the spot, but apparently a British liaison officer suggested instead that they make them go round with buckets and brushes and scrub their slogans off the walls. This fortunately appealed to their captors even more. The most serious incident took place in the south of the province, when EOK bands retaliated against the Communist stronghold of Koxaré and killed many ELAS men including their leader Limonias.

Just over ten days later, on 29 January, clashes occurred in Heraklion between ELAS and Bandouvas. This time it is hard not to suspect that personal pride was more at stake than political principle, but the casualties were just as real. They included a British officer and his driver: Captain Clynes of the Special Boat Squadron and Private Cornthwaite who were hit by an ELAS sniper in their jeep on the road to Rethymno.*

In the province of Canea the presence of the common enemy did not diminish tensions between ELAS and the British. Even the disarming of Axis prisoners and deserters had political implications:

* In November 1944, Bob Bury, the SBS officer who had come to cover the Kreipe evacuation, was shot in a caique off Salonika by Royalists in the belief that he and Andy Lassen were Communists.

ELAS would demand the weapons for themselves, and the British would refuse.

This happened after one of the most successful mass desertions of the occupation: that of an Italian battalion forced to soldier on by the Germans. Stephen Verney, after various indirect contacts with the Italian commanding officer, slipped into their camp hospital for a meeting. Verney lay disguised on an operating table while the colonel sat beside him hunched forward, almost as if hearing his confession. They discussed plans in a murmur while another officer played the part of surgeon.

Verney sought Xan Fielding's advice first, and the night was chosen. One company was taken off the beach near Maleme by caiques while the rest were led up into the hills. The Germans had no inkling until the last moment when the Italian colonel panicked and drove his staff car out with the headlights full on. A great deal of wild firing ensued in the dark and one of the Cretan *andartes* helping in the operation was killed.

After the Italians had been relieved of their weapons, they were marched down to Paleokhora and embarked in a Royal Navy warship for Egypt. Their armament meanwhile was stored in a garage in Kastelli Kissamou. ELAS wasted no time in demanding this large haul for themselves, but the British refused and once again suspicions were confirmed.

Kastelli Kissamou had been liberated by Major Digridis, a fearsome EOK leader who insisted that Jack Smith-Hughes accompany him into the town on horseback at the head of his *andartes*. Smith-Hughes who had never enjoyed an affinity with horses was obliged to overcome his alarm and hold on to the saddle with both hands when his mount caracoled nervously at the cheers of the crowd.

Dennis Ciclitira of SOE and John Stanley of ISLD set up their bases at Kastelli Kissamou, but the Communists were strong in that area and minor incidents could trigger a general mobilization on both sides. Ciclitira had a dozen men billeted in a school, mainly members of the Selino band including Antoni Paterakis. ELAS meanwhile requisitioned another school for a group of their men. The bulk of their volunteers, several hundred reserve *andartes*, could be summoned at short notice from the town and surrounding area.

On one occasion Antoni Paterakis encountered an ELAS guerrilla openly bearing arms in the street, which he considered a personal affront. In a flash he brought his own weapon to bear and disarmed the *andarte* in full public gaze. To a Cretan, this was a mortal insult. The ELAS *andarte* raced back to his base and within an hour, less than twenty miles from the German lines, both sides were ready for battle.

John Stanley sought out Father Spyrou, a prominent ELAS sympathizer, to find a formula to prevent a futile bloodbath. The two of them had to go to the ELAS strongpoint, 'a hair-raising walk', to discuss terms. Stanley, who was unfairly nicknamed the Red Captain for his efforts to keep the peace with ELAS, later advanced the view that in a curious way the Cretan tradition of family vendetta was an important influence in preventing civil war. The blood feuds engendered would have been so appalling that the very idea acted as a primitive equivalent of nuclear deterrence.*

An island with as long a history of occupation and revolt as Crete was bound to have developed an instinctive belief in merciless treatment for traitors. Collaborators knew they could expect no mercy if caught. One German agent captured by *andartes* begged to be allowed to commit suicide. They broke his legs with heavy stones some way from the edge of a cliff so he had to crawl the rest of the way to push himself over.

In Heraklion after the liberation, five collaborators were tried for having betrayed the assassins of a journalist who was a prominent German stooge. When only two received death sentences – the other three, younger and apparently influenced by their elders, were given long terms of imprisonment – armed *andartes* took over the court, hauled the prisoners into the prosecutor's office and began to hack off their heads, with only limited success. The bodies were then thrown through the window to the crowd outside.

Young bloods from mountain villages also made desperate attempts to prove themselves before the war ended. In Halepa, a few yards from General Benthag's residence, a shepherd boy shot down an officer. He spared two soldiers who rapidly raised their arms in surrender. The boy seized the officer's ceremonial dagger and ran. Later that day he swopped the dagger for ten sheep. No doubt the

---

* Family vendettas inevitably became enmeshed with politics. The Viglis clan of Samaria joined ELAS principally because their enemies, the Sartzetakis family, supported EOK.

new owner developed a good story about how he had killed the officer himself in single combat.

Another incident in the final week of the war (fourteen Germans died in the last ten days) involved two boys from the village of Asi Gonia. They too longed to seize the weapon of a German officer. In Ayios Ioannis on the edge of Canea, they grabbed a captain in the street to seize his Luger. During the struggle they shot him with his own gun. A German vehicle appeared, so they leaped over a wall and escaped. The locals when they heard of the incident were angry and grief-stricken: the officer killed by the boys was a German doctor much loved in the neighbourhood for having treated Cretan patients whenever possible.

A rash of spurious groups without political purpose suddenly emerged towards the end. These self-proclaimed *andartes* tried to pass themselves off as members of the resistance, partly for prestige, but also because there was the hope of a pension once peace came. Yet the ignoble opportunism of a few and several incidents of ferocious excess must be seen against a background of the Cretan resistance as a whole. Few other populations in occupied Europe had demonstrated such unity in the face of oppression. The courage of the real *andartes*, the saintliness of characters such as Father Ioannis Alevizakis and Alexandros Kokonas, and the brave generosity of villagers sheltering and feeding strangers – British, Dominion and Greek troops after the battle, fellow Cretans fleeing from other provinces, and members of the Allied Military Mission – rightly form a far more enduring memory.

The stalemate on Crete, having looked as if it could last indefinitely, suddenly came to an end because of events elsewhere. On 8 May, Dennis Ciclitira in Kastelli Kissamou received a signal telling him to contact the German commander to make arrangements for a formal surrender. Ciclitira did not speak German, but fortunately Costa Mitsotakis, a good linguist, was with him. Dressed in suits, not uniform, they approached the nearest German outpost and sent forward a messenger to the Kriegsmarine sentries.

After a long wait in the sun, a car arrived from headquarters. Ciclitira and Mitsotakis were driven to the Venizelos house in Halepa where Mitsotakis had been lectured by General Bräuer after his first release from prison. They were escorted to General Benthag's office where he awaited them flanked by Colonel Barge, his chief of staff, and Captain Wildhage, the officer in charge of counter-espionage.

All three were in their best uniforms and very stiff in manner. General Benthag, a tall, heavily built officer, announced that he had just received orders from Admiral Dönitz at Flensburg to surrender to Allied Forces Headquarters. Ciclitira confirmed that they were official representatives and began to discuss arrangements. Benthag then asked how they were going to contact the authorities in Heraklion. Ciclitira replied that this presented no problem. For some time their wireless had been operating secretly from an apartment next to his headquarters where the volume of signal traffic had concealed their own messages from German direction-finders.

The next day, a light aircraft flew from Heraklion to Maleme to collect the General. This was done with great secrecy to avoid a rush of last-minute attacks by Cretan irregulars. Benthag landed at Heraklion airport hatless and in a coat without insignia. From there he was driven to the Villa Ariadne where the proceedings – they were too brusque to merit the term ceremony – took place in Sir Arthur Evans's long dining-room. Major General Sir Colin Callander, the new GOC of the 4th Division, ordered to Greece during the Athens fighting the previous December, had sent Brigadier Dick Kirwan in his place. Benthag was shaken to find there were no terms, only unconditional surrender. He asked whether that meant commanders could be shot. Yes, if found guilty of war crimes, came the reply. Benthag flew back from Heraklion to Maleme looking 'very dejected'. The Villa Ariadne and the airfields at Maleme and Heraklion formed a fitting triangle for this last act.

Whatever Benthag's fears after his return from the Villa Ariadne, the Germans in the Canea area suffered no ill-treatment. Kirwan authorized them to keep their personal weapons for self-defence until British troops arrived to guard them, and told General Benthag to continue to administer German military discipline. Benthag ordered the execution of a soldier who raped and murdered a Cretan woman. In a tangle of military justice, General Benthag was charged some months later with the crime of having a soldier shot after the surrender. Fortunately, Kirwan, by then Deputy Director of Military Opertions in the War Office, heard of this and exonerated Benthag.

With Germans still in possession of formidable firepower yet deeply frightened of the Cretan population, the interregnum had a curious air of unreality. On the evening of Benthag's secret surrender at Knossos, British officers in the Canea area such as Ciclitira, Stanley and Verney entered the city. In an aberrant mood, they invited the German officers, who had been trying to track them down for so long, to a party in a café before their disappearance into captivity. The idea of introducing themselves, both by their code-names and their real names, held an irresistible appeal. A jazz band was furnished by the German garrison. The guests included several of the most hated members of the occupying power – Captain Herbert Glembin of the Feldgendarmerie and Sonderführer Emil Grohmann, who had interrogated Geoffrey Barkham. Grohmann, a mining engineer, was another German guerrilla-hunter who had lived most of his life in Greece. Schubert, although reputedly still in Canea at this moment, was not present, nor were any members of the Gestapo since they had left the island in September 1944.

The next morning, once more in uniform, the British took part in the unforgettably spontaneous celebrations eclipsing even those which had taken place in Heraklion the previous October. Crowds from the surrounding villages and towns converged merrily on Canea. Rival bands of *andartes* raced to be the first into the town, and rumours spread that fighting was inevitable between ELAS bands and the National Army troops under Colonel Gyparis. But the mood of shouting and chanting and singing was too strong that day. People danced everywhere: in the streets, in cafés and in private houses.

Verney, whose work switched to propaganda for the Allies, set up an office in Canea, this time openly. Within the next couple of days he received copies of the very first photographs taken in liberated concentration camps. He immediately organized an exhibition, but it provoked disbelief and outrage amongst the fully armed German soldiers, one of whom placed a grenade under his car.

On 13 May an advance party of 'Presforce', a battalion of the Royal Hampshires under Brigadier Patrick Preston, left Piraeus in a destroyer for Canea. Ten days later, the disarmament of German troops took place. The main body of the Hampshires marched up the road from Suda Bay in parade order: a very different sight from those exhausted and filthy soldiers who had retreated from the paratroopers and mountain troops almost exactly four years before.

The German troops, who had withdrawn for self-defence on to the Akrotiri, were held behind a protective cordon until shipped out from Suda Bay. According to Dennis Ciclitira, they were allowed to take all their booty home with them. They had so much that the captain said he could have taken twice as many British troops with full equipment. 'The Cretans', records the Hampshires' regimental history, 'strongly resented the restraint of the British troops towards their hated and conquered foes.'

After the shouting came the tidying up. Ralph Stockbridge's main priority was to single out Major Kleinschmidt of the Abwehr and fly him off to Athens for interrogation. As an extension of his propaganda activities, Verney set up an English school. This was taken over by the British Council and transferred to the former German Consulate. There one of its members discovered a hoard of silver bricked up at the end of a corridor.

For the SOE officers who stayed on for the next few months, the main task was to compensate those who had helped the British and to settle claims. But the flow of sovereigns from Cairo had ceased and local currency had become worthless: in Athens one sovereign bought 64 billion drachma. The price of expensive items was fixed in okas of olive oil and smaller items such as newspapers were priced in cigarettes.

Dennis Ciclitira, who came from a family of dried fruit traders, decided that the only way to settle SOE's obligations was to resort to commodity speculation in olive oil. He asked the Royal Navy to blockade Canea to prevent exports to Heraklion, and having thus driven down prices at one end of the island and raised them at the other, he rapidly borrowed, bought and sold to raise the sums required.

For many Cretans, victory over the Germans did not bring release from suffering; in fact times grew even harder. Many young resistance fighters soon found themselves drafted into the army to fight the civil war on the mainland which erupted again in July 1946 and lasted until the end of August 1949. Ralph Stockbridge, then a regular MI6 officer, became Vice-Consul in the Salonika Consulate-General to report on intelligence aspects of the conflict in the region.

Once again Cretans did not follow the mainland Greeks – 'those from above' as they were sometimes called. Venizelos would have approved: the island underlined its unusual, yet entirely coherent, position by rejecting the monarchy in the referendum of September 1946, while also decisively rejecting Communism.

Cretan politics were too trenchant. The Communists had never been able to manipulate the question of the monarchy and the Metaxas regime on an island as avowedly republican as Crete. Accusations of collaboration against Cretan conservatives and the centre-right fell flat because so few were tainted. Deprived of this handhold on the tail of their rivals, the Communists could not twist issues as they had on the mainland.

The other difference was that on the mainland the awe-inspiring eastward advance of the Red Army gave a much stronger impression of inevitability – that Marxist-Leninist argument which appealed to the visceral emotion of excited dread.

The island of Crete and the sense of individuality it engendered in the vast majority of its inhabitants also formed a fortress against internationalism, whether the New Order of Hitler or Russian Communism masquerading as a universal brotherhood. And the outcome of the civil war on Crete, although it dragged on until 1948, led relentlessly to the defeat of ELAS as even Cretan Communists must have known in their hearts.

Yanni Bodias, the ELAS renegade from Bandouvas's band, met the traditionally savage end of an outlaw. Having successfully evaded army units on Psiloriti, he was tracked by Bandouvas and his band in what was perhaps an inevitable finale to their curious relationship. But it was a gendarme who spotted Bodias hiding in a tall ilex tree in the foothills. He killed him with a single shot. The body fell across a branch, and hung there bent double. The gendarme went off to tell his superiors.

A shepherd, attracted by the shot, spotted Bodias's body and his binoculars swinging gently on the neckstrap. He climbed the tree to retrieve them and carried his booty away proudly. Bandouvas encountered him shortly afterwards and immediately recognized the binoculars, which he had given to Bodias before their split in 1943. The shepherd had no alternative but to lead him back to the corpse. One of Bandouvas's men was told to climb the tree and bring down the body, which was taken to his brother at Ay Varvára. There, the head and one hand were severed for identification. Next day, Bandouvas's men returned to Heraklion through the Canea Gate to carry the head in triumph on a stick through the streets. Bandouvas, who in his memoirs pretended rather unconvincingly to have been deeply shocked at such barbaric behaviour, claimed on other occasions to have fired the fatal shot.

Apart from the Mount Ida range, the main area of Communist resistance was around the gorge of Samaria where an ELAS unit several hundred strong held out until 1948. Eventually, National Army troops advanced from both ends in force, certain that they had the ELAS *andartes* trapped, but most managed to scale the cliffs and escape into the White Mountains. There, a number of them lingered on as outlaws, surviving off stolen sheep. The last two, Spyros Blazakis and Giorgios Tzobanakis, came down in the autumn of 1974 after the fall of the Colonels' regime.

One of the least deserved fates of the post-war years awaited George Psychoundakis. He first had to endure the squalid indignity of imprisonment as a deserter from the Greek army, because of a bureaucratic blunder over his papers. This injustice did not spare him from two years' active service in Northern Greece against the Communist forces there. On his return to Crete, he had to work as a navvy building mountain roads to provide for his family, all of whose sheep had been stolen in the war. Fittingly, it was during this period of purgatory that he wrote his masterpiece of the resistance, *The Cretan Runner*.

Many years later, in 1974, the Germans established their war cemetery on Hill 107 above Maleme. Psychoundakis, with a good dash of Cretan black humour, applied for the job of keeper. There, he was to bury the man who might be called the last German of the island's occupation.

In 1946, the Greek government demanded the return of generals in command of Axis occupying forces to stand trial for war crimes.* The accusation that government forces had depended on collaborators to crush the Communists still rankled.

The first two German commanders on Crete to be sent back to face trial in Athens were General Müller, notorious for his brutality, and General Bräuer, the least culpable of all. Both were condemned to death.

Paddy Leigh Fermor, who happened to be in Athens at the time, was taken to the last day of the trial by Greek friends. Afterwards they insisted on his visiting the two generals behind the scenes. Leigh Fermor was uneasy about the idea, but the German generals behaved as if it were a perfectly ordinary social occasion. When he was introduced as the captor of General Kreipe, Müller laughed. *'Ach, Herr Major. Mich hätten sie nicht so leicht geschnappt!'* — 'You would not have captured me so easily!'

Bräuer's execution was delayed, with distasteful symbolism, until 20 May 1947, the anniversary of the airborne invasion. His death shocked international opinion so much that Andrae and other senior officers, who were far guiltier, escaped with prison sentences. Few protested on behalf of Müller.

---

* General Student's trial at Luneburg had already collapsed. Colonel von der Heydte, inexplicably flown over from the prisoner-of-war camp at Colchester as a witness for the prosecution, caused consternation in the courtroom by stating that, along with Field Marshal Alexander, Student was the general he most admired.

Many years later, at the request of the Association of German Airborne Troops, General Bräuer's body was brought from Athens to the cemetery overlooking Maleme where he was reburied by George Psychoundakis.

During the 1970s George Psychoundakis and that other hero of the Resistance, Manoli Paterakis, worked in the German cemetery together. When taking a break from work, they would chat in the shade of a tree, looking out over Maleme to the sea. One afternoon, over thirty years after the war, an elderly visitor limping from an old injury, clearly a former German officer, suddenly came to a stop and began to stare at Manoli Paterakis with a disturbing intensity. His features – Paterakis had the profile of an eagle – were unmistakable.

'I have seen you before,' he said with a smile of grim certainty. Paterakis searched the German's face and his own memory. He was sure that he had never laid eyes on him in his life.

'You never saw me,' the German confirmed, 'but I saw you. You were with a man who had lost one hand, and rested his rifle on the stump of his forearm.' Amazed, Paterakis agreed that this was so. The German went on to explain that he had been lying hidden under a bush when the two of them had stopped next to it.

On the very first morning of the battle for Crete, severely hit soon after his descent by parachute, he had dragged himself out of sight like a wounded animal. His battalion had almost been wiped out, and Cretan irregulars were searching for survivors. The arrival of German reinforcements had then appeared a forlorn hope. In the end, he had lain there for three days without water before being found. He had never forgotten Manoli Paterakis's face.

Appendices

Appendix A: Secret Organizations

Military Intelligence (Research) was a War Office organization started in 1938 by Colonel J.C.F. Holland and Major Colin Gubbins who later became the head of SOE. The main purpose of MI(R) was to raise, train and supply guerrilla groups behind enemy lines.

Section D was an offshoot of the Secret Intelligence Service, and therefore did not come under the War Office although it was headed by a regular officer, Colonel Lawrence Grand. Section D mainly recruited businessmen with knowledge of a country, because it specialized in the sabotage of industrial plant and communications.

Section D and MI(R), together with Electra House (a black propaganda outfit under Sir Campbell Stuart), were amalgamated in the summer of 1940 into what was later known as the Special Operations Executive (SOE) and then split afresh between SO1 and SO2. Both came under the Minister of Economic Warfare whose organization was renamed the Political Warfare Executive.

SO1 was the black propaganda wing responsible to the Minister of Economic Warfare, the Minister of Information and the Foreign Secretary and later known as the Political Warfare Bureau (PWB). SO2, which concentrated on sabotage and the organization of resistance groups in enemy and enemy-occupied countries, was usually known as just SOE. Its regional groupings later took on other names. SOE Cairo and its assets became known as Force 133.

SOE had an intelligence-gathering competitor. This was the Secret Intelligence Service's military offshoot, the Inter Services Liaison Department (ISLD). Unlike in Cairo, or in the field in Greece where on one occasion the rivalry led to a fatal shooting, in Crete, SOE and ISLD personnel worked together very amicably.

Appendix B: The British and German Order of Battle

Creforce Order of Battle and Chain of Command

Creforce Headquarters — Major General Freyberg VC
Colonel Stewart

1st Bn. Welch Regt.

Maleme and Galatas Sectors
2nd New Zealand Division — A/Major General Puttick
    (HQ 1 km SW of Canea) — Lieutenant Colonel Gentry (CoS)
3rd Hussars (seven light tanks)

4th New Zealand Brigade — Brigadier Inglis
18th NZ Bn.
19th NZ Bn.
1st Lt. Troop RA

5th New Zealand Brigade — Brigadier Hargest
    (Maleme Sector, HQ Platanias)
7th Royal Tank Regt. (2 Matildas)
21st NZ Bn.
22nd NZ Bn.
23rd NZ Bn.
Engineer Det.
28th (Maori) Bn.
1st Greek Regt. (Kastelli Kissamou)

10th New Zealand Brigade — Colonel Kippenberger
NZ Divisional Cavalry
NZ Composite Bn.
6th Greek Regt.
8th Greek Regt.
20th NZ Bn. (Divisional Reserve)

Suda Sector
Mobile Naval Base Defence Organisation — Major General Weston
Lieutenant Colonel Wills

Naval Officer-in-Charge Suda — Captain Morse RN
15th Coastal Defence Regt.
Anti aircraft and searchlight batteries
Marine composite battalion
1st Bn. Rangers
Northumberland Hussars
106th Royal Horse Artillery
16th Australian Inf. Bde. Comp. Bn.
17th Australian Inf. Bde. Comp. Bn.
'Royal Perivolians' Comp. Bn.
2nd Greek Regt.

Georgioupolis
HQ 19th Australian Inf. Brigade   Brigadier Vasey
2/7th Australian Inf. Bn.
2/8th Australian Inf. Bn.

Rethymno
2/1st Australian Inf. Bn.   Lieutenant Colonel Campbell
2/11th Australian Inf. Bn.
7th Royal Tank Regt. (2 Matildas)
4th Greek Regt.
5th Greek Regt.
Cretan Gendarmerie

Heraklion Sector
HQ 14th Infantry Brigade   Brigadier Chappel
2nd Bn. Black Watch
2nd Bn. York and Lancaster Regt.
2nd Bn. Leicesters
2/4th Australian Infantry Bn.
7th Medium Regt. RA
7th Royal Tank Regt. (2 Matildas)
3rd Hussars (six light tanks)
3rd Greek Regt.
7th Greek Regt.

Tymbaki
2nd Bn. Argyll and Sutherland Hldrs.
7th Royal Tank Regt. (2 Matildas)

Strength
The total of Allied troops amounted to 42,460 of whom only about half were properly formed infantrymen. The Suda sector had the lowest proportion of armed servicemen: only 3,000 out of 15,000. The total of 42,460 included about 9,000 Greek soldiers of whom only a small proportion, because of insufficient arms and training, played a significant role. In addition there were 1,200 gendarmes and over 3,000 Cretan irregulars.

Losses
Killed and Missing   1,751
Wounded   1,738
Prisoners of War   12,254

Royal Navy: 1,828 killed and 183 wounded
Cruisers sunk: *Gloucester, Fiji, Calcutta*
Destroyers sunk: *Juno, Greyhound, Kelly, Kashmir, Imperial, Hereward*
Capital ships damaged: *Warspite, Barham, Valiant, Formidable*
Cruisers damaged: *Ajax, Naiad, Perth, Orion, Dido, Carlisle*
Destroyers damaged: *Kelvin, Nubian, Napier, Ilex, Havoc, Kingston, Nizam*

The German Order of Battle and Chain of Command

IV Air Fleet	General Löhr

VIII Air Corps   General Freiherr von Richthofen
120 Dornier 17s based at Tatoi
40 Heinkel 111s based at Eleusis
80 Junkers 88s based at Eleusis
150 Junkers 87b Stukas based at Mycenae, Molaoï and Skarpanto
90 Messerschmitt 110s based at Argos
90 Messerschmitt 109s single-engined fighters based at Molaoï

XI Air Corps   General Student
Brigadier Schlemm (CoS)
Colonel von Trettner (Ops)
Major Reinhardt (Int)

Three transport groups under command (approx. 500 Junkers 52s)
Glider wing (approx. 70 DFS 230 gliders)
Squadron of Fieseler Storch reconnaissance aircraft

Storm Regiment HQ	Brigadier Meindl (then Colonel Ramcke)
	Major Braun
I Battalion	Major Koch
II Battalion	Major Stentzler
III Battalion	Major Scherber
IV Battalion	Captain Gericke
7th Parachute Division HQ	Major General Süssmann
	Major Count von Uxküll
Parachute Engineer Battalion	Major Liebach
1st Parachute Regiment	Colonel Bräuer
	Captain Rau
	Captain Count von der Schulenburg
I Battalion	Major Walther
II Battalion	Captain Burckhardt
III Battalion	Major Karl-Lothar Schulz
2nd Parachute Regiment	Colonel Sturm
	Major Schulz
	Captain Paul
I Battalion (Rethymno)	Major Kroh
II Battalion (Heraklion)	Captain Schirmer
III Battalion (Rethymno)	Captain Wiedemann

3rd Parachute Regiment	Colonel Heidrich
	Lieutenant Heckel
I Battalion	Captain Freiherr von der Heydte
II Battalion	Major Derpa
III Battalion	Major Heilmann

5th Mountain Division	Major General Ringel
	Major Haidlen
	Captain Ferchl

95th Mountain Regiment	(Divisional troops)
Mountain Artillery	Lieutenant Colonel Wittmann
Pioneers	Major Schaette
Reconnaissance	Major Count Castell zu Castell

85th Mountain Regiment	Colonel Krakau
I Battalion	Major Treck
II Battalion	Major Esch
III Battalion	Major Fett

100th Mountain Regiment	Colonel Utz
I Battalion	Major Schrank
II Battalion	Major Friedmann
III Battalion	Major Ehal

141st Mountain Regiment (from 6th Mountain Division)	Colonel Jais

Strength
Landed by parachute and glider:

Maleme	1,860
Ayia valley and Canea	2,460
Rethymno	1,380
Heraklion	2,360

Landed by troop-carrier:

Maleme	13,980
Total	22,040

Losses
Killed and missing*

paratroopers	3,094
mountain troops	580
aircrew	312
Wounded	2,594

*17 of the missing were German officers shipped out to Egypt as prisoners of war.

Appendix C: Ultra Signals Sent to Crete Before the Battle

In this early stage of Ultra, signals were sent to Cairo in the OL or Orange Leonard series with three digits. The OL 2000 series was sent simultaneously or up to several hours afterwards to Crete. Cairo thus knew what had been sent to Crete — the OL 5000 series was for Malta. This system was intended to prevent the onward dispatch of unnecessary information which might risk compromising Ultra if intercepted or captured. Messages sent to Creforce were usually prefixed 'Personal for General Freyberg — Most Immediate'. Captain Sandover, the officer in the cave above the Creforce quarry, would decode the message, show it to Freyberg, and then burn it. The time and date of dispatch came at the end of each message, but here they are put at the beginning for easy reference.

OL 2151   1845 hours   28.4.41
OL messages sent to Cairo only will carry OL three digit numbers in current series. Messages to Cairo and A.O.C. Crete [Group Captain Beamish received Ultra for a few days before Freyberg's arrival] carry OL 2000 and up in current series. Numbers thus show distribution each message.

OL 2155   1615 hours   1.5.41
It is learnt that to enable the GAF [German Air Force] to carry out operations planned for the coming weeks, enemy will not mine Suda Bay nor destroy aerodromes on Crete. This message cancels OL 2154.

OL 2157   0325 hours   3.5.41
There are indications that air transport units will not be ready for large scale operations before 6th May earliest. Other preparations appear to be complete.

OL 2165   2150 hours   4.5.41
There is evidence that on May 4th staff of 7th Fliegerdivision moved to Salonika, and that it will move to Athens about May 8th.

OL 2167   2340 hours   6.5.41
Preparation for operation against Crete probably complete on 17 May. Sequence of operations from zero day onward will be parachute landing of 7th Fliegerdivision plus corps troops 11th Fliegerkorps to seize Maleme Candia [Heraklion] and Retimo [Rethymno]. Then dive bombers and fighters will move to Maleme and Candia. Next air landing of remainder 11th Fliegerkorps including headquarters and subordinated army units. Then flak units further troops and supplies. Third mountain regiment from 12th Army detailed, elements of armoured units motorcyclists anti-tank units to be detailed by supreme command army and all to be under 11th Fliegerkorps. Admiral South-East will provide protection with Italian torpedo boat [or boats?] flotillas minesweepers and possibly U boats. Sea transport by German and Italian vessels. Operation to be preceded before zero day by sharp attack on RAF military camps and anti-aircraft positions.

[Note: This third mountain regiment was the 141st Mountain Regiment from the 6th Mountain Division added to reinforce the 85th and 100th Mountain Regiments in the 5th Mountain Division. The 95th Mountain Artillery Regiment and other detachments would not have counted since they were divisional troops. Admiral South-East was Admiral Schuster.]

OL 2168   1005 hours   7.5.41
Flak units further troops and supplies mentioned our 2167 are to proceed by sea to Crete. Also three mountain regiments thought more likely than third mountain regiment.

[Note: The main misunderstanding arose when analysts read these two sentences together, and made two mistakes. They jumped to the conclusion that three mountain regiments were coming *in addition* to the XI Air Corps (7th Parachute Division and 22nd Airlanding Division). The 22nd Division's involvement had been described in OL 167 of 26 April, which detailed its transport from Bucharest to Athens, but no signal cancelling its move by the 12th Army and substituting the 5th Mountain Division appears to have been intercepted. The Directorate of Military Intelligence, but not the Directorate of Air Intelligence (see OL 2170 below), appear to have read the two sentences together and assumed that these three mountain regiments were also to be transported by sea along with the flak units. In OL 2/302 almost all the other follow-on elements detailed by the 12th Army are lumped into the seaborne convoy.]

OL 2169   1735 hours   7.5.41
Melos to be occupied by Germans on 7th May with a view to preparation aerodrome.

OL 2170   1830 hrs   7.5.41
Further to 2167 this series concerning projected German attack on Crete. Following is estimated scale of attack and suggested timetable. Suggested timetable. First day or first day minus one — sharp bombing attack on air force and military objectives. First day — parachute landings and arrival of some operational aircraft. On first or second day arrival of air landing troops with equipment including guns, motor cycles and possibly light AFVs [armoured fighting vehicles]. Second day — arrival of seaborne forces and supplies after arrival of airlanding detachments. Estimated scale of parachute and air landing attack. Number of troop carrying aircraft at present available in the area is about 450. This could be increased to 600 if required. Subject to operational facilities for the highest number being the scale of a parachute attack on the first day could be 12,000 men in two sorties. Scale of air landing of troops and equipment on second day could be 4,000 men, and four hundred tons of equipment or equivalent, carried by 600 Ju 52s. If an air landing operation took place on first day parachutists effort would be reduced by about 50%. A preliminary bombing attack would probably be made by long range bombers and twin engined fighters based in Bulgaria Salonika Athens and possibly Rhodes. Maximum effort for a day estimated at 105 long range bomber sorties and 100 twin engined fighter sorties. Aircraft available as occupying air force — 60 Me 109s and 90 Ju 87s. Start from landing grounds in Peleponnese. Position of landing grounds not known but Germans are believed to be searching for suitable sites. Athens area is the operational area from which airborne attack will probably start. All above scales of effort are the maximum weight which it is believed could be

attained. No account has been taken of effect of our action or possible lack of operational facilities in the Athens area for the maximum number of aircraft available. Foregoing from director of intelligence.

OL 2/284   1900 hours   13.5.41
Twin engined aircraft will probably attack aerodromes on Crete on May 14th.

OL 2/302   1745 hours   13.5.41
The following summarises intentions against Crete from operation orders issued.
Para 1. The island of Crete will be captured by the 11th Air Corps and the 7th Air Division and the operation will be under the control of the 11th Air Corps.
Para 2. All preparations, including the assembly of transport aircraft, fighter aircraft, and dive bombing aircraft, as well as of troops to be carried both by air and sea transport, will be completed on 17th May.
Para 3. Transport of seaborne troops will be in cooperation with admiral southeast, who will ensure the protection of German and Italian transport vessels (about twelve ships) by Italian light naval forces. These troops will come under the orders of the 11th Air Corps immediately on their landing in Crete.
Para 4. A sharp attack by bomber and heavy fighter units to deal with the allied air forces on the ground as well as with their anti-aircraft defences and military camps, will precede the operation.
Para 5. The following operations will be carried out as from day one. The 7th Air Division will make a parachute landing and seize Maleme, Candia, and Retimo. Secondly. Dive bombers and fighters (about 100 aircraft of each type) will move by air to Maleme and Candia. Thirdly. Air landing of 11th Air Corps, including corps headquarters and elements of the Army placed under its command probably including the 22nd Division. Fourthly. Arrival of the seaborne contingent consisting of anti-aircraft batteries as well as of more troops and supplies.
Para 6. In addition the 12th Army will allot three Mountain Regiments as instructed. Further elements consisting of motor-cyclists, armoured units, anti-tank units, anti-aircraft units will also be allotted.
Para 7. Depending on the intelligence which is now awaited, also as the result of air reconnaissance, the aerodrome at Kastelli [Pediados] south east of Candia and the district west and south west of Canea will be specially dealt with, in which case separate instructions will be included in detailed operation orders.
Para 8. Transport aircraft, of which a sufficient number — about 600 — will be allotted for this operation, will be assembled on aerodromes in the Athens area. The first sortie will probably carry parachute troops only. Further sorties will be concerned with the transport of the air landing contingent, equipment and supplies, and will probably include aircraft towing gliders.
Para 9. With a view to providing fighter protection for the operations, the possibility of establishing a fighter base on Skarpanto will be examined.
Para 10. The Quartermaster General's branch will ensure that adequate fuel supplies for the whole operation are available in the Athens area in good time, and an Italian tanker will be arriving at the Piraeus before May 17th. This tanker will probably also be available to transport fuel supplies to Crete. In assembling supplies and equipment for invading force it will be borne in mind that it will consist of some 30 to 35,000 thousand men, of which some 12,000 will be the parachute landing contingent, and 10,000 will be transported by sea. The strength

of the long range bomber and heavy fighter force which will prepare the invasion by attacking before day one will be of approximately 150 long range bombers and 100 heavy fighters.

Para 11. Orders have been issued that Suda Bay is not to be mined, nor will Cretan aerodromes be destroyed, so as not to interfere with the operations intended.

Para 12. Plottings prepared from air photographs of Crete on one over ten thousand scale will be issued to units participating in this operation.

[Note: The single-figure prefix to OL 302 has been defaced in the Public Record Office copy, but it is almost certainly the figure 2. The accumulation of misreadings reaches its peak in this signal, with inaccurately estimated figures taken as confirmed.]

OL 5/313   0420 hours   14.5.41
If reconnaissance fails to reveal shipping targets on 14th May Junkers 88 dive bombers gruppe 1 LG1 will attack Suda Bay.

[Note: The Junkers 88 was not a dive-bomber. Presumably the originator meant the Junkers 87, or Stuka.]

OL 6/314   1015 hours   14.5.41
In future the word Colorado will be used instead of the word Crete in all messages this series.

OL 8/337   0500 hours   16.5.41
On 16th May attacks by heavy fighters on British aircraft at Heraklion aerodrome intended also transfer to Scarpanto — aerodrome probably south point of island — of about 20 Junkers 87 aircraft to close Kaso strait.

OL 9/339   0805 hours   16.5.41
Further evidence indicates that day one for operation against Colorado [Crete] is 17th May but postponement by 48 hours appears likely.

OL 10/341   1410 hours   16.5.41
From further information postponement day one for operation against Colorado confirmed. 19th May seems earliest date.

OL 12/370   0155 hours   19.5.41
On May 19th at 0800 hours GMT conference of officers commanding air force units will take place at Eleusis aerodrome. Discussions concern operation against Colorado, particularly Malemes, Canea Retimo and Iraklion. Sorties by all units in spite of this conference. Single-engined fighters for Molaoi — in strength of about one flight at a time — will repeatedly attack aircraft on Malemes aerodrome on 19th. Dive bombers on Scarpanto also expected to operate probably on shipping. It seems today Monday may be day minus one.

Appendix D: Greek Political Organizations

Communist-Dominated

KKE   Communist Party of Greece.

EAM   National Liberation Front. A left and centre-left political coalition at first skilfully, then crudely, manipulated by the Communists. It managed to attract many with good democratic credentials, until the Communist Party's single-minded interest in power for itself alone became apparent.

ELAS   National Popular Liberation Army, EAM's military wing. On the mainland it had over 50,000 men under arms organized regionally in divisions. In Crete its armed strength never exceeded 5,000 men, including reserves. The naval side using armed caiques was called ELAN.

Non-Communist and Anti-Communist

EDES   National Republican Greek League. Originally a left-of-centre organization, it swung to the right, largely as a result of relentless Communist pressure. The urban political side especially became tainted with collaboration. The military wing was led by General Napoleon Zervas. British support for Zervas and counter-pressure on EAM–ELAS organized by Monty Woodhouse saved EDES from an all-out Communist attack. (Mainland only.)

EKKA   National and Social Liberation. EKKA, another centrist group, was led by Colonel Dimitrios Psarros. Smaller than EDES, it was vulnerable, and ELAS destroyed it in a treacherous massacre. (Mainland only.)

X   The X organization consisted of extreme right-wing nationalist groups led by Colonel George Grivas. Fanatically anti-Communist, and in many cases armed by the Germans, its members gave substance to the Communist epithet of 'monarcho-fascist'. (Mainland only.)

EOK   The National Organization of Crete. EOK was an informal alliance of non-Communist Cretans, mainly Venizelist in sympathy, and ranging from left of centre to republican right-wing. (Crete only.)

Notes

Part One   The Fall of Greece

Page   **1. Military Missions**
5   'Every Sunday . . .', Hunt, *A Don at War*, p.20.
8   'You're off . . .', Wisdom, *Wings over Olympus*, p.58.
8   'close-up information . . .', Churchill, *Their Finest Hour*, p.424.
8   'intelligent but not very wise', Caccia, conversation, 14.3.90.
9   'an avatar of Byron', Woodhouse, *Something Ventured*, p.9.
10   'astonishing repertoire . . .', Mott-Radclyffe, *Foreign Body in the Eye*, p.50.
10   'The Greeks were certainly brave . . .', Hollingworth, *Front Line*, p.97.
10   'The prize show . . .', Blunt, quoted Mott-Radclyffe, p.46.
11   'a second Scapa', PM to Gen. Ismay, 3 Nov., quoted Davin, *Crete*, p.6.
11   'We will look after Crete', Caccia, conversation, 21.3.90.
12   'clothing and footwear . . .', De Guingand, *Operation Victory*, p.59.

         2. Diplomatic Missions
14   'war of nerves . . .', Wavell to CIGS, quoted Connell, *Wavell*, p.310.
14   'to warn both . . .', Wavell to CIGS, quoted Connell, p.312.
14   'His Majesty's . . .', Chiefs of Staff to Cs-in-C, quoted Connell, p.310.
14   'it would be necessary . . .', Papagos, *The Battle of Greece*, p.312.
14   'all heaved a sigh of relief', Jacob, conversation, 10.4.90.
14   'Winston felt . . .', *ibid.*
16   'in some ways . . .', *ibid.*
17   'at whatever cost', Mack Smith, *Mussolini*, p.309.
17   'Do not consider . . .', Churchill, *The Grand Alliance*, p.63.
17   'in all matters . . .', Churchill, *The Grand Alliance*, p.60.
18   'formidable', De Guingand, *Operation Victory*, p.57.
18   'preened himself', De Guingand, *Generals at War*, p.29.
19   'normally a rather taciturn man . . .', Caccia, conversation, 14.3.90.
19   'War is an option...', De Guingand, *Operation Victory*, p.55.
19   'the haggling . . .', Coats, *Of Generals and Gardens*, p.88.
20   'Our representatives . . .', Blunt, quoted Mott-Radclyffe, p.66.

21   'full of Foreign Office . . .', De Guingand, *Generals at War*, p.33.
21   'the two weary soldiers . . .', Connell, p.354.
22   'MOST SECRET . . .', Wavell, quoted Connell, p.355.

3. Secret Missions

23   'It was the obsolete choice . . .', Leigh Fermor, *A Time of Gifts*, p.1.
23   'What a lot . . .', Hart-Davis, *Peter Fleming*, p.215.
24   'The whole thing . . .', Wilkinson, conversation, 20.3.90.
24   'Compton Mackenzie . . .', Household, *Against the Wind*, p.101.
24   'only one eye . . .', Fleming, quoted Hart-Davis, p.224.
25   'didn't have a clue . . .', Norman, conversation, 20.3.90.
25   'to stiffen Prince Paul's resolve,' *ibid.*
25   'bristling . . .', *ibid.*
26   'The most bogus . . .', Pendlebury, quoted Powell, *The Villa Ariadne*, p.113.
26   'My best . . .', Hammond and Dunbabin, *John Pendlebury in Crete*, p.x.
26   'I have been carried shoulder high . . .', *ibid.*
26   'Anglophily is rampant . . .', Powell, p.98.
26   'the island better than anyone . . .', Powell, p.113.
27   'not unlike a grown-up Cupid . . .', *Korero*, 27 March 1944, p.5.
27   'How on earth . . .', quoted Smith-Hughes, conversation, 21.8.90.

4. The Double Invasion

30   'Half the time . . .', Fletcher, conversation, 20.5.90.
31   'additional risks', CIGS to S of S for War, 7.3.41, quoted Connell, p. 352.
31   'I felt . . .', Bright, *History of the Northumberland Hussars Yeomanry*, p.39.
31   'They were . . .', Hobson, *Army Quarterly and Defence Journal*, April 1990.
32   'gasping for revenge', Schmidt, *Hitler's Interpreter*, p.223.
33   'Thursday's events in Belgrade . . .', Churchill, 30.3.41 to Acting PM of
      Australia, Churchill, *The Grand Alliance*, p.143.
33   'repulsed in [the] Rupel Pass,' Ultra signal OL 51 PRO DEFE 3/891.
34   'adverse situation', Papagos, p.363.
34   'Facing which way?' Bright, p.41.
35   'havoc of a spectacular and enjoyable kind', Hart-Davis, p.243.
35   'I must say that . . .', Hobson, 'The Episode in Greece'.
35   'I have to . . .', letter, Hobson to the author, 19.10.90.
36   'just like a picture . . .', de Winton, conversation, 28.9.90.
37   'My dear fellow . . .', Petre Norton, letter, 25.6.91.
37   'a hole twenty yards long . . .', de Winton, conversation, 28.9.90.
37   'You stay out', *ibid.*
37   'A hawk . . .', Norman, conversation, 20.3.90.
38   'Their great battle-cry . . .', Hunt, conversation, 11.4.90.
38   'Well, if the Boche . . .', Hobson, 'Episode in Greece'.
39   'fetishistic doctrine . . .', Wilson, p.80.
40   'On the Führer's birthday . . .', List, *Von Serbien bis Kreta*, p.96.
40   'fifth-column work', Wilson, p.95.
41   'standing in the centre . . .', Wisdom, p.199.
41   'not an impressive sight,' Hollingworth, p.115.
41   'having driven . . .', Bright, p.64.
42   'Come back with good fortune!' Stephanides, *Climax in Crete*, p.17.

5. Across the Aegean

43	'lorries were being . . .', Stephanides, p.16.
48	'Who do you . . .', Hobson, 'Episode in Greece'.
49	'I am going to do . . .', Leigh Fermor, conversation, 13.2.90.
50	'getting out of hand', Lee, *The Royal House of Greece*, p.90.
50	'grouped in two . . .', Stephanides, p.22.
51	'A sunny day . . .', Hadjipateras and Fafalios, *Crete 1941*, pp. 31–2.
54	'we have paid . . .', Churchill, quoted Coats, p.102.
55	'Few realise . . .', Blunt's diary, quoted Mott-Radclyffe, p.86.
55	'I am proud . . .', Household, p.132.

Part Two   The Battle of Crete

6. 'A Second Scapa'

60	'I am not surprised,' Cox, *A Tale of Two Battles*, pp.16–17.
61	'But we couldn't . . .', Smith-Hughes, conversation, 20.8.90.
61	'Good afternoon . . .', Wisdom, p.197.
61	'Carry on! Rule Britannia!', letter from Edward Hodgkin.
63	'the most essential . . .', Mott-Radclyffe, conversation, 5.4.90.
65	'Hey! What've you done . . .?' Cox, p.31.
65	'I think they . . .', Pumphrey, conversation, 19.2.90.
65	'one of the most . . .', Caccia, conversation, 21.3.90.
67	'We'd been there . . .', *ibid.*
68	'some extremely bolshie . . .', Wilkinson, conversation, 20.2.90.
68	'a great chap for . . .', Hammond, conversation, 1.3.90.
68	'speechless with . . .', Cox, conversation, 25.4.90.
69	'made that blighter . . .', *Korero*, 27 March 1944, p.5.
69	'No good RAF . . .', Cox, p.63.
69	'Every effort should . . .', Churchill, *Their Finest Hour*, p.476.
70	'The Greek General Staff', Report by Inter-Services Committee on Operations in Crete, PRO WO 106/3126.
70	'past the Venetian . . .', C.J. Hamson, *Liber in Vinculis*, p.26.
71	'In his house . . .', Memorandum by the German Command Concerning the Attitudes of the Civilian Population in Crete towards the German Armed Forces and the Reaction of These, para. 5, Canea, 18 December 1942.
71	'love and adieu', quoted Powell, p.113.

7. 'The Spear-point of the German Lance'

72	'Germany could . . .', Germany, Auswärtiges Amt, *Documents on German Foreign Policy*, Series D, Vol. XI, No. 242. See also Ciano, *Diplomatic Papers*, p.400.
73	'brusque good humour', Farrar-Hockley, *Student*, p.115.
74	'Far from being . . .', Creveld, *Hitler's Strategy 1940–1941*, p.168.
74	'The occupation of the island . . .', *DGFP*, D, Vol. XII, No. 403. See also Führer Directive No. 29 of 17 May 1941, *DGFP*, D, Vol. XII, No. 536.
75	'Our formation is young', Heydte, *Daedalus Returned*, p.21.
75	'idealism, ambition or adventure,' Heydte, p.25.
75	'A bit of spirit . . .', Pöppel, *Heaven and Hell*, p.9.
76	'had become . . .', Leigh Fermor, p.197.

76	'name was misspelled', Heydte, letter to the author, 30.10.90.
76	'a real god of war', Pöppel, p.10.
77	'rather on holiday . . .', Heydte, p.35.
78	'In a quiet . . .', Heydte, p.37.
79	'the island appeared lifeless', Student, in *Kommando*, quoted Stewart, *The Struggle for Crete*, p.89.
79	'The Cretans are . . .', 'Military and Geographical Description of Greece', p.84, 31 March 1941, quoted, Memorandum, 18 December 1942.
80	'overloaded donkey-carts . . .', Heydte, pp.39–40.
81	'we are almost foolish . . .', Emrich, unpublished journal.

8. 'Most Secret Sources'

82	'reached the rank of General', quoted Singleton-Gates, *General Lord Freyberg VC*, p.25.
82	'a certain amount of notoriety', quoted Singleton-Gates, p.26.
83	'You nearly . . .', Churchill, *The Grand Alliance*, p.242.
83	'he could not bear . . .', Stevens, *Freyberg VC*, p.41.
84	'the great St Bernard', Coats, p.74.
84	'Winston was a bad judge . . .', Jacob, conversation, 10.4.90.
84	'It seems clear . . .', Churchill, *The Grand Alliance*, p.241.
84	'Winston is always . . .', Channon, *The Diaries of Chips Channon*, p.362.
85	'I want you to go to Jerusalem and relieve Baghdad', Wilson, p.102.
85	'I told him . . .', quoted Davin, p.40.
86	'like a horde of hawks . . .', J.W. Clayton of A Troop 23rd Lt. AA Battery, letter to the author, 15.8.90.
86	'Our staff appeared . . .', Wilkinson report to Gubbins, 29 May 1941.
87	'Forces at my disposal . . .', quoted Churchill, *The Grand Alliance*, p.243.
87	'our information points insufficient . . .', Wavell, PRO PREM 3/109.
87	'our information points to . . .', Churchill, *The Grand Alliance*, p.245.
88	'a man of quickly changing moods . . .', Coats, p.102.
88	'Cannot understand . . .', quoted Churchill, *The Grand Alliance*, p.246.
88	'Please enquire of General Freyberg . . .', OL 2166, PRO DEFE 3/894.
89	'So complete . . .', Chiefs of Staff to Cs-in-C, No. 98, PRO PREM 3/109.
89	"Bear of Little Brain", Dorman-Smith, quoted Greacem, *Chink*, p.177.
89	'If they come as . . .', Freyberg, quoted Connell, p.454.
89	'The Germans could transport . . .', JIC report 27.4.41, PRO PREM 3/109.
91	'Freyberg was undaunted,' Churchill, *The Grand Alliance,* p.246.
91	'We for our part . . .', Freyberg, quoted Stewart, p.108.
91	'One thing stands . . .', Gefechtbericht XI Fl.Korps — Einsatz Kreta, in Freiburg archives, quoted Mabire, *La Crète*, p.32.
93	'a seaborne landing . . .', Freyberg, comment on draft of Churchill, Davin papers, quoted Stewart, p.128.
94	'somewhat unlikely possibility', De Courcy, *History of the Welch Regiment*.
94	'owing to policy matters . . .', Freyberg, comment on draft of Official NZ history, Davin papers, quoted Stewart, p.128.
95	'malaria-ridden little . . .', Kippenberger, *Infantry Brigadier*, p.49.
96	'handsome face . . .', quoted Powell, p.111.
97	'Satanas owed his name . . .', Woodhouse, *Something Ventured*, p.18.
97	'I baptize thee . . .', Smith-Hughes, conversation, 26.8.90.

98	'breathed blood and slaughter . . .', Hammond, conversation, 1.3.90.
98	'not to rush out . . .', quoted Davin, p.100.
99	'he was not according . . .', Stewart, p.135.
99	'Have completed plan . . .', Freyburg, quoted Churchill, *The Grand Alliance*, p.250.
101	'a man who presented himself . . .', Cox, p.33.
101	'I don't know what lies ahead . . .', Cox, p.67.

9. 'A Fine Opportunity for Killing'

102   'That is not a good enough . . .', Farrar-Hockley, p.91.
103   'Contrary to previous . . .', Leutnant Genz, *Der Zweite Weltkrieg*, Vol. 29, quoted Hadjipateras and Fafalios, p.46.
105   'Usual Mediterranean . . .', 22nd Bn. war diary, PRO WO 179/735.
106   'an angry throb,' *ibid.*
106   'eerie, acrid and ominous,' quoted Henderson, *22 Battalion*, p.41.
107   'It was not . . .', Hadjipateras and Fafalios, p.13.
107   'His attitude was . . .', Woodhouse, *Something Ventured*, p.13.
109   'the heavens shook . . .', Astley, p.76.
109   'What a remarkable sight!', quoted Hunt, p.39.
110   'sited for targets at sea', Davin, p.100.
113   'tell him that I . . .', Kippenberger, p.50.
113   'where they did nothing . . .', Kippenberger, p.52.
113   'a solid rectangle . . .', Kippenberger, p.50.
113   'in their silence . . .', Kippenberger, p.52.
113   'He yelled for mercy . . .', letter home, Fletcher.
113   '19 Battalion told us . . .', Kippenberger, p.55.
114   'the whole valley . . .', Kippenberger, p.56.
115   'The bastards are landing,' Farran, *Winged Dagger*, p.87.
116   'I do not think . . .', Farran, p.90.
116   'German callousness . . .', Farran, p.91.
116   'despatched by civilians . . .', Davin, p.145.
117   'which had been . . .', Memorandum, Canea, 1942.
117   'Pretty good shots . . .', Hollenden, conversation, 13.6.90.
118   *'der Furor Teutonicus'*, List, p.141.

10. Maleme and Prison Valley

122   'handicapped by hopelessly bad communications . . .', Davin, p.99.
124   'If you must, you must', Davin, p.110.
125   'Civilians, including women . . .', Memorandum, Canea, 1942.
126   'We just found . . .', Betts, conversation, 20.5.90.

11. Close Quarters at Rethymno and Heraklion

130   'Paratroopers never come under fire!', Pöppel, p.34.
134   'a very shaken . . .' and 'We do not . . .', Sandover, conversation, 12.10.90.
137   'signaller said solemnly . . .', Fergusson, *The Black Watch and the King's Enemies*, p.79.
138   'by the revolvers . . .', Bolitho, *The Galloping Third*, p.264.
139   'Mungo Stirling . . .', Fergusson, p.81.
139   'I nearly came along . . .', Fergusson, pp.81–2.

140   'south and west of the town . . .', Memorandum, Canea, 1942.
142   'He knew that for him . . .', C.J. Hamson, p.105.
142   'We also tried . . .', PRO PREM 3/109.

12. First Night and Second Day

145   'Today has been . . .', quoted Churchill, *The Grand Alliance*, p.254.
146   'quite satisfactory', NZ Division War Diary, quoted Davin, p.134.
150   'A striking . . .', Stewart, quoted Singleton-Gates, p.162.
150   'on the wall . . . ', Heydte, pp. 110--12.
153   'At one stage . . .', Captain Anderson, quoted Davin, pp.188--9.
153   'As we got to him . . .', Dyer, quoted Davin, p.90.
154   'Seventy seconds . . .', Cox, pp.80--1.
155   'the impression prevailed . . .', Davin, p.194.

13. 'The Seaborne Invasion'

156   'Our attention in the quarry . . .', Cox, p.81.
157   'Reliable information . . .', NZ Division War Diary, quoted Stewart, p.278.
158   'I could not leave . . .', Freyberg, quoted Stewart, p.309.
158   'a 1/500,000 map . . .', Harmeling, p.24, quoted Stewart, p.88.
160   'to comb . . .', Stitt, *Under Cunningham's Command*, p.146.
160   'Guns open fire!' Barratt, conversation, 13.8.90. See also Alfred M. de Zayas, *The Wehrmacht War Crimes Bureau*, pp.254--6.
161   'Suddenly, on the horizon . . .', Cox, p.82.
161   'Brigadier Stewart . . .', *ibid.*
162   'I for one . . .', Cox, p.83.
162   'torture to watch . . .', Lindsay, *History of the Sherwood Rangers*, p.22.

14. Disaster by Land and by Sea

164   'a well-trained battalion . . .', Long, *Australian War History — Greece, Crete and Syria*, p.235.
164   'a red open-faced . . .', Farran, p.94.
164   'no doubts were expressed . . .', Gentry, quoted Davin, p.197.
165   'the merits of simplicity . . .', Farran, p.94.
165   'The amount of . . .', Upham, quoted Davin, p.216.
166   'Steady flow of . . .', NZ Division War Diary, quoted Davin, p.229.
167   'a useful purpose . . .', Rawlings, Cunningham dispatch, para. 31.
168   'like Jesus Christ . . .', Coats, p.107.
170   'Who the bloody hell . . .', Caccia, conversation, 14.3.90.
171   'Palo and I met Dicky . . .', Queen Frederica, letter 30 May, *A Measure of Understanding*, p.43.
171   'Wait a moment . . .', Heydte, p.119.
171   'completely in the cart . . .', Kidson, *Petrol Company*, p.124.
171   'Well, that's that . . .', Farran, p.94.
172   'whose nerves . . .', Heydte, p.120.
173   'a most infernal uproar', Kippenberger, p.59.
173   'came Captain Forrester,' quoted Davin, p.234.
173   'tootling a tin whistle . . .', Bassett, quoted Davin, p.160.
173   'Over an open space . . .', Kippenberger, p.59.
173   'he would have been . . .', Emrich, unpublished journal.

173 'one of the coolest . . .' and 'the most thrilling . . .', quoted Davin, p.235.

16. The Battle of Galatas
182 'They all felt . . .', Thomas, *Dare to be Free*, p.14.
184 'to see them come in . . .', Kippenberger, p.60.
184 'ominously quiet', Kippenberger, p.61.
184 'almost oppressive', Heydte, p.19.
186 'gathered in stunned silence . . .', Stephanides, p.100.
187 'the Burgundian knight . . .', Heydte, p.143.
187 'swelled to a roar', Kippenberger, p.63.
187 'In a hollow . . .', Kippenberger, p.64.
187 'Back, back!', Thomas, p.19.
188 'tired, but fit . . .', Kippenberger, p.66.
188 'Everyone looked tense . . .', Thomas, p.21.
188 'There was Kip . . .', conversation, Forrester, 4.10.90.
189 'The Maoris . . .', *ibid.*
189 'The effect was . . .', Thomas, p.22.
189 'scores of automatics . . .', Kippenberger, p.67.
191 'a tarpaulin-covered hole in the ground', Kippenberger, p.69.

17. Laycock's Commandos and Force Reserve
194 'We were busy . . .', Wilkinson report to Gubbins, 29 May 1941.
194 'You're to be put . . .', Wilkinson, conversation, 20.2.90.
194 'was unimpressive . . .', Waugh, *The Diaries of Evelyn Waugh*, p.494.
195 'the smart set', Waugh, p.488.
195 'I saw few . . .', Waugh, p.491.
195 'Never in the history . . .', Waugh, p.495.
195 'raid enemy . . .', Laycock report, PRO DEFE 2/699 XC/A/60340.
195 'stated that . . .', Waugh, p.498.
195 'a nightmare of unreality . . .', Graham, *Cretan Crazy Week*, archive of Middle East Commando Historical Research Group (MECHRG).
196 'noticed that . . .', Laycock report.
197 'hovel . . .', *ibid.*
198 'Here we go . . .', Bevan, conversation, 19.5.90.
199 'Anyone watching . . .', Heydte, p.146.
200 'composed but obtuse', Waugh, p.500.
200 'General Weston popped out . . .', Waugh, p.501.
200 'flapping about . . .', Tanner, conversation, 2.12.90.
200 'the road was jammed,' Graham, *Cretan Crazy Week*.

18. South from Suda Bay
204 'I found it hard . . .', Stephanides, p.122.
204 'Funny thing . . .', Woodhouse, *Something Ventured*, p.14.
205 'walking very fast . . .', Kippenberger, p.71.
205 'If anybody . . .', Tanner, conversation, 2.12.90.
205 'After drawing water . . .', *The Account of Sergeant Charles Stewart who was himself taken prisoner at Crete*, MECHRG.
206 'It was pitiful to see . . .', Sergeant Stewart, *ibid.*
207 'unashamedly pleased', Kippenberger, p.71.

207   'The Black Watch . . .', Fergusson, p.86.
207   'the other end . . .', Hollenden, conversation, 13.6.90.
208   'astonished silence . . .', Sheffield, *The York and Lancaster Regiment*, p.84.
208   'one glass of sherry . . .', Underhill, *The Royal Leicestershire Regiment*, p.53.
208   'It was an eerie . . .', Fergusson, p.88.
210   'So it was . . .', Collins of 7th Cruiser Squadron, PRO PREM 3/109.
211   'They've fled . . .', C.J. Hamson, p.121.
211   'to pursue . . .', 5th Mountain Division War Diary, quoted Davin, p.392.
212   'The game's up . . .', Long, p.274.
212   'Major, my greatest . . .', Sandover, letter to the author, 2.10.90.

19. Surrender

213   'The Luftwaffe . . .', Stephanides, p.137.
214   'once a man . . .', quoted Long, p.299.
214   'like a setting . . .', Cox, p.100.
216   'My mind was fixed . . .', Hargest, quoted Long, p.304.
216   'HQ of each unit . . .', Kippenberger, p.75.
216   'Some begged . . .', Kippenberger, p.76.
217   'Navy voices . . .', Cox, p.105.
217   'My God, the faces . . .', Forrester, conversation, 4.10.90.
217   'formed the opinion . . .', Kippenberger, p.77.
217   'To the three Services . . .', Hunt, p.46.
218   'One of the worst . . .', Hamson, p.127.
218   'sharply overruled', quoted Davin, p.438.
219   'You were the last . . .', Waugh, p.507.
219   'Final orders from CREFORCE . . .', PRO WO 218/166.
219   'You and your staff . . .', Graham, *Cretan Crazy Week*.
219   '[Weston] first charged . . .', Waugh, p.509.
219   'Laycock still had two battalions . . .', Graham, letter of 9 June 1976 to
         Michael Davie, editor of *The Diaries of Evelyn Waugh*.
219   'General Weston asked me . . .', Graham, *Cretan Crazy Week*.
220   'On finding that entire staff . . .', PRO WO 218/166.
221   'Come on, Lofty . . .', Tanner, conversation, 2.12.90.
221   'had a personal . . .', Graham, letter to Davie.
221   'My orders were to go with the men . . .', Laycock, PRO DEFE 2/699.
222   'Presume Ivor . . .', *The Letters of Ann Fleming* (ed. Mark Amory), p.155.
222   'I replied that if . . .', Waugh, *The Diaries of Evelyn Waugh*, 6 July 1955,
         p.728.
223   'Then came the . . .', quoted Long, p.307.
224   'It's all right . . .', quoted Messenger, *The Middle East Commandos*, p.93.
224   'What are you . . .', quoted Long, p.307.
224   'There they proceeded . . .,' Hildyard diary.

20. Cairo and London

227   'There was Cairo . . .', Forrester, conversation, 4.10.90.
228   'The reaction of the US . . .', Eccles, *By Safe Hand*, p.274.
228   'I don't . . .', Killearn Diaries, 29 May 1941, St Antony's College, Oxford.
228   'hum of splenetic . . .', Lee, p.111.
228   'Everyone was . . .', Wilkinson, conversation, 20.2.90.

229   'I am far from reassured . . .', Churchill, 14 June 1941, PRO PREM 3/109.
229   'Of course, you know . . .', Farrar-Hockley, p.101.
230   'a bitter memory', Pöppel, p.67.
230   'attributed by the German command . . .', Memorandum, Canea, 1942.
230   'His attitude . . .', de Winton, conversation, 28.9.90.
231   'in my view . . .', Laycock, PRO DEFE 2/699.
231   'Our case was indeed . . .', C.J. Hamson, p.12.

Part Three   The Resistance

21. Reprisal, Evasion and Resistance
235   'Ten Commandments . . .', quoted Mabire, *La Crète*, p.449.
236   'Many parachutists . . .', quoted Zayas, *The Wehrmacht War Crimes Bureau*, p.155.
236   'It is certain that the civilian population . . .', General Student, Order of 31.5.41, quoted Memorandum, Canea, 1942.
237   'certain punitive measures . . .', PRO FO 371/28885, quoted Zayas, p.99.
238   'was inclined to agree', *ibid.*
241   'Ah yes, we have plenty of those', quoted Powell, p.164.
242   'thrash them . . .', Psychoundakis, *The Cretan Runner*, p.37.
242   'Usual drill . . .', Sandover, conversation, 12.10.90.
243   'to feel out the country . . .', Stockbridge, conversation, 27.6.90.
244   'the restless, furtive . . .', Smith-Hughes, conversation, 20.8.90.
245   'fruity, flippant and bloodthirsty', Rendel, *Appointment in Crete*, p.25.
246   'a few hasty words . . .', quoted Powell, p.155.
246   'immensely brave and . . .', Fraser, conversation, 12.6.90.
246   'It is ill-gleaning after Pendlebury', quoted Powell, p.159.
247   'One of Tom's . . .', Leigh Fermor, letter to the author, 28.8.90.
247   'The villagers were so hospitable . . .', quoted Powell, p.159.
247   'Everything depended . . .', Stockbridge, letter to the author, 20.8.90.

22. Into the Field
248   'SOE was a strange . . .', Woodhouse, *Something Ventured*, p.28.
248   'This rather surprised . . .', Diaries of Lord Killearn, 24 March 1941.
249   'outhouse over the road . . .', Smith-Hughes, conversation, 20.8.90.
249   'SOE and SIS were separated . . .', War Cabinet Defence Committee (Operations) SOE Operations in Europe: Note by Minister of Economic Warfare DO (44) 2 of 11 January 1944.
249   'SOE was basically . . .', Stockbridge, conversation, 27.6.90.
251   'I can't tell you . . .', Ward, conversation, 28.5.90.
252   'a subject which anyone . . .', Rendel, p.18.
253   'the personnel people . . .', Ward, conversation, 28.5.90.
253   'Four months after . . .', Woodhouse, *Apple of Discord*, p.45. See also Denys Hamson, *We Fell Among Greeks*, p.149.
253   'This part of our . . .', Rendel, p.22.
254   'more like a practical joke . . .', Rendel, p.27.
255   'like marching through . . .', Rendel, p.57.
256   'Some talk . . .', John Pendelbury, quoted Hammond and Dunbabin, p.47.

256   'What, never seen . . .', Stanley, conversation, 4.7.90.
257   *'pallikari*-complex', Fielding, *The Stronghold*, p.28.
258   'Stand still Turk . . .', Psychoundakis, p.87.
259   'Your knees began . . .', Verney, conversation, 17.7.90.

23. The Peak of German Power
262   'the deaths of . . .', Pitt, *Special Boat Squadron*, p.32.
263   'To be out of . . .', Fielding, *Hide and Seek*, p.79.
266   'a dynamic tubby . . .', Woodhouse, *Something Ventured*, p.8.
266   'Nobody who did not experience it . . .', Sweet-Escott, *Baker Street Irregular*, p.73.
267   'the reddish beard . . .', Leigh Fermor, letter to the author, 28.8.90.
268   'Mandakas wanted to be . . .', Psychoundakis, conversation, 24.5.90.
269   'Young man . . .', Manoussakis, conversation, 26.5.90.
269   'Nearly the whole population . . .', Memorandum, Canea, 1942.

24. The Year of Change
273   'Germans! You have now . . .', Leigh Fermor, letter, 26.7.90.
274   'a nice old boy', Stanley, conversation, 4.7.90.
274   'large, bluff . . .', Hammond, *Venture into Greece*, p.124.
277   'none of that Cretan swagger', Fraser, conversation, 12.6.90.
278   'rather as one would suggest coming to . . .', Stockbridge, conversation, 27.6.90.
282   'a fox-terrier quivering with eagerness', Rendel, p.18.
282   'I'm only lighting . . .', Psychoundakis, conversation, 24.5.90.

25. The Italian Armistice
284   'chiromantic belief . . .', Deakin, *The Brutal Friendship*, p.183.
287   'a lot of flattery . . .', Leigh Fermor, conversation, 26.7.90.
287   'so long the object . . .', Churchill, *Closing the Ring*, p.168.
287   'Should the Italian troops in Crete and Rhodes . . .', Churchill, *Closing the Ring*, p.167.
287   'this is a time . . .', Churchill, *Closing the Ring*, p.102.
290   'If there had been . . .', Leigh Fermor, letter to the author, 14.9.90.
292   *'Ah, ah, mon capitaine!'* Leigh Fermor, letter to the author, 12.10.90.
297   'And now Greco . . .', quoted Hadjipateras and Fafalios, p.300.
299   'rotten to the core', quoted Cooper, *Cairo in the War*, p.271.
299   'a shiny round . . .', Woodhouse, *Something Ventured*, p.8
299   'What will history . . .', Manoussakis, conversation, 29.9.90.
300   'more trouble than it was worth', Ciclitira, conversation, 26.6.90.

26. The Abduction of General Kreipe
303   'As far as the ultimate . . .', Moss, *Ill Met by Moonlight*, p.39.
305   *'Was wollen sie in Kreta?'* Akoumianakis, conversation, 22.5.90.
308   'NOTIFICATION . . .', *Paratiritis*, Friday, 5 May 1944.
311   'Everybody felt taller . . .', Manoussakis, conversation, 26.5.90.
311   *'Kreipe Befehl: Wir Folgen!',* Dunbabin, Final Report, p.45.
311   'care and foresight', text of Decree of Municipal Council of Heraklion 15.2.48, provided by Miki Akoumianakis.

27. The German Withdrawal

312 'gather political . . .', Fraser, conversation, 12.6.90.
313 'Ah, you're back . . .', Lodwick, *The Filibusters*, p.174.
315 'the stage was . . .', Moss, *A War of Shadows*, p.46.
316 'Since the . . .', quoted Kokonas, *The German Occupation of Crete*, p.339.
321 'the impression that . . .', Verney, conversation, 17.7.90.
321 *'Nicht boom-boom!'*, Manoussakis, conversation, 26.5.90.
321 'Keep calm . . .', Verney, conversation, 17.7.90.
323 'seated in a captured German . . .', Rendel, p.223.
326 'tell Major . . .', Manoussakis, conversation, 26.5.90, and Verney, 17.7.90.
328 *'Yassou*, Herr Glembin . . .', Psychoundakis, p.232.

28. The Last Days of the Occupation

330 'the high-spirited . . .', Psychoundakis, pp.225-6.
333 'looked like boarders . . .', Seferis, *A Political Diary*, Athens 1979, p.269, quoted Papastratis, *British Policy Towards Greece During the Second World War*, p.204.
333 'the Greek gendarmerie on the corner . . .', Sweet-Escott (an eye-witness to the event), p.226.
334 'aimed at a political solution', Grambas, 'The Greek Communist Party 1941-1945: The Internal Debate on Seizing Power', published in Sarafis, *Background to Contemporary Greece*, Vol. ii, p.194.
336 'a hair-raising walk', Stanley, conversation, 4.7.90.
338 'very dejected', Ciclitira, conversation, 26.6.90.
338 'an agreeable example . . .', Hunt, p.46.
339 'The Cretans strongly resented . . .', Scott Daniell, *Regimental History of the Royal Hampshire Regiment*, p. 207.
342 'Ah, Herr Major . . .', Leigh Fermor, conversation, 26.7.90.
343 'I have seen . . .', dialogue reconstructed, Psychoundakis, conversation, 24.5.90.

Bibliography

Published Sources

[Place of publication is London unless otherwise stated]

Bennett, Ralph, *Ultra in the Mediterranean*, Hamish Hamilton, 1989

Bitzes, John, *Greece in World War II*, Sunflower University Press, Kansas, 1989

Bolitho, Hector, *The Galloping Third*, John Murray, 1963

Bright, Joan, *History of the Northumberland Hussars Yeomanry, 1924–1949*, Mawson, Swan & Morgan, Newcastle-upon-Tyne, 1949

Britton, James, *Record and Recall*, Lightfoot, 1988

Carlton, D., *Anthony Eden*, Allen Lane, 1981

Churchill, Winston S., *The Second World War: Their Finest Hour* (Vol. II), *Grand Alliance* (Vol. III), *Closing the Ring* (Vol. V), Cassell, 1949, 1950 and 1952.

Ciano, Galeazzo, *Ciano's Diplomatic Papers*, Odhams, 1948.

Clark, Alan, *The Fall of Crete*, Blond, 1962

Coats, Peter, *Of Generals and Gardens*, Weidenfeld & Nicolson, 1976

Connell, John, *Wavell*, Collins, 1964

Cooper, Artemis, *Cairo in the War*, Hamish Hamilton, 1989

Cox, Geoffrey, *A Tale of Two Battles*, William Kimber, 1987

Davin D., *Crete*, Official History of New Zealand in the Second World War 1939–1945, War History Branch, Wellington NZ, and OUP, 1953

Deakin, F.W., *The Brutal Friendship*, Weidenfeld & Nicolson, 1962

De Belot, R., *The Struggle for the Mediterranean 1939–45*, Princeton, 1951

De Courcy, J., *The History of the Welch Regiment 1919–1951*, Western Mail & Echo, Cardiff, 1952

De Guingand, Major-General Sir Francis, *Operation Victory*, Hodder, 1947
Generals at War, Hodder, 1964

Eccles, David, *By Safe Hand*, Bodley Head, 1983

Elliott, Murray, *Vasili — the Lion of Crete*, Stanley Paul, 1987

Farran, Roy, *Winged Dagger*, Collins, 1948

Farrar-Hockley, General Sir Antony, *Student*, Ballantine, New York, 1973

Fergusson, *The Black Watch and the King's Enemies*, Collins, 1950

Fielding, Xan, *The Stronghold*, Secker, 1953

Fielding, Xan, *Hide and Seek*, Secker, 1954

Fleming, Ann (ed. Mark Amory), *The Letters of Ann Fleming*, Collins, 1985

Forgeat, Raymond, *Les Parachutistes de la France Libre*, Vincennes, 1990

Germany, Auswärtiges Amt, *Documents on German Foreign Policy 1918–1945*, Series D, Vol. XI, HMSO, 1961, and Vol. XII, HMSO, 1962

Greacen, Lavinia, *Chink: A Biography*, Macmillan, 1989

Hadjipateras, C., and Fafalios, M., *Crete 1941*, Efstathiadis, Athens, 1989

Halder, Generaloberst F., *Kriegstagebuch*, Vol. II, Kohlhammer, Stuttgart, 1963

Hammond, Nicholas, and Dunbabin, T.J., *John Pendlebury in Crete*, privately published, Cambridge, 1948

Hammond, N.G.L., *Venture into Greece*, Kimber, 1983

Hamson, C.J., *Liber in Vinculis*, Trinity College, Cambridge, 1989

Hamson, Denys, *We Fell Among Greeks*, Cape, 1946

Handel, Michael I., 'Intelligence and Military Operations', in *Intelligence and National Security Journal*, Vol. 5, No. 2, April 1990

Hart, Captain Basil Liddell, *The Other Side of the Hill*, Cassell, 1951

Hart-Davis, Duff, *Peter Fleming*, Cape, 1974

Henderson, Jim, *22 Battalion*, Official History of New Zealand in the Second World War 1939–1945, War History Branch, Wellington NZ, 1958.

Heydte, Freiherr E. von der, *Daedalus Returned*, Hutchinson, 1958

Hinsley, F.H., *British Intelligence in the Second World War*, Vol. I, HMSO, 1981

Hobson, Brigadier R.W., 'The Episode in Greece', *Army Quarterly and Defence Journal*, April 1990

Holland, Jeffrey, *The Aegean Mission*, Greenwood Press, 1989

Hollingworth, Clare, *Front Line*, Cape, 1990

Household, Geoffrey, *Against the Wind*, Michael Joseph, 1958

Hunt, David, *A Don at War*, William Kimber, 1966

Kaloudis, Pantelis, *Sprung über Kreta*, Druffel Verlag, Munich, 1981

Kidson, A.C., *Petrol Company*, Official History of New Zealand in the Second World War 1939–1945, War History Branch, Wellington NZ, 1961

Kippenberger, Major General Sir Howard, *Infantry Brigadier*, OUP, 1949

Kiriakopolous, G.C., *Ten Days to Destiny*, Franklin Watts, New York, 1985

Kokonas, N.A., *The German Occupation of Crete, from the Archives of Colonel Christos Tsiphakis*, Rethymno, 1989

Kurowski, Franz, *Der Kampf um Kreta*, Moewig, Munich, 1988

Lee, Air Marshal Arthur Gould, *The Royal House of Greece*, Ward Lock, 1950 *Special Duties*, Ward Lock, 1947

Leigh Fermor, Patrick, *A Time of Gifts*, John Murray, 1977

Lindsay, T.M., *The Sherwood Rangers*, Burrup, 1952

List, Generalfeldmarschall, *Von Serbien Bis Kreta, Erinnerungen vom Feldzug*, Aspioti, Athens, 1942

Llewellyn, Peter, *Journey Towards Christmas*, Official History of New Zealand in the Second World War 1939–1945, War History Branch, Wellington NZ, 1949

Lodwick, John, *The Filibusters*, Methuen, 1947

Long, Gavin, *Australian War History — Greece, Crete and Syria*, Australian War Memorial, Canberra, 1953

Mabire, Jean, *La Crète — Tombeau des Paras*, Presses de la Cité, Paris, 1982

Mack Smith, Denis, *Mussolini*, Weidenfeld & Nicolson, 1981

Messenger, Charles, *The Middle East Commandos*, William Kimber, 1988

Michaelopolos, André, *Greek Fire*, Michael Joseph, 1943

Moss, W.S., *Ill Met By Moonlight*, Harrap, 1950
       A War of Shadows, Boardman, 1952

Mott-Radclyffe, Sir Charles, *Foreign Body in the Eye*, William Kimber, 1975

Papagos, General Alexander, *The Battle of Greece*, Scaczikis Alpha, Athens, 1949

Papastratis, Procopis, *British Policy Towards Greece During the Second World War*, Cambridge, 1984

Pitt Barrie, *The Crucible of War*, Vol. I, Macmillan, 1986
       Special Boat Squadron, Century, 1983

Playfair, Major General I.S.O., *History of the Second World War: The Mediterranean and the Middle East*, Vol. I, HMSO, 1954, Vol. II, HMSO, 1956

Pöppel, Martin, *Heaven and Hell*, Spellmount, Tunbridge Wells, 1988

Powell, Dilys, *The Villa Ariadne*, Hodder & Stoughton, 1974

Psychoundakis, George, *The Cretan Runner*, John Murray, 1955

Rendel, A.M., *Appointment in Crete*, Wingate, 1953

Sarafis, M. (ed.), *Background to Contemporary Greece*, Vols. I and II, Merlin, 1990

Sarafis, S., *ELAS — Greek Resistance Army*, Merlin, 1980

Schmidt, Paul, *Hitler's Interpreter*, Heinemann, 1951

Scott Daniell, D., *Regimental History of the Royal Hampshire Regiment*, Vol. III, Gale & Polden, Aldershot, 1955

Sheffield, Major O.F., *The York and Lancaster Regiment, 1919—1953*, Gale & Polden, Aldershot, 1953

Singleton-Gates, Peter, *General Lord Freyberg VC*, Michael Joseph, 1963

Smith, Major General A.C. (ed.), *The German Campaign in the Balkans*, Superintendent of Documents, Washington DC, 1953

Stephanides, Theodore, *Climax in Crete*, Faber & Faber, 1946

Stevens, Major General W.G., *Freyberg VC*, Wellington NZ, 1965

Stewart, Ian, *The Struggle for Crete*, OUP, 1955

Stitt, Commander George, *Under Cunningham's Command*, Allen & Unwin, 1944

Stout, T., *New Zealand Medical Services*, Official History of New Zealand in the Second World War 1939—1945, War History Branch, Wellington NZ, 1956

Sweet-Escott, Bickham, *Baker Street Irregular*, Methuen, 1965

Thomas, W.B., *Dare to be Free*, Allan Wingate, 1951

Tsivimonakis, E.M., *The National Resistance in the Nome of Rethymno, 1941—1944*, Estia, Athens, 1985

Underhill, Brigadier W.E., *The Royal Leicestershire Regiment*, South Wigston, 1958

Van Creveld, Martin, *Hitler's Strategy, the Balkan Clue*, CUP, Cambridge, 1973

Vrba, Leopold, *Kreta — Invasion auf Flügeln*, Moewig, Rastatt, 1985

Waugh, Evelyn (ed. Michael Davie), *The Diaries of Evelyn Waugh*, Penguin, Harmondsworth, 1976
       Officers and Gentlemen, Chapman & Hall, 1955

Wilson, Field Marshal Henry Maitland, *Eight Years Overseas*, Hutchinson, 1950

Wisdom, T.H., *Wings over Olympus*, Allen & Unwin, 1952

Woodhouse C.M., *Apple of Discord*, Hutchinson, 1948
       Something Ventured, Granada, 1982

Zayas, Alfred M. de, *The Wehrmacht War Crimes Bureau, 1939—1945*, University of Nebraska Press, 1990

Zotos, Stephanos, *Greece — The Struggle for Freedom*, New York, Crowell, 1967

Unpublished Sources

Reports, diaries, letters in private collections
Public Record Office
    ADM 1/11056, 202
    DEFE 2/ 711
    DEFE 3/ 686, 687, 891 and 894
    PREM 3/ 109
    WO 169/ 914, 915, 919, 923, 1334A, 1500, 1736 and 1751
    WO 179/ 723, 724, 721, 732, 733, 734, 735, 736 and 746
    WO 201 and 202
Imperial War Museum
Middle East Commando Historical Research Group
National Army Museum
War Museum, Athens

Acknowledgements

The extract from General Wavell's verse 'The Jug' is quoted by kind permission of the joint owners of the Wavell papers. Crown copyright material in the Public Record Office is reproduced by permission of the Controller of Her Majesty's Stationery Office.

Conversations and Correspondence

Part One The Fall of Greece
Lord Caccia GCMG, GCVO (First Secretary, British Legation, Athens); Sir Geoffrey Cox CBE (New Zealand Division); Major G.W.F. de Winton (Middlesex Yeomanry and HQ 1st Armd. Bde.); Sergeant R. Fletcher (New Zealand Division); Major General M. Forrester CB, CBE, DSO, MC (Queen's Regiment and British Military Mission); Professor Nicholas Hammond CBE, DSO, FBA, DL (MI(R)); Brigadier R.W. Hobson CBE (Brigade Major, 1st Armoured Bde.); Sir David Hunt KCMG, OBE (Welch Regiment, intelligence staff BAFG); Major Patrick Leigh Fermor DSO, OBE (Intelligence Corps, British Military Mission); Lieutenant Colonel Guy May (Northumberland Hussars and W Force HQ); Sir Charles Mott-Radclyffe DL (Rifle Brigade and British Military Mission); Lieutenant Colonel Mark Norman CBE (Hertfordshire Yeomanry and Yak Mission); Lieutenant Colonel John Pumphrey MBE, TD (Northumberland Hussars); Brigadier Ray Sandover DSO (2/11th Australian Infantry Battalion).

Part Two The Battle of Crete
Miki Akoumianakis; Tom Barratt (HMS *Dido*); Tom Bevan (Welch Regiment); R.B. Brown (RFA *Olna*); Lord Caccia; Evangelos Christou (Heraklion); Marine J.W. Clayton (MNBDO); Horace Cowley (HMS *Kos*); Sir Geoffrey Cox (Creforce HQ); Alexander Dow (Black Watch); Gefreiter Gottfried Emrich (3rd Parachute Regiment); Sergeant Ron Fletcher (19th Battalion, New Zealand Division); Major General Michael Forrester (British Military Mission); Vassilios Fourakis; Alfred

Gotts (Royal Artillery and 'Royal Perivolians'); Professor Nicholas Hammond (SO2 and HMS *Dolphin*); Professor Freiherr von der Heydte (3rd Parachute Regiment); Captain Myles Hildyard (Sherwood Rangers Yeomanry); Lord Hollenden [Lt Gordon Hope-Morley] (Black Watch and HQ 14th Infantry Brigade); Sir David Hunt (Welch Regiment and intelligence staff Creforce HQ); F.M. Hutton (HMS *Glenroy* and *Thurland Castle*); Lieutenant General Sir Ian Jacob GBE, CB, DL (Military Assistant Secretary to War Cabinet); Manolis Kougoumtzakis; Major Patrick Leigh Fermor (HQ 14th Infantry Brigade); Clifford Pass (Welch Regiment); Lieutenant Colonel John Pumphrey (Northumberland Hussars); Brigadier Ray Sandover DSO (2/11th Australian Infantry Battalion); Major J. Smith-Hughes OBE (RASC); K. Stalder (RAMC); Norman Swift (Leicesters); Dr R.E.S. Tanner (Layforce); Eleutheris Tsinakis; Sir Peter Wilkinson KCMG, DSO, OBE (Royal Fusiliers and SOE).

Part Three The Resistance
Miki Akoumianakis; Major Dennis Ciclitira (Staffordshire Regiment and SOE); Major Xan Fielding DSO (Cyprus Regiment and SOE); Captain Hugh Fraser (7th Hussars and SOE); The Earl Jellicoe PC, DSO, MC (SAS and SBS); Major Patrick Leigh Fermor (Intelligence Corps and SOE); Manoussos Manoussakis; George Psychoundakis; Major Jack Smith-Hughes (RASC and SOE); Niko Souris; Captain John Stanley MC (Sudan Defence Force and ISLD); Captain Ralph Stockbridge MC and Bar (Field Security and ISLD); Major Stephen Verney MBE (RAOC and PWE); Major Michael Ward (Green Howards and SOE Cairo).

Index

For listing of formations and regiments, see under national army headings: *Australian Imperial Force, British Army, German air force, German army, Italian army, New Zealand Army* and *Royal Hellenic Army*. For British warships see under *Royal Navy*.

Koryzis, Alexandros, 16; suicide of, 39
Koustoyérako, 281, 295—7
Koxaré, 334
Kreipe, Gen H., 239; operation to kidnap, 303—11; 342
Kroh, Maj, 130, 131, 132, 133, 175, 176
Kroussonas, 207, 324
Kyriakosellia, 280, 281

Lampson see Killearn
Langouvardos, Fr A., 241, 244
Larissa, 39
Lasithi, 225; resistance organization, 277; 286; ELAS in, 295; 301, 302
Lassen, Capt Anders, VC, 285, 328, 334
Lawrence, Prof A.W., 27
Laycock, Maj Gen R., 194, 195, 200, 203, 204, 218—22, 231
Leigh Fermor, Joan, 280
Leigh Fermor, Maj P.M.: with British Military Mission in Greece, 9, 10, 23, 48, 52; in Crete, 76, 96; with British Military Mission in Crete, 207—8, 247, 250, 252, 252, 255, 257, 265, 268, 272, 277—80, 285—6; and Italian negotiations, 286—8; 289, 290; with Bandouvas, 288—9; escape of Gen Carta, 291—3; promoted to major, 297; parachute in for Kreipe operation, 301; and Kreipe operation, 302—11; returns to Crete, 330—1; leaves Crete and end of war, 332; trial of Gens Bräuer and Müller, 342
Leivada, 295
Leros, 287
Levidis, Col, 119, 120, 168—70
Liebach, Maj, 114
Limonias (ELAS leader), 317, 334
List, FM Wilhelm, 40, 77, 150
Lodwick, Capt J., 313, 327
Löhr, Gen Alexander, 77, 151
Lokhria, 308, 309, 311
Longmore, Air Marshal A., 18, 21, 22

Lukas, Maj Stanislas, 322

MI9, 280
MI(R), 3, 23, 24, 46, 194, 344
MacGlasson, Col, US Army (OSS), 312
Mackay Force, 34, 35
Mackay, Maj Gen I., 34
Maclean, Brig Fitzroy, 298
Maleme airfield, 66, 78, 84, 85; Ultra warning of attack on, 91; 93, 94; just before invasion, 100; 104; morning of invasion, 105—7; paratroop attack, 109—11; misunderstanding over defence, 145—8; defenders withdraw, 152; 192, 195, 229, 261; and German surrender on Crete, 338
Mandakas, Gen E., 246, 268, 269, 274—5, 283, 299, 330
Maniadakis, Constantinos, 6, 10, 28, 39, 47, 62
Manoussakis, Manoussos, 238, 251, 269, 277, 301, 311, 326
Margarikari, 308, 309, 311
Margarites, 314
Matapan, Cape: Battle of, 32
Matsuoka, Mr, 32
Maxwell, Lt P.V.H., 165—6
Maxwell, Col T., 249, 265
May, Capt Guy, 47
Mazarakis, Gen, 39
Meindl, Brig E., 110, 111, 113, 151
Melidoni: Dunbabin meeting with EAM, 317
Mellisinos, Gen, 10
Mercury (Merkur), Operation, 74
Metaxas, Gen I., 5, 6, 10, 13, 14; death of, 16; 55
Metaxas line, 33, 35
Miers, Cdr, VC, 242
Milos, 158, 159, 166,
Mincemeat, Operation, 284
Missolonghi, 43
Mitsotaki, Kaite, 327
Mitsotakis, Constantinos, 268, 278, 299, 320; arrested, 321, 326, 327, 337—8
Moir, Sgt T., 280—1
Monastir Gap, 18, 25, 34